SEMANTICS

Volume 1

JOHN LYONS

Professor of Linguistics, University of Sussex

CAMBRIDGE UNIVERSITY PRESS

Cambridge

London · New York · Melbourne

Published by the Syndics of the Cambridge University Press
The Pitt Building, Trumpington Street, Cambridge CB2 1RP
Bentley House, 200 Euston Road, London NW1 2DB
32 East 57th Street, New York, NY 10022, USA
296 Beaconsfield Parade, Middle Park, Melbourne 3206, Australia

First published 1977
Reprinted 1978, 1979

Printed in Great Britain at the
University Press, Cambridge

Library of Congress Cataloguing in Publication Data

Lyons, John.

Semantics.

Includes bibliographies and indexes.

1. Semantics. 2. Semiotics.
3. Grammar, Comparative and general. I. Title.
P325.L96   410   76–40838
ISBN 0 521 21473 4 hard covers
ISBN 0 521 29165 8 paperback

Contents to Volume 1

Contents to Volume 1

Contents to Volume 2

Contents to Volume 2

Figures

Typographical conventions

SMALL CAPITALS
For sense-components and other more abstract elements, or correlates, of meaning (cf. 9.9).

Italics
1. For forms (as distinct from lexemes or expressions: cf. 1.5) in their orthographic representation.
2. For certain mathematical and logical symbols, according to standard conventions.

Single quotation-marks
1. For lexemes and expressions (cf. 1.5).
2. For the citation of sentences (i.e. system-sentences: cf. 1.6).
3. For titles of articles.

Double quotation-marks
1. For meanings (cf. 1.5).
2. For propositions (cf. 6.2).
3. For quotations from other authors.

Asterisk
For technical terms when first introduced and occasionally thereafter to remind the reader of their technical sense.

Notes
1. When a term has been furnished with an asterisk, single quotation-marks are not used.
2. Single quotation-marks are omitted when a sentence, expression or lexeme is numbered and set on a different line; but italics and double quotation-marks are still used in such circumstances.
3. In quotations from other authors, the original typographical conventions have usually been preserved. Occasionally adjustments have been made in order to avoid confusion or ambiguity.

Preface

When I began writing this book six years ago, it was my intention to produce a fairly short one-volume introduction to semantics which might serve the needs of students in several disciplines and might be of interest to the general reader. The work that I have in fact produced is far longer, though in certain respects it is less comprehensive, than I originally anticipated; and for that reason it is being published in two volumes.

Volume 1 is, for the most part, more general than volume 2; and it is relatively self-contained. In the first seven chapters, I have done my best, within the limitations of the space available, to set semantics within the more general framework of semiotics (here defined as the investigation of both human and non-human signalling-systems); and I have tried to extract from what ethologists, psychologists, philosophers, anthropologists and linguists have had to say about meaning and communication something that amounts to a consistent, if rather eclectic, approach to semantics. One of the biggest problems that I have had in writing this section of the book has been terminological. It is frequently the case in the literature of semantics and semiotics that the same terms are employed in quite different senses by different authors or that there are several alternatives for what is essentially the same phenomenon. All I can say is that I have been as careful as possible in selecting between alternative terms or alternative interpretations of the same terms and, within the limits of my own knowledge of the field, in drawing the reader's attention to certain terminological pitfalls. At one time, I had hoped to be able to follow the practice of never using non-technically any word that was also employed anywhere in the book in some technical sense or other. I soon had to abandon this rather quixotic ambition! Some of the most ordinary words of English (e.g., 'case', 'feature', 'aspect') are employed in a highly specialized sense in linguistics and related disciplines; and, however hard I tried, I found it impossible to get by without them. I trust that the context (and the device of using asterisks for introducing technical terms) will reduce, if it does not entirely eliminate, ambiguity and the possibility of misunderstanding.

The last two chapters of volume 1 are devoted to structural semantics (or, more precisely, to structural lexicology). This is a topic that I have been concerned with, on and off, for the best part of 20 years; and, although the so-called structuralist approach to semantics is no longer as fashionable among linguists as it once was, I still believe that it has much to contribute to the analysis of language.

Volume 2 may be read, independently of volume 1, by anyone who is already familiar with, or is prepared to take on trust, notions and distinctions explained in volume 1. In volume 2, which (apart from the chapter on Context, Style and Culture) is concerned with semantics from a fairly narrowly linguistic point of view, I have been tempted to do something more than merely clarify and systematize the work of others; and this accounts for the fact that the book, as a whole, has taken me far longer to write than I had expected. Five of the eight chapters in volume 2 – two of the three chapters on Semantics and Grammar, the chapter on Deixis, Space and Time, the chapter on Mood and Illocutionary Force, and the chapter on Modality – contain sections in which, unless I am mistaken, there are a few ideas of my own. *Caveat lector!*

As I have said, the book is, in certain respects, less comprehensive than I intended. There is nothing on etymology and historical semantics, or on synonymy; and there is very little on the structure of texts (or so-called text-linguistics), or on metaphor and style. If I had dealt with these topics, I should have had to make my book even longer. Sometimes one must stop even if one has not finished!

As I write this Preface, I am all too conscious of having just moved from Edinburgh where I have now spent twelve years, in one of the finest Departments of Linguistics in the world. Throughout this time I have benefited, in my writing and in my teaching, from the advice and criticisms of my colleagues in several Departments. Many of them have helped me, as far as the present book is concerned, by reading sections of it for me in draft and commenting upon them or by discussing (and in some instances originating) the ideas that have found their way into my text: John Anderson, R. E. Asher, Martin Atkinson, Gillian Brown, Keith Brown, John Christie, Kit Fine, Patrick Griffiths, Stephen Isard, W. E. Jones, John Laver, Christopher Longuet-Higgins, J. E. Miller, Keith Mitchell, Barry Richards, and James Thorne. Ron Asher and

Bill Jones have been especially helpful: each of them has read the whole typescript; and Bill Jones has undertaken to do the index for me. Apart from these Edinburgh and ex-Edinburgh colleagues, there are many others to whom I am indebted for their comments on drafts of parts of the book: Harry Bracken, Simon Dik, R. M. Dixon, Françoise Dubois-Charlier, Newton Garver, Gerald Gazdar, Arnold Glass, F. W. Householder, Rodney Huddleston, R. A. Hudson, Ruth Kempson, Geoffrey Leech, Adrienne Lehrer, David Makinson, P. H. Matthews, G. A. Miller, R. H. Robins, Geoffrey Sampson, the late Stephen Ullmann, Anthony Warner. There are doubtless many errors and inadequacies that remain but without the aid of so many friends, whose specialized knowledge in many of the relevant fields is far greater than my own, I should have gone astray more often than I have done.

Like all teachers, I have learned more from my students over the years than they have learned from me. It has been my privilege to conduct several research seminars and to supervise a fair number of Ph.D. dissertations on semantics during the period when I was writing this book. Two of my students I must mention by name, since I am very conscious of having derived directly from them some of the points that appear in the book: Marilyn Jessen and Claudia Guimãraes de Lemos. I have no doubt, however, that others of my students are also responsible for much of what I think of as being original in the second volume.

I owe a special debt of gratitude to Rena Somerville who, as my secretary in the last few years (the best secretary that I have ever had), has typed so many versions of certain sections of my manuscript that she could probably reproduce at least the gist of them from memory! Much of this work she has done at home in the evenings and at the week-end: I trust that her family will forgive me for the time that I have stolen from them in this way.

Finally, I must record my gratitude to my wife and children for their willingness to put up with my frequent bouts of depression, ill-temper or sheer absent-mindedness while I was writing the book and the post-ponement of so many promised outings and holidays. More particularly I wish to thank my wife for the love and support that she has always given me, in my writing as in everything.

J. L.

Falmer, Sussex
November 1976

I
Introduction:
some basic terms and concepts

1.1. *The meaning of 'meaning'*

In this chapter I will make a number of general points and introduce certain distinctions which will be taken for granted in all that follows. The reader's attention is drawn especially to the fact that any term that is introduced here and given a technical interpretation will be used exclusively in that sense, in so far as it is employed as a technical term, throughout the book. Such terms will be marked with a following asterisk when they are introduced in their technical sense in this or succeeding chapters too. Asterisks will also be used occasionally to remind the reader that a term which has been introduced earlier is being employed in a technical sense and should not be interpreted in any of its non-technical senses. All asterisked terms are explained in the body of the text or in the footnotes.

Semantics is generally defined as the study of meaning; and this is the definition that we will provisionally adopt: what is to be understood by 'meaning' in this context is one of our principal concerns in later chapters. Ever since Ogden and Richards (1923) published their classic treatise on this topic, and indeed since long before that, it has been customary for semanticists to emphasize the fact (and let us grant that it is a fact) that the noun 'meaning' and the verb 'to mean' themselves have many distinguishable meanings.[1] Some idea of the range of their meanings may be obtained from a consideration of the following sentences:

(1) What is the meaning of 'sesquipedalian'?
(2) I did not mean to hurt you

---

[1] Leech (1974: 1ff) suggests that the reason why "semanticists have often seemed to spend an immoderate amount of time puzzling out the 'meanings of *meaning*' as a supposedly necessary preliminary to the study of their subject" is that they have been trying "to explain semantics in terms of other disciplines". I think that there is more to it than that. It is at least arguable that linguistic meaning cannot be understood or explicated except in terms of other kinds of non-linguistic meaning.

(3) He never says what he means
(4) She rarely means what she says
(5) Life without faith has no meaning
(6) What do you mean by the word 'concept'?
(7) He means well, but he's rather clumsy
(8) Fame and riches mean nothing to the true scholar
(9) Dark clouds mean rain
(10) It was John I meant not Harry.

It has just been said that the various meanings of the noun 'meaning' and the verb 'to mean' illustrated above are distinguishable, not that they are unrelated. Just how they are related to one another is, however, a difficult and controversial question.

Certain of the meanings (or senses) can be distinguished by the technique of substituting other words in the same context and enquiring whether the resulting sentences are equivalent. For example, it seems that 'intend' could be substituted for 'mean' in (2) without changing the total meaning of the sentence; and that 'significance' (or perhaps 'value') is equivalent to 'meaning' in the context of (5). The notion of intention seems to be relevant also to our understanding of (4), (6), (7) and (10), though each use of the verb 'mean' here appears to be somewhat different from the others and the substitution of 'intend' for 'mean' (where this operation can be carried out without awkwardness) might be held to effect some change in the meaning of the sentence. The sense in which 'mean' is used in (8) is close to the sense of 'meaning' in (5): it would be generally agreed that 'Life without faith means nothing' and 'Fame and riches have no meaning for the true scholar' are roughly equivalent to (5) and (8) respectively. Neither 'intention' nor 'significance' is equivalent to 'meaning' in the context of (1): the former word could hardly occur at all here, and the substitution of 'significance' for 'meaning' would produce a sentence ('What is the significance of 'sesquipedalian'?') with a quite different meaning from that of (1).

Sentences (3) and (4) are especially interesting. Each of them presupposes the possibility of saying one thing and meaning another. This in itself is puzzling enough. How can one use a particular word, or combination of words, to mean something other than what it means? (Humpty Dumpty, it will be recalled, took a characteristically extreme and dogmatic attitude with regard to this question, but our sympathies surely lie more with Alice!) The notion of meaning relevant to the interpretation of (3) would seem to be rather different from, though not completely unrelated to, the notion of meaning relevant to the interpretation of (4). The same is true of (10), and perhaps also of (6), where what seems to be involved is the speaker's intention to identify (or, as we shall say later, refer* to) a particular person, thing or situation which the hearer has presumably failed to identify correctly. In this respect, there are similarities with and differences from (3) and (4). The nature of these similarities and differences, however, is, to say the least, elusive and may vary considerably with the circumstances in which the sentences might be appropriately uttered.

It is worth pointing out also that, whereas (1) may be paraphrased as 'What does 'sesquipedalian' mean?', a sentence like 'Who(m) did you mean – John or Harry?' cannot be paraphrased as 'Who was your meaning – John or Harry?' (or even as 'What was your meaning – John or Harry?'). Nor can (3) and (4) be paraphrased, except very unnaturally, with sentences containing the noun 'meaning' rather than the verb 'to mean'. This point, obvious enough when put like this, is of some importance, as we shall see later, particularly in the discussion of naming and reference (chapter 7).

We will not proceed further at this stage with our analysis of the various meanings of the verb 'to mean' and the noun 'meaning'. From our brief discussion of the examples given above it will be obvious that the meanings (or senses) of 'to mean' and 'meaning' exhibit a network of similarities and differences such that it is impossible to say that any one of these meanings is totally unrelated to the others. Most linguists and some philosophers would be inclined to dismiss all but (1), and possibly (10), as exemplifying uses or senses of the words 'meaning' and 'mean' that are of no concern to the semanticist; and in this book we too will be concentrating upon the sense of the noun 'meaning' that is exemplified in (1) above. It is arguable, however, that this sense of 'meaning' cannot be explained or understood except in relation to the notions of intention, on the one hand, and significance (or value), on the other, which, as we have seen, are relevant to the interpretation of at least some of the other senses of 'meaning' and 'to mean'.[2] Indeed,

---

[2] Morris (1964: vii) has suggested, on the basis of the fact that "in many languages there is a word like English 'meaning'" with the twin poles "that which something signifies and the value or significance of what is signified" that there is an essential relation between signification and significance. I would not deny that this is so. However, I do not believe that all linguistic meaning can be analysed satisfactorily in terms of signification

as we shall see in a later chapter, it is highly desirable, if not essential, to draw this distinction. But the fact remains that the meaning of words and sentences is learned and maintained by the use to which language is put in communicative situations. The notion of communication, as will be emphasized in chapter 2, presupposes the notions of significance and intention; and what the words and sentences of a language mean is, in the last resort, both theoretically inexplicable and empirically unverifiable except in terms of what the speakers of that language mean by their use of these words and sentences.

A rather different point may now be made – a point which at first sight may seem to be hardly worthy of mention, let alone of emphasis. It is simply this: 'meaning' is a word of the ordinary, everyday vocabulary of English. (It can be matched at least roughly with words in other languages: 'signification' in French, 'Bedeutung' in German, etc. But this process of matching is itself of considerable interest, in that there may be no other language in which all the senses of the English verb 'to mean' or the noun 'meaning' are covered by a single word.) Unless and until we choose to give the word 'meaning' a more restricted technical sense, we should not expect to be able to bring everything we call 'meaning' within the scope of a unified and consistent theory of semantics. That this is so is perhaps clear enough with respect to differences in the use of the words 'meaning' and 'to mean' of the kind illustrated in the sentences listed above. It is important to realize, however, that the point also holds for any representative set of sentences, like (1), of the form 'What is the meaning of (the word) X?'. According to the circumstances in which this question is asked, the kind of word that X is and the context in which it is being employed, so we should expect the answer to this question to differ, not only in detail, but even in general type. That there is a distinction to be drawn between the meaning of a word and the meaning of a (non-idiomatic) phrase or sentence is obvious enough, as also is the fact that the meaning of a phrase or sentence is a product of the meaning of the words of which it is composed. It is, however, the besetting temptation of semanticists to attempt to force all answers to the question 'What is the meaning of the word X?' into the same theoretical mould. This temptation is to be resisted. We will introduce a number of different

(cf. chapter 4). Furthermore, the notion of intentionality seems to be no less important than that of significance in the complex of interrelated notions subsumed under 'meaning'.

technical terms for the various aspects or kinds of word-meaning (as also of sentence-meaning and utterance-meaning) to which we shall, in due course, be giving theoretical recognition, but we will not insist that any one of these is more basic (meaning properly so called, as it were) than the others. The term 'meaning' itself will be used throughout in what might be called an ordinary-language, or everyday, sense; that is to say, in what will be described later as an intuitive, pre-theoretical, sense (cf. 1.6).

1.2. *Use and mention*

One of the most characteristic features of natural languages (and one which may well distinguish them, not only from the signalling-systems used by other species, but also from what is commonly referred to as non-verbal communication in human beings: cf. 3.4) is their capacity for referring to, or describing, themselves. The term we will employ for this feature, or property, of language is reflexivity*.[3] Language can be turned back on itself, as it were.

We have already had occasion to draw upon the reflexivity of ordinary language in our discussion of meaning in the previous section. A sentence like 'What is the meaning of 'sesquipedalian'?' is not only a sentence of English: it is also (under a standard interpretation and when uttered in the appropriate circumstances) a sentence that may be used to ask a question about English. Another typical example is 'The word *Socrates* has eight letters', in which the word *Socrates* is used not, as normally, to refer to a particular person, but, in a certain sense, to refer to itself. (It will be observed that two different conventions have been used in citing the words 'sesquipedalian' and *Socrates* – quotation-marks *vs.* italics. The reason for this notational difference will be explained more fully in section 1.5.)

The fact that we not only can, but must, use language in order to talk about language creates particular problems for the linguist, and more especially for the semanticist. He must make sure that he has available the technical vocabulary and notational conventions that he requires in order to distinguish between the reflexive and the non-reflexive (or normal) use of language. One terminological distinction proposed for this purpose and now quite commonly found in the literature is that

---

[3] The term 'reflexive' is also used later in its more traditional sense, in the phrase 'reflexive pronoun' and with reference to the property which distinguishes reflexive from non-reflexive pronouns. It will always be clear from the context which of the two senses of reflexive is involved.

of use* and mention*.[4] In a sentence like 'What is the meaning of 'sesquipedalian'?' the word 'sesquipedalian' is said to be mentioned; in a sentence like 'He is inordinately fond of the sesquipedalian turn of phrase' it is said to be used. Although the terms 'use' and 'mention' have been employed in the title of this section and, because they are of frequent occurrence in the literature, have been introduced into the discussion, we will make no further use of them as technical terms in the following sections. It would be almost impossible to avoid the non-technical employment of the verb 'use' and potentially confusing to allow such a common word to have both a technical and a non-technical sense in a book on semantics. Furthermore, it is arguable that to mention a word is also to use it – to use it, however, in a rather special way.

One reason why logicians have insisted upon the importance of distinguishing between what we are calling the reflexive* use of a word and other uses of the word will be clear from a consideration of the following obviously fallacious argument:

(1) He hates 'John',
(2) The man over there is John,
(3) Therefore he hates the man over there.

I have said that this is an obviously fallacious argument, because it is clear that the word 'John' is being used reflexively in the major premiss (1): it is being used to refer to a name rather than to a person bearing that name. Just how it is being used in the minor premiss (2) is a question we need not go into at this stage: it suffices for our present purposes that its use in (2) is evidently different from its use in (1). The fact that 'John' is being used reflexively in (1) is indicated, in the written form of this sentence, by the quotation marks. In the spoken language this fact might be clear from the context; if not, it can be made clear by inserting the phrase 'the name', or some similar descriptive expression, before 'John': 'He hates the name 'John''.

Much theoretical discussion of the reflexive use of language has been

---

[4] There is now a large body of philosophical literature devoted to the use-*vs.*-mention distinction. Zabeeh *et al.* (1974: 20–31) gives a useful summary with bibliographical references. Of the several philosophical articles devoted to this topic, Garver (1965) is possibly the most helpful and, linguistically, the most sophisticated. Not to be confused with the use-*vs.*-mention distinction is the use-*vs.*-meaning distinction, which has been much discussed by the so-called ordinary-language philosophers (cf. note 6) and was promoted to a position of peculiar prominence by Wittgenstein's (1953: 43) famous and, out of context, misleading slogan "the meaning of a word is its use in the language".

confused by ambiguities in such terms as 'word' and 'phrase'. Consider for example the following two sentences:

(4) *John* has four letters
(5) I hate 'John'.

The majority of philosophers, linguists and logicians would say that it is the same word that is being used in both instances and that in each instance it is being used reflexively (or that it is being mentioned, rather than used). It is by no means clear, however, that the same entity is in fact being referred to in (5) as the entity that is referred to in (4); and by employing italics in the one case and quotation marks in the other we are in fact presupposing that there is a difference in the entity that is being referred to. What is being referred to in (4) is reasonably clear (if we discount, for the present, the distinction between token* and type*: cf. 1.4): it is a sequence of four shapes. This entity is in principle unpronounceable; but, by virtue of the fact that it is correlated by convention with a complex of speech-sounds identifiable as the spoken form of the name 'John', it is itself identifiable as the written form of this name.

But let us now consider just two of the ways in which one might wish to interpret (5). It might mean that I hate the English name referred to, in whatever medium* (i.e. whether it is written or spoken: cf. 3.3) and in whatever form* (i.e. in the form *John* or the form *John's*: cf. 1.5), but I have no objection, let us say, to the French 'Jean', the German 'Johann', the Italian 'Giovanni' or the Russian 'Ivan'. Another interpretation is that which rests upon that notion of identity or equivalence in terms of which we say that the French 'Jean' and the English 'John' constitute the same name. There are very many other interpretations possible (some of them no doubt more plausible than others). It will suffice for the present to call attention to the two that have just been mentioned and to point out that the difference between them is obvious as soon as we are faced with the problem of translating (5) into another language. (There are occasions when it is appropriate to translate proper names and there are occasions when it is not: cf. 7.5.) It was in fact the former of these two interpretations that was intended; and it was for this reason that single quotation marks, rather than either italics or double quotation-marks, were used.

The distinction between *John* and 'John' may appear to be, not only rather subtle, but unnecessary, since proper nouns in English are uninflected, except for the possessive form, *John's* (and one might be inclined to treat *John's*, as many linguists do, as an extension of *John*, the true or underlying form of the name). In an inflected language, however, a single word may have several different forms associated with it and these forms may very well differ with respect to the number of letters in their written representations. In Latin, for example, the name 'Johannes' appears in several different forms according to the grammatical function that is performed by the word in any particular sentence: *Johannes, Johannem, Johanni,* etc. Now, it so happens that the conventional citation-form* of 'Johannes' (i.e. the form of the word that is conventionally used to refer to the word: cf. 1.5) has, when written, eight letters. But the citation-form of a word is to be distinguished, in principle, from the word itself. Much confusion has been engendered in the discussion of the reflexive use of language by the failure to draw this distinction.

We will not dwell further at this point upon the importance of distinguishing clearly between such different linguistic entities as are exemplified by *John* and 'John'. One example may be given, however, of the problems that can arise if some kind of distinction is not maintained between the written form of a word (or expression) and the word (or expression) itself. In his classic discussion of use and mention, Quine (1940: 23–6) employs as examples the following sentences

   (6) 'Boston' has six letters
   (7) 'Boston' is a noun
   (8) 'Boston' is disyllabic;

and he says that, unlike

   (9) Boston is populous,

they each ascribe properties to the name 'Boston', rather than to the city, Boston, that is named by 'Boston'. Quine is here following the standard philosophical convention, according to which single quotation-marks are employed to indicate that an expression is being mentioned, rather than used. As he puts it: "The name of a name or other expression is commonly formed by putting the named expression in single quotation marks." He goes on to say: "To mention Boston we use 'Boston' or a synonym, and to mention 'Boston' we use ' 'Boston' ' or a synonym." It follows that 'Boston' is an expression which names Boston, and ' 'Boston' ' is an expression which names 'Boston'.

At first sight, this is straightforward enough. But what are we to make of the term 'expression' in this context? It is the expression itself which, when named, is said to be enclosed in quotation-marks. Now, what is put between quotation-marks is obviously nothing other than a string of letters; and in this case it is the string of letters that constitutes the conventional written form of the expression that names Boston. It would seem to follow therefore that an expression is nothing other than the string of letters which constitutes its conventional written form. Quine interprets (6) as a statement which ascribes to 'Boston' the property of having six letters; and this is consistent with his identification of the expression with its conventional written form. But he also interprets (7) as ascribing to 'Boston' the grammatical property of being a noun, and (8) as ascribing to 'Boston' the phonetic property of being disyllabic. But if being a noun and being disyllabic are properties on a par with having six letters, the expression which has these properties cannot be identified with the string of letters which constitutes the conventional written form of the expression. For it obviously does not make sense to say that a sequence of visually perceptible shapes has a certain phonetic property. Nor does it seem reasonable to associate the grammatical properties of an expression directly with its conventional written representation and only derivatively with its spoken form. This argument for drawing a distinction between an expression and its written or spoken form is independent, it should be noted, of the distinction that was hinted at, though not explained, in our discussion of (4) and (5).

It is independent also of the way in which the difference between *John* and 'John', or between *Boston* and 'Boston', is formulated in any particular description of the structure of English. A more precise account of this difference must be postponed until we have furnished ourselves with the necessary technical terms (cf. 1.6). For the present, it is sufficient to say that there are at least two defensible ways of formulating the difference between *John* and 'John'; and which way we adopt will depend partly upon our theory of grammar and partly upon our conception of the relation between written and spoken language. We can say that *John* is the conventional written representation of 'John' – that it is the citation-form of 'John' in the written language – and that this, its written shape as it were, is one of its properties, as its phonetic shape is another of its properties. (The fact that most linguists would take the spoken form to be primary and the written form of a word to be derivative is at this point irrelevant: cf. 3.3.) Alternatively, we can say that what is put between quotation-marks is neither the expression itself nor a representation of one of its properties, but another kind of entity, which is distinct from, but correlated with, the expression of which it is the conventional citation-form.

If we adopt either of these alternatives we can handle the fact that, under a certain interpretation of the expression 'this sentence', the following two sentences (or the statements made by uttering them) are true

(10) This sentence contains the word *contains*
(11) This sentence contains the word 'contain',

whereas the following sentence (given the convention that we have adopted for the use of italics) is patently false:

(12) This sentence contains the word *contain*.

For (12), though it does indeed contain the form *contain*, does not (under any standard definition of the term 'word') have the form *contain* functioning as a word.

1.3. *Object-language and metalanguage*

This distinction is similar to, and by some authors identified with, the distinction between use and mention. It is nonetheless worthy of separate discussion.

The terms object-language* and metalanguage* are correlative, in the sense that the one depends upon the other. As we saw in the preceding section, we have to use language to talk about or describe language. Instead of using a given language, reflexively, in order to describe itself, we can employ one language to describe another. In this case, we may say that the language being described is the object-language and the language which is used to make the descriptive statements is the metalanguage. We might use English to describe French, or French to describe English, and so on. For example, the following sentence

(1) The French word 'homme' is a noun

might be used to make a metalinguistic* statement in English about a word in French – the object-language. Here we have one natural language serving as a metalanguage with respect to another.

It is perhaps more common, however, to restrict the term 'meta-language' to specially constructed and formalized systems; and we will use the term 'metalanguage' (though not 'metalinguistic') throughout in this sense. The metalanguage will then normally contain terms for identifying and referring to the elements of the object-language (words, sounds or letters, etc.) and, in addition, a certain number of special technical terms which can be used to describe the relations between these elements, how they may be combined to form phrases and sentences, and so on. According to the customary conception of the relationship between metalanguage and object-language, expressions of the metalanguage which refer to words and phrases of the object-language do so by naming them; and the metalanguage name of an object-language word or phrase is constructed, as we saw in the previous section, by enclosing the conventional written citation form of the latter in single quotation-marks. Looked at from this point of view, therefore, 'man' is the name of a particular English word and 'homme' is the name of a particular French word.

One must be careful not to misunderstand the point that has just been made. The metalanguage is in principle a quite different language from the object language: it need not therefore have in its vocabulary any of the actual words or phrases belonging to the object-language. It is a matter of convenience, rather than necessity, that the metalanguage-expression 'man' should be related systematically to the English word that it names by enclosing the conventional written citation-form of the word in quotation-marks. Any other convention would serve for the purpose of constructing metalanguage-names provided that it was clear which object-language word or phrase was being named by which metalanguage name. We might number the words in the vocabulary of the object-language, for example, and then use numerals to refer to any word about which we wished to make a metalinguistic statement. Thus, given that '239' has been assigned (by whatever principle) to the French word whose citation-form is *homme*, we could make the same statement that is made by the utterance of (1) by uttering

(2) The French word 239 is a noun.

Indeed, if we wished, for our own whimsical purposes, to identify the words and phrases of the object language by christening them with such names as 'Tom', 'Dick' and 'Harry', there is nothing to prevent us from doing so. The connexion between a metalanguage-name and what that name stands for in the object-language (whether the object-language is a natural language or not) is in principle arbitrary. This principle holds true even when the metalanguage is developed on the basis of some subpart of an existing natural language. Formalization involves the regimentation of ordinary language even when it is grounded in and based upon the grammar and vocabulary of ordinary language.

It will now be clear why it is undesirable to identify metalinguistic statements made about a particular language with reflexive statements made in that language. For the reflexive use of language does not depend upon the prior formalization of the language or the acceptance of explicit conventions as to what kinds of descriptive statements are permissible. Nor does it seem reasonable to say of the reflexive use of ordinary language (although certain philosophers have taken this view) that in sentences such as 'What is the meaning of 'sesquipedalian'?' or '*Socrates* has eight letters', we are not using the word 'sesquipedalian' or the form *Socrates*, but naming them.

Having made this point and given it due emphasis, we can go on to admit that the difference between metalinguistic statements and reflexive statements is far less sharp than has just been suggested in the kind of linguistic discussion that we are embarking upon; that is to say, in a discussion about language which, though it will aim to be as precise as possible and will make use of very many technical terms, will none-theless be conducted in more or less ordinary English, as indeed it must be, rather than in some specially constructed formal language or in some subpart of English, duly constrained and treated as a formal language. It is a debatable and controversial question whether a com-plete formalization of the everyday use of ordinary language is even in principle possible. It is also a matter of considerable philosophical con-troversy whether we should take ordinary language, with all its richness, complexities and alleged inconsistencies as something basic and irre-ducible or think of it as being, in some sense, derived (or derivable) from a simpler and more regular kind of language with properties similar to those embodied in formal constructed languages.[5] The so called ordinary-language philosophers have tended to take the first view, and formal semanticists the second.[6] It is no accident, therefore, that the ordinary-language philosophers have customarily talked in terms of use and mention and the formal semanticists in terms of language and metalanguage.

---

[5] It is probably far more widely accepted than it was at one time that any formalization is parasitic upon the ordinary everyday use of language in that it must be understood, intuitively, on the basis of ordinary language (cf. 6.1).

[6] For so-called ordinary-language philosophy (notable representatives of which are Austin, Ryle, Strawson and Urmson) cf. Caton (1963), Chapell (1964), Cohen (1966), Passmore (1957), Urmson (1956), Warnock (1958). For formal semantics: cf. chapter 6. A somewhat tendentious discussion of ordinary-language philosophy and formal semantics from the point of view of generative grammar (cf. 10.3) is to be found in Fodor & Katz (1964).

In this section, the term 'language' has been used in the sense in which it is commonly used in formal logic, and 'ordinary language' or 'natural language' has been used in contrast with 'constructed language' or 'formal language'. Elsewhere in this book the term 'language' will be employed without qualification in the sense of 'natural human language', examples of which are everyday English and French. Some of the more general features of language will be discussed in a later chapter (3.4).

The distinction between language and metalanguage is crucial, as we shall see later, in Tarski's definition of truth; and Tarski's definition, together with a certain convention associated with it, is the foundation-stone upon which all modern formal semantics is built (cf. 6.5).

1.4. *Type and token*

The terms type* and token* were introduced into semantics, as were a number of other terms that we shall meet later, by the American philosopher C. S. Peirce (cf. 4.1).[7] The distinction is now widely employed, although it is frequently confused with other important distinctions. The relationship between tokens and types will be referred to as one of instantiation*; tokens, we will say, instantiate* their type. Let us begin by considering the following two sentences:

(1) There are nine letters in the word *reference*
(2) There are five (different) letters in the word *reference*.

Each of these sentences is true under a certain interpretation of what constitutes identity and difference. There is an obvious sense in which the word *reference* contains nine letters; and there is a no less obvious sense in which, since the letter *e* occurs four times, the letter *r* twice and every other letter only once, the word *reference* contains five (different) letters. So far, so good. But can we make this more precise?

Invoking the type-token distinction, we can say that on each and every occasion on which the word *reference* occurs (i.e. whenever it is correctly written or printed), the letter *e* is instantiated four times, the letter *r* twice and the letters *f*, *n* and *c* once. Is the letter in position 2 of the sequence the same as the letter in position 4 (in any given occurrence of the word *reference*)? Yes, if by 'letter' we mean letter-type;

---

[7] Cf. Peirce *Collected Papers*, 4.537 & 2.245. The type-token distinction has been explained and invoked in numerous recent works on semantics and semiotics. It has all too frequently been misinterpreted.

no, if by 'letter' we mean letter-token. Similarly, for words (more precisely, for word-forms: cf. 1.5). In any particular occurrence of the following sentence there are two tokens of the same word-type, *a*:

(3) I sold a book to a friend.

Sentence (3), incidentally, illustrates yet another kind of ambiguity. Looked at from one point of view *a* is a letter (and as such it is not a form); from another point of view it is a word (and, more precisely, a word-form: cf. 1.5). This ambiguity (which we may describe as an ambiguity of level*: cf. 3.4) is obviously distinct from type-token ambiguity.

Tokens are unique physical entities, located at a particular place in space or time. They are identified as tokens of the same type by virtue of their similarity with other unique physical entities and by virtue of their conformity to the type that they instantiate.

This explanation of the difference between types and tokens and of the relationship between them will serve for the present; and it will be clarified further by the use that we make of it throughout the book. The important point to grasp at this stage is that, when we say that the same letter occurs twice in a written word or that the same word occurs twice in the same sentence (or indeed that the same letter occurs in different words or the same word in different sentences), the kind of identity that is involved is what we are calling type-token identity. This does not mean, it should be noted, that the notion of type-token identity is directly applicable to sentences like (1) and (2). Generally speaking, (1) and (2) will be construed as making generic* statements (cf. 7.2); i.e. as saying something about the word-type *reference*, and not about any particular token of the type. This interpretation of (2) can be accounted for, however, in terms of the notion of type-token identity by generalizing from any particular occurrence of *reference* (i.e. from any single token) to the class of all its tokens. It is only within the word-token that letters can be described as tokens (i.e. as unique physical entities) which instantiate one type or another. At the same time, it obviously makes sense to say, generically, of the word-type *reference* (and not merely of each of its tokens) that it contains nine letters.

It is only rarely that we shall have occasion to cite tokens, rather than types, since the statements that we shall be making about particular languages will be, for the most part, generic. Should one wish, exceptionally, to cite tokens, rather than types, one can make use of Reichenbach's (1947: 284) device of token-quotes*. These are little arrows, whose function it is to indicate that what they enclose is to be considered as a token of the type that it instantiates. Making use of this device, one can write sentences like the following in such a way that the intended interpretation is clear:

(4) There are nine letter-tokens and five letter-types in the word ˋreference˰

(5) ˋThis sentence contains the word 'contain'˰

(6) ˋThis sentence contains the word *contains*˰

(7) ˋThis sentence contains the word ˋ*contains*˰ ˰.

All of these sentences (more precisely, all of these text-sentences*: cf. 1.6) manifest a particular kind of reflexivity, which may be described as token-reflexivity*: i.e. they are to be interpreted as referring to the very entity that is enclosed by the token-quotes.[8] The device of token-quotes is of very restricted application (cf. Linsky, 1950);[9] and we shall make no further use of it in this volume. It has been introduced here simply to make clear the notion of token-reflexivity, which, as we shall see later, is of considerable importance in connexion with Austin's (1962) distinction between performative* and constative* utterances (cf. 16.1).

At first sight the type-token distinction may appear to be quite trivial, if not pointless. After all, we do not usually fall victim to type-token ambiguities in everyday life. We know which sense of 'word' is intended when we are told that telegrams cost so much a dozen words (or whatever it might be). Consider, however, such questions as the following. Does a capital letter instantiate the same type as the corresponding lower-case letter? Does a word printed in italics instantiate the same type as a word printed in Roman? Is a word handwritten by X ever the same as a word handwritten by Y? The answer to these questions does not depend upon some notion of absolute identity. The relationship of instantiation involves the recognition of identity relative to some purpose or function. What kind of identity is involved may be clear enough in most practical situations. But it is

[8] Reichenbach's term 'token-reflexive' is far more frequently encountered in the literature than is his device of token-quotes. But it is often used, rather loosely, as the equivalent of 'indexical' (in one of the senses of this term: cf. 4.2 and Bar-Hillel, 1954) or 'egocentric particular' (cf. Russell, 1940: 96).

[9] Linsky (1950) makes use of Reichenbach's token-quotes to point out and clarify a number of confusions.

important to realize that it cannot be specified in terms of a certain degree of physical or perceptual similarity. Indeed, it is doubtful whether any sensible measure of physical or perceptual similarity can be determined that is totally independent of functional considerations in questions of pattern recognition of the kind that are at issue here. Our immediate and easy decision that in the written word *reference* (more precisely, in particular tokens of the written word-form *reference*) there are nine letter-tokens, but only five letter-types, is very largely due to the standardization of English spelling and our school training in what counts, from this point of view, as the same letter of the alphabet. The identification of spoken forms as tokens of the same type is far more difficult.

The categorization of tokens into types has just been described in terms of the process of pattern-recognition; and we have emphasized the importance of functional factors and conventional standards of identification in what is all too often regarded as a purely perceptual process. It may be worth adding that, looked at from a psychological point of view, there is perhaps no sharp distinction to be drawn between pattern-recognition and what is commonly called concept-formation. Before a child can be said to have learned the meaning of the word 'table' (i.e. to have formed the concept associated with the word 'table'), he must be able to recognize that there are certain objects, of various shapes and sizes, that are correctly referred to as tables and other objects that are not. The fact that this kind of concept-formation cannot be accounted for purely in terms of the perceptual similarity of the objects that are identified as tables is frequently pointed out in general treatments of semantics. So too is the arbitrariness, or conventionality, of the relation between meaning and form (cf. 3.4). The fact that what counts as identity of form is also grounded, at least partly, in the conventions tacitly accepted by the members of a particular language-community is less frequently emphasized, except in books on linguistics.

We have taken some care to distinguish clearly between tokens and types, and we will draw upon this distinction frequently in the course of this book. It would be unnecessarily pedantic, however, to distinguish terminologically or notationally between types and tokens in cases where the context makes it clear which is intended. The important point is to have grasped the nature of the type-token relationship, to be alive to the possibility of ambiguities which result from it, and to be able to draw upon the terminology when it is helpful to do so.

A simple example may be offered, at this point, of the importance of being able to give some account, at least in principle, of the criteria for type-token identity. The philosophical literature in semantics is full of articles dealing with what is traditionally called indirect discourse (or reported speech) and the problem of specifying the conditions under which such sentences as the following might be true or false (where p stands for any arbitrary proposition):

(8) John said that p and so did Mary.

It is obvious that, for (8) to be true, it is unnecessary that John and Mary should have produced the same string of words: they might even have been speaking two quite different languages. The problems of indirect discourse are real enough for the semanticist. But what about so-called direct discourse (which is presumably more basic)?

Sentences which conform to the following pattern (where X stands for the conventional orthographic representation of any utterance-type in any language) could not be true, it would be generally agreed, unless John and Mary had produced two different tokens of the same type:

(9) John said X and so did Mary.

So much is clear enough. The difficulty lies in specifying precisely what X can cover and the criteria for type-token identity between different instances of X. As long as we restrict our attention to some standardized written language or operate solely with written representations of spoken forms (and especially so, if we make use of non-cursive, printed representations in an alphabetic script), we may be inclined to under-estimate the difficulty of specifying the conditions under which (9) would be true or false. We shall be devoting some space, in a later chapter, to a discussion of what constitutes the verbal component of an utterance (cf. 3.1). For it is a necessary, if not sufficient, condition for type-token identity between utterances that two utterance-tokens of the same type should be formally identical with respect to their verbal component: i.e. that they should instantiate the same forms in the same sequence. What else is required over and above this, however, is unclear. Ever since Bloomfield (1926) explicitly formulated the principle (as one of his postulates for linguistics) that every utterance is wholly made up of forms (as every form is wholly made up of phonemes), it has usually been taken for granted by linguists that the question of type-token identity for any language is decidable. Great difficulty has been experienced, however, in giving empirical content to the linguist's theoretical commitment to Bloomfield's postulate.

Before we leave this topic of type-token identity, we must mention another kind of identity-relationship, similar to that of type-token identity but to be distinguished from it. This is the relationship which holds between an original and a copy, or reproduction, of it (cf. Cohen, 1966: 4–5). Suppose X writes the word *reference* and Y copies it, imitating X's handwriting (whether deliberately or not is irrelevant). Both the word written by X and the word written by Y will be judged (under the appropriate criteria of type-token identity) to be tokens of the same type: from this point of view they are of equivalent status. The relationship which holds between an original and what I will call its replicas* is nonetheless clearly distinct from the relationship which holds between a type and its tokens. The example just given of the relationship of replication* is rather trivial. More interesting is the identity-relationship which holds between a speech and a tape-recording of that speech played back subsequently; and even more complex and theoretically more interesting, as we shall see, is the relationship between speech and writing (cf. 3.3). Within certain limits it would seem to be appropriate to describe written words as replicas of spoken words, even though they do not normally replicate particular word-tokens.

1.5. *Forms, lexemes and expressions*

In this section, a threefold distinction will be drawn which, as far as I am aware, has not been drawn in these terms before: between forms, lexemes and expressions. The term 'form' has already been used in previous sections. So too, without any explanation, has 'expression'. We have been careful to use 'form' in the sense in which it was defined by Bloomfield (1926) and has been used ever since by most linguists. The term 'expression' has been taken from philosophical semantics. But philosophers and logicians rarely, if ever, draw a consistent distinction between forms and expressions, on the one hand, and between lexemes and expressions, on the other.

The distinction between forms and lexemes will be introduced first. It is seen most clearly in relation to words. One way of defining 'word' for written English (and, once again, we will first of all confine our attention to the written language) might be: a word is any sequence of letters which, in normal typographical practice, is bounded on either side by a space. This definition allows as it should, for variations in the house style adopted by different newspapers and publishing firms; and it defines 'word' in the sense appropriate to the costing of telegrams and other such practical concerns. Words of this kind are forms*: more

precisely, they are word-forms*. As we have seen, the normal convention in linguistics for the citation of forms (when they are represented
orthographically, rather than phonetically or phonologically) is to use
italics. This was the convention adopted in the section on use and
mention above, where it was said that *John* has four letters.

Let us now consider the following metalinguistic proposition about
English: "The words *found* and *find* are different forms of the same
word". The term 'word' is clearly being used in two different senses
here (both of them quite normal in technical as well as non-technical
discussion). In the sense of 'word' in which *find* and *found* are said to be
forms of, or belong to, the same word, it is a vocabulary-word that is
being referred to; and vocabulary-words constitute one subclass of what
(with some support in current linguistic usage) we are calling
lexemes*.[10] Lexemes will be referred to throughout by enclosing their
citation-forms in single quotation-marks. By the citation-form* of a
lexeme is meant the form of the lexeme that is conventionally employed
to refer to it in standard dictionaries and grammars of the language.
(This may not always be the same as the citation-form that is used in
the everyday reflexive use of a language in a particular language-
community; and there may be alternative conventions in operation,
e.g., the use of the infinitive form of the verb *vs.* its first-person singular
form in Latin.) It is important to realize that the citation-form is
indeed a form of the lexeme (being used for a particular reflexive or
metalinguistic purpose): it is not to be identified with the lexeme itself.
Given our notational conventions for distinguishing between word-
forms and lexemes we can say, without confusion or ambiguity, that *find*
and *found* are forms of 'find'. The reader is warned, however, that this
is not a standard notational convention. Most linguists use italics for
both forms and lexemes; and philosophers tend to use quotation-
marks to refer to forms, expressions and lexemes.

Something may now be said about our use of double quotation-
marks. They are employed in this work primarily for two purposes:
first, for quotation proper (as distinct from citation); and, second, to
refer to the meaning of a form or lexeme (in the widest sense of
meaning). It has not seemed necessary to distinguish systematically

[10] The term 'lexeme' has been used in several different senses in linguistics.
The distinction between 'form' and 'lexeme', as it is drawn here, is intended
to be consistent with that drawn by Matthews (1972, 1974), who has done
much to make it more precise. The term 'expression' has never been defined,
as far as I know, in linguistics, except in the very different glossematic sense
in which it is opposed to 'content' (cf. Hjelmslev, 1953).

between these two uses of double quotation marks, since the context of the discussion always makes it clear which is intended. We shall be mainly concerned with the meanings of lexemes; and these may be referred to by putting the citation form of the lexeme, unitalicized, in double quotes. Given that 'X' is a lexeme, "X" is the meaning of 'X'. Thus "door" is the meaning of 'door'; and on the assumption that the French lexeme 'porte' has the same meaning as 'door', we can say, in English, that 'porte' means "door". (The reader is reminded that 'meaning' is being reserved as a conveniently loose and imprecise term. At this stage, we do not wish to raise such questions as whether lexemes of different languages can ever be said to have the same meaning in one or other sense of 'meaning', and so on. These are questions that will come up for investigation in later chapters.) Our notational conventions for the citation of sentences and utterances will be explained below. So far they have been cited within single quotation-marks, except when they have been numbered and set out on a different line (or enclosed in token-quotes).

As we saw in the previous section, the type-token relationship is relevant to the identification of two or more word-forms as the same. Since the type-token distinction does not apply to lexemes, there is never any need to use the terms 'word-form-token' and 'word-form-type'; and consequently there is no possibility of confusion or ambiguity arising from the use of 'word-token' and 'word-type' to refer to what would indeed be more strictly called word-form-tokens and word-form-types. Wherever the context makes it quite clear which sense is intended, 'word' will be used in any one of the four senses so far distinguished. As was remarked earlier, the type-token relationship has been confused in much of the literature with other distinctions: in particular, it has been confused with the quite different form-lexeme relationship. Even more commonly, especially in frequency-counts, it has been confused with the compound relationship which holds between a lexeme and a word-token: what is called the type-token ratio for words in texts is often, though not always, a measure of the ratio of lexemes to word-tokens.[11]

We may now look a little more closely at the question of identifying forms as tokens of the same type. We will take it to be a necessary and sufficient condition of identity for written English that the tokens in question should be composed of the same letters in the same order. Forms, it should be noted, may be (morphologically) simple or com-

[11] As in such classic works as Cherry (1957) and Miller (1951).

plex. What is meant by morphological complexity need not be made very precise at this point, nor indeed could it be made precise without going into considerable detail. The distinction between morphological simplicity and complexity can be made clear enough for our present purpose with reference to the following two sentences:

(1) Ignatius of Loyola was the founder of the Society of Jesus
(2) With any other hand at the helm the ship of state would surely founder.

In sentence (1) there occurs the form *founder*; in sentence (2) there occurs the same form *founder*; and by our definition of 'form', they are tokens of the same type (instances of the same form). Morphological analysis of *founder* in (1) would show that it is complex, being composed of *found* and *er* (each of which may be regarded as morphologically simple); whereas *founder* in (2) is simple in that it is not further analysable into grammatically functioning parts. (When necessary, the morphological composition of a complex form may be indicated by using a hyphen: thus *found-er*.)

Some linguists might wish to impose the condition that forms identified as tokens of the same type should be forms of the same lexeme. However, it seems to be terminologically more convenient not to do so. We will say that the form *found* identified above as a component of *found-er* is not only identical with the citation form of 'found' (meaning either "establish" or "melt and pour into a mould"), but also with the past-tense form of 'find'. The advantage of this terminological decision is that we can now say (in accordance with another fairly usual application of the word 'form') that forms are identified as tokens of the same type solely on the grounds of their form, independently of their meaning or their assignment to lexemes. Our terminological decision accords with that of Bloomfield (1926) and most of his followers, including (in this respect) Chomsky (cf. 10.3). That we are not simply equivocating with the term 'form' here will be clear from a brief consideration of homonymy*.

Most dictionaries of English will have separate entries for 'found' meaning "establish" and 'found' meaning "melt and pour into a mould". They may also have an entry for *found* as the past tense of 'find'; this is because it is morphologically irregular, and convenience dictates a single alphabetic listing of lexemes (in their citation form) and irregular forms (cf. 13.1). The fact that there are two separate entries means that the compilers or editors of the dictionary have decided that two distinct lexemes are involved (and not one lexeme with two meanings): 'found₁' and 'found₂'. In this instance, their decision may have been partly determined (as it frequently is in standard dictionaries of English and other European languages) by the historical derivation of the words (cf. Latin 'fundare' *vs.* 'fundere', still distinct in modern French 'fonder' *vs.* 'fondre'). Etymological considerations, however, may be regarded, from our present point of view, as being theoretically irrelevant (cf. 8.2). Independently of their historical source 'found₁' and 'found₂', however, might have been distinguished on the grounds that their meanings are not only different, but unrelated. By contrast, there will probably be only one entry for 'eye' whether it means "organ of sight" or "hole in a needle", for here the two meanings are taken to be related: 'eye', therefore, is treated as one lexeme with a number of meanings. We shall be concerned later with this distinction between relatedness and unrelatedness of meaning: we need not examine it too closely now.

As the term is commonly defined, homonyms* are said to be words (i.e. lexemes) which have the same form, but differ in meaning. We have already seen that it is not difference, but unrelatedness, of meaning that is in fact the criterion in deciding for example that 'found₁' and 'found₂' are homonyms. But what about having the same form? Lexemes as such, as we have seen, are abstract entities and do not have a form. They are associated with a set of one or more forms. It is in the following sense, therefore, that we must understand the customary definition of homonymy: homonyms are lexemes all of whose forms have the same form.

A further condition of homonymy, which is more frequently assumed to be necessary than explicitly mentioned or discussed, is identity of grammatical function. The expressions 'found₁' and 'found₂' satisfy both conditions: (i) each of them has the same set of forms: *found*, *founds*, *founding* and *founded*; (ii) there is identity of grammatical function, not only in the sense that each lexeme is a verb, but also in that the same form has the same grammatical function whether it is associated with 'found₂' or 'found₁': in either case, *founds* is the third-person singular, present-tense form, *founded* is the past-tense form, and so on. It requires but little reflexion to see that these two conditions are, in principle at least, independent, so that they do not necessarily both hold simultaneously. We may therefore recognize various kinds of partial homonymy (including homography* and homophony*) in addition to full homonymy (cf. 13.4).

The distinction of lexemes and forms is applicable, not only to words, but also to phrases. That this is so is clear from the fact that a conventional dictionary of English will list, not only words, but phrases, as items of vocabulary. Many of these phrasal* lexemes are idiomatic in one way or another: 'red herring', 'kick the bucket' (meaning "die"), 'in full swing', etc. This is a question we will not discuss further. The point being emphasized here is that word-lexemes are but a subclass of lexemes. Roughly speaking, we can say that lexemes are the words and phrases that a dictionary would list under a separate entry.

We may now introduce the term expression*, which, as was remarked earlier, is commonly employed by philosophers and logicians in their discussions of language. The fact that the term 'expression' is in existence does not, of course, constitute sufficient reason for distinguishing it from 'lexeme', on the one hand, and from 'form', on the other. The question is whether it is necessary, or at least convenient, to have all three terms.

Let us begin by saying that a term is required for the linguistic units that serve to identify (or refer to) whatever we are talking about when we make a statement about something. The term that is most commonly used in philosophical semantics for this purpose is 'referring expression'. We also want a term for the linguistic units that are employed in order to ascribe particular properties to whatever is being referred to. Once again, the term that is generally used by philosophers is 'expression', and more particularly 'predicative expression': an expression denoting a certain property is said to be predicated of the entity to which the property that it denotes is being ascribed. To take Quine's example (cf. 1.2): we can use 'Boston' to refer to Boston and we can predicate of Boston the expression 'populous' in order to ascribe to it the property of being populous. These semantic notions of reference, denotation, ascription and predication will all be discussed in some detail later. The very simple example that has just been given will serve for the present. We are assuming, then, that there are certain linguistic units whose function it is to refer (referring expressions) and certain linguistic units (predicative expressions) whose function it is to be predicated, or predicable, of entities that are referred to. Let us also concede that (whether or not some or all of these units have one, but not the other, function) both sets of units are appropriately called expressions. Our question is whether expressions, so defined, can be identified with either forms or lexemes, which are established by grammarians (for certain languages at least) on independent grounds.

That expressions cannot be identified with forms – if 'Boston' is an expression in 'Boston is populous' – has been demonstrated already (cf. 1.2). Now, it so happens that 'Boston' might be described, not only as an expression, but also as a lexeme (provided that we think of proper names as belonging to the vocabulary of a language: cf. 7.5). But there are indefinitely many complex expressions, which are clearly not lexemes, but whose meaning is determined by the meaning of their component lexemes and the productive grammatical rules of the language: 'the city where he has lived, loved and lost'; 'the home of one of the world's greatest living logicians and philosophers of language'; 'the place where, some two hundred years ago, several hundred chests of tea were thrown into the harbour in protest against the taxes imposed on tea by the British'; etc. Such complex expressions are not lexemes. Nor can they be identified with the forms that occur in particular sentences. For the argument that was deployed earlier against the identification of simple expressions with forms is valid also against the identification of complex expressions with forms. Furthermore, there are occasions when we want to say that two or more different forms of the same expression occur in different sentences according to the grammatical function of the expression in the sentence in which it occurs. For example, the Latin expression 'ille homo' (meaning "that man") may appear in the form *ille homo, homo ille, illum hominem, hominem illum, illius hominis,* etc. according to its grammatical role. If we want to be able to handle the contradictoriness of the following two translationally equivalent sentences by means of the same principle, we must be able to say that the Latin sentence (2) contains two occurrences of the same expression 'ille homo', just as the English sentence (1) contains two occurrences of the same expression 'that man':

(1) I know that that man is my father, but that man is not my father
(2) Scio illum hominem meum patrem esse, sed ille homo meus pater non est.

There is some sense, then, in which we wish to be able to say that there is an underlying complex linguistic entity of which the forms that actually occur in sentences are the grammatically determined realizations*; and it is this underlying entity, not one or other of its forms, that functions as a referring expression. At the same time, it is obvious that the relation between an expression and its forms is similar to, if not identical with, the relation between a lexeme and its forms. Furthermore, as we shall see later, some lexemes at least, in English and in other languages, can function as referring or predicative expressions. For that reason therefore no notational distinction will be drawn between lexemes and expressions: single quotation-marks will be used for both.

One of the problems that arises in describing precisely the relationship that holds between lexemes and expressions, on the one hand, and between forms and lexemes, on the other, is that this cannot be done except within the framework of some specific grammatical theory. Furthermore, the relationship might require to be stated somewhat differently for different languages. Indeed, there are languages in the description of which the distinction between forms and lexemes is, arguably, dispensable; and many linguists would say that English (though less obviously than, say, Classical Chinese or Vietnamese) is one such language. Something further will be said about this question in a later chapter (10.1). Meanwhile, however, it will be assumed that the explanation given here of forms, lexemes and expressions is sufficient for the terms and notation relating to them to be employed without confusing the reader. It should be clear at least that many philosophical treatments of language (in particular, treatments of use and mention and of object-language and metalanguage) are confused, if not actually vitiated, by the failure to make precise just what kind of linguistic entities are under discussion. This is also true, as we shall see later, of the usual accounts of duality of structure (or double articulation) in linguistics and semiotics (3.4).

1.6. *Theories, models and data*

It is not generally realized by non-linguists how indirect is the relationship between observed (or observable) utterances and the set of grammatical sentences postulated (and cited by way of example) by the linguist in his description of any particular language. The precise nature of this relationship is a matter of controversy among linguists themselves. As is commonly the case, much confusion has been caused by a failure to secure agreement on terminology. Terminological agreement would not, of itself, resolve the theoretical disputes that have been taking place in linguistics about the relationship between data and theory; but it would clarify the issues and perhaps eliminate a certain amount of misunderstanding. It is my purpose in this section, therefore, to explain briefly how I conceive of the relationship between data and theory and to introduce a number of terminological conventions by means of which we can distinguish clearly, when the necessity arises, between the observable phenomena, on the one hand, and a variety of theoretical constructs, on the other.

We may begin by distinguishing between language-behaviour* and the language-system* which underlies it.[12] When we say that someone is speaking a particular language, English for example, we imply that he is engaged in some kind of behaviour, or activity, in the course of which he produces vocal signals of greater or less duration, as well as various non-vocal signals which interact with, and may determine the interpretation of, these vocal signals. The vocal signals we will call utterances*.

Now the term 'utterance' (unlike, for example, the French 'énonciation' and 'énoncé') is ambiguous in that it may refer to a piece of behaviour (an act of uttering: French 'énonciation') as well as to the vocal signal which is a product of that behaviour (French 'énoncé'). These two senses may be distinguished, when this is necessary, by means of the term utterance-act* and utterance-signal*. Philosophers are perhaps more accustomed to using the term 'utterance' in the sense of an act (or activity), linguists in the sense of a signal.[13] It may be worth pointing out, in view of the confusion that surrounds the term 'utterance' in linguistics, that, as it was explicitly defined by both Bloomfield (1926) and Harris (1951), it could be construed as denoting either portions of signalling-behaviour or the transmitted products of that behaviour: it is quite clear, however, that, as it was actually used, not only by Bloomfield and Harris, but by most linguists until recently, 'utterance' was intended to apply to signals, rather than to the behaviour of which the signals are the product. Whenever the term 'utterance' is used without further qualification in this book it is to be understood as being equivalent to 'utterance-signal'.

As defined by Harris (1951: 14) an utterance is "any stretch of talk, by one person, before and after which there is silence on the part of that person"; and this is the definition that we will adopt (extending it, however, to cover written, as well as spoken, language). It follows from the definition that an utterance may be of any length: it may consist of

[12] The terms 'language-behaviour' and 'language-system' are intended to translate Saussure's (1916) 'parole' and 'langue', respectively (cf. 8.2). They are modelled upon Hjelmslev's (1953) 'process' and 'system'.

[13] As we shall see later, utterances are commonly discussed by philosophers of language nowadays within the framework of the theory of speech-acts, initiated by Austin (1962). In this context the term 'speech-act' has a rather special sense, which distinguishes it from 'utterance-signal' (cf. 16.1).

a single word, a single phrase or a single sentence (in a sense of 'sentence' to be explained presently); it may consist of a sequence of sentences; it may also consist of one or more grammatically incomplete sentence-fragments; and it may have one sentence or sentence-fragment parenthetically included within another. In short, there is no simple relation of correspondence between utterances and sentences.

Both the speaker's behaviour and the utterances he produces are observable and, up to a certain point, can be described in purely physical, or external, terms. The terms 'language-behaviour' and 'utterance' (as it is being used here) belong to the pre-theoretical or observational vocabulary of the linguist's metalanguage: they are terms that he can use to talk about his data prior to and independently of its description within a particular theoretical framework. But the linguist also has another set of terms at his disposal, which, as we shall see, relate less directly to the primary data. These we will call theoretical terms, since, in contrast with the pre-theoretical or observational terms, their definition and interpretation is fixed within a particular linguistic theory.

The terms 'pre-theoretical' and 'observational' have just been used in a way which might suggest that they are equivalent.[14] This is not so. For the pre-theoretical vocabulary of linguistics will include a number of terms taken from everyday discourse about language. One of these, and the most important for our purposes, is 'meaning'. Another, as far as spoken language is concerned, is 'word'; for word-tokens, physical entities though they might be, cannot be identified as separate units in the stream of speech on purely external criteria. Terms like 'meaning' and 'word', when they are used prior to and independently of any particular theoretical framework, we will call intuitive*: they rest upon the intuitions of the native speaker about his language. These intuitions have no doubt been very much affected by our formal schooling in the standardized written language and must never be taken on trust as a reliable guide to our actual usage in spontaneous speech. But there is no reason to doubt that there is some degree of correspondence between the way we speak and the way we think we speak. And one of the aims of

[14] This point must be emphasized in view of the role played by observational terms in empiricist versions of scientific methodology. The necessity of distinguishing between the theoretical and pre-theoretical vocabulary of linguistics has been stressed, on several occasions, by Bar-Hillel (cf. 1964, 1970). It must not be supposed, however, that the distinction can be drawn as sharply as such scholars as Carnap, Hempel or Reichenbach suggested in the hey-day of logical positivism: cf. Carnap (1956), Popper (1968).

linguistics, and more particularly of semantics, should be to explicate the native speaker's intuitions as to the acceptability or equivalence of certain utterances, the unacceptability of others, and so on.[15] It will generally be found that intuitive notions, referred to pre-theoretically by means of such terms as 'acceptability', 'meaning', 'equivalence', etc., cover a multiplicity of distinguishable phenomena; and it must then be decided, as a matter of convenience, whether it is better to keep the pre-theoretical term, giving to it a narrower theoretical application, or to introduce a completely new technical term instead. As has been explained above, 'meaning' will be used throughout this book as a pre-theoretical, intuitive term; and a variety of theoretical terms will be introduced in due course to refer to various aspects of meaning. 'Acceptability' will also be employed throughout as a pre-theoretical term, its application being determined, as appropriate to the context, by either observation or intuition.[16]

Utterances are unique physical events; as such, they can be referred to in terms of the observational metalanguage of linguistics. The linguist, however, is not generally concerned with utterances as unique observational entities. He is interested in types, not tokens; and the identification of utterance-tokens as instances of the same utterance-type cannot be carried out in terms solely of external, observational criteria. When we say that two utterances are tokens of the same type, we are implying that they have some structural or functional identity by virtue of which native speakers will recognize their sameness. The pre-theoretical recognition of type-token identity is based, it should be stressed, upon intuition. One might expect that it should be possible to give a theoretical account of the structural identity of two utterances in terms of an acoustic analysis of the two signals; and of their functional identity, or meaning, in terms of a purely behavioural analysis of the two acts of utterance. This is not so. It is now generally agreed by linguists that two utterance-tokens might differ quite grossly acoustically and yet count as structurally identical for the native speaker. Nor does it seem possible to identify utterances as tokens of the same

---

[15] Someone like Itkonen (1974) would say that linguistics, like the social sciences in general, is hermeneutic, rather than truly empirical, in that its aim is restricted to that of explicating and systematizing what is already known intuitively. But this is, so far, a minority view.

[16] The term 'acceptability' was originally used in this way by Chomsky (cf. 1957: 13). More recently, it has been employed in a somewhat different sense (cf. Chomsky, 1965: 11). For a recent discussion of the notion of acceptability cf. Al (1975).

type, as far as the vast majority of utterances are concerned at least, in terms of their functional identity as responses to the same stimuli (when the stimuli themselves have been independently and appropriately grouped together as tokens of a particular type).

What the linguist does when he describes a language, English for example, is to construct what is commonly referred to by scientists as a model, not of actual language-behaviour, but of the regularities manifest in that behaviour (more precisely of that part of language-behaviour which the linguist defines, by methodological decision, to fall within the scope of linguistics): he constructs a model of the language-system. When we say that someone speaks English, or can speak English, we imply that he has acquired the mastery of the principles which govern that kind of language-behaviour which we identify, pre-theoretically, as speaking English. To use Chomsky's (1965) terms: he has acquired a certain competence*, and it is this which makes possible, and is manifest in, his performance*. It will be noted that a distinction has been drawn here between the underlying language-system and the linguist's model of the language-system.[17]

Something should now be said about the relationship between utterances and sentences. The term 'sentence', like 'word', is used in everyday non-technical discourse about language; and, as far as the written language is concerned, what constitutes a sentence is made more or less clear by the conventions of punctuation and the use of capitals. It is a commonplace of traditional grammar that the utterances of everyday conversation tend to be, in some sense, grammatically incomplete or elliptical. It will be assumed that what is meant by the term 'complete sentence' (by contrast with 'incomplete sentence'), for written English, is reasonably clear and that the term can be made applicable in essentially the same sense to the spoken language. We will come back later to the role played by stress and intonation in speech (3.1).

We can now distinguish between the sentence as something that can be uttered (i.e. as the product of a bit of) language-behaviour and the sentence as an abstract, theoretical entity in the linguist's model of the language-system. When it is necessary to distinguish terminologically between these two senses we will use text-sentence* for the former and system-sentence* for the latter. Following what is now coming to

[17] This distinction is not maintained by Chomsky, who deliberately uses the term 'grammar' (in a very general sense: cf. 10.1) with systematic ambiguity, to refer both to the native speaker's competence and also to the linguist's model of that competence (cf. Chomsky, 1965: 25).

be the standard usage in linguistics, we will employ the term text* for any connected passage of discourse, whether it is spoken or written and whether it is a conversation or a monologue. Text-sentences, it will be obvious, can be identified as tokens of the same type: for text-sentences are either utterances (whether written or spoken) or parts of utterances. Text-sentences may be complete or incomplete, in the sense referred to earlier.

The relationship between text-sentences and system-sentences, especially in informal or casual speech, may be quite complex; and it has been the subject of considerable theoretical controversy among linguists. We will return to this question in a later chapter (14.6). In the meantime, we will operate with the simplifying assumption that system-sentences are sequences of words in a one-to-one order-preserving correspondence with what would be judged, intuitively by native speakers, to be grammatically complete text-sentences.

Following a suggestion of Bar-Hillel (1970: 365), we will now draw a systematic distinction between the terms 'statement', 'question', 'command', etc., on the one hand, and 'declarative', 'interrogative', 'imperative', etc., on the other. We will use the former set of terms in relation to utterances, whether acts or signals, and the latter in relation to system-sentences, and then derivatively to such text-sentences as correspond closely in grammatical structure to system-sentences. What might be described as the characteristic function, or use, of a declarative sentence is to make a statement (i.e., to inform someone of something); of an interrogative sentence, to ask a question; and of an imperative sentence, to issue a command (or request). But 'declarative sentence' and 'statement' do not always correspond in this way, nor do 'interrogative sentence' and 'question'; nor 'imperative sentence' and 'command'. Questions may be asked by uttering declarative sentences, commands may be issued by uttering interrogative sentences, and so on. We must therefore distinguish between the grammatical structure of a sentence and the kind of communicative act that is performed, in a particular situation or in an identifiable class of situations, by the utterance of that sentence.

Provided that we are sensitive to the distinctions outlined here we need not be unnecessarily pedantic in our use of the terminology. From what has been said above, it will be clear that system-sentences never occur as the products of ordinary language-behaviour. Representations of system-sentences may of course be used in metalinguistic discussions of the structure and functions of language; and it is such representations that are customarily cited in grammatical descriptions of particular languages. In what follows, expressions like 'the utterance of a sentence' will therefore be understood to refer to the production of a text-sentence and will not be held to imply any identification of system-sentences with utterances.

It remains to make one final point about notation. So far no clear notational distinction has been drawn between system-sentences and utterances (including text-sentences): single quotation-marks have been used for both. Henceforth, single quotation-marks will be reserved for system-sentences, expressions and lexemes (and, by convention, they will be dispensed with whenever any of these units is numbered and set on a different line).[18] Italics will be used for utterances (as well as being used for word-forms, phrasal forms, etc.). For example, *I saw him yesterday* is the text-sentence that corresponds to the system-sentence 'I saw him yesterday'; *John Smith – I saw him yesterday – told me he's getting married* is an utterance whose grammatical structure can be accounted for in terms of the parenthetical embedding of 'I saw him yesterday' within 'John Smith told me he's getting married'; *Next Friday* is an utterance which consists of a sentence-fragment and might be related, according to the context in which some token of it occurs, to indefinitely many system-sentences. It should be clear, of course, that the use of single quotation-marks for system-sentences and of italics for utterances does not imply that the former are expressions and that the latter are forms.[19]

---

[18] It will also be noted that quotation-marks are omitted when a term has an asterisk attached to it. This has the effect of obliterating, from a notational point of view (though not of course otherwise), the distinction between the use and the mention of asterisked terms. It should be added that no attempt has been made to draw a notational distinction between the use and the mention of symbols.

[19] Utterance-signals are indeed forms; but utterance-signals do not stand in the same relation to sentences as forms do to expressions.

2

Communication and information

2.1. *What is communication?*

To say that language serves as an instrument of communication is to utter a truism. Indeed, it is difficult to imagine any satisfactory definition of the term 'language' that did not incorporate some reference to the notion of communication. Furthermore, it is obvious, or has appeared so to many semanticists, that there is an intrinsic connexion between meaning and communication, such that it is impossible to account for the former except in terms of the latter. But what is communication? The words 'communicate' and 'communication' are used in a fairly wide range of contexts in their everyday, pre-theoretical sense. We talk as readily of the communication of feelings, moods and attitudes as we do of the communication of factual information. There can be no doubt that these different senses of the word (if indeed they are truly distinct) are interconnected; and various definitions have been proposed which have sought to bring them under some very general, but theoretical, concept defined in terms of social interaction or the response of an organism to a stimulus.[1] We will here take the alternative approach of giving to the term 'communication' and the cognate terms 'communicate' and 'communicative' a somewhat narrower interpretation than they may bear in everyday usage. The narrowing consists in the restriction of the term to the intentional transmission of information by means of some established signalling-system*; and, initially at least, we will restrict the term still further – to the intentional transmission of factual, or propositional, information.

The principal signalling-systems employed by human beings for the transmission of information, though not the only ones, are languages. We shall be discussing the similarities and differences that exist between linguistic and non-linguistic signalling-systems in the next chapter. The concepts and terminology introduced here are intended to be appli-

[1] A now classic work is Cherry (1956). Smith (1966) gives a broad coverage of the field, with reprints of some of the most important articles.

cable to both. It will be assumed that the sense in which the terms 'signal', 'sender', 'receiver' and 'transmission' are being employed in this section is clear enough from the context. They will be introduced and incorporated in a simple model of a signalling-system in the next section; and they will be discussed with particular reference to language in later chapters.

A signal is communicative*, we will say, if it is intended by the sender to make the receiver aware of something of which he was not previously aware. Whether a signal is communicative or not rests, then, upon the possibility of choice, or selection, on the part of the sender. If the sender cannot but behave in a certain way (i.e. if he cannot choose between alternative kinds of behaviour), then he obviously cannot communicate anything by behaving in that way. This, we say, is obvious; and upon it depends one of the most fundamental principles of semantics – the principle that choice, or the possibility of selection between alternatives, is a necessary, though not a sufficient, condition of meaningfulness. This principle is frequently expressed in terms of the slogan: meaning, or meaningfulness, implies choice.

'Communicative' means "meaningful for the sender". But there is another sense of 'meaningful'; and for this we will reserve the term 'informative' and the cognate expressions 'information' and 'inform'. A signal is informative* if (regardless of the intentions of the sender) it makes the receiver aware of something of which he was not previously aware. 'Informative' therefore means "meaningful to the receiver". If the signal tells him something he knew already, it tells him nothing (to equivocate deliberately with the verb 'tell'): it is uninformative. The generally accepted slogan, that meaningfulness implies choice, can thus be interpreted from either the sender's or the receiver's point of view. It is worth observing, at this point, that sender's meaning involves the notion of intention and receiver's meaning the notion of value, or significance. These two notions were referred to in our preliminary discussion of the meanings of 'meaning' (cf. 1.1).

Under a fairly standard idealization of the process of communication, what the sender communicates (the information put into the signal, as it were, by the sender's selection among possible alternatives) and the information derived from the signal by the receiver (which may be thought of as the receiver's selection from the same set of alternatives) are assumed to be identical. But there are, in practice, frequent instances of misunderstanding; and we must allow for this theoretically.

The communicative component in the use of language, important though it is, should not overemphasized to the neglect of the non-communicative, but nevertheless informative, component which is of such importance in social interaction. All utterances will contain a certain amount of information which, though put there by the speaker, has not been intentionally selected for transmission by him; and the listener will commonly react, in one way or another, to information of this kind. We will come back to this point in the following chapter (3.1).

There are two further points having to do with the notion of communication which should be mentioned, though they will not be discussed in detail here. The first has to do with the distinction between the actual and the intended receiver of a signal. It is not uncommon for there to be more than one receiver linked to the sender by a channel of communication and for the sender to be communicating with only one (or some subset) of these receivers. The sender may then include as part of the signal some feature which identifies the intended receiver, or addressee*, and invites him to pay attention to, or respond to, the signal. The most obvious case of this in communication by means of language is when the sender uses a name or some other term of address in what we will later refer to as the vocative* function (7.5). But the distinction between receiver and addressee is more widely relevant in communication, since, as we shall see later, the sender will often adjust what he has to say according to his conception of the intended receiver's state of knowledge, social status, and so on (14.2).

The second point is of more general theoretical importance: that successful communication depends, not only upon the receiver's reception of the signal and his appreciation of the fact that it is intended for him rather than for another, but also upon his recognition of the sender's communicative intention and upon his making an appropriate behavioural or cognitive response to it. This has long been a commonplace of non-philosophical treatments of meaning and communication (e.g., Gardiner, 1932); and it has been forcefully argued more recently, from a philosophical point of view, by such writers as Grice (1957) and Strawson (1964).

As far as statements of fact (or what purport to be statements of fact) are concerned, it is generally the case that the sender will intend that the receiver should believe what he is told: that he should hold it to be true and should store it in memory as a fact. Furthermore, the sender's desire to convince the receiver that such-and-such is true commonly derives from, or is associated with, some other purpose. For example, there are all sorts of reasons why we might wish to draw someone's attention to the fact that it is raining: we may think that he will be pleased to know that he need not water the garden; we may be concerned that he should not forget to take his raincoat or umbrella; we may want him to close the window or bring in the washing. The particular purpose that we have in telling someone that it is raining will vary, but there will usually be some purpose over and above our desire to inform him of a fact of which he was previously ignorant. Indeed, it may be the case (and it commonly is) that what we actually say is of itself uninformative, in that the receiver knows (and we may know that he knows) whatever fact it is that we are drawing to his attention. This does not invalidate in any way the notions of communication and information with which we are operating here. There is nothing paradoxical in the suggestion that a non-informative utterance should be produced with the intention that the receiver should infer from it (and from the fact that, despite its banality, it is uttered) something that is not said and in the context need not be said. It may be assumed, however, that the interpretation of non-informative utterances trades upon our ability to interpret the same utterances in contexts in which they would be informative; so too does our ability to infer the very specific and context-bound purposes that the sender might have had for producing such-and-such an utterance-token on some particular occasion. The sentence 'It's raining' has a certain constancy of meaning which is independent of the specific purposes that someone might have in uttering it. The question is whether this constant meaning of 'It's raining' and of any arbitrary sentence that might be uttered in order to make a statement of fact can be said to depend intrinsically upon some more general notion of communicative intention.

We will not go into this question here. Certain aspects of the question will be taken up, however, in our discussion of speech-acts* in a later chapter (16.1). Meanwhile, it may be pointed out that, whereas it is clearly not essential to the notion of making a communicative and informative statement that the person making the statement should be speaking what he believes to be the truth or should intend the addressee to believe what he is being told, these are arguably the conditions under which the communication of factual information is normally assumed to operate. We will tacitly make this assumption throughout most of the book.[2]

[2] Lewis (1969) argues, on philosophical grounds, that a convention of truthfulness is a necessary condition for the operation of language.

2.2. *A simple model of communication*

The model introduced here is not restricted in application to communication by means of language. Nor is it intended to cover all aspects, or all kinds, of linguistic communication. The sense in which the term 'communication' is being used falls within the scope of the restrictions explained in the previous section; and we are for the present concerned with an even more restricted kind of communication, namely with the communication of what we have been calling factual information.

Our simple model of communication is cast in the terminology of communications-engineering; it is based upon the model described in the now classic work by Shannon and Weaver (1949). Similar block diagrams to the one given here in figure 1 have appeared in a number of

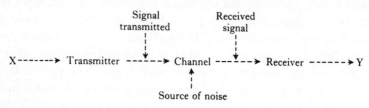

Figure 1. A model of communication

publications in the last twenty years; and the terminology, with certain minor modifications, has been widely employed by psychologists, and to a lesser extent by linguists, in general discussions of communication. It is important to realize that the terms in question are of much wider applicability than their origin in communications-engineering might suggest; and they should not be thought of as referring solely to some electrical, mechanical or electronic system of signal-transmission. To give just one example from linguistics: Jakobson (1960) has used an analysis of essentially this kind to classify different aspects or functions of language and different kinds of information that is transmitted in language-utterances (cf. 2.4). Much general discussion of language was cast in these terms in the late 1950s.

Let us now interpret the diagram (see figure 1). X is the source* and Y is the destination*. We can describe this by saying, as we have done so far, that X sends some information to Y. But 'send' is ambiguous, as far as the present model is concerned, as between the origination of what in communications-engineering is generally referred to as the message* and the actual transmission; and we must distinguish, in principle, between the source of the message and the transmitter. But we can continue to use the word 'sender' when, as is commonly the case, the same machine or organism is both source and transmitter, or incorporates both mechanisms within it, or when it is not important to distinguish between origination and transmission. The message originated by X is encoded* by the transmitter* into a signal*. The signal is sent over a particular communication channel* to the receiver*. The receiver decodes* the signal into a message and passes the message on to Y. (It would be convenient to have a distinct term subsuming 'receiver' and 'destination' as 'sender' subsumes 'source' and 'transmitter'. We have previously used 'receiver' in this wider sense and will continue to do so when there is no conflict between the general sense and the more technical sense just introduced. The distinction between 'receiver' and 'addressee' was explained in the previous section.) It will be observed that the signal transmitted may differ from the signal that is received due to distortions introduced by noise* in the channel. This may, but does not necessarily, lead to a failure in communication. We will come back to this point later: meanwhile we may neglect the source of noise and the difference between the signal transmitted and the received signal.

As was said above, we must be careful to interpret all the theoretical terms introduced here in a sufficiently general sense. Telephone signals are transmitted along a wire as a varying electric current; vocal signals, used in speech, are transmitted as sound waves through the air. Other signalling systems make use of odours, gestures, etc.; and different channels may be distinguished according to the nature of the encoding or decoding systems that are used and the operations that are carried out. Some authors have distinguished the channels according to the sense employed by the receiver, and have talked of the visual, aural or tactile channel; but this is perhaps to use the term in a slightly different sense from the sense it bears in communications engineering. A distinction will be drawn later between channel and medium* (3.3).

Not only is it the case that the source and transmitter, as well as the receiver and destination, may be parts of the same machine or organism, but they may be interconnected by making use of the same processing mechanisms. This is typically so in human and animal communication, where the brain is involved in both the origination and encoding of messages. And there is the further complication that the sender may monitor the signal as he is transmitting it and use feedback from this process, whether consciously or not, to modify the signal, and even the message, during transmission itself. All these complexities will be ignored for the present.

Some messages, or types of messages, may be channel-dependent, in the sense that they can be signalled only along a particular channel of communication. But most messages of the kind we would describe as factual are, we will assume, channel-free: they could be transmitted along one of various alternative channels, and might be sent simultaneously along several, or partly along one and partly along another.

Not only one-to-one communication is possible (where both X and Y are single organisms or machines), but also one-to-many and, in principle, many-to-one communication. Of these, the former type of communication, where one source, X, sends the same message simultaneously to several destinations, Y, Y′, Y″, etc., is common enough: X might be giving a lecture to a group or talking to a number of friends. Many species make use of channels of communication characterized by the properties of broadcast transmission and directional reception. That is to say, the signals are transmitted, like ordinary radio signals, in all directions: they are not beamed to particular points. But the receiver must be turned towards, or otherwise directed to, the transmitter in order to pick up the signals. Broadcast transmission and directional reception are particularly appropriate to one-to-many communication.

More important for semantic theory than properties of the channel, are the following possibilities: (i) that two or more signals may be equivalent, each encoding the same message; and (ii) that a particular signal may be ambiguous, encoding more than one message. Equivalence and ambiguity of utterances are common phenomena in language.

Both the source X, and the destination, Y, will be in a certain state of knowledge or belief: each will have stored in his memory or brain a certain number of propositions*. What precisely is meant by the term 'proposition' we need not at this point enquire (cf. 6.2). It is sufficient to say that propositions are expressed by sentences (and contained in utterances) and may be either true or false.

The communication of factual, or propositional, information can now be described, in terms of our simple model, as follows. X has accessible to him a set of propositions $\{p_1, p_2, p_3, \ldots, p_n\}$. He selects one of the set, p_i, and encodes it (or has it encoded) as a signal and transmits it (or has it transmitted) along the channel of communication; the signal is decoded and reaches Y as a message (which we will assume has not been distorted or garbled). Provided that the proposition, p_i, is not already included in Y's store of knowledge and is not in conflict with any of the other propositions known to Y (or held to be true by Y), it will be accepted and stored by him; and Y's store of factual knowledge (or belief) will be thereby augmented. As far as normal communication by means of language is concerned, we can say that X makes a statement expressing what he holds to be a true proposition, and that, if the communication is successful, Y believes the proposition and remembers it. If Y is already in possession of p_i, the signal encoding p_i, as we saw in the previous section, is uninformative and Y's state of knowledge is unaffected. But if p_i is in conflict with any other proposition, p_j, in Y's possession, Y can do one of various things: he can reject p_i as untrue; he can store p_i in place of p_j, which it conflicts with; he can suspend judgement, storing in effect the information that either p_i or p_j (but not both) is true.

The account that has just been given of the communication of propositional knowledge is admittedly very schematic and highly idealized. But it is not without value. One of the advantages of putting things in the way that we have done is that, by drawing our attention to the deficiencies of our simple model, it enables us to see more clearly the various factors that are involved in the process of communication and their interaction. Let us now list some of the more obvious deficiencies.

(i) Nothing has been said about the possibility that some propositions may be more accessible than others, and that their accessibility may vary from time to time; and no allowance has been made for the possibility that facts can be temporarily or permanently forgotten. Our assumption has been that all propositions are either held in store and are immediately accessible or are not held in store at all. This is clearly unrealistic. If we were to attempt to implement our model of communication on a general-purpose computer, these questions of accessibility and storage would have to be resolved at the outset.

(ii) No distinction has been drawn between propositions that are known a priori* (i.e. independently of experience) and propositions that are known a posteriori* (i.e. on the basis of experience). The status of the distinction between truths of reason and truths of fact, as Leibniz called them (cf. Russell, 1949: 207), has been a central issue in philosophy from the earliest times; and in one form or another it will be of concern to us throughout this book. Its relevance in the present context is that if two propositions are in conflict, it obviously makes a difference that one should be held to be contingent and the other to be an irrefutable truth of reason. Even if we reject the distinction between truths of reason and truths of fact (between the necessary and the contingent, between the analytic* and the synthetic*: cf. 6.5), we must admit that some of the propositions that we hold to be true occupy a more central place than others do in our view of the world; and this holds, not only with respect to propositions that tend to excite the interest of philosophers, but also with respect to the most mundane propositions descriptive of our everyday life. Not all the propositions that are put to us compete for our attention and acceptance on equal terms.

(iii) No distinction has been drawn within the set of propositions that are held to be true as a matter of empirical fact between those that derive from one's own observation and immediate experience and those that have been learned from others or arrived at by a process of reasoning. And yet the source of our beliefs will surely make a difference to the degree of conviction with which we adhere to them; and it may make a difference to the form in which they are stored.

(iv) No account has been taken of the fact that the participants in the communicative process will always have some knowledge or beliefs about one another and will be continually adjusting their view of one another (and, in particular, of one another's sincerity and reliability) in the course of their communicative interaction. When X informs Y of p_i, Y will not only accept or reject p_i himself, but (unless he has reason to doubt the sincerity of X) he will also store the fact that X holds p_i to be true; and that X holds p_i to be true will itself be a proposition whose truth Y can assume in any further dealings he has with X. Similarly, provided that X has no reason to doubt that he has been successful in communicating p_i to Y and in getting him to believe it, he can henceforth act on the assumption, not only that Y now holds p_i to be true, but also that Y knows that X knows that Y holds p_i to be true. Obviously, Y's evaluation of the sincerity and the reliability of his informant is going to be an important factor in the determination of whether Y accepts p_i as true or not. It is not only the inherent plausibility of p_i or its relationship to other such propositions in Y's store of factual knowledge that is relevant. The same proposition might be communicated to Y, in what are otherwise the same circumstances, by two different informants and be accepted as true from the one, but rejected as false from the other.

These are perhaps the most serious of the deficiencies in the deliberately simplified model of communication that has been presented in this section. Since we are not concerned with the construction of a realistic model of communication as such, but only with the way in which the structure of language is determined by the communicative functions that it is called upon to perform, we shall not go into the questions that have been raised here in any detail. However, the points that have just been made are important and should be borne in mind throughout this chapter. So too should the more general point that not all of our knowledge is correctly described as propositional.

2.3. *The quantification of information*

So far we have been using the term 'information' in more or less its everyday sense. There is, however, another sense in which the term has come to be used in the study of communication. In order to avoid confusion we will draw a terminological distinction between these two senses of 'information'. The first kind we will call signal-information*; the second we will call semantic information*.

The distinction between these two senses of 'information' (and they are not always kept clearly apart in the literature) has to do with the difference, between identifying a signal (as s_i rather than s_j) and interpreting it in terms of the message (p_i or p_j) that it encodes. For example, if the sentences *He had a book* and *He had a look* are produced as spoken utterances (i.e. as signals in the vocal-auditory channel: cf. 3.1) they will differ acoustically in that where one has what we may here refer to as a *b*-sound the other has an *l*-sound. Any physical properties of the signals which enable the receiver to identify a particular sound as *b* rather than *l* (or any other potentially occurrent sound), and consequently to identify a particular form as *book* rather than *look* (or any other potentially occurrent form), may be described as signal-information: this is acoustic information in the case of spoken utterances, and visual information in the case of written utterances. 'Semantic information', on the other hand, is closer to, and, if it is defined as a theoretical term, can be said to explicate the non-technical, or everyday, term 'information'. It will be clear that 'information' was used in the sense of "semantic information" in the first section of this chapter. When we say that a signal is informative we imply that it conveys some semantic information to the receiver (that it tells him something). Signal-information and semantic information, though they must be distinguished, interact, as we shall see, in the process of decoding and interpreting utterances.

It is the notion of signal-information that has been quantified within the mathematical theory of communication: or information-theory*, as it is often called. Information-theory, which was originally developed with reference to the very practical problem of maximizing the efficiency of signal transmission in terms of cost and reliability, has not so far justified all the claims that were made for it by some of its early enthusiastic proponents. But it has been the source of much speculation and experiment in the last twenty years or so; and the basic concepts are of the greatest importance in any discussion of communication. Only the very briefest summary need be given here.[3]

Let us begin by supposing that there is a fixed and finite set of potential messages any one of which X may wish to send to Y. Let us further suppose that each message can be encoded by means of one and only one signal. Y knows that X is about to send him a signal, but he does not know which one of the inventory of signals it is to be. We will now define signal-information content, as a function of Y's expectancy, interpreting 'expectancy' in terms of probability of occurrence. We will first assume that Y's expectancy is the same for all signals; that is to say, he no more expects to receive any one signal than he does any of the others. Identifying expectancy with probability, we can say that Y regards all the signals as being equiprobable. Y's knowledge or calculation of the probabilities might depend, in principle, on various factors. However, it is customary to define 'probability' in this context as being equivalent to 'statistical probability': i.e. in terms of frequency of occurrence in a statistically stable system. This means, in effect, that Y's expectancy is assumed to be determined solely by the relative frequency with which he has received such signals in the past. Given that the signals are equiprobable we can say that they all contain the same amount of signal-information.

How signal-information content is quantified (in terms of bits*) is of no consequence for our present purpose. The important point is that signal-information content is inversely proportionate to probability of occurrence: the greater a signal's probability of occurrence the less signal-information it contains; and if the occurrence of a particular signal is totally predictable (i.e. if it has a probability of 1) it carries no signal-information. Given that we have some measure of signal-information based on these principles, we can calculate both the capacity of the channel and the signal-information content of any signal. If a signal takes up more of the channel-capacity than is necessary, it will be to that degree redundant*. Redundancy in a signalling-system is measured as the difference between its maximum potential capacity and its actual

[3] A more popular exposition than Shannon & Weaver (1949) is Weaver (1949). For further details and possible applications, cf. Miller (1951), Cherry (1957), Smith (1966). Hockett (1953) did much to familiarize linguists with the general principles.

capacity. By reducing the redundancy in a system we reduce the cost of transmission; but, as we shall see, we also lessen its reliability. To summarize: there are two principles of general importance deriving from information-theory. The first is the principle that information content is inversely proportionate to probability of occurrence; the second – to which we will return – is that a certain amount of redundancy is not only inevitable, but desirable.

So far we have taken messages as unanalysable wholes and have thought of them as being encoded holistically as signals. Linguistic signals, however, are not holistic; or, at least, not characteristically so. Utterances have an internal structure. In fact, they have two levels* of internal structure: the level of forms and the level of sounds (cf. 3.4). Statistical considerations are relevant at both levels.

Let us first take the lower, or secondary, level and, for simplicity, illustrate its statistical structure with reference to written English. It is well known that different letters of the alphabet vary in their overall frequency of occurrence in any sufficiently large and representative sample of English: *e* occurs more often that *t*, *t* more often than *a*, *a* more often than *i*, and so on. We can calculate these relative frequencies of occurrence and assign to each letter an overall probability of occurrence: distinguished from the overall probability of occurrence, however, are various kinds of conditional* probabilities, which we may group under two main heads: positional* and contextual*. By the positional frequency of occurrence we mean the relative frequency with which a given letter occurs in a particular position in the structure of a word-form: in initial position, in final position, and so on. For example, in English *b* has a high probability of occurrence in word-initial position, but a low probability in word-final position. By the contextual frequency of occurrence is meant the relative frequency with which a given letter occurs in the context of one or more other letters. It is important to appreciate that 'context' does not here imply contiguity. Where the context is contiguous with the letter whose contextual probability we are calculating we may use the more specific term transitional* probability. For example, the transitional probability of occurrence of *r* in the context of an immediately preceding *t* is relatively high; but in the context of an immediately preceding *s* (in the same word-form) it is very low.

Applying the general principle that signal-information content is inversely proportionate to statistical probability and using the same formula as before, we can calculate the signal-information content of any given letter for particular structural positions and particular contexts. In the limiting case the conditional probability of a given letter will be 1 (i.e. its occurrence will be completely determined by either structural position or context). For example, this holds in English (apart from a small number of borrowed words and transliterated proper names) with respect to the letter *u* after an immediately preceding *q*. In this context, therefore, *u* has no signal-information content: it is completely redundant.

Exactly the same principles apply at the level of word-forms. The overall probabilities of particular word-forms in English have been calculated for different kinds of texts and published in various so called word counts. It is more tedious to calculate positional and contextual probabilities; and very little useful information about conditional probabilities at this level is available. However, it is intuitively clear that our ability to guess what word has been omitted from a text is increased by our being able to draw upon our knowledge of its structural position and context; and this ability has been experimentally verified on many occasions. Just as the letter *u* is redundant after *q*, so the word-form *to* is redundant in a context like *want...come* (regardless of what precedes *want* or follows *come*) provided that it is known that only a single word-form (or alternatively a form of such-and-such a length in terms of transmission-time or the number of lower-level units it contains) has occurred: in contexts like this *to* has no signal-information content. It could be omitted without affecting the message that is being sent.

We come now to the second main point in our discussion of information-theory: this is that a certain degree of redundancy* is essential, not only in language, but in any communication system, in order to counteract the distorting effects of noise*. The term 'noise', which is here being employed in the technical sense that it bears in communications-engineering, refers to any disturbances or defects in the system which interfere with the faithful transmission of signals. Every channel of communication, whatever its physical properties, is subject to a greater or less amount of random noise; and the noise will obliterate some of the signal-information transmitted along the channel. Consequently, the information content of the received signal will differ, to a greater or less degree, from that of the transmitted signal (see figure 1). If the transmitted signal were free of redundancy, the information lost in the course of transmission could not be recovered by the receiver and the signal would be incorrectly decoded. Misprints in the written language fall within the scope of the concept of noise: they are often not noticed by the reader because the redundancy of even quite small sections of written text is high enough to outbalance the loss of information. As far as the spoken language is concerned, noise can be taken to comprehend any kind of distortion of the utterance, whether this is due to the imperfect performance of the speaker and hearer or to the acoustic conditions of the physical environment in which the utterance is produced.

The ideal system is one which encodes just enough redundant information in signals to enable the receiver to recover any information lost as a result of noise. If the conditions of transmission are relatively constant, and if the degree of reliability expected is also relatively constant and does not vary according to the kind of message that is being transmitted, it is possible to design a system which approximates to this ideal. It should be clear that the conditions under which linguistic signals are transmitted vary enormously from one occasion to another, and that hearing exactly what is said is more important in some situations than in others. One might not, therefore, expect languages to approximate very closely to the ideal of signalling efficiency. That some general principle of signalling efficiency is operative in the historical development of languages has often been suggested, though it has never been convincingly demonstrated that signalling efficiency, in this sense, is a major determinant of language-change. One manifestation of the principle of efficiency is the tendency to shorten the most frequently used forms; and the operation of this factor in the historical development of languages, on a small scale at least, is well attested.

Signal-information content, as measured by the mathematical theory of communication, has frequently been referred to as surprise-value; and it is this aspect of the theory, if any, which links the two senses of 'information', which we are distinguishing by means of the terms 'signal-information' and 'semantic information'. For, in a general way, it does seem reasonable to say that the greater the surprise-value of a certain item of news, the more significant it is (in some sense of 'significant'). "Man bites dog", as they say, is a more significant item of news than "Dog bites man". As we have seen, when a signal (or some portion of a signal) has a probability of 1 (i.e. when its occurrence is totally predictable), it is defined to carry no signal-information. This seems to be intuitively acceptable also as far as its semantic information is concerned. If the receiver is aware that a certain message will necessarily be transmitted, reception of the signal which encodes that message, when it is transmitted, will not augment his store of knowledge. The information-theory principle that what is completely determined by its context carries no information is in accord, therefore, with the principle introduced in the previous section that meaningfulness implies choice.

The illustration given earlier of information-theory principles was artificially simplified. It was assumed that there was a fixed and finite number of potential messages and that each of these could be encoded holistically into one and only one signal. There are certain situations in which a restricted part of a language is used in this way. But they can hardly be regarded as typical of the use of language. There are alternative ways of encoding the same message (i.e. different utterances can have the same meaning) and one signal can encode more than one message (i.e. utterances can be ambiguous); and it is certainly not the case that speaker and hearer have stored in their brain a table listing all possible messages together with the appropriate signals for encoding them. Furthermore, the reception of utterances cannot be split sharply into two distinct processes: first the identification of the signal and then its interpretation. In the decoding of the acoustic signal, the listener draws upon his knowledge of the positional and contextual probabilities of words even for the identification of sounds; and his calculation of these conditional probabilities of words is not determined solely by his knowledge of the statistical structure of the language, if indeed he can be truly said to know the statistical structure of his language. He is influenced also by his more general expectations of what the speaker wants to say in the particular situation; that is to say, he decodes the signal, partly at least, in the light of what he thinks the message will be. That is to say, signal-information and semantic information interact, in a very complex manner, in the processing of language-utterances; and any theoretical model of the production and reception of speech must take account of this. Because of this complex interaction between signal-information and semantic information, and for other reasons too, there are immense, and perhaps insuperable, problems attaching to any precise application of information-theory to the processing of language-utterances. It does not follow, however, that the general principles are not applicable; in particular, the principle that signal-information content is inversely proportionate to the expectancy of the receiver. The main difficulty is that the receiver's expectancy is not solely a function of the statistical probabilities of sounds (or letters) and words. Probabilities of a different, and perhaps more subjective, kind are also relevant.

We may now raise the question whether semantic information content is quantifiable, as signal-information content is. Certain proposals have been made relating to the quantification of semantic information. Although they have not so far been developed to the point that they can be profitably applied to the everyday use of language (and it is not clear that they are in principle capable of being developed to this point), they are worth discussing briefly for their explication of at least certain aspects of what it means to inform someone of a fact of which he was not previously aware. We will restrict ourselves to a very informal account of the theory of semantic information put forward some years ago by Bar-Hillel and Carnap (1952).

Let us consider a situation in which X is describing some state-of-affairs to Y; and let us assume that this state-of-affairs is totally describable by means of the assertion of just four propositions: p_1, p_2, p_3 and p_4. We might, for example, be concerned with the question whether each of four persons (a, b, c and d) is married or not. Y's initial state of knowledge with respect to this question, we will assume, is minimal. There are sixteen possible states-of-affairs, any one of which might be the actual state-of-affairs. Consider now the effect of communicating to Y any one of the four propositions: e.g. the proposition p_1, that a is married. If he accepts this as true he will put it into his store of factual knowledge; in effect, he will eliminate from the set of sixteen possible states-of-affairs each of the eight which is incompatible with the fact that a is married. His prior doubt about the actual state-of-affairs is halved. Let us now suppose that subsequently another and different proposition, p_2, that b is married, is communicated to Y and accepted as true. The set of states-of-affairs that he is prepared to entertain as possible is again reduced by a factor of two (from eight to four). If p_1 and p_2 had been combined and communicated together, the effect, it will be noted, would have been the same.

It is on the basis of considerations such as these that Carnap and Bar-Hillel have developed their theory of semantic information. They first define a state-description* as a complete set of propositions describing some possible state-of-affairs, and then define the semantic content of a proposition to be the set of state-descriptions that it eliminates. What this means should be clear from the simple example just given. It should also be clear that, although we do not usually talk in this way about what it means to be informed of some fact, this notion of semantic content agrees well enough with our pre-theoretical notion of what constitutes the semantically informative aspect of a proposition. A

tautology, such as the proposition that *a* is either married or not, tells the
recipient of a signal communicating to him such a proposition nothing
of which he was not previously aware; and it would fail to exclude any
of the sixteen states of the universe which Y is prepared to entertain,
initially, as possible. A contradiction, such as the statement that *a* is
both married and not married, is uninformative, however, in the different, and somewhat paradoxical, sense that it has too much content:
"it excludes too much, and is incompatible with any state of the
universe" (Bar-Hillel, 1964: 301). To put it in psychological terms, it
baffles him by purporting to tell him more than he can accommodate in
his conceptual scheme. Finally, if the class of state-descriptions
excluded by proposition *p* includes, and is not included in, the class of
state-descriptions excluded by another proposition *q*, then *p* is semantically more informative than *q*. Thus *p*-and-*q* is semantically more
informative than either-*p*-or-*q*. Carnap and Bar-Hillel deliberately
refrain from making their notion of semantic content relative to a recipient's state of knowledge. It seems clear, however, that, within
certain limits at least, it can be interpreted in this way. For example,
it can be maintained that, after Y has been informed that *p* is true the
subsequent transmission to him of both *p* and *q* is no more informative
than would be the communication of just *q*.

At this point, a cautionary remark should be made in qualification of
the principle that tautologies are semantically uninformative. Whilst
this is intuitively acceptable as far as many tautologies are concerned,
there are certain propositions, which are tautologous, or necessarily
true, in that they follow logically from other propositions taken to be
axiomatic and which nonetheless would normally be held to be informative. The most obvious examples are mathematical propositions.
For example, it is demonstrable that "$(x^2-y^2) = (x+y)\,(x-y)$" is
necessarily true for all values of x and y; and yet the communication of
this proposition to someone who had not previously known or realized
that it was true would generally be taken to augment his store of
knowledge. The status of such tautologous, but apparently informative,
propositions has been of central importance in modern philosophical
semantics (cf. 6.5 and 7.3).

Carnap and Bar-Hillel go on to define the amount of semantic information conveyed by a proposition in terms of Carnap's (1950)
notion of logical probability. As we have seen, the notion of probability
upon which the Shannon–Weaver measure of signal-information
content is founded is defined in terms of relative frequency: we have

referred to this as statistical probability. Many modern treatments of the theory of probability suggest or imply that there can be no objective definition of probability other than in terms of relative frequency of occurrence. Carnap disagrees, and claims that two fundamentally distinct senses of the pre-theoretical expression 'probable' are being confused and that each has its own range of applicability. When we say *The probability of throwing a six with this dice is 1/6* we are presumably making an appeal to the notion of statistical probability. But when we say *The probability of rain (on the evidence of certain meteorological observations) is 1/6* we are ascribing a certain logical relationship (of an inductive kind) to two propositions: the first proposition is the hypothesis "It will rain"; the second is the evidence reporting the relevant meteorological observations (this will normally be a complex proposition composed of many simple propositions). This kind of probability, which Carnap calls logical and which, in his view, is the basis for inductive inference, is often described as subjective and explained in terms of degree of belief or certainty. But Carnap defines it in terms of the degree of confirmation of a hypothesis with respect to a given body of evidence. It would be a separate question whether anybody's degree of belief in the hypothesis, however measured, was equal to the degree of confirmation. The point is that logical probability can be defined, and measured, as a property of some system of propositions in abstraction from the beliefs of the users of the system; and Carnap's theory is intended to measure logical, or inductive, probability in this sense. We will make reference to this notion of logical probability in our discussion of modality in a later chapter (cf. 17.1).

It is within this general framework that Carnap and Bar-Hillel define their notion of semantic information. The basic idea is that semantic information, like signal-information, is equivalent to the elimination of uncertainty. The difference between the two kinds of information can be expressed by saying that the one eliminates uncertainty as to what the signal is and the other uncertainty as to what the message is. In both cases, however, there will be the same kind of inverse relationship between probability and information content; the greater the statistical probability of a certain signal, the smaller will be its signal-information content; the greater the logical probability of a proposition (whether transmitted as a message or not), the smaller will be its semantic information content. It turns out, however, that there are alternative ways of interpreting, and then measuring, the semantic information contained in a proposition, according to whether we have in mind the absolute number of state-descriptions that it enables us to eliminate or the relative number of state-descriptions with respect to the number of state-descriptions not eliminated by previously given propositions. Without going into the numerical relationship which holds between these two measures of semantic information in terms of the theory proposed by Carnap and Bar-Hillel, we can perhaps see that it would be reasonable to distinguish two senses of 'informative' along these general lines, and thus to make precise (in perhaps various ways) that particular sense of 'informative' (or 'significant') in which we say that some facts are more informative (or significant) than others. It is in this sense that semantic information content is analogous to signal-information content. Whether it should be measured in terms of logical probability, or in relation to some other notion of expectancy is, however, another matter; and we will not pursue the question further. It is the notion of a state-description as a set of propositions describing some actual or possible state-of-affairs that will be taken up later (cf. 6.5).

2.4. *Descriptive, social and expressive information*

So far in this chapter we have deliberately restricted our attention to a consideration of what is involved in the transmission of factual, or propositional, information. It is difficult, and at this stage of the discussion it would be impossible, to make more precise than we have done already what is meant by factual information. For the present, we will rest content with the statement that a piece of information is factual if it purports to describe some state-of-affairs.

Many semanticists have talked as if language was used solely, or primarily, for the communication of factual information. Others have maintained that making statements descriptive of states-of-affairs is but one of the functions of language; that it also serves, as do our other customs and patterns of behaviour, for the establishment and maintenance of social relationships and for the expression of our attitudes and personality. We will not go into this question in detail at this point. Let us simply assume that these are three more or less distinguishable functions: the descriptive*, the social* and the expressive*. Correlated with these three different functions we can recognize three different kinds of semantic information encodable in language-utterances. Descriptive information (or descriptive meaning) is factual in the sense explained above: it can be explicitly asserted or denied and, in the most favourable instances at least, it can be objectively verified. An example of an utterance with descriptive meaning is the statement *It is raining* *here in Edinburgh at the moment.* Whether this utterance necessarily or normally contains any additional non-descriptive information is a question we may leave on one side for the present. It is descriptive meaning, as we shall see later, that has been of central concern in philosophical semantics. Other terms that have been used in the literature for this aspect of meaning include 'referential', 'cognitive', 'propositional', 'ideational' and 'designative'.

The distinction between expressive and social meaning is far from clear-cut, and many authors have subsumed both under a single term ('emotive', 'attitudinal', 'interpersonal', 'expressive', etc.). If we define expressive meaning (in a narrower sense than it often bears) to be that aspect of meaning which "covaries with characteristics of the speaker" (Brown, 1958: 307) and social meaning to be that aspect which serves to establish and maintain social relations, it is clear that the two are interconnected. For it is only by virtue of our membership of social groups that we are able to interact with others and, in doing so, to establish our individual identity and personality (cf. Argyle, 1969). The most appropriate term for what is common to the social and expressive functions of language (and of other human signalling-systems) is interpersonal* (cf. Halliday, 1970: 143). It is convenient, however, to allow for the terminological distinction of the two functions, since one of the points of controversy in linguistic theory is the degree to which the individual is constrained by social conventions in the use of language. Such writers as Croce (1902) and Vossler (1932) have perhaps exaggerated the role of individual creative expression in language, whereas others, like Malinowski (1935) and to a lesser extent Firth (1950), may have given undue emphasis to the force of social constraints.[4]

A somewhat different tripartite classification of the functions of language from the one that we have adopted here was put forward some years ago by Bühler (1934) and figures prominently in many influential

[4] Benedetto Croce is very rarely mentioned by English-speaking linguists and philosophers of language. On the other hand, as Lepschy (1966: 98) points out, he is one of the very few scholars whose influence Sapir (1921) explicitly acknowledges. Croce's work is set in the more general context of the development of semantics by De Mauro (1965). Although I have contrasted Croce and Vossler with Firth and Malinowski, no-one can read the works of any of these four scholars (or Sapir) without realizing that each of them acknowledges the role both of social constraints and of individual creativity in the use and development of language: it is at most a question of balance. The Prague School linguists, too, have always been appreciative of the complementary roles of the social and the expressive functions of language (cf. Garvin, 1955; Vachek, 1964).

treatments of language. Two of Bühler's functions, for which he employed the German terms 'Darstellung' ("representation") and 'Ausdruck' ("expression"), correspond closely with what we are calling the descriptive and the expressive functions, respectively. The third, for which Bühler used the term 'Appell', is what we will call the vocative* function. Bühler's classification is based upon his analysis of the typical speech-act (Sprechakt) in terms of three essential components: the speaker, the addressee and the external situation to which reference may be made in the utterance.[5] According to whether reference is made primarily to one rather than the other two of these three components, so the utterance will be primarily expressive, vocative or descriptive in function. There is an obvious connexion between Bühler's analysis and the traditional analysis of the typical situation of utterance as a drama in which three roles are given grammatical recognition by means of the category of person* (cf. 15.1); and Bühler and his followers have explicitly mentioned this connexion. They have emphasized, however, that it is not only utterances with a first-person subject that are expressive and not only utterances whose subject is a second-person pronoun that have a vocative function. They have also stressed the fact, as we are doing here, that few, if any, utterances have one function to the exclusion of the others. As we shall see later, Bühler's tripartite classification is also relevant to his distinction of symptoms, symbols and signals: every utterance is, in general and regardless of its more specific function, an expressive symptom of what is in the speaker's mind, a symbol descriptive of what is signified and a vocative signal that is addressed to the receiver (cf. 4.1).

Bühler's scheme has been modified and extended by Jakobson (1960). The principal modification consists in the substitution of 'conative' for 'vocative' (i.e. 'Appell'). This is not a purely terminological substitution (as is perhaps Jakobson's substitution of 'referential' for 'representational' and 'emotive' for 'expressive'). By using the term 'conative' and explicitly associating it with Bühler's notion of orientation towards the addressee, Jakobson is presumably implying (as others have done) that it is primarily as an instrument in the satisfaction of the speaker's wishes and desires that the addressee is invoked. The conative* function of language is thus closely linked with what is commonly called its instrumental* function: i.e. its being used in order to achieve some practical effect. Furthermore, as we shall see in our discussion of mood

---

[5] This is a different sense of 'speech-act' from the sense in which it is used in work based on Austin (1962): cf. 16.1.

and modality later, it is not always possible to draw a sharp distinction between utterances expressive of the speaker's wishes and utterances which serve as directives imposing upon the addressee some obligation (cf. 15.1). But we may leave this particular point for the present, noting only that what Jakobson and others have referred to as the conative function of language merges with the expressive function, on the one hand, and the instrumental function, on the other.

Bühler's scheme is extended by Jakobson by bringing into consideration three further components of the communicative process and recognizing that each of these may be the focal point, as it were, of the utterance. The first of these additional components is the language that is used (or, in Jakobson's terms, the code*). Any utterance whose primary function it is to verify that the interlocutors are using the same language or dialect, or using expressions of the language in the same way, is said to be metalinguistic*. Enough has been said about this function of language in the previous chapter (1.2; 1.3).

The second additional factor is the channel of communication (cf. 2.2). Many utterances of everyday conversation have as their primary communicative function that of opening up or keeping open the channel. For example, there are all sorts of conventional greetings (*Good morning!*, etc.) or ritualized gambits (*Wonderful weather we are having!*, etc.) with which we can initiate a conversation. There are others with which we can bring a conversation to a mutually acceptable conclusion (*It's been lovely to see you again!*, *Give my regards to your wife*, etc.); and others that serve to prolong the conversation or to indicate to the speaker that the addressee is still in contact and following what is being said. Much of this interaction-management information, as it has been called (i.e. "the information that the participants exchange in order to collaborate with each other in ordering the temporal progress of the interaction": Laver & Hutcheson, 1972: 12), is transmitted by means of paralinguistic* signals (eye-movements, gestures, posture, etc.: cf. 3.2). But some of it is encoded in the verbal component of language-utterances. Malinowski (1930) had coined the term 'phatic communion' for that kind of speech "in which ties of union are created by a mere exchange of words" – a kind of speech which, he says, "serves to establish bonds of personal union between people brought together by the mere need of companionship and does not serve any purpose of communicating ideas"; and Jakobson borrows the term phatic* in order to refer, more particularly, to that function of language which is channel-oriented in that it contributes to the establishment and maintenance of communicative contact. Thus interpreted, the phatic function is very close to, or at least is a very important part of, what we have been calling the social function of language.[6]

Finally, there is what Jakobson calls the poetic* function – in a very broad sense of 'poetic', which relates it, not just to poetry, but to the artistic or creative use of language in general. The poetic function is defined in terms of its orientation towards what Jakobson calls the message, but which is perhaps better referred to as the message-encoded-as-a-signal. For it is characteristic of the poetic use of language that it tends to blur, if it does not obliterate, the simple distinction of form and meaning in terms of which the structure of language is so often analysed. Many of the devices of poetry – rhythm, rhyme, assonance, alliteration, metre, chiasmus, etc. – exploit the properties of the medium* (cf. 3.3); and it is a commonplace of literary criticism that a line like Tennyson's *And murmuring of innumerable bees* would lose much of its meaning (in some relevant sense of 'meaning': cf. 1.1) if *murmuring* or *innumerable* were replaced with word-forms that did not manifest the same pattern of sounds, even if the forms that were substituted for them were forms of words that had the same meaning generally as 'murmur' and 'innumerable'. All that needs to be added to this commonplace observation is that, if Molière's Monsieur Jourdain had spoken prose all his life without knowing it, we all go through life speaking poetry at times, whether we do so deliberately or not and whether we are conscious of doing so or not: we all exploit, to some degree, those resources of our native language which depend upon the properties of the medium in which language is manifest. In the poetic use of language signal-information and semantic information tend to be fused in a way that our simple model of communication does not allow for (cf. 2.3).

Bühler's analysis of the functions of language and Jakobson's modification and extension of this have been briefly summarized here primarily because they have been very influential and a knowledge of the terms in which their analyses are formulated is often taken for granted by later writers. Another reason is that our discussion of these two approaches, brief though it has been, has shown us that there are several ways in which utterances, and the various kinds of information encoded in utterances, can be classified in terms of an analysis of the necessary, or at least typical, components of an act of communication. There is

---

[6] Laver (1975) argues that the notion of 'phatic communion' should be given a somewhat broader interpretation.

perhaps no single classificatory scheme that can be described as the only one that is correct. Furthermore, it requires little reflexion to see that the metalinguistic and the poetic function are closely connected: it is not always possible in the everyday use of language to draw a sharp distinction between object-language and metalanguage, and it may be an important part of the poetic employment of a particular form that attention should be directed to the form itself rather than to what would normally be thought of as the meaning of the expression of which it is a form. Similarly, it is difficult to draw a sharp distinction between the metalinguistic and the phatic function, or between the phatic and the conative. If X uses the word 'sesquipedalian' and Y asks him what it means, Y is clearly making use of the metalinguistic, or reflexive, function of language (cf. 1.2). But he may also be trying to prevent the breakdown of communication; and he is presumably making an appeal to the addressee.

The fact that there is perhaps no unique and obviously correct classificatory scheme does not render the various schemes that have been put forward valueless. Many of the terms that have been introduced here for different kinds of utterances, and for different kinds of information encoded in the same utterance, will be utilized in later chapters. Meanwhile, however, we will operate with the global tripartite distinction of expressive, social and descriptive information; and we will use the term 'interpersonal' (as far as language is concerned) to subsume both 'expressive' and 'social'.

Granted that language has both a descriptive and an interpersonal function, various questions arise. Do any semiotic systems other than languages (or systems derived from or parasitic upon languages) have the one function to the exclusion of the other? This is a question that will be taken up in the following chapter. A further, and more complex, question has to do with the way in which the descriptive and interpersonal functions of language are interrelated. Utterances can be classified, partly in terms of the grammatical structure of the sentences uttered in making them, as statements, questions, commands, requests, wishes, exclamations, and so on. Of these, it is only statements that can ever be said to describe states-of-affairs. It does not make sense to enquire whether a question, command, wish or exclamation, is true or false; it does not therefore make sense to ask what proposition is explicitly asserted by utterances other than statements. However, as we shall see later, we can enquire what propositions are implied or presupposed by certain utterances other than statements (and also, what propositions are implied or presupposed, in addition to those that are explicitly asserted, by certain statements). We can also ask whether there is some notion analogous to the logical notion of truth in terms of which questions, commands, etc., are validated or judged successful. Intuitively, it seems that the refusal to obey a command is analogous to the denial of an assertion. These topics will be dealt with in a later chapter (cf. 16.2). It will be obvious even now that questioning and answering, as well as the issuing of commands, necessarily involves the social function of language; and that any discussion of such utterances as wishes and exclamations must appeal to the expressive function.

Here it may also be mentioned, in anticipation of what will be discussed in greater detail later, that some of the most interesting of recent work in semantics draws its inspiration from Austin's (1962) thesis that to make a statement descriptive of some state-of-affairs is to engage in a particular kind of social activity regulated by conventions similar to, and in part identical with, those which regulate such other acts as making promises, asking questions or issuing commands. If we accept this point of view, however narrowly we circumscribe the descriptive function of language, we must grant that it depends upon, and to that extent is less basic than, the social and expressive function; and this is the view taken by perhaps the majority of linguists, anthropologists and social psychologists who have been concerned with semantics. It can be argued (and this point will in fact be made in the following chapter) that the descriptive function of language is more distinctive of natural languages than is the interpersonal function, which is shared by other human and non-human signalling systems. But this does not mean that the descriptive function is more basic than the other functions. This point must be borne in mind when we come to deal with logical semantics (in chapter 6).

3
Language as a semiotic system

3.1. *Verbal and non-verbal signalling*

The terms 'verbal communication' and 'non-verbal communication' are quite widely employed to distinguish language from other semiotic* systems: i.e. systems of signalling-behaviour. They are terms which, from the point of view adopted in this book, are doubly unfortunate: (i) 'non-verbal communication' is commonly applied to signalling-behaviour in man and animals of a kind which, though it may be informative, is not necessarily communicative (cf. 2.1); (ii) 'verbal communication', in so far as it refers to communication by means of language, might be taken to imply that language-utterances are made up solely of words, whereas, as we shall see in this section, there is an important, and indeed essential, non-verbal component in spoken language. The use of such expressions as 'verbal communication' or 'verbal behaviour' to refer to language-behaviour is, at least potentially, misleading.[1]

We may begin our discussion of spoken language by distinguishing between vocal* and non-vocal* signals, according to whether the signals are transmitted in the vocal-auditory channel or not. The vocal-auditory channel* is here defined it will be observed, in terms of its two end-points and of the manner and mechanisms by means of which the signals are produced at the source and received at the destination, rather than simply in terms of the properties of the channel itself which links the terminals and along which the signal travels. This point in itself is worth noting, since there are alternative definitions to be found in the

---

[1] It may seem pedantic to make this terminological point. But it is arguable that the use of the terms 'verbal behaviour' to refer to what is in fact language behaviour and of 'non-verbal communication' (frequently abbreviated by social psychologists nowadays as NVC) to refer to non-linguistic communication has been detrimental to the study of language and non-language. Much of what appears in the present chapter is a revised and expanded version of Lyons (1972). For criticism of this article, and of other chapters in Hinde (1972): cf. Mounin (1974).

literature. By making our primary classification one of vocal *vs.* non-vocal signals (rather than for example acoustic *vs.* non-acoustic or auditory *vs.* non-auditory signals) we are deliberately taking the view that the so-called speech-organs enjoy a position of pre-eminence among the signal-transmitting systems employed by human beings. It is because the vocal-auditory channel serves for the transmission of language and because, by common consent, languages are the most important and most highly developed semiotic systems employed by human beings, that we start by distinguishing vocal from non-vocal signals. We are for the present concerned solely with speech, which we will assume to be (in a sense to be explained later: cf. 3.3) more basic or more natural than written language.

Not all vocal signals are linguistic. First of all, we must exclude such vocal reflexes* as sneezing, yawning, coughing and snoring. Usually they are physiologically determined; and, although they are signals, in the sense that they are transmitted (for the most part involuntarily) and can be interpreted by the receiver, no-one would wish to regard them as being other than external to language. When they occur as physiological reflexes during speech, they merely introduce noise into the channel (cf. 2.3); and when, by prior individual or cultural convention, they are deliberately produced for the purpose of communication (when, for example, we cough to warn a speaker that he might be overheard by someone approaching), they operate outside and independently of language.

Rather more debatable, from a linguistic point of view, is voice-quality* (also called voice-set*), by which term is meant "the permanent background vocal invariable for an individual's speech" (Crystal, 1969: 103). Unlike the vocal reflexes, voice-quality is a necessary concomitant of speaking. Furthermore, it plays an important expressive and social role by signalling the identity of the speaker and information about him that is of great importance in interpersonal relations. Voice-quality, which may have both a physiological and a cultural component, is very relevant to the phenomenon known as self-presentation* discussed by social psychologists (cf. Argyle, 1967). We will here follow the majority of linguists in describing voice-quality as extra-linguistic. It must be emphasized, however, that in describing it as extra-linguistic, we are not suggesting that it should be regarded as irrelevant to the investigation of language proper (cf. Laver, 1977).

We now come to the distinction of verbal*, prosodic* and paralinguistic* features or components. Every normal English utterance is produced with a particular intonation-pattern or intonation-contour, which is determined partly by the grammatical structure of the utterance and partly by the attitude of the speaker (as dubious, ironical, surprised, etc.). Moreover, each word is pronounced with a certain degree of stress*, or emphasis, according to its grammatical function and a variety of other factors including the contextual presuppositions of the utterance, the attitude of the speaker, and so on. For example, if I stress the form *seen* in *I haven't seen her* (in reply, let us say, to *Have you seen Mary?*) it might be taken to imply that, although I haven't seen her, I have news of her. By contrast, if I make *Mary* prominent it will imply that, although I haven't seen Mary, I have seen someone else. Intonation and stress are the principal prosodic* features operative in English; and they are the only ones that need be mentioned here. They are superimposed, as it were, upon the string of forms which constitutes the verbal component of the utterance. They may be non-verbal, in the sense that they do not serve to identify the word-forms of which the utterance is composed. And yet they are an essential part of what are commonly referred to as verbal signals.

The acoustic correlates of intonation and stress both in English and in other languages are quite complex, and will not be dealt with here. One point that should be made, however, is that, not only intonation, but also stress involves variation in pitch; and, in each case, other factors as well as pitch are involved. It suffices for our purpose that native speakers of a given language (e.g., English) should be able to distinguish one intonation-pattern from another and should be able to say whether a particular word or phrase in an utterance is stressed or unstressed; and this they can certainly do, even if they cannot identify the acoustic features in the utterance-signal which enable them to distinguish intonation from stress, on the one hand, and different kinds of intonation and different degrees of stress, on the other.

In some languages, including English, stress may serve to distinguish one word-form from another. For example, the citation-form (and base-form) of the verb 'produce' is distinguished from the citation-form of the noun 'produce' in that the former is stressed on the second syllable and the latter on the first syllable: viz. *prodúce vs. próduce* (where the acute accent indicates the position of stress within the word). There are several pairs of derivationally* related verbs and nouns in English which are distinguished by stress in this way (in the spoken language). In this case, word-stress plays the same role as does the presence or absence of a suffix like -*ment* or -*al* in distinguishing the forms of nouns like 'amazement' or 'refusal' from the forms of the verbs from which they are derived* (cf. 13.2). In other cases, word-stress may serve to distinguish inflexionally*, rather than derivationally, related forms: i.e. distinct forms of the same lexeme (cf. 1.5). There are no instances of inflexional word-stress in English. But it can be readily illustrated from Spanish: *canto* ("I sing") *vs. cantó* ("he/she sang"). Or from Russian: *góroda* ("of the city") *vs. gorodá* ("the cities"). In yet a third class of cases, word-stress serves to distinguish forms of morphologically unrelated lexemes: e.g. English *differ vs. defer*. Word-stress is, in all three classes of cases illustrated in this paragraph, functionally distinct from either normal or emphatic sentence-stress; and it is as much part of the verbal component of the vocal signal as are the consonants and vowels of which word-forms are composed.

In certain languages (commonly referred to as tone-languages*), word-forms are kept apart, by differences of pitch: one form being pronounced with a rising tone and an otherwise identical form with a falling tone, or one form being pronounced with a high tone and another form with a low tone.[2] In Chinese, for example, different lexemes are distinguished by tone as readily and as normally as English lexemes are distinguished by contrasting vowels and consonants; and in Twi or Ewe (and in many other West African languages) different inflexional forms of the same lexeme (e.g., different tenses of the same verb) are distinguished by tone as regularly as inflexionally distinct forms of the same lexeme in English are distinguished by the presence or absence of particular suffixes. It is customary in linguistics to employ the term 'intonation' for the tonal pattern or contour that is super-imposed upon the verbal component rather than to use it for tonal differences of the kind that have been mentioned in this paragraph, which serve to distinguish one word-form from another and thus constitute an integral part of the verbal component itself (cf. Bolinger, 1972).

So much then for differences of stress and pitch, which, as we have seen, may or may not have to be taken account of in describing the verbal component of utterances. Languages vary considerably in this respect. It is fair to assume, however, that in all languages such prosodic

---

[2] The term 'tone-language', though well established in linguistics, is far from being precisely defined; and it may be construed, wrongly, as implying that what are not classified as tone-languages make no systematic use of tone. A classic treatment of tone-languages, from a particular point of view, is Pike (1948).

features as stress and intonation constitute an important part of the non-verbal component of utterances.

The term paralinguistic* has been used in a variety of senses in the literature. Here it will be employed to cover, not only certain features of vocal signals (e.g., loudness and what may be described loosely as tone of voice), but in addition those gestures, facial expressions, eye-movements, etc., which play a supporting role in normal communication by means of spoken language. The paralinguistic component of language behaviour will be discussed briefly in the following section. The important point at this stage is that it is impossible to distinguish between prosodic and paralinguistic features on general phonetic grounds. Functional considerations have to be taken into account.[3]

It will be clear from what has been said so far that there is room for considerable disagreement as to where the boundary should be drawn between language and non-language; and, consequently, as to what should be included in the linguist's model of the language-system. We can of course decide, as a matter of methodological fiat, that the boundary should be drawn between the prosodic and the paralinguistic; and this is where most linguists do in fact draw the boundary. But this apparent agreement conceals a fair amount of disagreement. For linguists differ as to what vocal features apart from intonation and stress should count as prosodic and what as paralinguistic. The fact that there is such a complete and intimate interpenetration of the verbal, the prosodic and the paralinguistic should always be borne in mind in considering the relationship between linguistic and non-linguistic signalling. It should also be borne in mind that the paralinguistic and the non-verbal prosodic components of an utterance are an essential part of it.

We can now make certain generalizations about language on the basis of this classification of the various components of utterances. First, it would probably be agreed by linguists that, although all the components that we have recognized are essential, the verbal component is more central than the non-verbal component and that prosodic features are more central than paralinguistic features; that within the set of prosodic features some, like stress and intonation, are more central than others; and that paralinguistic features are more central (or perhaps

---

[3] There has been an enormous increase of interest in paralinguistic and prosodic phenomena recently: (cf. Key, 1975). My own treatment is heavily dependent upon Crystal (1969, 1975), which summarize the work that has been done so far and are invaluable for their comprehensive bibliographies. A convenient summary of recent work on both vocal and non-vocal paralinguistic features is Laver (1976).

one should say less peripheral) than voice-quality. The reason why the linguist evaluates centrality in this way would seem to be that the more central a particular component is, the more highly structured it is grammatically and the more specific it is to human language by contrast with the signalling-systems of other species and human signalling-systems other than languages. In this sense, therefore, the verbal component can be taken to be the most distinctive, though it is not the sole, or even the most essential, part of language-behaviour.

The second generalization has to do more particularly with the semiotic functions of the different components of language. It is sometimes suggested that linguistic and non-linguistic signals typically convey two different kinds of semantic information, the former descriptive, the latter expressive or social. We have already seen (in 2.4) that it is impossible to draw a very sharp distinction between these three kinds of information or meaning. They interpenetrate as intimately as do the verbal and non-verbal components of utterances; and they are complementary, rather than contrasting. Whether a spoken English utterance is interpreted as a statement, descriptive of some state-of-affairs, will depend at least partly, and in certain cases wholly, upon its having the appropriate stress-pattern and intonation-contour. The difference between a statement and a yes–no question may be indicated by the presence or absence of certain forms or by the arrangement of the forms in one order rather than another (cf. *They go to school now vs. Do they go to school now?* or *They are going to school now vs. Are they going to school now?*), but it will also be indicated, in most cases, by intonation. So too will the difference between a statement and a request or command. Uttered with the appropriate prosodic and paralinguistic features *He will do it by Tuesday* will be taken as a statement (though predictive or promissory, rather than purely descriptive); uttered with a different set of prosodic and paralinguistic features it may be interpreted as a command or request. The non-verbal component is therefore relevant to the descriptive function of language at least to the extent of distinguishing statements from utterances other than statements. Furthermore, as we shall see below, what may be referred to as the prosodic or paralinguistic modulation* of an utterance may have the effect of contradicting the descriptive meaning that is expressed, or appears to be expressed, in the verbal component. What it cannot do, however, is to change completely the descriptive meaning of a statement in the way that the substitution of one word for another can (cf. *He is tall vs. He is angry*). In this sense, therefore, we can say that the verbal component is more closely associated with the descriptive, and the non-verbal component with the social and expressive function of language. But this generalization, as we have seen, should not be understood to imply that the non-verbal component can be disregarded in any discussion of how spoken language is used to make descriptive statements. Nor should it be supposed that the verbal component of descriptive statements will always contain purely descriptive information. All writers on semantics emphasize the fact that many words are not purely descriptive. They may have expressive (or, more narrowly, emotive) connotations over and above their descriptive meaning. The speaker's choice of one word rather than another is often indicative of his attitude towards what he is describing and may have the effect, whether intended or not, of pleasing or antagonizing the listener.

It has frequently been observed that the semantic information signalled non-verbally in an act of utterance will at times be in conflict or contradiction with the information transmitted by the verbal component. (This point is commonly made in terms of the differences in the information signalled in different channels or different modalities, but neither 'channel' nor 'modality' is the appropriate term here. There is not necessarily any difference of channel involved: there may be contradiction between different components of the composite signal transmitted in the vocal-auditory channel. And 'modality' is best reserved, in linguistics as it is in logic, for distinctions of possibility, necessity, obligation, etc.: cf. 17.1.) The phenomenon of semiotic conflict may hold, it should be noted, not only between vocal and non-vocal signals, or between the linguistic and paralinguistic components of an utterance, but also between the verbal and the prosodic components. An utterance may have the grammatical structure of a declarative sentence (as far as its verbal component is concerned) and yet have superimposed upon this the intonation characteristic of a question. Given that this is so, we may now venture a further generalization; whenever there is a contradiction between the semantic information conveyed by the verbal part of an utterance and the information conveyed by the associated prosodic or paralinguistic features, it is the latter which determine the utterance as a question rather than a statement, as a tentative suggestion rather than a question, and so on.

3.2. *Paralinguistic phenomena*

The most typical form of language-behaviour is that which occurs in face-to-face conversation between members of the same culture; and this is what will be meant by the term 'normal language behaviour'. All other uses and manifestations of language, both written and spoken, are derived in one way or another from normal language-behaviour understood in this sense.

Normal language-behaviour, as we have seen, has a non-verbal, as well as a verbal component; the non-verbal component consists of non-vocal, as well as vocal, phenomena; and the vocal part of the non-verbal component comprises a prosodic and a paralinguistic part. It has already been pointed out that the term 'paralinguistic' (together with 'para-language' and 'paralinguistics') is used in a variety of different ways in the literature. Indeed, it has been said that "the tendency has been to broaden its sense to a point where it becomes almost useless" (Crystal, 1969: 40). In this book, however, the term will be used in a fairly wide sense (though not in as wide a sense as that favoured by certain other authors). It will be held to include both non-prosodic vocal phenomena (variations of pitch, loudness, duration, etc.) and non-vocal phenomena (eye-movements, head-nods, facial expressions, gestures, body-posture, etc.). But non-vocal phenomena will be referred to as paralinguistic only in so far as they are integrated with and further determine the structure or meaning of utterances and serve to regulate the development of a conversation and the interpersonal relations of the participants. Paralinguistic phenomena, thus defined, are parasitic upon and presuppose language. We shall therefore have no technical use for the terms 'paralinguistics' or 'paralanguage'; the former might suggest that the investigation of paralinguistic phenomena falls within the province of some discipline independent of linguistics; the latter that such phenomena constitute an independent, though language-like, signalling-system. This is not the view taken here.

It is important to realize – and this point was made in the previous section – that paralinguistic signals, both vocal and non-vocal, are an essential part of all normal language-behaviour. As Abercrombie puts it: "We speak with our vocal organs, but we converse with our entire bodies... Paralinguistic phenomena...occur alongside spoken language, interact with it, and produce together with it a total system of communication... The study of paralinguistic behaviour is part of the study of conversation: the conversational use of spoken language cannot be properly understood unless paralinguistic elements are taken into account" (1968: 55). If the appropriate paralinguistic elements are omitted, the participants in a conversation get confused, nervous or angry; they may lose the drift of what they are saying and become more or less incoherent, and they may stop talking altogether; in short, conversation is inhibited, if not rendered impossible, by the absence of the appropriate paralinguistic cues (cf. Argyle, 1967: 37–9).

The functions of the paralinguistic phenomena in normal language-behaviour can be classified under two main headings (though neither of these functions, as will be clear from the previous section, is exclusive to the paralinguistic component): modulation* and punctuation*.

By the modulation* of an utterance is meant the superimposing upon the utterance of a particular attitudinal colouring, indicative of the speaker's involvement in what he is saying and his desire to impress or convince the hearer. As we have already seen (cf. 3.1), the paralinguistic features of an utterance may, on occasion, contradict, rather than supplement, the information contained in the verbal and prosodic components: the term 'modulation' is equally appropriate in either case. What is commonly referred to as tone of voice summarizes the most important of the vocal features with a modulating function; and the frequency with which one hears the remark *It's not what he said but the way that he said it* testifies to the recognition by listeners of their importance.

By the punctuation* of an utterance is meant the marking of boundaries at the beginning and end of an utterance and at various points within the utterance to emphasize particular expressions, to segment the utterance to manageable information units, to solicit the listener's permission for the utterance to be continued, and so on.

The more technical discussion of what is loosely described as tone of voice involves the recognition of a whole set of variations in the features of voice dynamics: loudness, tempo, pitch fluctuation, continuity, etc. (cf. Abercrombie, 1967: 95–110). It is a matter of everyday observation that a speaker will tend to speak more loudly and at an unusually high pitch when he is excited or angry (or, in certain situations, when he is merely simulating anger and thus, for whatever purpose, deliberately communicating false information). Other variations in the features of voice dynamics are less easily described by the untrained observer. They are nonetheless present, and the participants react to them, in all normal language-behaviour. Some progress has been made in analysing them phonetically and in correlating them with variations of attitude and emphasis. Among the most obvious non-vocal phenomena classifiable as paralinguistic, and having a modulating, as well as a punctuating, function is the nodding of the head (in certain cultures) with or without an accompanying utterance indicative of assent or agreement.

There are many other movements of the head and hands, as well as changes of facial expression, which modulate and punctuate language-utterances; and these also have been fairly extensively investigated in recent years. One general point that has been continually stressed in the literature is that both the vocal and non-vocal phenomena are to a considerable extent learned rather than instinctive and differ from language to language (or, perhaps one should say, from culture to culture). It is well-known, for example, that a speaker of Greek or Turkish will throw his head back, rather than move it from side to side, when he expresses disagreement or dissent. If one wishes to speak a language correctly and fluently, in the fullest sense, and to avoid being misunderstood, one must be able to control, not only the linguistic, but also the paralinguistic, elements.

Paralinguistic features of the kind referred to in the previous paragraph can also be discussed in terms of the more general role they play in social interaction; and they have been investigated from this point of view by social psychologists. It has been pointed out, for example, that during a conversation the speaker requires continual feedback from the listener, assuring him that the listener is following him, is sympathetic to what he is saying, is willing for him to continue, and so on. Much of this feedback consists in head-nods, grunts and eye-movements. Speaker and listener must also solve the problem of floor-apportionment*, assuming or yielding the right to speak by turns. Looked at from this point of view, a conversation is a piece of social interaction, like any other; and, what is actually said in words, may be of relatively little importance. Its primary function is to establish and maintain social relationships; to indicate that one belongs to a particular group within the society, to assert one's identity and personality, to present a certain image of oneself to others (cf. Goffman, 1956). All these functions we have subsumed under the term 'interpersonal', in the distinction of interpersonal and descriptive meaning; and we have emphasized that both kinds of meaning are indissolubly associated in language (cf. 2.4).

Non-linguistic signalling can, of course, be studied independently of its interaction with utterances in language-behaviour; and it has been investigated from this point of view by a number of scholars. Indeed, this is what is commonly meant by 'non-verbal communication' and 'paralanguage'. The semiotic functions fulfilled by non-linguistic signals outside language-behaviour are almost exclusively social and expressive, rather than descriptive, and do not appear to differ significantly from the functions that they fulfil, concomitantly with their paralinguistic function, when they operate as a part of language-behaviour. Since our main concern is with linguistic semantics, we will not go further into the role of non-linguistic signalling in social interaction (cf. Laver & Hutcheson, 1972). Nor will we discuss in any detail the proposals that have been made for the analysis of the non-linguistic signalling-systems used by man. Mention may be made, however, of two technical terms that have been coined in this connexion. The first is kinesics* (cf. Birdwhistell, 1970), which is now commonly employed to refer to the investigation of signalling-systems making use of gestures and other body movements; the second is proxemics* (cf. Hall, 1959), which is applied to the study of the way in which the participants in social interaction adjust their posture and relative distance from one another according to the degree of intimacy that obtains between them, their sex, the social roles they are performing, and so on. The use made of the interpersonal space in social interaction varies, as do gestures and other body movements, from one culture to another and, within one culture, along a number of identifiable socio-personal dimensions.

3.3. *Language and medium*

Languages, as we know them today in most parts of the world, may be either spoken or written. Western traditional grammar, which originated in Greece and was taken over and further developed by Roman and medieval scholars, was concerned almost exclusively with the language of literature, and comparatively little attention was given to the analysis of everyday colloquial speech. During the nineteenth century immense progress was made in the investigation of the historical development of languages; and scholars came to realize more clearly than before that changes in the language of written texts of different periods – changes of the kind that over the centuries transformed Latin into French, Italian or Spanish, for example – could only be explained in terms of changes that had taken place in the corresponding spoken language. All the great literary languages of the world are derived, ultimately, from the speech of particular communities. Furthermore, from a linguistic point of view, it is a matter of historical accident that the speech of one region or of one social class should have served as the basis for the development of a standard literary language in particular language communities and that the variant dialects of other regions or of other social classes should now be regarded, as they often are by educated members of the language community in question, as inferior or substandard versions of the language (cf. 14.5). It is important to realize that non-standard dialects are in general no less regular or systematic than standard literary languages. It is because they have been taught the grammar of the standard written language at school, but have never studied the grammar of a non-standard dialect (even though they might speak one at home), that many people think of non-standard dialects as being essentially unsystematic.

It is one of the cardinal principles of modern linguistics that the spoken language is basic. This does not mean, however, that language is to be identified with speech. For we must draw a distinction between the language and the medium* in which the language is manifest. This concept of medium is related to, but, as we shall see, must be distinguished from the notion of the channel* of communication introduced in an earlier chapter (2.2). According to a common formulation of the relationship between speech and writing, and one which we will adopt here, the spoken language is prior to the written in the sense that the latter results from the transference of the former from a primary to a secondary medium (cf. Abercrombie, 1967: 1–19).[4] This implies that sound, and more specifically, phonic* sound (i.e. the range of audible sound which can be produced by the human speech organs) is the natural, or basic medium in which the language-system is realized and that written utterances result from the transference of language from this primary phonic* medium to a secondary graphic* medium.

It should be noticed that we have used the term 'phonic' for the medium of spoken language, but 'vocal-auditory' for the channel along which it is normally transmitted (3.1). The reason why it is important to distinguish between channel and medium is that both spoken and written language can be transmitted along a variety of different channels. For example, a message written in Braille is decoded by means of the sense of touch, rather than sight. But it is composed of configurations of dots in one-to-one correspondence with the letters of the written language, and the word-forms of Braille are also in one-to-one correspondence with the word-forms of the written language. In short, a message written in Braille and a message written in the normal orthography are structurally isomorphic; and this is the crucial point. When

---

[4] My definition of 'medium', however, differs in certain respects from Abercrombie's. My own views have been influenced by Hjelmslev's notion of substance (cf. Hjelmslev, 1953). There are alternative ways of classifying and analysing the phenomena.

we use the term 'medium', rather than 'channel', we are concerned, not with the actual transmission of signals, but with the systematic functional and structural differences between written and spoken language. Many of these differences, it is true, can be attributed, in origin at least, to physical differences in the characteristically distinct channels of transmission employed for spoken and written language. But they are not necessarily determined by the actual channel of transmission on each occasion of utterance. Spoken English can be transmitted in writing, though not very satisfactorily in the normal orthographic script; and the written language can be transmitted, and commonly is nowadays, along many different channels. It requires but a moment's reflexion to appreciate that there are many complexities that need to be accounted for in relating medium to channel. Many formal lectures, for example, though they are delivered orally and have the phonological structure of the spoken language, are composed, as far as grammar and vocabulary are concerned, in the written medium. Verbatim transcripts of spontaneous conversations illustrate the converse possibility: at the level of orthographic structure they are in the written medium, but in grammar and vocabulary they are constructed according to the principles which determine the selection and combination of words in the spoken medium. Passages of dialogue in novels, on the other hand, though they purport to be transcripts of conversations, are frequently rather unrealistic; and much of what is written in newspapers or in advertisements (and is intended to be read) is strongly influenced by the spoken language. Despite these complexities, the fact that the spoken language can be written and the written language spoken is important; and it depends upon the principle of duality* and upon the relative independence of the two levels of structure (cf. 3.4). Some indication of this interrelationship and of the fact that ordinary native speakers are aware of it may be given here by simply mentioning the everyday employment of the terms 'bookish', on the one hand, and 'colloquial', on the other.

Having emphasized the fact that languages are to some considerable degree independent of the medium in which they are manifest, we must now give due recognition to the functional and structural differences between spoken and written languages. There are, in fact, important grammatical and lexical differences between the two; and the prosodic and paralinguistic features of speech are only crudely and very incompletely represented by punctuation marks and the use of italics, etc., in writing. Written texts may be composed, reflected upon and edited, before any part is transmitted; and the fact that they are more enduring than spoken utterances (or were so until ways of recording sound were developed) and have therefore been used throughout history in literate communities for the codification, preservation and citation of important legal, cultural and religious documents has contributed to the greater formality and prestige of the written language. It has encouraged people to think of written words, in Firth's felicitous phrase, as "graven images" (1937: ch. 4) and it has led to the development of the concepts of literature and scripture. Any account of language and the role it fulfils in modern society must recognize that written languages, despite the fact that they have in all cases derived from spoken languages, now have a considerable degree of structural and functional independence.[5]

3.4. *The design features of language*

The term 'design features' is taken from Hockett and refers to a number of general properties in respect of which languages may be compared with other semiotic systems used by man or animals. The original list of features, or key properties, has been extended in successive publications from seven to sixteen (cf. Hockett, 1958, 1960; Hockett & Altmann 1968). Some of these design features have to do solely with the channel of communication and with the physical properties of vocal signals (cf. Householder, 1971: 24–42); and we will take no account of them here. Of the others, four are of particular importance for the understanding of how languages operate as signalling systems, and these will be discussed in some detail: arbitrariness, duality, productivity and discreteness. The remainder will be referred to more briefly.

(i) Arbitrariness. The term arbitrariness* is used, in a somewhat narrow sense, by Hockett to contrast with iconicity* (cf. 4.2). Any signal, or component of a signal, which is, in some way, "geometrically similar" to what it means or stands for is iconic; otherwise it is said to be arbitrary (Hockett, 1958: 577). It is legitimate, however, to use the term 'arbitrary' to describe any feature that cannot be said to derive from the

---

[5] The partial independence of written and spoken language is something that many linguists have failed to recognize. It has always been recognized by linguists of the Prague School (cf. Vachek, 1945/9, 1964) and, within a different theoretical framework, by the glossematicians (cf. Uldall, 1944; Spang-Hanssen, 1961). Generally speaking, post-Bloomfieldian American linguistics (including Chomskyan versions of generative grammar: cf. 10.3) has emphasized the principle of the priority of the spoken language to the point of distortion. Notable exceptions are Bolinger (1946) and, more recently, in a stimulating and very original discussion of the whole topic, Householder (1971: 244–64).

properties of the channel along which language is normally transmitted, from the physiological and psychological mechanisms employed in the production or reception of language or from the functions language is called upon to perform. The importance of arbitrariness in the narrow sense in which Hockett uses the term (i.e. to refer to the absence of iconicity) has long been recognized (notably by Saussure, 1916), not only in connexion with the problem of accounting for the origin of language, but also with respect to the semiotic versatility and adaptability of the system; and we shall discuss it in greater detail later (cf. 4.2). In the present context it is sufficient to point to the difficulty of deciding upon a suitable pictographic representation of the meaning of every English word. For words denoting physical objects and spatial relationships it is perhaps easy enough to find suitable signs. But for other words it would be difficult, and for some words perhaps impossible. If the meanings that can be signalled in a system are restricted to those in which there is some kind of geometrical similarity between a signal and its meaning, the system will be incapable of signalling much of the information that we can signal quite freely in languages as we know them. Arbitrariness therefore contributes to the versatility and flexibility of language.

Symptomatic* signals (cf. 4.2) are especially interesting when they are considered from the point of view of iconicity. It would be generally agreed, for example, that the correlation of increasing loudness of voice and rising pitch with increasing anger or excitement is iconic; and moreover that it is natural rather than conventional – i.e. that it is biologically, rather than culturally, determined. What may be called natural iconicity is undoubtedly an essential and important feature of language-behaviour (though it may be described as paralinguistic, rather than linguistic), and it is very characteristic of other kinds of signalling behaviour used by man and animals.

(ii) Duality. What Hockett calls duality* (or more fully 'duality of patterning') is also referred to in the literature by means of the terms 'double articulation' (cf. Martinet, 1949); and it is generally recognized as one of the universal features of language. Indeed, some scholars (notably Hjelmslev, 1953) have proposed that it should be made an essential and defining property of language on a priori grounds.

It is important not to confuse duality with the property of being meaningful: the principle of duality can be stated without making any mention of meaning at all. To say that languages have the property of duality is to say that they have two levels* of structural organizations, phonological* and grammatical*, and that the two levels are related in that higher-level segments, forms, are composed of lower-level segments, phonemes.[6]

The relationship between the phonological and the grammatical levels of analysis, in many languages at least, is such that we cannot simply say that combinations of lower-level (phonological) units, constitute higher-level (grammatical) units; and that, whereas the higher-level units are meaningful the lower-level units are not. For this, as we have seen in a previous chapter (1.5), would involve us in the confusion of a form with the lexeme of which it is a form. In the analysis of languages of the so-called isolating* type, such as Classical Chinese or Vietnamese, where (to make the point very loosely) all the words are invariable (i.e. where every lexeme is associated with one and only one form), the distinction between forms and lexemes would not need to be drawn, if it were not for the fact that even in isolating languages there are instances of homonymy* (cf. 13.4). In languages of the so-called agglutinating* type, such as Turkish and Japanese (and possibly the majority of the world's languages), it is also arguable that the distinction between forms and lexemes would be unnecessary, if it were not for the phenomenon of homonymy. For an agglutinating language is one in which the word-forms can be analysed as sequences of morphemes*, each of which is invariable, in the same sense that the words of isolating languages are invariable; and it is morphemes, rather than words, that are the basic grammatical units. But in inflecting* languages like Latin

[6] This is something of a simplification, as it stands, in that phonemes, though they may be regarded as the minimal segments of the phonological level, are not necessarily the minimal units, since they may be further analysed as sets of simultaneous components (or distinctive features*). The notion of distinctive features (i.e. of minimal contrasting phonological components) goes back to Trubetzkoy (1939). It was subsequently modified by Jakobson (cf. Jakobson & Halle, 1956) and, with further modifications, incorporated in Chomskyan generative grammar (cf. Chomsky & Halle, 1968). Hjelmslev (1953) had a somewhat different conception of distinctive features, which he referred to as cenemes*. For some discussion of the status of distinctive features, cf. Householder (1971: 147–93). It should also be added that the phonological analysis of an utterance is far from exhausted by a specification of what segmental phonemes occur in the verbal part of the utterance. Such prosodic features as stress and intonation must also be accounted for; and whether these so-called suprasegmental* features are characterized by duality or not is a matter of dispute. The necessarily simplified statement of the principle of duality given here will, however, suffice for our present purpose. The point to be stressed is that nothing has been said here about higher-level units being meaningful.

and Greek, with which Western traditional grammar was primarily concerned (and from which some of its concepts were inappropriately transferred to languages of a different type), the distinction of word-forms and lexemes would seem to be essential. In such languages the analysis of word-forms into smaller grammatical segments (where they can be so analysed) does not result in sequences of morphemes, each of which is invariable.[7]

English, as far as most of its regular word-forms are concerned, is either isolating or agglutinating. Adjectives like 'beautiful' have only one form, *beautiful*; and this, in comparative and superlative phrases, is modified by *more* and *most*. But adjectives like 'rich' are associated with three word-forms *rich, richer* and *richest*; and *rich-er* and *rich-est* are agglutinating in character. The -*s* suffix which occurs at the end of third-person singular verbs in the simple present tense of verbs (as in *come-s*) is grammatically complex, as Latin or Greek suffixes tend to be: it marks the form simultaneously as both third-person singular and present tense. But the same form when it marks the plural of regular nouns (as in *boy-s*) is not grammatically complex in the same way; and this is again typical of the agglutinating character of the regular patterns of inflexion in English.

We have already recognized two senses of 'word' (cf. 1.5). There is also a third sense of 'word' that can be usefully distinguished with reference to English. Is *loved* in *I loved* the same word as *loved* in *I have loved*? That it is the same word-form which occurs in both instances is clear enough; for the same simple forms are combined in the same way, *love-ed*. It is also obvious that the *loved* of *I loved* and the *loved* of *I have loved* are forms of the same lexeme 'love'. But there is another point of view from which one might wish to say that the two forms (though tokens of the same type: cf. 1.4) are different words; or, more precisely that they realize different words. In *I loved* the form *loved* realizes the past tense of 'love', but in *I have loved* it realizes the past participle (of the same verb). We will refer to the past tense of 'love' and the past participle of 'love' as two distinct morphosyntactic* words; and we will say that morphosyntactic words underlie (or are realized by) word-forms. As we have just seen, two distinct morphosyntactic

---

[7] The tripartite typological classification of languages as inflecting (or fusional), isolating or agglutinating is no longer thought to be as important as it appeared to be to many nineteenth-century linguists (cf. Pedersen, 1931; Jespersen, 1924). But, properly interpreted and stripped of its evolutionary implications, it has its uses (cf. Bazell, 1958).

words may be realized by one word-form: this is traditionally known as syncretism*. The converse situation may also hold, and this we will call alternation*: for example, *dreamed* and *dreamt* are alternative realizations of the same underlying morphosyntactic word.[8]

These distinctions between lexemes, morphosyntactic words and word-forms have been drawn here primarily to emphasize the point that the relationship between the phonological and the grammatical level of analysis can be quite complex. They are useful for talking about languages fairly informally, even if the more formal grammatical description of any particular language does not give theoretical recognition to lexemes, morphosyntactic complexes and forms as distinct entities. Our discussion of language in this book is intended to be as neutral as possible with respect to alternative theories of grammar (cf. 10.1).

Looked at from a semiotic point of view, the advantage of duality lies in the fact that it makes it possible to distinguish a very large number of forms (and indirectly therefore a very large number of lexemes and expressions) by combining a relatively small number of lower-level elements in a variety of different ways. Taken in conjunction with the property of grammatical productivity (which we will be discussing below), duality accounts for the fact that indefinitely many formally distinct utterances can be constructed in any natural language out of a relatively small set of phonological elements.

Duality, as it operates in language, is also bound up with arbitrariness. If each phonological element in a given form had to bear an identifiable iconic relationship, whether conventional or natural, to some aspect of its meaning, it is obvious that there would be severe constraints upon the possibility of combining phonological elements with one another. This would still be true if there were a constant, but non-iconic, relationship between a given phonological element and the meaning of the forms in which it occurred, as is the case in systems of the kind that were constructed by Dalgarno (1661) and Wilkins (1668).[9] The alleged superiority, in terms of consistency and logicality, of a language in which (let us say) all forms relating to location in space began with the same phoneme, all forms having to do with marriage ended with the

---

[8] For further discussion and references, cf. Matthews (1972, 1974). The terminology that I have used here conforms to that of Matthews (1974) and, in certain respects, differs from that of Lyons (1968).

[9] A modern example is Loglan (cf. Brown, 1966); cf. Zwicky (1969) for a sympathetic, but critical, review, which makes several points of general theoretical interest. For the background to the works of Dalgarno and of Wilkins, cf. Salmon (1966).

same phoneme, and so on, would be more than outbalanced by its lack of flexibility and the limited number of word-forms of a given length that could be composed out of a small set of elements.

The dissociation of duality and arbitrariness happens only on a small scale in natural languages: most notably, in cases of sound-symbolism and onomatopoeia (cf. 4.2). It is not uncommon, however, for certain phonological elements or certain types of phonological structure to be invested with a specific grammatical function; and this reduces the arbitrariness of the language-system, even though it may not increase its iconicity. For example, there are languages in which the phonological structure of the forms of nouns differs from that of the forms of verbs; there are languages in which pronouns, prepositions or conjunctions are characteristically different in phonological structure from the forms of nouns, verbs or adjectives; and so on. Mention should also be made in this context of what Trubetzkoy (1939) called boundary-signals (Grenzsignale): i.e. phonemes or prosodic features whose function it is to mark the boundaries of forms and so make them more prominent in the stream of speech (cf. Martinet, 1960). Stress functions in this way in many languages; as, for example, in Czech, where the first syllable of every word-form in an utterance is stressed, or Turkish, where (with some exceptions) the last syllable receives the stress. Vowel-harmony, as it operates in such languages as Turkish or Hungarian, can also be seen as having this function; in other languages, however, it may serve to mark word-forms as members of particular grammatical classes or to link grammatically related forms.[10]

The dissociation of duality and arbitrariness imposes certain limits, then, upon the combination of phonological elements in particular languages. Over and above such restrictions upon the permissible combinations of phonological elements as have just been mentioned, there are others, both systematic and random, which are independent of grammatical function and meaning. For example, there are no word-forms in English (other than the forms of some proper names) beginning *tv-* or *sr-*. Such combinations of consonants are not inherently difficult to pronounce and occur frequently at the beginning of word-forms in many languages (e.g. Russian). It is because all languages have such constraints or limitations that we say they have a level of phonological structure, rather than simply an inventory or repertoire

---

[10] The phenomena treated by Trubetzkoy and his followers in terms of the notion of boundary-signals are handled rather differently by phonologists of the so-called London School (cf. Palmer, 1970).

76   *Language as a semiotic system*

of phonological elements. What is meant by saying that certain restrictions upon the combination of phonemes are random, rather than systematic, may be illustrated with reference to such non-existent word-forms as *gred* or *blick*. The fact that there is no such form in English as *blick* has nothing to do with its phonological structure; unlike *bnick*, it does not violate any of the systematic principles of English phonology (cf. Chomsky & Halle, 1968). It is a potential word-form, as it were, which has not been actualized in the language-system. Clearly, the more limitations there are, whether systematic or random, upon the combination of phonological elements, the greater will be the redundancy in the signals; and redundancy, as we have seen, is essential to counteract channel-noise (2.3).

(iii) Productivity. By productivity*, as we shall employ the term, is meant that property of the language-system which enables native speakers to construct and understand an indefinitely large number of utterances, including utterances that they have never previously encountered. The importance of this property has been stressed in the recent linguistic literature with special reference to the problem of accounting for the acquisition of language by children (cf. Chomsky, 1957, 1965). The fact that children, at a quite early age, are able to produce utterances that they have never heard before is sufficient proof, if proof were needed, that language cannot be learned solely by means of the memorization and imitation of whole utterances. Much earlier speculation about the origin and acquisition of language failed to give due emphasis to productivity and concentrated solely on the problem of explaining how isolated words and utterances acquired their meaning. This is by no means a trivial question; but, even if it were answered to our complete satisfaction, the answer would not suffice to account for either the origin of languages or their acquisition, in childhood, by native speakers.

It is important, in evaluating semiotic systems in terms of the property of productivity, not to overlook the formal complexity of the principles by virtue of which new utterances may be constructed. The number of new utterances that are coined in relation to the number of utterances previously encountered will not necessarily reflect this complexity. To say that bee-dancing, for example, has the property of productivity, because the bee can produce indefinitely many different signals (as it indicates the direction and distance of a source of honey) by systematically varying both its position in relation to the sun and the intensity of its body movements during the dance (cf. Hockett, 1958; Thorpe, 1972) is therefore rather misleading. The formal simplicity of the principle which determines the productivity of bee-dancing is in striking contrast with the complexity and heterogeneity of the formal principles of syntax which govern the productivity of language.

Productivity has been interpreted here solely in terms of the grammatical structure of language; and this kind of productivity, it should be noted, is characterized, to some considerable degree at least, by the feature of arbitrariness. For example, the simple attributive adjective precedes the noun that it qualifies in English and German, but it generally follows the noun in French; the verb normally comes at the beginning of the sentence in Irish, but at the end in Turkish. Word-order is to this extent arbitrary, as is much else in the grammatical structure of languages. Having made this generalization, however, we must immediately qualify it by saying that not everything in grammar is arbitrary. For example, the fact that in *John came in and he sat down*, but not in *He came in and John sat down*, 'he' can refer to John is not just an arbitrary and inexplicable fact of English. It is explicable in terms of the principle that (unless they occur in subordinate clauses) pronouns refer either to entities that are present in the environment or to previously mentioned entities (cf. 15.3); and this in turn depends partly upon the fact that language-utterances, in their natural medium and transmitted in the normal vocal-auditory channel (cf. 3.3), are produced and processed in real time and partly upon the fact that what is said earlier serves to amplify or modify the context for what is said later. Other examples of non-arbitrariness in grammatical structure could be given; and it is important that they should be borne in mind in any discussion of the nature of language.

There are of course utterances whose novelty does not consist solely in the fact that they have never occurred in the previous experience of the speaker or writer, but in their acknowledged orginality of style; and it is for this kind of novelty or originality that the term 'creativity' is most appropriate (though it is not uncommonly used by linguists for what we are calling productivity). Whether creativity is a property of languages or a characteristic feature of the use made of languages by particular speakers and writers on particular occasions is debatable. Whatever one may decide about this question, creativity as it manifests itself in the metaphorical use of lexemes or their unusual, but stylistically effective, combination, clearly depends upon the semantic structure of the language-system, and it has traditionally been of great concern to the semanticist. Whether creativity, like productivity, is rule-governed and to what degree it is arbitrary, rather than motivated are questions upon which no firm stand will be adopted in this book.

(iv) Discreteness. The term discreteness* applies to the signal-elements of a semiotic system. If the elements are discrete*, in the sense that the difference between them is absolute and does not admit of gradation in terms of more or less, the system is said to be discrete; otherwise it is continuous*.

The verbal component of language is discrete in the sense that two word-forms, considered solely from the point of view of their form, are either absolutely the same (as tokens of the same type) or absolutely different. One might be in some doubt as to which of two different word-forms has been uttered in speech or writing; and the signal itself might be quite indeterminate in respect of the physical properties which would normally distinguish the two forms. But it must have been uttered and must be interpreted as one or the other; it cannot be taken as some third form midway between the two and combining the meaning of both.[11]

Discreteness, it will be clear, is not logically dependent upon arbitrariness; but it interacts with it to increase the semiotic flexibility of the system. Two word-forms may differ minimally (i.e. by just one discrete element) and may be forms of lexemes that are not at all similar in meaning: cf. *bear*:*pear*. The fact that minimally-distinct forms may be forms of lexemes that differ considerably in meaning and belong to different grammatical classes also has the effect of enhancing and pre-serving their discreteness when channel-noise would tend to obliterate or destroy the physical differences in the signal which would normally keep them apart. Very often the occurrence of the one will be so much more probable than the occurrence of the other (judged by the expec-tancy of the receiver: cf. 2.3) that there is in practice no possibility of misunderstanding.

In contrast with the verbal component of language a semiotic system of the kind exemplified by bee-dancing referred to above is continuous, rather than discrete; and its productivity is dependent upon this fact. The bee's body movements vary in intensity, both directly and con-tinuously, with a correspondingly continuous variation in the distance of the source of nectar. It should also be noted that bee-dancing is non-arbitrary in that distance is represented by the intensity of the

[11] Certain qualifications are required here: cf. Bolinger (1961).

movements of the bee's abdomen and direction by the orientation of the bee's body in relation to the sun.

The four design features of language that have been singled out for more detailed discussion in this section – arbitrariness, duality, productivity and discreteness – are, as we have seen, interconnected in various ways. They are present in all languages, and they are independent of both channel and medium. Whether they are to be found in any semiotic system other than language is questionable. But, if they are, they do not appear to be present on the same scale or to be interconnected in the same way. It is also worth pointing out that these four design features, although they are incontrovertibly characteristic of the verbal component of language, are not so obviously characteristic of the non-verbal part. It is a matter of dispute among linguists whether such prosodic features as intonation and stress manifest the property of duality, as also is the degree to which they are arbitrary and discrete. In this respect, therefore, as well as in respect of their characteristic function (cf. 3.1), the prosodic and paralinguistic features of language-behaviour more closely resemble other kinds of non-verbal signalling than the verbal component does.

(v) Semanticity. It would seem to be little short of tautological to say of any semiotic system that it has semanticity*: i.e. the property of being able to convey meaning. Whether it is useful to discuss different systems in respect of semanticity or not depends upon a more precise definition or explication of 'meaning'. Semanticity is defined by Hockett in terms of the associative ties that hold between signals and features of the external environment. This definition, however, is far too general to be useful for the subclassification of semiotic systems. It says nothing about the nature of the association; and it does not say whether the external features are a necessary or sufficient cause of the signal. If we define the nature of the putative association more closely, we will find, as we shall see in our discussion of behaviourism below (chapter 5), that very many language-utterances have no discernible association with any independently identifiable external feature. There is little point in adopting a definition of semanticity which has the unfortunate consequence that it allows as meaningful an enormous variety of behaviour, both human and non-human, and yet excludes a considerable amount of obviously meaningful language-behaviour.

As we have seen, there are many different kinds or aspects of meaning that must be taken into account in the description of language-behaviour; and no single gloss or definition can be expected to capture all of these. We have drawn one broad distinction between communicative and informative signals (2.1); and, since this distinction rests upon the notion of intentionality, it is doubtful whether any non-human signals can be shown to be communicative rather than merely informative in terms of this distinction. We have drawn another broad distinction between descriptive, social and expressive meaning (2.4); and we have seen that the non-verbal component tends to convey the latter rather than the former (3.1). Once again it is very doubtful whether any non-human signals can be properly described as being descriptive rather than as being expressive or socially informative. Discussion of this question is complicated by the fact that in the case of non-human semiotic systems it is often difficult to decide whether a particular signal conveys information about the sender or about the environment (or both). As Hinde puts it (1972: 93); "when the matter is pressed it becomes arbitrary to draw a hard line anywhere in the series. "There is a predator behind that tree"; "I know there is a predator behind that tree"; "I am afraid because there is a predator behind that tree"; "I am afraid"." But it is at least arguable that all non-human signalling is expressive. To discuss non-human signalling in terms of all the different kinds of meaning that we shall recognize in the course of our exploration of the field of semantics, would be difficult and would take us too far from our central purpose. The main point to be made here is that there are certain kinds of meaning that appear to be unique to language (and more especially to its verbal component) and there are others which language shares with non-human semiotic systems.

(vi) Displacement. This is the property of language which makes it possible for us to refer to objects and events that are remote in time and place from the act of utterance itself. The term displacement* can be traced back to the behaviourist conception of language and meaning, according to which the primary function of words and utterances is to refer to features of the immediate situation, with which they are associated as stimuli to responses (see chapter 5), and the correlation of linguistic expressions with objects and events outside the situation-of-utterance is a matter of secondary development.

Hockett's formulation of the notion of displacement, in his earlier discussion of the design features of language, was as follows: "a message is displaced to the extent that the key features in its antecedents and consequences are removed from the time and place of transmission" (1958: 579). Elsewhere in the same book he maintains that the earliest language-utterances of children, like their non-verbal signals, are not displaced; and he goes on to say "linguistic signals are often displaced: we refer to things when they are not around" (pp. 354-5). That language has the property of displacement, in this sense, is indisputable; and research into the acquisition of language by children supports the view that displacement is indeed something that comes later, rather than earlier, in this process. But whether we say that any non-human signalling-system (or indeed any human non-verbal system) is characterized by displacement will depend upon our definition of spatiotemporal remoteness and reference.

There is little point in so defining the notion of displacement that an utterance like *War was declared in 1939* and the alarm call of a bird responding to a predator that is still some considerable distance away or the honey bee's reference to a distant source of nectar are brought together under the same head. Recent work with chimpanzees, on the other hand, has shown that they are capable of producing and interpreting signals that make reference to entities absent from the immediate environment (cf. 3.5).

(vii) Interchangeability. By interchangeability* is meant that "any organism equipped for the transmission of messages in the system is also equipped to receive messages in the same system" (Hockett, 1958: 589). There is some degree of idealization involved in Hockett's further statement that "any speaker of a language...is theoretically capable of saying anything he is able to understand when someone else says it". For we can often understand utterances containing expressions which we never heard before and which we could not ourselves have used appropriately. However, the theoretical idealization involved in identifying competence as a speaker with competence as a hearer (provided that it is acknowledged as an idealization of the facts) is perfectly legitimate; and it is an important fact about language that we can be both senders and receivers using essentially the same system. In many kinds of animal signalling behaviour, this is not so. For example, it is not uncommon for members of one sex to produce mating signals which only members of the other sex will respond to.

(viii) Complete feedback. This property, which is dependent upon interchangeability, has to do with the fact that a speaker hears and is able to monitor his own performance. This is not solely a matter of monitoring the signal for audibility in the particular physical conditions in which it is produced. It also involves the checking of one's own utterances for comprehensibility and correctness of formation as they are produced and making adjustments when these are judged necessary. Whether any other species can be said to control its signals by feedback in this sense is unknown, but the fact that human beings can, and do, control language-utterances in the course of production by feedback is extremely important.

(ix) Specialization. This is defined in terms of the behaviouristic notion of triggering, which refers to the indirect influence that one organism exerts upon the behaviour of another. A signal is said to be highly specialized if the direct physical consequences of the signal and its effect upon the behaviour of the receiving organism are not functionally interrelated. For example, setting the table in the sight of other members of the family might have the same effect of causing them to come to the table as would the utterance *Dinner is almost ready*. But setting the table is said to be functionally interrelated with its effect in a way that the language-utterance is not. Hockett maintains that specialization is a matter of degree and that the most that one can say about language in this respect is that "it shows much more extensive specialization than known examples of animal communication" (1958: 579). It would surely be preferable to say (as we will maintain in our treatment of behaviourist semantics in chapter 5) that the whole concept of triggering is inapplicable to much of our language-behaviour; and the fact that it is inapplicable is a more distinctive feature of language than is the degree of specialization in those cases where triggering does apply.

(x) Cultural transmission. This is opposed to genetic transmission, and it has to do with the fact that the ability to speak a particular language is passed on from one generation to the next by teaching and learning, rather than by instinct. We need not here discuss the question whether a knowledge of the more general aspects of the grammatical structure of languages is genetically, rather than culturally, transmitted (cf. 3.5). Even the strongest form of the hypothesis that children are born with a knowledge of certain universal principles which determine the structure of language (cf. Chomsky, 1965) must allow that a very considerable part of the structure of particular languages is acquired by learning. At the same time, it must be recognized that much of the signalling-behaviour of other species that was once thought to be purely instinctive is now known to be acquired by a combination of instinct and learning. It has been demonstrated, for example, that the general pattern of a chaffinch's song may be determined by instinct, but that its more elaborate development and correction depends upon the bird's being able to hear other mature chaffinches singing. The difference between language and non-human semiotic systems in respect of cultural transmission is not, therefore, very clear cut.

(xi) Learnability. This is the property which makes it possible for any human being of whatever race or ancestry to learn in childhood any language equally well (provided that he is not physically or psychologically defective in some way that would impair the process of language-acquisition and provided that he is exposed to samples of the language in question under the appropriate environmental conditions). As with cultural transmission, it is difficult to decide to what degree learnability, in this sense, applies in non-human semiotic systems. Some birds can imitate the songs characteristic of other species; and it is now known that the song characteristic of certain species is distinguished by what might be called differences of dialect which depend upon the particular community in which the birds hatch and come to maturity. It seems clear, therefore, that bird song at least has to some degree the property of learnability (cf. Thorpe, 1972).

(xii) Reflexivity (referred to by Hockett as reflectiveness). This property has already been discussed (cf. 1.2). All that needs to be said here is that, as far as we know, no non-human semiotic systems other than languages have this property. But it is difficult to imagine that any system could be used to refer to itself in the way that languages can be so used unless the system in question has a descriptive, and not merely an expressive or social function.

(xiii) Prevarication. By prevarication* is meant the possibility of using a semiotic system to deceive or misinform. Many authors consider that prevarication is the property which, with reflexivity, most clearly distinguishes language as a semiotic system from all other signalling-systems. There has been some discussion, however, about the occurrence of prevarication in the behaviour of certain mammals and birds. Does the luring of one species by another into a trap by the emission of reassuring signals count as deception or not? Does the behaviour of a bird which shams injury and tempts a predator to pursue it away from the nest justify the use of the term 'prevarication'? The fact that we can raise such questions reminds us, once again, that in the study of animal signalling we are obliged to give an external account of the phenomena, in terms of the observable behaviour of the sender and the observable behaviour of the receiver. In the study of human signalling, on the other hand, it would be stultifying to impose upon oneself such gratuitous and unnecessary restrictions and to eschew, on principle, any appeal to beliefs and intentions.

Furthermore, it might be argued that prevarication should not be regarded as a property of the semiotic system as such, but as a feature of the behaviour and intentions of those using the system. In his original account of the key properties of language, Hockett included under displacement the phenomena that were later held to fall within the scope of prevarication. He notes, for example, that a child cries from hunger only when it is actually hungry, but that the linguistic signal *I'm hungry* can be uttered whether the person uttering it is hungry or not (1958: 354–5). As used in relation to this example, 'displacement' looks suspiciously like a behaviouristic term that is introduced in order to describe a characteristic feature of language-behaviour which is more accurately described as freedom from stimulus-control (cf. 5.3). Freedom from stimulus-control is presumably a precondition of mendacity and deception in the strict sense of these terms: and it is therefore a precondition of prevarication.

We have now covered, in greater or less detail, all the design features (other than those relating to the channel of transmission) which have been proposed by Hockett for the classification of semiotic systems. The most obvious conclusion to be drawn from our discussion is that no classification based simply on the number of properties manifested by particular systems is likely to be of much theoretical interest. Many of the properties are defined in such general terms, not to say so loosely, that they conceal rather than reveal the salient differences between languages and non-human signalling-systems; and whether a particular system has or has not a particular property is often, as we have seen, uncertain. These problems have not been overlooked, but they have not been given sufficient emphasis by scholars who have applied this classificatory scheme. It is partly for this reason, no doubt, that a classification of animal signalling-systems that is based solely on the presence or absence of these design features fails to correlate at all with a biological classification of species according to their evolutionary development (cf. Hinde, 1972: 93). It does not follow, of course, that a more sophisticated classification of semiotic systems in terms of their design features would necessarily fail to correlate in the same way. It might even be the case that a suitable measure of grammatical complexity and of the different kinds of meaning that various semiotic systems can express would of itself serve to classify those systems more satisfactorily than the rather disparate list we have considered in this section.

3.5. *The origin of language*

One question which inevitably arises in any discussion of language from a semiotic point of view is whether language, as we know it, can be shown or plausibly assumed to have evolved from some non-linguistic signalling-system. Only the briefest treatment of this question can be given here (cf. Hewes, 1973; Liebermann, 1974/5).

Men have been debating the origin of language from the very earliest times. Long before the publication of Darwin's *Origin of Species* (1859) scholars had been putting forward theories designed to account for the evolution of language from such systems of non-verbal communication as instinctive emotional cries, gestures, rhythmic communal chanting, and so on. But it was the work of Darwin, including his own speculations on the origin of language, that gave particular impetus to the attempt to construct an evolutionary theory of the origin of language in the late nineteenth century. At that time linguistics was very strongly influenced by the theory of evolution. Over the last fifty years or so, however, most linguists have shown little interest in the origin of language. The reason is simply that no sign of evolution from a simpler to a more complex state of development can be found in any of the thousands of languages known to exist or to have existed in the past. If we had interpretable records of the forms of communication employed by earlier hominid species we might be in a better position to discuss the origin of language. As things are, most linguists would say that the question is unanswerable and, in any case, totally irrelevant to the construction of a general theory of the structure of language and the description of particular languages within the framework of this general theory. The attitude of most linguists to evolutionary theories of the origin of language tends, therefore, to be one of agnosticism. Psychologists, biologists, ethologists and other might say, if they so wish, that language must have evolved from some non-linguistic signalling-system;

the fact remains, the linguist might reply, that there is no actual evidence from language to support this belief.

It can be argued, however, that, although there is no evidence of evolution from a more primitive to a more advanced form of structure in existing languages, there are two other kinds of evidence that can be drawn upon in discussing the origin of language: evidence derived from the study of children's language, on the one hand, and evidence derived from a comparison of the structure and functions of language and non-linguistic signalling, on the other. The acquisition of language by children is a topic to which we will return presently. Evidence of the second kind has already been mentioned in earlier sections of this chapter. The problem is how to evaluate it. One of the points that has been continually stressed throughout this chapter is that there is no clear distinction in language-behaviour between what is purely linguistic and what is non-linguistic and that many of the semiotic functions one finds manifest in language-behaviour (in particular those which have been classified as expressive and social, rather than descriptive) can be identified also in both human and animal non-linguistic signalling. Does it follow from the intimate interpenetration of the linguistic and non-linguistic features of language and from the fact that some aspects of meaning, or semanticity, are common to language and non-language that the former has evolved from the latter? Clearly it does not. In default of any explanation of what is meant by 'evolve', and of the mechanism by means of which the evolution of language from non-language is presumed to have operated, evidence based on the structural and functional continuity of verbal and non-verbal communication is purely circumstantial, compatible with, but not conclusively demonstrative of, the evolutionary development of the one from the other. The verbal component in language might have been of totally distinct origin and its interpenetration with the non-verbal component a matter of subsequent and gradual development. The one hypothesis is as plausible, a priori, as the other.

The question of the vocalization of language is important in this context. Let us suppose that we were suddenly to discover a society of human beings making no use of vocalization (except for the emission of vocal reflexes and a limited set of expressive signals symptomatic of such emotional states as anger, fear, sexual arousal, etc.), but communicating by means of a complex system of gestures. Let us further suppose that, upon analysis, these gestures were found to have the same kind of grammatical structure (or a grammatical structure of a similar degree of complexity) as our own spoken languages; that they were used for the same or a similar variety of communicative functions, and had various other properties (arbitrariness, duality, productivity and discreteness) which we think of as being characteristic and distinctive of language by contrast with other semiotic systems. Faced with this hypothetical discovery, we would surely say that the society in question had a language.

The point is that languages, or at least the verbal component of languages, can be considered independently of the medium in which they are primarily and naturally manifest (3.3); and, as we have seen, written languages already have some degree of independence as one of man's principal means of communication. So too have the various gestural sign-languages used by the deaf and dumb in different cultures, although, like writing, many of them were originally derived from spoken languages. In any comparison of human signalling with animal signalling, or of verbal and non-verbal signalling in man, due weight should be given to the fact that people can learn, fairly easily and successfully for the most part, to transfer, not only from one channel to another, but also from one medium to the other, holding invariant much of the verbal part of language (cf. 3.3). What might be referred to as the medium-transferability* of language is at least as important a design feature of language as what Hockett called learnability (cf. 3.4). As Householder (1971: 34f) has shown, little purpose is served by defining language in such a way that it is necessarily, rather than contingently, associated with speech.

Is it not possible, we might ask, to conceive of a group separating itself from the main body of our own society and forswearing all use of the spoken language? In what sense would their written or gestural language still be dependent upon the spoken language that elsewhere in the society was associated with it? Could it not then develop independently, as the written language has in fact developed in partial independence of speech? And could it not be taught to children without their first having acquired some spoken language in partial correspondence with it? The answer to these questions is at present unclear. There is, however, a certain amount of evidence bearing upon them.

It has been argued, notably by Lenneberg (1967), that language is species-specific and depends upon particular biological propensities not found in animals other than man. There is a considerable body of anatomical and physiological evidence to suggest that human beings are designed, as it were, for the production and reception of speech. It has been observed that the vocal apparatus of the other primates most closely related to man is singularly ill-adapted for the production of speech-sounds and that (in striking contrast with some species of birds) they normally make use of only a limited number of vocal signals. All normal children go through a fixed developmental sequence in the acquisition of spoken language. The first stage in this sequence is babbling, characterized by the production of a comparatively rich set of different sounds; and it is at this stage that the child begins to acquire the prosodic patterns of his native language. It seems clear, therefore, that the child is physiologically adapted at birth for vocalization and that he is genetically predisposed to rehearse, as it were, a wide range of speech-sounds and subsequently to develop and refine his control of the sound-patterns of the language he hears around him.

It is also well attested that children can acquire language even when they are congenitally handicapped by deafness, blindness and various other physical disabilities. This fact speaks strongly in favour of the hypothesis that all children are very strongly motivated to acquire language, as they are no less strongly motivated to acquire other systems of behaviour employed in the society in which they are reared. The further fact, if it is a fact, that there is a critical period in childhood, during which the brain is, as it were, tuned to language and that, if language is not acquired during this period, it may not be properly acquired at all, suggests that the child's motivation and ability to learn the society's principal system of communication are innate.

The evidence just summarized indicates that human beings are biologically disposed (i) to vocalize and (ii) to communicate. What it does not prove – though it is often so interpreted – is that they are genetically programmed to learn spoken language as such. For it is in principle possible that the predisposition to vocalize and the predisposition to communicate are genetically unconnected. It has also been argued recently that language is much more likely to have evolved from a system of manual gestures and to have been only subsequently associated with vocalization than it is to have developed directly from the somewhat limited set of vocal signals found in mammals (cf. Hewes, 1973). The biological advantages of the phonic medium, in the conditions in which early man is known to have lived, are obvious and have often been mentioned: vocal signals, unlike visual signals, can be transmitted by night as well as by day; they are not obstructed by trees, boulders, etc., between the sender and the addressee; they can be transmitted simultaneously to a group of widely scattered addressees; and their production does not interfere with other activities.

The neurophysiological evidence so far available is inconclusive. It has long been known that the human brain is distinguished from that of the higher apes by its size and by the greater development of the parietal regions, especially in the left hemisphere; and it has been hypothesized that the development of the left hemisphere is causally connected with the evolution of language. As far as the reception of speech is concerned, it seems that the verbal component is usually processed by the left hemisphere, but that the prosodic features of vocal signals can be interpreted equally well by either hemisphere. Visual input, however, is processed by the right hemisphere. Furthermore, it appears that both hemispheres are involved in the grammatical and semantic processing of language; but once again with some degree of specialization, the right hemisphere being able to interpret expressions referring to concrete objects, the left hemisphere alone being capable of interpreting more abstract expressions. If this is so, it certainly seems to confirm the hypothesis that the evolution of language is connected with the phenomenon of cerebral dominance. But it also implies that the processing of language is not carried out solely in what has often been referred to as a language-centre in the left hemisphere. It is interesting that cerebral dominance appears to be especially relevant to what on other grounds we have described as the more linguistic part of language: the part which is characterized by the design features of arbitrariness, discreteness, productivity and duality, which operate jointly to produce a complex and flexible semiotic system; the part which is readily transferable from one medium to another; the part which has a descriptive function. But cerebral dominance also appears to be relevant to the development of man's general cognitive abilities. In saying that there is a connexion between cerebral dominance and the evolution of language we may be saying no more than that the evolution of language depended upon the evolution of man's cognitive abilities; and this is hardly an original thesis![12]

Reference was made above to the relatively constant developmental sequence through which the child passes in his acquisition of language and to the fact that the first stage in this sequence, which begins about three months after birth, is characterized by babbling. The second stage, which starts towards the end of the first year, is the stage of

---

[12] For some discussion, cf. Caplan & Marshall (1975), Dimond & Beaumont (1974), Lenneberg (1967), Schmitt & Worden (1974), Whitaker (1971).

holophrastic* speech, consisting of grammatically unstructured one-word utterances. This stage is succeeded, in the course of the second year, by the production of simple two-word and three-word utterances of a so-called telegraphic character, lacking an overt marking of such grammatical distinctions in English as present *vs.* past tense, singular *vs.* plural, or the use of the definite and indefinite article. In passing through the second and third stage of language-acquisition, the child gradually improves his control of the system of segmental phonological distinctions utilized in the spoken language. It is only when the child reaches the third stage of development that we can say that he has acquired, as far as production is concerned, some kind of language. It is possible, however, that the child is able to identify sounds and to interpret certain grammatical distinctions in the speech of adults long before he demonstrates in his own speech-production the ability to make these phonological and grammatical distinctions. If this is so (by virtue of the features of interchangeability and complete feedback: 3.4), we are perhaps entitled to conclude that his acquisition of the language-system in the early stages is somewhat in advance of his development of the mechanism of speech-production; and there is evidence to suggest that this is the case. However this may be, it seems clear that the acquisition of language proceeds through a succession of recognizable stages.[13]

What is not so clear at the present time is whether the child's acquisition of language proceeds independently of his more general cognitive development and whether the inability of other species to get beyond a certain stage in the acquisition of language is due to their inability to reach a certain higher level of cognition, rather than to their lack of a more specific innate faculty for language. Chomsky (1968, 1976) has argued strongly that the grammatical structure of all human languages is determined by a very specific set of principles and that the child is born with a predisposition to recognize these principles in any language to which he is exposed at the critical period. The force of this argument is reduced, however, by the fact that linguists are far from being in agreement about the universality of the principles of grammatical structure. That the grammar of all languages is of considerable for-

---

[13] There is a vast and growing literature on the acquisition of language by children: cf. Bates (1976), Brown (1973), Clark & Clark (1977), Ferguson & Slobin (1973), Flores d'Arcais & Levelt (1970), Greenfield & Smith (1974), Hayes (1970), Huxley & Ingram (1972), McNeill (1970), Moore (1973), Slobin (1971).

mal complexity is beyond dispute; and it may also be true that, at a very
general level, all similarities among languages are perhaps equally well
explained by the similarity in the semiotic functions which all languages
fulfil and by the fact that all human beings have the same general cognitive abilities. In this connexion, it is worth noting that many scholars
have suggested a correlation between the developmental sequence for
language-acquisition and the stages of cognitive development recognized by such psychologists as Piaget (1923).

Attempts have been made on several occasions in the past to train
chimpanzees to use spoken language; and they have met with little
success. In one of the best known experiments, a young chimpanzee
called Viki, after six years of intensive training, was able to produce
only four vocal signals resembling English words (Hayes & Hayes,
1955). More recently, two further experiments have been carried out
with considerably greater success, the one with a chimpanzee called
Washoe (Gardner & Gardner, 1971), and subsequently with a second
generation of chimpanzees interacting with Washoe, and the other with
a chimpanzee named Sarah (Premack, 1970). In neither case, however,
is it spoken language that the animals have been taught; for, as was
pointed out above, it is now recognized that the vocal apparatus of the
higher non-human primates is not well adapted for the production of
speech-sounds and this fact alone, it was thought, may account for past
failures to teach them spoken language. Washoe was taught a gestural
system used in the United States by the deaf and known as the American
Sign Language. Unlike some other systems used by the deaf and dumb,
this is not based on finger spelling, and the principles which govern the
combination of the manual gestures of which utterances are composed
differ from those which govern the grammatical combination of words
in English. After about three years Washoe had a vocabulary of eighty-
seven signs and was able to use these appropriately in nearly three
hundred different two-sign combinations, many of which, it seems, she
had not previously encountered. She also produced a number of longer
utterances. The second generation of chimpanzees have made even
more striking progress.

The other chimpanzee, Sarah, was trained to learn a vocabulary consisting of over a hundred pieces of plastic, differing in size, shape and
colour; to associate them with particular meanings, identifiable as the
meanings of certain proper names, common nouns, verbs, adjectives
and adverbs in English; and to combine these plastic word-forms in a
particular linear order according to the syntactic structure of the system

designed by the experimenters. Sarah, like Washoe, was able to produce correct combinations that she had not previously seen. Both chimpanzees, therefore, have demonstrated the ability to acquire a semiotic system with some degree of syntactic structure and productivity. Whether we say that their ability differs from the human capacity for language in degree or in kind is perhaps largely a question of how we define 'language'. Neither of the two systems that the chimpanzees have learned has the grammatical complexity of the language-systems used by adult human beings. But they do not appear to differ significantly, in terms of formal complexity, from the language-systems of young children or the American Sign Language, as it is employed by competent adult users; and this is particularly true of Sarah's signalling-behaviour.

What is especially interesting is that the chimpanzee's utterances are grammatically and semantically comparable with the utterances of children in what was described above as the third stage of language-acquisition. It has often been suggested that the utterances of children at this period can be accounted for partly in terms of expressive and social meaning and partly in terms of a small set of more specific structural meanings (vocative, desiderative, attributive, locative, agentive, etc.), such that the same combination of words may be associated with different structural meanings in different contexts (cf. Bloom, 1973). The chimpanzees' utterances, it has been claimed, can be analysed in terms of the same structural meanings and, considered in isolation from the context in which they occur, have the same kind of ambiguity or indeterminacy. Brown (1970) relates the set of structural meanings required for the analysis of children's two-word and three-word utterances more particularly to the sensory-motor intelligence postulated by Piaget (cf. Sinclair, 1972, 1973), with which, not only human beings, but also animals may operate and which develops in the infant, over many months, on the basis of his interaction with animate and inanimate entities in his environment. The implication is that the earliest, but not the later, stages, of language development are under the control of sensory-motor intelligence; and that, as a consequence, we might expect certain species of animals to reach, but not go beyond, these earliest stages. In view of the structural and functional parallels that have been drawn between human non-verbal communication (including the non-verbal component in language) and animal signalling-systems, one might perhaps go on to hypothesize that non-verbal communication, in general, is under the control of sensory-motor intelligence, whereas language in its fully developed form (though it continues to make use of the sensory-motor basis) requires a higher kind of cognitive ability. This hypothesis would also seem to be compatible with cerebral dominance and with what we know at present about the role played by the left and the right hemispheres of the brain in language-behaviour. However that may be, the fact that parallels can be drawn between the signalling-behaviour of children and the signalling-behaviour of chimpanzees casts doubt upon the views of those who would say that there is an unbridgeable gap between human and non-human signalling.[14]

But there is a more important conclusion to be drawn from our discussion of the evolution of language and our earlier comparison of the verbal and non-verbal components of language. This is that the question whether language evolved from some non-verbal signalling-system is not formulated precisely enough to be answered positively or negatively; and it is not just that we lack the evidence which would enable us to answer it. Although there is perhaps no sharp distinction between human and non-human signalling and between language and non-language, there are certain properties of adult language at least, having to do with its grammatical complexity and its descriptive function, which, as we have seen, appear to be unique to language and associated more particularly with its verbal component. If we decide to make the possession of these properties a defining characteristic of what we will call language, we can then say, correctly, that languages are fundamentally, or qualitatively, different from all other signalling-systems. We might equally well have framed a definition of 'language', however, according to which one would be inclined to say that the difference between language and non-language is a matter of degree rather than kind. This purely definitional aspect of the question should be borne in mind when one considers the question whether language is or is not unique to the human species. So too should the fact that, whether we define language

[14] This question, needless to say, is highly controversial and what I have said in the text seems to me to be no more than what prudence dictates. It is of course possible that future, and as yet unforeseen, developments in the study of neurophysiology or ethology could dramatically shift the balance of scholarly opinion in one way or the other. In writing this section, I have drawn heavily upon relatively few sources of a fairly general character. Among them (apart from those referred to in the text or listed in earlier notes) the following have proved useful and will serve as an introduction to the field for the non-specialist: Adams (1972), Bateson & Klopfer (1974), Bower (1974), Hinde (1972), Sebeok (1968, 1974), Sebeok & Ramsay (1969), Whitaker (1971). Some of the philosophical issues are discussed in Chomsky (1968, 1976), Cooper (1973), Hook (1969) and Sampson (1975).

in such a way that it turns out to be unique to the human species or not, there is much in the everyday use of language that links it with other kinds of signalling-behaviour in both men and animals. The rationalist approach to semantics, confining itself, as it does, to the descriptive function of language and neglecting, as it tends to, all but the verbal component, gives a very inadequate account of language as a semiotic system. To make this point, without at the same time denying that the descriptive function of language is its most characteristic, if not its most basic, semiotic function has been the central aim of this chapter.

4

Semiotics

4.1. *Signification*

The meaning of linguistic expressions is commonly described in terms of the notion of signification*: that is to say, words and other expressions are held to be signs* which, in some sense, signify*, or stand for, other things. What these other things are, as we shall see, has long been a matter of controversy. It is convenient to have a neutral technical term for whatever it is that a sign stands for: and we will use the Latin term significatum*, as a number of authors have done, for this purpose.

Many writers, in discussing the notion of signification, have drawn a distinction between signs and symbols, or between signals and symbols, or between symbols and symptoms. Unfortunately, however, there is no consistency in the way in which various authors have defined these terms. For example, Ogden and Richards (1923: 23) distinguish symbols as "those signs which men use to communicate with one another", whereas Peirce (1940: 104), who also treats symbols as a subclass of signs, defines them, as we shall see, on the basis of the conventional nature of the relation which holds between sign and significatum. So too does Miller (1951: 5). But Morris (1946: 23–7), who follows Peirce quite closely in certain respects, says that "a symbol is a sign...which acts as substitute for some other sign with which it is synonymous" and that "all signs not symbols are signals". Bühler (1934: 24–33) describes the utterance as a symptom of what is in the speaker's mind, a symbol of what is meant or signified, and a signal to the hearer (cf. Ullman, 1957: 68; 1962: 12), whilst Cherry (1957: 7) employs the word 'sign' for "any physical event used in communication" and reserves 'symbol' for "religious and cultural symbols interpretable only in specified historical contexts", such as the Crown, the Cross or Uncle Sam.[1]

---

[1] This is but a small selection of references: cf. also Baldinger (1957), Barthes (1964), Buyssens (1943), Eco (1971), Greimas *et al.* (1970), Guiraud (1971), Langer (1942), Mounin (1970), Mulder & Hervey (1972), Prieto (1966), Spang-Hanssen (1945). It is interesting to note that, in many respects, Indian theories of signification ran parallel to, or antedated, Western theories: cf. Kunjunni Raja (1963).

It will be clear from these various definitions of 'sign', 'signal', 'symbol' and 'symptom' that there is no single standard interpretation of any one of them in the literature. The term signal* has already been introduced in order to refer to whatever is transmitted along some channel of communication and can be interpreted by the receiver as encoding some message (chapter 2); and we will continue to use it in this sense. As we have seen, language-utterances (that is, the products of acts of utterance) are signals, which may be grouped as tokens of the same type (1.4, 1.6). Accepting for the moment the view that all communication is by means of signs, we can say that messages are signs, which may or may not be composed of simpler signs. Signals therefore encode signs.

Signification is commonly described as a triadic relation, which may be further analysed into three dyadic relations; two basic and one derivative. This kind of analysis is conveniently illustrated, as it was by Ogden and Richards (1923: 11) and subsequently by many others writing on semantics or communication, by means of a diagrammatic representation in the form of a triangle. In figure 2, we have used letters

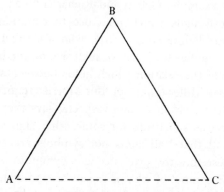

Figure 2. The triangle of signification

to name the corners of this triangle. Various terms are employed in the literature: for the present at least, we will employ sign* for A, concept* for B, and significatum* for C. This is in accordance with at least one traditional analysis of signification – the one that is expressed, for example, in the scholastic maxim: "vox significat [rem] mediantibus conceptibus" (cf. Ullmann, 1957: 71). This may be translated as "the word signifies [the thing] by means of mediating concepts". The Latin word 'vox' is the standard technical term for phonic sound and was commonly employed for words considered from the point of view solely of their form (and, more particularly, of their spoken form), but it was used rather inconsistently to refer sometimes to word-forms and sometimes to either lexemes or expressions. As has already been pointed out, the distinction between these different senses of 'word' is seldom drawn, and many of the standard modern analyses of signification are vitiated by their failure to take it into consideration (1.5): we will interpret 'vox' in the present context as referring to lexemes, and we will for the present disregard (as the work that we are summarizing does) the distinction between lexemes and expressions. It should also be pointed out that there is some discrepancy in the interpretation of 'significatum' among those authors who use the term. Morris (1946), for example, would say that it is B rather than C that is the significatum of A and that C is its denotatum*. We shall not go into these terminological differences or the somewhat different conception of the notion of signification upon which they depend. Nor shall we deal with extensions of the triadic analysis of signification which also bring in, as a separate component, the user of the sign or the context in which it is used.

The fact that the relationship between a lexeme (A) and its significatum (C) is indirect, being mediated by a concept (B), is indicated in the diagram by making AC a dotted line, unlike AB and BC, which being continuous represent two more basic relationships. This graphic device is adapted from Ogden and Richards. Before we consider their analysis in more detail it may be observed that, according to certain traditional accounts, both AB and BC represent relations of signification: the lexeme signifying the concept and the concept signifying the thing.

It has already been mentioned that Ogden and Richards distinguished a variety of meanings of 'meaning' (1.1). They were especially concerned with problems of misunderstanding and misinterpretation; and they believed that much of this was due to the tendency to think that there is some inherent and indissoluble link between signs and what they stand for. Communication would be improved and clarity of thought facilitated, they claimed, if it was realized that the relationship between words and things was purely derivative – an imputed, non-causal relationship, resulting from their association in the mind of speaker and listener (or writer and reader) during the process of communication. (The so-called general semantics movement, initiated by the work of Korzybski (1933) in the United States, and further developed by such writers as Chase (1938) and Hayakawa (1949) is inspired by a similar desire to make people aware of the alleged dangers of treating words as something more than conventional and rather inadequate symbols for things. It would be perhaps more appropriately described as therapeutic semantics.) The AB and BC relations, however, were said to be true causal relations; and the account that Ogden and Richards gave of them can be described in a very general sense, as behaviouristic. Some object (C) in the external world calls forth a thought (B) in the mind of the speaker and this thought in turn elicits from him a sign (A). Ogden and Richards do not draw the distinction that we have drawn between sign and signal; they therefore think of the sign as being transmitted, without further processing as it were, to the listener. However, we can easily insert an encoding and decoding stage in the process of communication without otherwise affecting their scheme. The sign will call forth a thought in the mind of the listener and the thought will direct his attention to C. The important point to notice here is that the genesis of thoughts in the mind of the speaker is held to be determined by causal factors, or stimuli, in the external environment. It is for this reason that I have said that the Ogden and Richards theory is, in a general sense of the term, behaviouristic; the fact that they use such mentalistic expressions as 'thought', which the behaviourist finds abhorrent (5.1), is irrelevant. There is no reason why thoughts or concepts should not be postulated as theoretical constructs within the framework of a mechanistic theory of knowledge and communication. We will discuss more explicitly behaviourist theories of meaning in the next chapter.

The term used for C by Ogden and Richards is referent*; and this term is now quite widely employed by semanticists. It is worth noting, however, that the relation of reference, for Ogden and Richards, holds between B and C, and not between A and C. As we shall see later, it is far more common to say that words or expressions, not concepts, refer to (or stand for) things (7.2).

Attempts have often been made to eliminate either B or C, whilst still maintaining the view that the meaning of a word is what it signifies. Ullmann (1957: 72) argues that C is of no direct concern to the semanticist and that those properties of things which are relevant to determining the meaning of words are abstracted from things and represented in B. Following Saussure's (1916) analysis (in terms of which the sign is not A, but the composite entity A+B), he describes not only B, but also A, as a mental entity, saying that they are dynamically and reciprocally related in the mind: "If I hear the name 'table', I shall think of a table; if I think of a table, I shall articulate the name if required" (1957: 69–70). Meaning is therefore a reciprocal relation between A and B, which "enables them to call up one another". Other scholars, being suspicious of the mentalistic mould within which this account of meaning is cast, have questioned the need for B, thoughts or concepts mediating between words and things. For them the meaning of a word is simply the object or class of objects that it stands for. We will not stop to discuss either of these two views of meaning at this point, since they are subject to the more general criticisms of the definition of meaning in terms of signification that will be made later in this chapter.

There is considerable disagreement about the details of the triadic analysis of signification even among those who accept that all three components, A, B and C, must be taken into account. Should A be defined as a physical or a mental entity? What is the psychological or ontological status of B? Is C something that is referred to on a particular occasion? Or is it the totality of things that might be referred to by uttering the sign (or a signal encoding the sign)? Or, yet a third possibility, is it some typical or ideal representative of this class? We need not go into these questions here: but we should keep them in mind. They are important and they will come up again later, though in a somewhat different form.

4.2. *Symbols, icons, indices and symptoms*

Much recent work in the theory of signs has been strongly influenced by the writings of C. S. Peirce; and in this section we will look at some of the terms he employs for different kinds of signs. Unfortunately, Peirce is not only one of the subtlest and most original of writers on the subject; he is also one of the most difficult, and there is no one place in his collected works to which one can go for an integrated and definitive account of his theory. Since we are not concerned with the details of his theory, but only with the most general distinctions that he draws, this is however of little consequence. Much of Peirce's influence has, in any case, been indirect.

The term that Peirce uses to refer to the theory of signs is 'semiotic'. This is the same term that Locke used in his *Essay on Human Understanding* (1690). It comes from the Greek word meaning "to signify" and, having originated in Greek medicine for diagnosis by means of bodily symptoms, it was employed by the Stoic philosophers to include both logic and epistemology. Most authors nowadays, however, use semiotics* as the noun and semiotic* as the corresponding adjective;

and this is the usage that will be adopted here. For the present, we will take semiotics to be the theory of signs, or signification; later it will be argued that, as it has now come to be used by most authorities, 'semiotics' is better understood as referring to the analysis of signalling-systems; and the reader will recall that it has already been employed in this sense in the previous chapter. How semiotics differs from semantics is also a question that we will take up later. An alternative (and more or less equivalent) term to 'semiotics' is semiology, which Saussure (1916) introduced for the more general science (itself a branch of social psychology) of which linguistics would be a part. The term 'semiology' is most widely used perhaps by scholars who adopt a characteristically Saussurean point of view (cf. 8.1).

Peirce recognized up to ten different classes of signs, with further subdivisions. But these were based on intersecting criteria. We shall be concerned with only one of the dimensions of his classification, which yields a distinction of three kinds of signs: symbols, icons and indices.

(i) Symbol. Peirce's definition of symbol* rests upon the conventionality or arbitrariness of the relationship between the sign and its signification. The importance of arbitrariness as one of the design features of language has already been mentioned (3.4). One of the philosophical controversies which gave birth to traditional grammar and determined its subsequent development turned on this very question: is the relationship between the form of a word and its meaning natural or conventional? Few linguists would put the question in such general terms these days.

Saussure (1916) made what he called "the arbitrariness of the linguistic sign" (that is to say, the conventionality of the relationship between form and meaning) one of the most basic principles of his whole theory; and most linguists have followed him on this point (even though they have not always accepted the Saussurean notion of the linguistic sign). They are agreed that, whatever might have been the case at some earlier stage of man's evolutionary development, in all known languages the connexion between a word and what it stands for is, with relatively few exceptions, arbitrary. What is meant by the term 'arbitrary', in this context, may be explained, as it commonly is, by means of an example. In English there is a word 'tree', in German there is a word 'Baum' and in French there is a word 'arbre'; and each of these words, we will assume, has the same signification: it may be used to refer to the same class of objects. These three words are quite different in form; and no one is more naturally appropriate to signify trees than are the other two. To make this point rather more precisely none of the forms of 'tree' (viz. *tree, trees*) or of 'Baum' (viz. *Baum, Baüme*, etc.) or of 'arbre' (viz. *arbre, arbres*) whether written or spoken is naturally representative of trees or of their distinctive properties. In contrast, the words 'cuckoo' in English, 'Kuckuck' in German and 'coucou' in French are, in their spoken form, naturally representative of the characteristic cry of the species of birds that they signify (cf. Ullmann, 1957: 88). What is traditionally called onomatopoeia*, as illustrated here, is a universally recognized exception to the generality of the Saussurean principle of the arbitrariness of the linguistic sign; and onomatopoeic forms constitute only a small minority of the word-forms in any language-system. Furthermore, there is some arbitrariness, or conventionality, even in onomatopoeic forms, since they are made to conform to the phonological systems of particular languages, rather than being directly imitative of what they (or, more precisely, the lexemes they encode) stand for.

We have just interpreted the principle of arbitrariness in the way in which it is customarily interpreted by linguists. It should be noticed, however, that in the Saussurean analysis of the linguistic sign, what is signified (the signifié) is to be identified with B rather than C in the triangle of signification (cf. 4.1). One might therefore argue, as some scholars have done, that the principle of arbitrariness should be applied, within a Saussurean framework to the bond which unites A with B, rather than to the relationship holding between A and C (which Ogden and Richards said was indirect and not truly causal). This question has been extensively discussed in the linguistic journals, as have other issues relating to Saussure's theory of signification (cf. Ullmann, 1962: 81). We will not go into the details of the Saussurean analysis of signification here or of the discussion that has ensued from it. All that needs to be said, in the present context, is that it is now appreciated that the notion of arbitrariness is rather more complex than at first sight it appears to be. In particular, it has become clear that 'arbitrary' and 'conventional' are not equivalent.

Granted that there is no intrinsic reason (no reason in nature, to use a traditional formulation) why the English lexeme 'tree' should be associated with the forms *tree* and *trees* (rather than, say, with *bodge* and *bodges*), a number of more interesting questions can be raised in connexion with the principle of arbitrariness; and here we will find considerable disagreement among scholars. Must there be some lexeme 'tree' in English, regardless of the forms with which it is associated?

Indeed, what does it mean to say that a language must have (or need not have) a lexeme semantically equivalent to the English 'tree'? We shall see later that one of the points that Saussure and other structural seman- ticists have insisted upon is that each language has, not only its own stock of forms, but also its own system of meanings or concepts (cf. 8.1.)

(ii) Icon. Peirce's term for non-arbitrary signs is icon*. He distinguishes icons from symbols, in one passage, as follows: "An icon is a sign which would possess the character which renders it significant, even though its object had no existence; such as a lead-pencil streak as representing a geometrical line... A symbol is a sign which would lose the character which renders it a sign if there were no interpretant. Such is any utter- ance of speech which signifies what it does only by virtue of its being understood to have that signification" (1940: 104). Peirce's definition, it will be observed, makes use of the term 'interpretant'. In Peirce's theory this is the mental effect produced by the sign: we may think of it as the concept associated with the sign in the triangle of signification. The conventionality, or arbitrariness, of symbols, in contrast with what might be called the naturalism of iconic* signs is grounded in the user's knowledge or awareness of the convention. As we have seen, there are many iconic features in language, in addition to onomatopoeia, which relate it to non-verbal signalling-systems (3.4).

The distinction between icons and symbols, as Peirce describes them, is far from clear. Iconicity is said to be dependent upon some natural resemblance, geometrical or functional, between the sign and its object. But the whole notion of resemblance holding independently of our recognition of the relevant features by virtue of which two things are similar is, to say the least, suspect. And our recognition of the re- semblance between a sign and its object (to talk in Peirce's terms) is frequently based upon our knowledge of certain cultural conventions of interpretation. It follows that 'iconic' cannot be equated with 'natural'. Granted that a distinction can be drawn between what is natural (i.e. unlearned) and what is cultural, on the one hand, and between what is arbitrary and what is non-arbitrary, on the other, it would appear that icons are a subclass of non-arbitrary signs in which the resemblance may be either natural or cultural. Furthermore, in so far as resemblance may be of many different kinds, in languages as in other semiotic systems, iconicity is at best a complex and heterogeneous property (cf. Eco, 1972). Many of the onomatopoeic forms of spoken language and of the characters and hieroglyphs of so-called ideographic writing systems are only weakly iconic, in the sense that, knowing their meaning, we can see that there is some resemblance of form and meaning, but we could not deduce their meaning solely on the basis of their form. It is worth pointing out also that the term 'ideogram' is misleading in relation to writing systems of the kind that were used by the Egyptians and the Maya and are still used by the Chinese: these so-called ideograms stand for, or are in correspondence with, forms or lexemes of the spoken language; they do not directly represent meanings or ideas, and relatively few of them represent, pictorially, classes of things. Furthermore, all such systems have become more flexible and semiotically more efficient as the so-called ideograms have become progressively less iconic (cf. Gelb, 1963). In general, it is a relatively weak kind of iconicity that is found in language; and when we do make use of more strongly iconic signals, in the paralinguistic gestures that accompany speech for example, or in miming, these are generally interpretable only by virtue of redundancy in the situation and the receiver's ability to discern our intentions.

Iconicity has been discussed so far in terms of resemblance (of various kinds) between form and meaning. This may be described as primary iconicity*; and this type of iconicity is clearly medium-dependent. For example, the English word-form *cuckoo* is iconic in the phonic, but not in the graphic, medium. Of far greater significance for the analysis of the vocabulary of natural languages is the notion of resemblance, or relatedness, between different meanings associated with some form (or set of forms); and we will discuss this in greater detail later (13.4). Here it may be pointed out that a more complex type of iconicity may hold between form and meaning, mediated by what, from a historical point of view, may be described as an extension of meaning from a basic to a transferred, or metaphorical*, sense. Suppose, for example, that there were an onomatopoeic word in English which, as pronounced, resembled the cry of an owl (in the way that the pronunciation of the citation-form of 'cuckoo' resembles the cry of the cuckoo). If the word meant "owl", this would be a case of iconicity. (True, like 'cuckoo', the word would refer to the source of the sound, rather than to the sound itself; but the characteristic sounds made by birds and animals are as distinctive a part of them as their shape. It is their characteristic sounds that will be iconically represented in the phonic medium, but their characteristic shapes in a graphic medium, as, for example, in Egyptian hieroglyphs.) Let us suppose, however, that the word no longer meant "owl" (though it may have done so originally), but "wise" or "wisdom". This would be an instance of what may be called secondary iconicity*, based, as far as the forms of the word are concerned, on the primary iconic association with the characteristic sound of the bird and, as far as the meaning of the word is concerned, on a generally accepted association of owls with wisdom. Both of these associations have usually been regarded, in the past, as natural rather than conventional; and the traditional figures of speech (metaphor, metonymy, synechdoche, etc.) were employed by the Stoics and their successors, to account for the allegedly natural extension of meaning from an original or basic to a secondary related sense. More recently, they have been used to codify historically documented changes of meaning (Bréal, 1897; Stern, 1931). Secondary iconicity has often been invoked, though not in these terms, as one of the factors operative in the origin and evolution of language.

What has been called secondary onomatopoeia is a special case of secondary iconicity. Examples given by Ullmann, who classifies them in this way, are such forms as *dither, dodder, quiver, slink*, having to do with movement of various kinds, and *gloom, grumpy, mawkish, slatternly*, which are forms of lexemes denoting "some physical or moral quality, usually unfavourable" (Ullmann, 1962: 84). All these examples of secondary onomatopoeia, in which the sound of the spoken word-forms is felt to be appropriate to the meaning of the lexemes of which they are forms, though the words do not actually denote sounds or the source of sounds, illustrate the phenomenon known as sound-symbolism* (or phonaesthesia*). This has been extensively treated in the literature of phonetics, semantics and stylistics (cf. Ullmann, 1962: 84ff). Although it is undoubtedly the case that in particular languages certain sounds or combinations of sounds are associated with aspects of meaning (and great use of these associations is sometimes made in poetry), it is uncertain to what degree the principles of sound-symbolism are shared by different languages. In so far as it exists, sound-symbolism appears to be restricted to a relatively small part of the vocabularies of languages.

The main point that has emerged from our discussion of the relationship between the iconic and the conventional is that they do not as sharply oppose one another as, not only Peirce's, but also many other schemes of classification, would suggest. For example, the culturally recognized relationship between owls and wisdom may or may not be based on anything in nature. Within the culture in which we live, however, supported as it is by convention, the relationship is certainly not arbitrary. In any case, in this matter, as in many others, it is perhaps impossible in the last resort to draw a line between what is biologically and what is culturally determined, between nature and nurture.

The term 'iconic' is now well established in the literature and, though it is no more than a label for a rather disparate set of non-arbitrary relationships of form and meaning, it is a useful technical term. It is important, however, not to interpret it as being synonymous with 'natural'. Unlike 'symbolic', 'iconic' has the advantage of not having a different non-technical sense outside semiotics. Although anyone reading the literature of semiotics and semantics should be aware of the technical use made of the terms 'symbol' and 'symbolic' by Peirce and his followers, there is no good reason to perpetuate their usage. It would seem to be preferable to use the term symbolic* for relations of the kind that hold between owls and wisdom, saying, for example, that the owl is a symbol* of, or symbolizes*, wisdom. Apart from anything else, this is closer to the non-technical usage of everyday language.

The best technical term for any non-arbitrary form-meaning or meaning-meaning relationship that can be shown to be based on some general principle is perhaps Saussure's term, motivated*, which is already quite widely used by linguists (cf. Ullmann, 1973: 352ff). If the relationship is one of form and meaning and the general principle is resemblance of some kind, the form may be described as iconic. Iconicity understood in this sense will be a more specific kind of motivation; it may be either primary or secondary, but it will always be dependent upon properties of the medium in which the form is manifest. There is little point in applying the term 'iconicity' to meaning-meaning relations, such as metaphor (though, as we have seen, metaphor may be a constitutive factor in secondary iconicity).

(iii) Index. Peirce's third main category of signs is even more heterogeneous than the other two. The explicit definition which he gives of the term index* runs as follows: "An index is a sign which would, at once, lose the character which makes it a sign if its object were removed, but would not lose that character if there were no interpretant" (1940: 104). This definition, it will be observed, is so phrased as to make symbols, icons and indices, in theory at least, non-intersecting categories. Peirce goes on to say, by way of illustration, that a piece of mould with a bullet-hole in it is an index: "for without the shot there would have been no hole; but there is a hole there, whether anybody has the sense to attribute it to a shot or not". Just how his definition applies to other examples that he gives is, however, unclear: a man's rolling gait is "a probable indication that he is a sailor"; "a sundial or a clock indicates the time of day"; "a rap on the door is an index" – and, in general, anything which "focuses the attention" or "startles us" is an index (1940: 108). So too are demonstrative pronouns, because "they call upon the hearer to use his powers of observation, and so establish a real connection between his mind and the object" (1940: 110).

None of Peirce's followers appears to have used the terms index*, indexical* and indicate* in as general a sense as he did. Morris (1946: 76) employs the term 'identifier' for signs "signifying location in space and time", which "direct behavior towards a certain region of the environment" and 'indicators' for non-linguistic signals, such as the gesture of pointing, which function as identifiers. His term 'indicator' is therefore narrower than, though related to, Peirce's 'index'. As far as 'index' and 'indexical' are concerned, there now appear to be two quite distinct senses current in the literature. Abercrombie (1967) employs the term 'indices' to refer to "signs which reveal personal characteristics of the writer or speaker"; and this definition would clearly cover Peirce's example of the sailor's rolling gait and some, though presumably not all, of the signs, or signals, which focus our attention or startle us. Certain philosophers, on the other hand, use the term 'indexical' of sentences (e.g. "I am hungry") which are context-dependent in the sense that the truth-value of the propositions expressed in statements made by uttering them may vary from one occasion of their utterance to another (cf. Bar-Hillel, 1954b). This philosophical use of 'indexical' seems to derive from the fact that Peirce applied it to demonstrative pronouns and other words which call the attention of the hearer to aspects of the immediate situation. The definition of 'index', 'indexical' and 'indicate' that we will adopt will be closer to Abercrombie's.

We will take it as criterial for the application of the term indexical* that there shall be some known or assumed connexion between a sign A, and its significatum C such that the occurrence of A can be held to imply the presence or existence of C. This is not yet specific enough for our purposes: it is intended to capture the spirit of Peirce's general definition (without introducing the condition that A and C should be contiguous or that the connexion between them should be independent of the existence of an interpretant). When we say that smoke means fire or that slurred speech is a sign of drunkenness we imply, in terms of the general definition just given, that smoke and slurred speech are indices: they imply the presence of fire or drunkenness (by pointing to them, as it were). But there is a more particular condition which is also satisfied in these two instances; and it is one that we will make a defining condition for indices. Smoke does not merely imply that there is somewhere a fire; it indicates* the fire as the source of the smoke. Slurred speech does not merely imply that somebody is drunk; it indicates the drunken state of the speaker. We will take it as the essential feature of all indices that they should convey information, in this way, about their source.

An alternative term for 'indexical' which is quite common in the linguistic, psychological and ethological literature is expressive*; and we have already used this latter term in this way in distinguishing different kinds of meaning (2.4). 'Expressive', however, has the disadvantage that it is also used regularly in other senses in stylistics: we talk of a phrase, as being more expressive than another, for example, if it is more vivid or otherwise more effective, and regardless of whether it reveals anything about the state of mind or personality of the author. The reader should note that 'expressive' in essentially the same sense as 'indexical' is a key term in Bühler's (1934) theory and in the work of Jakobson and other Prague School linguists, who were much influenced by Bühler. However, now that we have introduced a more suitable general term for the information in utterances which covaries with, and therefore reveals, characteristics of the sender (cf. 3.1), we can restrict the term 'expressive' to those indexical features of an utterance by means of which a speaker or writer establishes or reveals his individuality in a particularly original manner. Expressivity, in this sense, will therefore be a part of creativity* (cf. 3.4); and it will fall within the province of stylistics, rather than semantics (in so far as these two branches of semiotics, or linguistics, can be distinguished from one another: cf. 14.5).

Indexical signs and signals may be subclassified in various ways. Abercrombie (1967: 7) distinguishes those which "indicate membership of a group", those which "characterize the individual" and those which "reveal changing states of the speaker". Laver (1968) makes a slightly different tripartite classification: into biological, psychological and social. Both Abercrombie and Laver are concerned primarily with speech, and more particularly with voice-quality* and paralinguistic* features (3.1). But 'indexical' is usefully applicable to other features of utterances also, and to written as well as spoken utterances. Not only may a person's pronunciation or handwriting indicate his membership of a particular regional or sociocultural group, his sex and age, who he is, what his emotional state or attitude is, and so on; so too may his employment of a particular form or lexeme, or a particular grammatical construction. Indeed, much of what is often described as an author's individual style is indexical in this sense of the term.

The subclassification to be adopted here is essentially the same as Abercrombie's. Indices and indexical features which characterize the source of the signal as a particular individual may be called individual-identifying* (or idiosyncratic*); and indices and indexical features which correlate with his membership of particular social groups within the community (being of a certain age, of a particular sex, of a certain physical build and personality, etc.) may be called group-identifying*. The latter may be subdivided, as necessary, into region-identifying* (or regional*) indices, based on the geographical provenance of the individual, status-identifying* (or status*) indices, based on his social standing, occupation-identifying* (or occupational*) indices, and so on. Features of this kind have long been studied by linguists; and they are frequently recognized within a language-community as falling within the scope of such terms as 'accent', 'dialect', 'jargon', in their everyday, pre-theoretical sense.

Within the class of indices there is one particular subclass worthy of special mention. This is the third of Abercrombie's subtypes ("those that reveal changing states of the speaker"), to which he (in common with many other authors) gives the label 'affective'. Indexical features of this kind are often referred to as attitudinal. It seems desirable, however, to adopt a rather wider definition of 'state of the speaker' than 'affective' or 'attitudinal' would suggest; and for the correspondingly wider subclass of indices so defined we will use the term symptom*. Any information in a sign or signal which indicates to the receiver that the sender is in a particular state, whether this be an emotional state (fear, anger, sexual arousal or readiness, etc.), a state of health (suffering from laryngitis, etc.), a state of intoxication, or whatever, will be described as symptomatic* of that state. In many cases, though not in all, the state in question can be plausibly interpreted as the cause of the symptom. This use of the term 'symptom', it may be observed, is close to the sense in which it is used in medicine; and, as was mentioned above, it was of the art of diagnosis, by interpreting symptoms as signs, that the word 'semiotic' was first used in Greek (cf. Morris, 1946: 285). The term 'symptom' is in fact quite widely employed in the literature in the sense it has just been given here; it is not subject to the same degree of fluctuation from one author to the next as 'symbol' or 'signal' are.

Our definition of 'symptom', it will be noted, would also allow for Bühler's use of the term, referred to above (4.1), according to which every utterance is a symptom for the receiver of what is in the sender's mind. It is doubtful, however, whether there is any point in giving to the expression 'state of the speaker' as general an interpretation as this. But some might wish to argue that every utterance is symptomatic of the internal state of the sender in a somewhat different sense: in that it is determined by a particular neurophysiological program and carries information which can be used to infer the nature of the program. This may be true; though in the present state of research it would be premature to conclude, as far as the production of spoken utterances is concerned, that every token of what listeners would regard as the same utterance-type, is the product of a distinctive and characteristic neurophysiological program. Even if this is the case, utterances would be symptomatic of the neurophysiological state of the speaker only for trained observers, and not for the customary receivers of the signals.

It should be noted that 'indexical' (including 'symptomatic') has been defined here in such a way that it is not incompatible with either 'arbitrary' or 'iconic'. Many symptoms and many idiosyncratic indices are either naturally or conventionally motivated; others are arbitrary. It should also be stressed that language-signals, as we have seen (3.1), are quite complex: some components of an utterance-signal may be indexical and others non-indexical. According to the subclassification of indexical features proposed in this section, the term 'indexical' covers many aspects of social meaning. We have already pointed out that it is only by virtue of the interpersonal relations established within social groups that we can assert our own distinctive personality as individuals (2.4).

4.3. *Nominalism, realism and conceptualism*

We must now look a little more closely at the role played by concepts in many traditional and modern theories of meaning. As we shall see, this is a philosophically and psychologically controversial topic. It is important that all semanticists should be aware that these controversies exist, even if they are not themselves philosophers or psychologists. The issues that are involved are crucial in any theory of semantics that claims to give an account of the relationship that holds between language and the world. In the course of our discussion a certain amount of more

or less standard terminology will be introduced which we can draw upon
later.

Let us grant that there exist in the external world a variety of entities
of various kinds (persons, animals, plants, etc.); that each such entity is
an individual* and that it is characterized by, or possesses, certain
perceptible or otherwise intelligible properties*. In saying this we are
adopting the metaphysics of everyday usage.

By a concept* is to be understood an idea, thought or mental construct
by means of which the mind apprehends or comes to know things. As
we have already seen, in one traditional analysis of signification, concepts mediate between words and objects. "Words signify [things] by
means of mediating concepts", it will be recalled, is the slogan which
sums this up (4.1); and we have called the object that is signified by a
word its significatum*. Let us now introduce the term signification*
for the mediating concept, so that we can say that what a word signifies
directly is its signification and what it signifies indirectly is its significatum. In a number of modern theories of semantics this distinction is
made by calling the concept the 'meaning' of the word and the object
'the thing-meant' (cf. Gardiner, 1932; Ullmann, 1957: 70).

Concepts have often been classified in terms of a number of dichotomies: as simple or complex, concrete or abstract, singular or common, universal or particular. We need not go into the details of this
scheme here; it should be noted, however, that such traditional grammatical distinctions as those drawn between concrete and abstract nouns,
and proper and common nouns, are partly dependent upon it, by virtue
of the close association of grammatical and logical theory in the Western
tradition (cf. 11.3). It is the distinction between universals and particu-
lars that especially concerns us at this point; for this was the source,
terminologically at least, of the so-called problem of universals, which
has been the subject of intense philosophical controversy from the time
of Plato down to our own day and, in the form of the conflict between
nominalism* and realism*, dominated later medieval logic and
metaphysics. It is associated especially with the name of the fourteenth-
century English philosopher, William of Ockham.

By a universal* is meant a concept of the kind that is associated with
such words as 'man' or 'beautiful' when they are used predicatively
to ascribe to individuals the property of being a man or being beautiful.
The traditional problem of universals has to do with their ontological,
not their psychological, status. Did universals have any existence of their
own outside the mind of a knowing or perceiving subject? That is to say,

did they have extra-mental, or objective, existence? What might be described as the orthodox view, until it was challenged by the nominalists, was that they did. The term 'concept' could be used, therefore, in two senses; not only for what we will now call mental concepts* (and it is in this sense that we introduced the term earlier in this section), but also for the postulated extramental entities that were apprehended by the mind in its knowledge and perception of the external world. We will call these objective concepts*. There were two major versions of realism in antiquity, the one deriving from Plato, which might be called transcendental*, or extreme, realism, and the other from Aristotle, which might be called in contrast immanent*, or moderate, realism. According to Plato, the objective concept (or idea, in the Platonic sense of the term) exists outside and apart from the individuals which, in some way or another, can be said to manifest it. It was, however, the alternative, more moderate version of realism, stemming from Aristotle, which prevailed in the construction of the scholastic synthesis of logic, epistemology and metaphysics; and it was this version that the nominalists were primarily attacking. Some influential modern scholars, such as Frege and Russell, however, have held a position which is closer to Plato's; and latter-day nominalists have criticized them for it.

The Aristotelian view was that every individual (or substance*) was composed of two distinct, but inseparable, principles, matter and form. Matter was the raw stuff of which something was made: it was the individuating principle; that which made an individual unique and different from all other individuals. Form (in a different sense of the term 'form' from the sense in which we are using it as a technical term in this book: cf. 1.5) was the intelligible and perceptual essence or nature of things; immanent in them and having no independent existence; and it was universal in that different individuals could have the same form. For example, the objective universal concept Man (which might well be analysed into simpler concepts) was immanent as form in all individuals to whom one could correctly ascribe the property of being a man.

The nominalists rejected this view of the relationship between words and things. They held that universals were names (hence the label 'nominalist') which signified individuals and which referred to them in propositions in one mode or another. Only individuals existed; and there were no objective, extramental universals. It is important to emphasize, at this point, that the medieval nominalists did not deny the objectivity of our knowledge of the external world; nor that individuals had properties. They were saying that there was no such entity as redness, but only red things: i.e. individual objects to which, by virtue of their similarity in colour, we apply the name 'red'. Universals, therefore, fell victim to what is generally known as Ockham's razor* – the principle of ontological parsimony or economy, according to which "Entities should not be multiplied beyond necessity" or, in what is apparently a more authentic, but less usual, form, "Plurality should not be assumed unnecessarily". It was objective concepts, not mental concepts, that the medieval nominalist rejected as unnecessary.

Nominalism, as we have seen, does not necessarily imply subjectivism or scepticism with respect to the possibility of our acquiring knowledge of the external world. Ockham, at least, seemed to have held that our knowledge of individuals is direct and intuitive, and is caused by the individuals themselves. What he has to say on this topic is of considerable interest. The intuitive apprehension of an object causes a concept of that thing to arise naturally in the mind. This individual concept is a natural sign of the object; and it can be regarded as the meaning of the written or spoken word which, by convention, signifies it in particular languages. "Perceiving a cow results in the formation of the same idea or "natural sign" (*terminus conceptus*) in the mind of the Englishman and of the Frenchman though the former will express this concept in words or writing by means of one conventional sign, 'cow', while the latter will express it by means of another conventional sign, 'vache'" (Copleston, 1953: 54).[2] According to this interpretation of Ockham, therefore, he held that the association between a word and a concept was a matter of convention: but that there should be such a concept was not, and all languages would have words for the concepts formed by direct apprehension of objects in the world.

We will now introduce the term conceptualism* to refer to any theory of semantics which defines the meaning of a word or other expression to be the concept associated with it in the mind of the speaker and hearer. In this rather wide sense of the term, not only traditional realism and nominalism may be described as conceptualist, but also a variety of alternative theories, including the one to which the term is sometimes applied in a more technical and more restricted sense by philosophers: namely, the theory that universal concepts have psycho-

---

[2] Whether this representation of Ockham's view is accurate in every detail is perhaps debatable. But it does make the general point clearly and succinctly.

logical, but not ontological, validity and are constructed, rather than directly apprehended, by the mind.[3]

Conceptualism, of whatever form, in semantics is open to two serious lines of criticism.[4] First, even if we grant that there are concepts associated with words, such that (to echo the quotation from Ullmann given above: 4.1) when I hear the word 'table', the concept of a table will come into my mind and, if I think of a table, the word 'table' will be called up for use as required, there is no evidence to show that concepts of this kind play any part in ordinary language-behaviour. Introspection is notoriously unreliable; but there is no other way of determining whether a succession of concepts accompany the production and understanding of utterances, and introspection does not give any clear support to the view that this is the case. Of course, one may be able to form some mental image of a table, if asked to do so (in a context of mention, rather than use); and one might well do the same occasionally whilst processing certain utterances in either production or reception. But this does not prove that we normally do so, and need to do so, for all words. Nor should it be objected at this point that, if we did not have a concept of table, we should not be able to identify tables and should not therefore be able to use the word 'table' correctly. This may be, not only true, but tautologous. For it could be argued that what is meant by having a concept of table is being able to identify members of the class of objects to which the word 'table' can be correctly applied when one is required to do so; and this is all that is implied by the term concept-formation*, as it is employed by many psychologists. It does not follow, however, from the fact that we must have acquired the concept of a table before we can be said to know the meaning of 'table' that this concept is involved in the production and understanding of most utterances containing the word 'table'. As the term 'concept' is used by many writers on semantics, it is simply not clear what is meant by it; and that is perhaps of itself a sufficient criticism of their use of the term. It is after all a term with a long and controversial history; and anyone who defines the meaning of a word to be the concept correlated with that word owes his readers some explanation of what kind of thing this concept might be.

---

[3] The term 'conceptualism' will never be used in this work in the sense in which it is customarily employed by philosophers.

[4] It must be emphasized that the criticisms of conceptualism put here have no bearing whatsoever upon the postulation of concepts as theoretical constructs within a psychological theory.

The second line of criticism can be directed not only against conceptualism, but against any theory of semantics which defines the meaning of a word in terms of what it signifies, regardless of whether meaning is said to be the signification or the significatum of the word. As long as we restrict our attention to objects like tables, it might seem reasonable to say that the words which are used to refer to them are signs. At least we can give a fairly clear account of the relationship between word and object in cases like this. Once we extend the notion of signification to cover all lexemes, however, we run the risk of trivializing it completely. For to say that what a word means is what it signifies – unless we then go on to recognize different kinds of signification – is to say no more than what a word means is what it means. It would seem to be preferable, therefore, to restrict the notion of signifying, or standing for, to that subclass of lexemes or expressions in language which do stand for things in some clearly interpretable sense of 'signify'. We return to this question in chapter 7. Meanwhile, the reader should be warned that throughout this chapter we have restricted the discussion of signification to the signification of lexemes; we have deliberately not drawn upon our distinction of forms, lexemes and expressions (cf. 1.5). It will be made clear later that, once this distinction is drawn, it is possible to apply the notion of a linguistic unit standing for something else with greater consistency.[5]

4.4. *Syntactics, semantics and pragmatics*

It is nowadays customary to recognize three areas within the field of semiotics: syntactics (or syntax), semantics and pragmatics. This threefold classification goes back ultimately to Peirce, but was first clearly drawn and made more generally familiar by Morris (1938: 6). It was taken up by Carnap (1942: 9), who, like Morris (and Bloomfield), was a contributor to the *International Encyclopaedia of Unified Science* (Neurath *et al.*, 1939), which had a strong reductionist and physicalist bias; and it was subsequently reformulated by Morris (1946) within the framework of his behaviouristic theory of signs. By then Morris felt obliged to point out that the terms 'pragmatics', 'semantics' and 'syntactics' had "already taken on an ambiguity which threatens to cloud rather than illumine the problems of this field, being used by

---

[5] The issues with which we have been dealing in this section are often discussed in terms of the relationship between language and reality (cf. Urban, 1939). For a selection of writings exemplifying more recent approaches, cf. Olshewsky (1969: 653–731).

some writers to designate subdivisions of semiotic itself and by others to designate kinds of signs in the object languages with which semiotic deals" (1946: 217).

There are slight differences in the way in which the distinction is drawn even among authors who use it to refer to three subdivisions of semiotics (or semiotic, as Morris and Carnap call it). In his earlier work Morris defined pragmatics as the study of "the relation of signs to interpreters", semantics as the study of "the relations of signs to the objects to which the signs are applicable", and syntactics as the study of "the formal relations of signs to one another" (1938: 6). Subsequently he proposed a more refined analysis which was designed to "retain the features of the prevailing classification, while freeing it from certain restrictions and ambiguities" and to make the three terms "interpretable within a behaviorally oriented semiotic" (1946: 218–19). The revised definitions run as follows: "pragmatics is that portion of semiotic which deals with the origin, uses, and effects of signs within the behavior in which they occur; semantics deals with the signification of signs in all modes of signifying; syntactics deals with combinations of signs without regard for their specific significations or their relation to the behavior in which they occur".

Carnap's distinction of the three areas of semiotics is close to Morris's earlier formulation, except that it is restricted to natural languages and logical calculi: "If in an investigation explicit reference is made to the speaker, or, to put it in more general terms, to the user of the language, then we assign it to the field of pragmatics... If we abstract from the user of the language and analyze only the expressions and their designata, we are in the field of semantics. And if, finally, we abstract from the designata also and analyze only the relations between the expressions, we are in (logical) syntax" (1942: 9). The reader will observe that 'user' is substituted as a more general term for 'speaker'; but it is not made clear whether the increased generality of this term comes from its inclusion of writers of written language as well as speakers of spoken languages (so that 'sender' or 'producer' would still be sufficiently general) or whether it is intended to cover hearers and readers also as users. What does seem clear is that Carnap, in pragmatics, appears to take the point of view of the producer of the sign more naturally than that of the receiver (even when he refers to "the whole situation – comprising speaker, hearer and environment" (1958: 79)), whereas Morris, in his earlier formulation defines pragmatics in terms of the effects signs have on their interpreters (though he subsequently includes the study of the origin and uses of signs, in addition to the study of their effects, in pragmatics). More popular formulations of the distinction of the three areas of semiotics are less than precise. Typical of these is the one given in the editorial introduction to a collection of articles by a large number of authors which makes the distinction an important organizing principle in the plan of the book: "...syntactics studies how signs are related to each other. Semantics studies how these signs are related to things. And pragmatics studies how they are related to people" (Smith, 1966: 4–5). Later in the book 'pragmatics' is defined in terms of the effects of signals (or signs) on people (p. 519).

For Carnap the distinction between semantics (or at least pure semantics) and pragmatics matches, or is related to, the distinction between languages and logical calculi (which Carnap calls 'constructed language-systems'): semantics and pragmatics are "fundamentally different forms" of the "analysis of meanings of expressions", the one, pragmatics, having to do with "the empirical investigation of historically given natural languages" and the other, pure semantics, with "the study of constructed language-systems". Descriptive semantics (i.e. the investigation of the meaning of expressions in "historically given natural languages"), he says, "may be regarded as part of pragmatics" (1956: 233). The reason why Carnap wanted to incorporate descriptive semantics within the field of pragmatics seems to have been that he believed that differences in the use of particular expressions were not only inevitable in language-behaviour, but must be taken account of in the description. However, despite his reference to pure semantics and descriptive semantics as "fundamentally different forms of analysis", he made it clear in some of his later work that he thought of pure semantics as serving as a model for descriptive semantics; and Bar-Hillel (1954a) took the same view in his advocacy of the application of the work of Carnap and other logical semanticists to the analysis of natural languages.

In his contribution to a volume devoted to the philosophy of Carnap (Schillp, 1963), Morris pointed out that, although Carnap has tended "to regard pragmatics as an empiricial discipline, and not to recognize the possibility of a pure pragmatics co-ordinate with pure semantics and pure syntactics" (p. 88), there is no reason why both pure and descriptive terms should not be introduced for the discussion of the relations which hold between signs and their users. The term 'logic' could then be extended (as Peirce suggested) to cover the whole field of pure semiotics. Carnap, in his reply, conceded these points (Schillp,

1963: 861); and had by then published his paper "On some concepts
of pragmatics" (1956: 248–50), in which he took the same view. Morris,
Carnap and Bar-Hillel are all agreed, however, that, whatever distinction may be drawn between pure semantics and pure pragmatics, the
analysis of meaning in natural languages will necessarily involve pragmatic considerations; and, in particular, that the distinction of
analytic* and synthetic* statements rests upon a decision as to what
meanings are accepted by users of the language that is being described
(cf. 6.5). The "essentially pragmatic character" of ordinary language
is stressed with particular force by Bar-Hillel in one of his most recent
papers (1970: 206–21).

From the summary that has just been given of the development of the
distinction between syntactics, semantics and pragmatics by Morris,
Carnap and Bar-Hillel, it will be obvious that its applicability to the
description of languages, in contrast with the description or construction of logical calculi, is, to say the least, uncertain; and, until
recently, few linguists have drawn the distinction in these terms. If
linguistics were to be included within the field of semiotics, as Morris
(1946: 220–23) and others have proposed, it is obvious that both the
whole field and its subdivisions would need to be circumscribed and
described with greater care and precision than they have been in these
terms so far. The distinction of pragmatics and semantics in relation to
the analysis of meaning in natural language is, as the summary just given
makes clear, generally recognized as controversial. We will come back
to this at several points in later chapters, but more especially in our
discussion of context* (cf. 14.4).

At this point, let us turn our attention instead to the distinction of
syntax (or syntactics) and semantics as this is drawn in the quotations
from Morris and Carnap. The first point to notice is the vagueness of
the definition of syntax. Carnap's definition does not explicitly restrict
syntax to combinatorial relations between words (though it is clear from
his subsequent formalization of a system of pure semantics that these
are what he has in mind); and one of the definitions make it clear what
the conditions of syntactic well-formedness are. Traditionally, linguists
and philosophers have distinguished between two principles of well-
formedness in the construction of sentences and phrases: one in terms
of which they are said to be grammatical (*vs.* ungrammatical); the other
in terms of which they are said to be significant (*vs.* meaningless). If
semantics is the study of meaning, then there is presumably a combinatorial aspect to semantics, as well as to syntax: but this is not

allowed for in the definition of syntax given by Carnap and Morris. A further criticism of the definition of syntax (or syntactics) is that it does not distinguish between forms, lexemes and expressions (cf. 1.5); so that it is uncertain how, or where, in the description of a language, morphology or inflexion would be distinguished from syntax.

As far as the definition of semantics goes, it rests heavily on the notion of signification, which was criticized in the previous section. To define meaning as a relationship between words and things, as we have seen, will not do; and the postulation of theoretical entities, such as Carnap's designata or Morris's dispositions to respond, must be justified, not by demonstrating their ontological or psychological validity, but their usefulness for the purpose of describing how language is used in everyday life. To set up a variety of modes of signifying (as Morris does) is at best an unsatisfactory way of giving recognition to the fact that most expressions of language are simply not used as signs at all (except, perhaps, when they are used reflexively: cf. 1.2). Signification is but one of a number of different semiotic functions.

Finally, the term semiotics* itself. The most useful way of defining this is to identify it with the theory, not of signs, but of signalling-systems: i.e. systems for the transmission of information along some channel (cf. 2.1). Among signalling-systems (i.e. semiotic systems), we can distinguish those that are natural* from those that are artificial*: natural, not in the sense that the signals are iconic, rather than symbolic (in Peirce's sense: 4.2); nor yet in the sense that they are partly or wholly instinctive (rather than acquired by learning); but natural in the sense that they are "historically given" (as Carnap might say) and have not been deliberately constructed. Whether it is possible or useful to incorporate linguistics within some all-embracing general theory of semiotics applicable to all natural and artificial signalling-systems, human or non-human, is an open question. What I have tried to do in this and the previous chapter is to point out the similarities and differences between linguistic and non-linguistic systems that emerge when these are considered from a semiotic point of view. Henceforth we shall be concerned more or less exclusively with language; and we will draw upon the semiotic concepts introduced above in so far as they are useful for this purpose without commitment to the possibility of incorporating linguistic semantics within a general theory of semiotics.

It was mentioned above that, until recently, the tripartite distinction of syntax, semantics and pragmatics, whose development we have traced in the works of Morris, Carnap and Bar-Hillel, is one that few linguists have made use of. It should perhaps be added, at this point, that, although an increasing number of linguists are now beginning to use the term 'pragmatics' in contrast with 'semantics', most of them do so without associating themselves with the view that linguistics is, or should be, a branch of semiotics. This is also true of the majority of logicians and philosophers who draw a distinction between semantics and pragmatics. Indeed, it is arguable that, by now, the origins of the tripartite distinction in Peirce's conception of an overall science of semiotics are more or less irrelevant to the way in which this distinction is currently drawn by either linguists or philosophers. Even less relevant (and we have said nothing about this) is the connexion, in Peirce's work, between pragmatics as a subdivision of semiotics and the philosophical movement known as pragmatism, which, though it was historically independent of positivism or behaviourism, has much in common with them (cf. 5.1).[6] It is a curious fact that many of the logicians and philosophers who currently appeal to the tripartite distinction of syntax, semantics and pragmatics do so in support of quite traditional metaphysical doctrines of the kind that logical positivists like Carnap and, in a more general way, all those who contributed to the *Encyclopaedia of Unified Science* were concerned to combat.[7] But the association of this distinction with the movement for the unification of science was perhaps no more than a short-lived historical contingency; and there is really very little that Morris, Carnap and Bloomfield share, apart from a set of quite general attitudes towards science.

[6] On this aspect of Peirce's work cf. Feibleman (1946), Gallie (1952).
[7] For a selection of views cf. Bar-Hillel (1971) and Davidson & Harman (1972).

5

Behaviourist semantics

5.1. *General attitudes*

In this chapter we shall be concerned with behaviourist theories of meaning. Although behaviourism is nowadays less widely accepted than it was a decade or so ago, it was for a long time dominant in American psychology and it exercised a considerable influence upon the formulation and discussion of some of the basic issues in semantics, not only by psychologists, but also by certain linguists and philosophers.[1]

It is perhaps useful to begin by distinguishing between behaviourism as a general attitude, on the one hand, and behaviourism as a fully developed psychological theory, on the other. In this section, we will discuss behaviourism in the more general sense, recognizing four characteristic principles or tendencies which give it its particular force or flavour.

First to be noted is a distrust of all mentalistic terms like 'mind', 'concept', 'idea', and so on, and the rejection of introspection as a means of obtaining valid data in psychology. The reason for the rejection of introspection is readily understood. Everyone's own personal thoughts and experience are private to him and what he will say about them to others is notoriously unreliable. Indeed, he is just as likely to deceive himself involuntarily as he is deliberately to mislead others about the beliefs and motives which inspire his conduct. Since this is so, the fact that there might be wide agreement among a number of persons reporting upon the results of their introspection is not a sufficient guarantee that these reports are trustworthy. Unless this introspective evidence concurs with evidence derived from an examination of their actions, the behaviourist argues, it is useless (or at least potentially misleading); and, if it does concur with the more reliable, publicly accessible evidence of

---

[1] What follows is not intended as a comprehensive account of behaviourism. Only such points are made as are of importance for the development of semantics. A classic textbook is Osgood (1953). For general background, cf. Carroll (1953), Osgood & Sebeok (1954).

observation, it is superfluous. Psychology, then, should restrict itself to what is directly observable; it should be concerned with overt behaviour, not with unobservable mental states and processes.

The rejection of mentalism* (in this sense of the term) lies at the very heart of the movement known as behaviourism*, founded by J. B. Watson. His classic textbook was published in 1924, but he had been advocating the main principles of the doctrine in articles and lectures for some years before that. As applied to the study of language, the rejection of introspection led to a concentration upon observable and recordable utterances and upon their relationship with the immediate situation in which they were produced. (It is worth noticing, in this connexion, that many psychologists use the term 'verbal behaviour' as the equivalent of, and frequently in preference to, 'language'. We have given reasons above for preferring the term 'language-behaviour' to 'verbal behaviour', and we have drawn a distinction between language-behaviour and the underlying language-system: 3.1, 1.6.) Language was a particularly important kind of behaviour for the psychologist to investigate; for it enabled him, in theory at least, to treat even thought as behaviour and thus dispense with the notion of consciousness. For all thought could be regarded, it was held, as inaudible speech, consisting in very slight and imperceptible movements of the vocal organs. Since what was inaudible could if necessary be amplified, as it were, and made publicly observable, thought was a form of behaviour as amenable to scientific investigation as any other.

The second general feature of behaviourism to be listed here is the belief that there is no essential difference between human and animal behaviour. As we have just seen, thought, or what is commonly described as consciousness, could in principle be treated as subvocal language-behaviour; and language-behaviour was to be accounted for in the same way as one accounted for other kinds of behaviour in human beings and animals. The belief that there is no essential difference in the principles which determine animal and human behaviour links behaviourist psychology with evolutionary biology and zoology and, as we have seen in the preceding chapter, supports the attempts of such scholars as Morris (1946) to construct a general theory of semiotics applicable to all natural signalling-systems. In the light of the alleged continuity of human and animal behaviour it becomes interesting and appropriate to ask such questions as the following in relation to semantics. Is animal behaviour meaningful in the same sense in which human behaviour, and in particular language-behaviour, is said to be meaningful? What are the features, if any, that distinguish languages from the signalling-systems used by other species and what are the features, if any, which they share? These questions have already been discussed in sufficient detail (in chapter 3) and will be touched on again only briefly in our treatment of behaviourism.

The third aspect of behaviourism is its tendency to minimize the role of instinct and other innate drives or faculties and to emphasize the part played by learning in its account of how animals and human beings acquire their behaviour patterns; to stress nurture rather than nature, to attribute more to environment and correspondingly less to heredity. In this respect behaviourism is a natural ally of empiricism in its opposition to rationalism. For empiricism claims that experience (and more especially experience channelled through the senses) is the principal source of knowledge, while rationalism stresses the role played by the mind in the acquisition of knowledge and emphasizes the mind's ability to reason from a priori principles. The conflict between rationalism and empiricism confronts us at almost every turn in any discussion of the principles of semantics. Logical semantics, as we shall see later (6.1), has been closely linked with empiricism, and more particularly with positivism: the doctrine that scientific knowledge of the kind that is sought and attained by the physical sciences is the only true form of knowledge, that this is based exclusively on sense-experience and that it is futile to indulge in metaphysical speculation about ultimate causes or the nature of reality. More traditional theories of meaning, as we have seen (4.3), were cast in a rationalist (or conceptualist) mould.

The fourth, and final, general feature of behaviourism to be mentioned at this point is its mechanism or determinism. These terms (which we will here treat as equivalent, though they are sometimes distinguished) are to be understood as referring to the view that everything that happens in the universe is causally determined according to the same physical laws and that this holds true of human action no less than it does of the movements and transformations of inanimate matter. Holding this view it is only to be expected that the behaviourist will lay great stress on predictability as the principal criterion for the evaluation of any theory of human behaviour that he might put forward; it is also perhaps natural that in his account of the way language behaviour is initiated he should look to the external environment, whenever he can, for the causal element in the production of utterances.

Before moving on, it is worth stressing that the four general features of behaviourism listed above do not belong indissociably together, in the sense that any one presupposes or implies any other. One can be an opponent of introspection without being a mechanist; one can deny that there is any gulf between man and the animal kingdom without thereby being committed to the denial of mind; and so on. Still less does the acceptance of any one, or even all four, of the attitudes listed here commit a scholar to the acceptance of behaviourism as a psychological theory. It simply is not true, and never has been in any previously recognized sense of the term 'mentalism', that one must be either a mentalist or a behaviourist.

5.2. *More particular features of behaviourism*

The behaviour of any organism can be described, according to the behaviourist, in terms of the responses* which the organism makes to stimuli* presented by the environment. Looked at from this point of view, other organisms may be taken as being part of the environment. The formula commonly used to symbolize this relationship between stimulus and response is

$$S \rightarrow R$$

The arrow here represents a causal relationship: the stimulus is a cause and the response its effect. The combination of the two is a stimulus–response reflex.

If the response which the organism makes to a given stimulus results in the satisfaction of some need or desire (more technically, if it alleviates some state of deprivation) it is thereby reinforced and becomes more probable as a response when the same stimulus is next presented. It is important to realize that the response may have been made originally by chance. We do not need to invoke the notion of purpose or intention; and, strictly speaking, we should not describe the behaviour that is reinforced as successful (since success presupposes intention). If a response is not reinforced, it will become progressively less probable and ultimately will be extinguished; it will be more quickly extinguished by aversive stimulation, or punishment. Talking in more usual terms, we can say that an organism will gradually learn to refrain from doing some things because they lead to pain or punishment and will learn to do other things because they bring pleasure or some alleviation of its pain or distress. It is upon these basic principles that the behaviourist theory of learning is founded.

A behaviour-pattern is learned as a chain of stimulus–response reflexes, as may be illustrated by

$$(S_1 \dashrightarrow R_1) \dashrightarrow (S_2 \dashrightarrow R_2) \dashrightarrow (S_3 \dashrightarrow R_3) \dashrightarrow \ldots$$

It is in this way, for example, that the grammar of a language is assumed to be learned. The first word of an utterance is produced as the response (R_1) to some external stimulus (S_1); the production of R_1 then serves as a stimulus (S_2) to which the second word is a response (R_2); and so on. The causal relationships between the S–R reflexes are built up on the basis of their previous association. Generally, of course, there will be more than one possible transition from one word to the next in a grammatically acceptable utterance, and the strength of the associative bond between a particular word and its possible successors will vary according to the frequency with which they have been associated in the past and their association reinforced. It will be clear that this view of the grammatical structure of utterances lends itself very naturally to further development in terms of information-theory (see 2.3). For statistical probabilities can be assigned to each of the set of possible successors at each point of transition from one S–R reflex to the next.

Particularly prominent in the earlier versions of behaviourism, in what is now often described as classical behaviourism, is the notion of the conditioned reflex. In fact, behaviourism was born, as a distinctive psychological doctrine, when Watson drew from Pavlov's work on the conditioning of physiological reflexes the implication that this notion could be used to account for the development of an association between a stimulus and its response. Pavlov had shown that salivation in dogs, which occurred naturally or instinctively as an unconditioned physiological response in the presence of food, could be evoked as a reaction to the ringing of a bell, when the bell had been rung a number of times in association with the presentation of the food. The food was an unconditioned stimulus, the ringing of the bell a conditioned stimulus, and the salivation an unconditioned response to the food, but a conditioned response to the bell. Similarly, reactions of fear or love, unconditioned (or instinctive) in relation to a small set of stimuli, could be conditioned to other substitute stimuli by virtue of the association, whether fortuitous or experimentally devised, of the substitute stimulus with the original stimulus. Reinforcement could convert an originally instinctive response into a learned response, as when a baby's crying is reinforced by parental attention in various states of deprivation or aversive stimulation. Finally, a response could be generalized to all stimuli that resembled the stimulus with which the response was originally associated, and the greater the similarity in the stimuli the stronger would be the associative S–R bond that is developed.

So much, then, for the basic notions of behaviourism. One more general point may be made before we pass on to consider behaviourist theories of meaning. The mechanism of reinforcement was assumed to operate in very much the same way as the mechanism of natural selection in evolutionary biology: as we have seen, a small number of reflexes were assumed to be innate, but the vast majority of responses were first made at random, their association with particular stimuli being established by reinforcement.

5.3. *Behaviourist theories of meaning*

An early formulation of the behaviourist conception of meaning was Watson's: "Words function in the matter of calling out responses exactly as did the objects for which the words serve as substitutes".[2] Here we find invoked the notion of the conditioned reflex: the word (i.e. the word-form) commonly occurs in the presence of a certain object, and the object evokes a particular response; an associative link is established between word and object (as between the food and the ringing of the bell in Pavlov's experiments); and, in the absence of the object the word acts as a substitute stimulus. Watson's views on this and other points was further developed by A. P. Weiss (1928).

Bloomfield's behaviouristic analysis of an imaginary speech-event rests upon the same notion of words or utterances as substitute stimuli and responses. It deserves to be discussed in some detail: partly because it is typical of the kind of analysis that any early behaviourist would give; but also, and this is the more important reason for paying particular attention to it here, because Bloomfield was one of the most influential figures in the development of the scientific study of language in the first half of the century and he, more than anyone else, was responsible for introducing the behaviourist point of view into linguistics.

In one of his early works Bloomfield (1914) had declared his adherence to what he was later to condemn as the mentalistic approach to the psychology of language advocated by Wundt (1912). By 1926, however, he had abandoned this approach; and in his "A set of postulates for the science of language" (Bloomfield, 1926), explicitly modelled on Weiss's behaviouristic postulates for psychology, he put

---

[2] According to Skinner (1957: 86–7), who quotes this passage from Weiss, "it is a superficial analysis which is much too close to the traditional notion of words 'standing for' things".

forward the view that meaning consists in the observable stimulus–reaction features in utterances. This is the view he took in all subsequent publications. In his classic textbook of linguistics, first published in 1933, he drew a contrast between what he described as the traditional mentalistic theory of language and "the materialistic (or, better, mechanistic) theory", according to which "human actions...are part of cause-and-effect sequences exactly like those we observe, say, in the study of physics or chemistry" (1935: 33).[3] (He went on to suggest that, although we could in principle foretell whether a certain stimulus would cause someone to speak and, if so, exactly what he would say, in practice we could make the prediction "only if we knew the exact structure of his body at the moment" (1935: 33). Bloomfield, then, shared at least two of the general attitudes which he noted as characteristic of behaviourism in the first section of this chapter: a distrust of mentalism and a belief in determinism. Moreover, as the quotations show, he accepted that particularly strong form of determinism to which the labels 'positivism' and 'physicalism' are often applied: that is to say, he believed that all science should be modelled upon the so-called exact sciences and that all scientific knowledge should be reducible, ultimately, to statements made about the properties of the physical world as these were described by physics and chemistry. It is worth noting, in this connexion, that Bloomfield was a contributor, together with such scholars as Carnap and Morris, to the *Encyclopaedia of Unified Science* (Neurath *et al.*, 1939), which was inspired by the thesis of physicalism (cf. 4.4).

Bloomfield's example of a speech-event is as follows (1935: 23ff). Jack and Jill are walking down a lane; Jill sees an apple on a tree and, being hungry, asks Jack to get it for her; he climbs the tree and gives her the apple; and she eats it. In this situation, Jill's being hungry and her seeing the apple constitute the stimulus (S). Instead of making the more direct response (R) of climbing the tree to get the apple herself she makes a substitute response (r) in the form of a particular utterance; and this acts as a substitute stimulus (s) for Jack causing him to respond (R) as he would have done if he himself had been hungry and had seen

[3] In abandoning the so-called mentalism of Wundt for the behaviourism of Weiss, Bloomfield did so in the belief that linguistics could, and should, remain neutral in psychological disputes: cf. Bloomfield (1926: 153). In traditional philosophical usage the term 'mentalism' often refers to the doctrine that the objects of knowledge have no existence outside the mind of the perceiver. The term is employed here in the more general sense in which it was used by the founders of behaviourism: to describe any philosophical theory according to which there is a radical difference between mind and matter.

the apple. The whole situation is symbolized by Bloomfield as follows:

$$S \longrightarrow r...s \longrightarrow R$$

The difference between lower-case and capital letters represents the distinction between a direct and a substitute stimulus or response. The meaning of the utterance ($r...s$) is "the situation in which the speaker utters it and the response which it calls forth in the hearer" ($S \longrightarrow R$) (1935: 26).[4] Later in the same book Bloomfield talks of the stimulus part of the S-R complex as being the meaning of the utterance (p. 139) and ultimately identifies meaning with the recurrent features of the situation in which forms are used (p. 158; cf. also Bloomfield, 1943). One point that is not clear in Bloomfield's analysis of meaning, it should be noted, is the relationship between the meaning of utterances and the meaning of lexemes. Jill's substitute response (r) is not a lexeme, but an utterance, which may be either a single word-form (what Bloomfield elsewhere calls a minimal free form) or a sequence of word-forms and will in either case have superimposed upon it some appropriate prosodic and paralinguistic modulation (cf. 3.1).

The analysis of meaning, in Bloomfield's opinion, is "the weak point in language-study" and will necessarily remain so "until human knowledge advances very far beyond its present state" (1935: 140). This is because a precise account of the meaning of words was held to depend upon a complete and scientific description of the objects, states and situations for which words operate as substitutes. For a small number of words we were already in a position to give a reasonably precise scientific description. Jill's hunger could be described in terms of the contraction of her muscles and the secretion of fluids in her stomach; her seeing the apple could be analysed in terms of light waves reflected from the apple reaching her eyes; and the apple itself could be given a botanical classification (ultimately reducible, no doubt, to a purely physical description). For the meaning of the vast majority of words, however, no such scientific analysis could be provided. Love and hate were not so readily

---

[4] Bloomfield's theory of meaning is therefore a causal theory, as is that of Ogden & Richards (cf. 4.1): it is also, like theirs, a contextual theory of meaning, in that it makes the meaning of an utterance dependent upon the context in which it is uttered. On causal theories of meaning in general, cf. Black (1968: chapter 7). Not all contextual theories of meaning are based on the principles of behaviourism. In particular, it should be emphasized that Firth, who explicitly adopted a contextual theory of meaning (cf. 14.4), was not a behaviourist; and Ogden and Richards were behaviourists only in a rather loose sense of the term.

identifiable in physical terms, as hunger is. Still less easy to characterize in this way was the meaning of such words as 'good' or 'beautiful'.

Bloomfield's positivism, or physicalism, should be distinguished from his behaviourism and, for convenience of exposition and discussion, if for no other reason, can be treated separately. Many philosophers have proposed theories of meaning based on positivism without being behaviourists; and it is quite conceivable that someone should wish to define meaning in terms of a stimulus–response model of behaviour without being committed thereby to the view that the only scientific description of the stimuli is by means of a reductive analysis to the theoretical constructs of the physical sciences. Let us therefore postpone all discussion of the physicalist thesis for the present.

What then can we say about the more specifically behaviourist element in Bloomfield's analysis of meaning? The first and most obvious comment is that, for a theory which is supposedly constructed on the solid basis of observable data, it takes a lot of unobserved, and indeed unobservable, evidence for granted. Let us concede as plausible that a sufficient, though presumably not necessary, condition for Jill's utterance of *I am hungry* is that she should in fact be hungry and should see something edible, such as an apple, in the evironment. If Jill's utterance serves as a substitute stimulus to Jack causing him to behave as he would have done if he had been hungry and had seen the apple, why did he not, after climbing the tree, eat the apple himself? Clearly something else must be introduced to account for the fact that Jack interprets and accepts Jill's utterance as a request that he should give the apple to her. Furthermore, casual observation and experience would suggest that the situations in which tokens of the utterance-type *I am hungry* are produced are extremely diverse and that the kind of behaviour which follows upon such an utterance is, not only diverse, but in many cases unpredictable. Nor is there any reason to believe, on the basis of casual observation and experience that there is something independently identifiable that is common to all the situations in which tokens of a given utterance-type are produced.

It may be objected that casual observation and experience can hardly be accepted as a reliable foundation upon which to construct a scientific theory of meaning; and this is true. But nothing more reliable has been offered in its place. It is one thing to say, because of some prior commitment to a certain philosophical view, that particular utterances must be fully determined by the situation (or some factor in the situation) and must themselves interact with the situation to determine the reaction of the listener; it is quite a different matter to show that this is so in the face of even casual and anecdotal evidence to the contrary. Suppose Jack's reaction is to say *You can't be; we've only just had lunch* or *Are you sure you want the apple? You know they give you indigestion.* Do we now say that the situation giving rise to Jill's utterance and Jack's reaction must have been different in all three cases, on the ground that Jack's reaction was different? And will we now insist that Jill's utterance has a different meaning in all three cases? For the meaning of an utterance, it will be recalled, is defined in terms of the reaction that it provokes as well as the stimulus that it is provoked by. Elsewhere Bloomfield says: "A needy stranger at the door says *I'm hungry*. A child who has eaten and merely wants to put off going to bed says *I'm hungry*. Linguistics considers only those vocal features which are alike in the two utterances, and only those stimulus–reaction features which are alike in the two utterances" (1926: 153). But what are the stimulus–reaction features common to these utterances? And how would one identify them? Are we not inclined to say that the listener's recognition of the meaning of *I am hungry* is independent of and prior to his reaction to it? This would certainly be a more usual way of looking at things; and the advantages of abandoning it in favour of a behaviouristic definition of meaning are far from clear. We will take up this point in the next section.

Bloomfield's notion of meaning, as we have seen, was very close to that of Watson and Weiss. Skinner, who belongs to a later generation of behaviourists and has constructed a far more elaborate theory, is very critical of this, saying: "Only when the concepts of stimulus and response are used very loosely can the principle of conditioning serve as a biological prototype of symbolization" (1957: 87).[5] He points out that it is only in a very limited set of cases that the verbal stimulus will have the same effect upon the organism as would the object with which it is associated; and he rejects the terms 'sign' and 'symbol' to denote the relationship of association. He bases his analysis on the concept of stimulus control*. This involves the three factors of stimulus, response and reinforcement, no two of which, however, can be identified as a

---

[5] The title of Skinner's book (1957) is somewhat misleading. The term 'verbal behaviour', as used by Skinner, includes much else besides language; on the other hand, as we have already seen, there is much in language that is not part of the verbal component (cf. 3.1). Though Skinner's book was not published until 1957, an earlier version had been circulating for some years previously and had exerted considerable influence upon the psychology of language in America.

symbol and what is symbolized. The point is that reinforcement depends solely upon the contingencies of the environment in which the stimulus occurs. If what is at first a random response to a given stimulus is reinforced, the organism will associate the response with the prior stimulus and be the more likely to emit the same response to the same stimulus on future occasions. The word-form *fox*, for example, is not a substitute stimulus, standing for a particular kind of animal; it is a word-form whose association with the animals in question has been established by its occurrence in utterances which "have been, and probably will be, reinforced by seeing a fox" (Skinner, 1957: 88).

Utterances, for Skinner, are verbal operants*. (The term 'operant' is intended to suggest "activities which operate upon the environment" in contrast with "activities which are primarily concerned with the internal economy of the organism" (p. 20).) They fall into two main classes, according to whether the prior stimuli that control them are (a) non-verbal or (b) verbal; and the first of these two classes is divided into two subclasses, mands and tacts.

The term mand* is mnemonically related to 'command', 'demand', 'countermand', etc. and refers to a verbal operant "in which the response is reinforced by a characteristic consequence and is therefore under the functional control of the relevant conditions of deprivation or aversive stimulation" (pp. 35–6). Utterances such as *Hand me that book* or *Give me an apple*, in their most characteristic use, would therefore be mands. If we temporarily disregard the behaviourist's rejection of the notions of purpose and intention, we can say that mands are utterances by means of which the speaker gets the listener to do something for him. Many authors refer to this as the instrumental* function of language and think of it as being especially basic or primitive (cf. 2.4). It should be noted that, for Skinner, mands include not only commands, requests and entreaties, but also questions: for a question is characteristically reinforced by a verbal response which alleviates the state of deprivation or aversive stimulation which gave rise to the question. Skinner also extends the term to cover what he calls 'magical' and 'superstitious' mands, such as wishes and oaths.

The second subclass of verbal operants under the functional control of prior non-verbal stimuli are tacts*. ("The invented term 'tact'... carries a mnemonic suggestion of behaviour which 'makes contact with' the physical world" (p. 81).) Just what utterances count as tacts, however, is rather unclear. A tact is defined as "a verbal operant in which a response to a given form is evoked (or at least strengthened) by a particular object or event or property of an object or event" (1957: 81-2). But this definition would presumably admit mands as a subclass of tacts. What Skinner is mainly concerned with in his discussion of tacts is the way in which linguistic expressions come to be associated with objects and events in the immediate situation. He says that "the presence of a given stimulus raises the probability of occurrence of a given form of response" (p. 82). But by this he does not mean that statements, say, rather than questions, commands or requests are more likely to occur (although he does at this point restrict his attention to statements, and moreover statements descriptive of the immediate physical environment): he appears to be far more concerned to argue that the presence of a particular object or the occurrence of a particular event in the immediate environment raises the probability that the speaker will produce an utterance containing an expression which refers to that object or event. We have just used the term 'refer', although Skinner expressly warns us against employing the notion of stimulus control "to redefine concepts such as sign, signal or symbol or a relation such as reference, or entities communicated in a speech episode such as ideas, meanings, or information" (p. 115). However, other authors, most notably Quine (1960), have redefined both signification and reference in behaviouristic terms; and Quine at least has explicitly related his view of the child's acquisition of the linguistic means of reference to Skinner's theory of operant-conditioning. We also employed the term 'expression', rather than 'form': this is because, within the terminological framework that we have adopted in this book, it is expressions, not forms, that are said to have reference (cf. 1.5, 7.1).

Skinner's own discussion of abstraction and reference, apart from his introduction of the specifically behaviourist notion of reinforcement (under conditions of deprivation or aversive stimulation) is strikingly similar to that found in such works as Ogden and Richards (1923), which we described above as being itself behaviouristic in a broad sense (cf. 2.1). His use of the term abstraction* is, in fact, quite traditional: every object serving as a stimulus will have a set of properties and the response may initially be to the same object or to a class of objects sharing all the same properties or some subset of them; eventually however, by virtue of the community's reinforcement of the response in the presence of a stimulus with the property which the community associates with the response and the community's failure to reinforce the response in the presence of objects lacking the criterial property, the response is appropriately specialized* and the property is correctly abstracted* from the objects which manifest it. It is in this way for example that we come to learn the meaning of words like 'red' or 'round'. Apart from the postulation of the mechanism of reinforcement by the community, what is said here about abstraction is identical with what many philosophers have said about the way in which so-called universal concepts are formed (cf. 4.3). It relates most obviously perhaps to the empiricist theories of Locke and Hume; but rationalist theories of abstraction are not strikingly different, except insofar as they emphasize the role of innate knowledge or predispositions.

Skinner has no special term for the class of verbal operants under the functional control of prior verbal stimuli. This includes a very substantial proportion of the utterances that we produce in any everyday conversation. But there are a number of subclasses which Skinner distinguishes and which are worthy of separate mention: echoic responses, textual responses and intraverbal responses. Echoic responses are those in which the listener repeats part or the whole of what a speaker has just said. They are said to be especially common in children; at the same time, it is emphasized that echoic behaviour does not depend upon or demonstrate any instinct or faculty of imitation (p. 59). Textual responses are those in which the prior verbal stimulus is a written text and the response that operation which we call reading. Most important of all are the intraverbal responses. They include, not only the relatively trivial instances of social formulae like *Fine, thank you* (uttered in response to the stimulus *How are you?*), but also a good deal of what we call knowledge. For factual knowledge, it is assumed, is stored in chains of intraverbal associations and is learned much as we might learn a poem or prayer by heart, the first line or phrase being the stimulus to which the second is linked associatively as a response, and so on to the end of the poem or prayer.

We will not discuss the details of this subclassification of verbal operants controlled by prior verbal stimuli or indeed any of the other distinctions drawn by Skinner in his book; and we shall postpone a more general criticism of his approach until the next section. Here one may simply say that the most valuable aspect of the book, and it should not be under-estimated, is that it does work out in considerable detail the implications of adopting a behaviourist attitude towards language and thought. Some features of Skinner's classification of utterances, as we have seen, are traditional enough (his recognition of a class of instrumental utterances, his notion of abstraction); others are both new and challenging (his distinction of textual and intraverbal responses, his uncompromising acceptance of the consequences of the behaviourist's view that thought is merely suppressed speech, his exclusion of everything but the mechanism of reinforcement from his theory of language learning). Semantic theory cannot but benefit from being obliged to confront them.

5.4 *Evaluation of behaviourist semantics*

The most striking feature of any behaviourist theory of meaning so far proposed is its inadequacy to deal plausibly with more than a very small fraction of the utterances of everyday life. And this is true not only of the earlier theories of Watson, Weiss or Bloomfield, but also of the more sophisticated and more highly developed theory of Skinner. An enormous leap of faith is required before one can accept that the apparatus sufficient to account for illustrative utterances like *I'm hungry, It's raining, Water!* or *Pass me the salt, please* is in principle capable of accounting, without further theoretical extension, for the full complexity of language-behaviour. There is no evidence to support the view that more than a very small number of Skinner's mands and tacts are under the functional control of some determinate and recurrent stimulus in the environment. In these circumstances, the behaviourist's claim to have brought the relations between words and things "within the scope of the methods of natural science" (Skinner, 1957: 115) is, to say the least, premature. As for the class of verbal operants under the functional control of prior verbal stimuli, their status is perhaps even less satisfactory. Here it is only in the case of highly ritualized exchanges or monologues that the notion of stimulus-control has any kind of prima facie plausibility.

As a framework within which to state the meaning of language-utterances or their constituent words and expressions, behaviourism is, for the present at least, of very restricted value. It has the merit of attempting to account for meaning in terms of observables (which, unlike purely introspective evidence, can be verified by others); and we might grant that some important aspect of the meaning of words like 'chair' or 'book' can be brought within the scope of a stimulus–response model by showing how they (or expressions containing them) come to be associated with certain classes of observable things, namely chairs or books, in the environment; and that the meaning of words denoting the observable properties of things, such as their shape, colour, weight and texture, can also be accounted for satisfactorily in this way. But many words do not denote observable things and properties; and behaviourism has nothing helpful to say about the way in which such words acquire their meaning.

Nor indeed is the stimulus–response account of the association between words and observables quite as straightforward as it might appear at first sight. It has often been pointed out that we do not normally react to words in the same way as we would react to the things, situations or properties with which they are associated. As Brown puts it: "Someone who knows that *rain* refers to rain does not always react to the word as he would to the thing itself, any more than he says *rain* whenever he sees, hears or feels it" (1958: 96). There have been various attempts to resolve or circumvent this difficulty. Some authors have maintained that, even though there may be no overt behavioural response, there will always be some kind of covert response: according to one theory, deriving from Watson, this will take the form of imperceptible muscular activity; according to another, it will consist in a characteristic mediating reaction in the nervous system. Needless to say, neither of these postulated reactions is any more directly observable than are the mental concepts or images of traditional semantic theory; and so far it has not been proved that such reactions do in fact occur. Other authors have suggested that the association between a stimulus and the characteristic response to it is dispositional: that is to say, we will not necessarily react, even covertly, in the presence of the stimulus, but, once the association is established, we will have a disposition to respond appropriately and this disposition will issue in an overt response, provided that all the determining conditions for this are fulfilled. We will refer to this as the dispositional* theory of meaning: two of its most influential advocates were Stevenson (1944) and Morris (1946).

The first question that must be asked in relation to this theory of meaning is what is meant by a disposition to respond. There can be no objection in principle to the notion of dispositional concepts; and the behaviourist is not necessarily committed to the existence of any kind of mental states or entities by his recognition of dispositions to respond as well as of actual responses to stimuli. After all, as has often been pointed out, many of the properties we attribute to inanimate objects, such as solubility or brittleness, can be described as dispositional. If we were to talk of the solubility of common salt as a disposition to dissolve in water, no-one would accuse us of animism, saying that we were explicitly or implicitly committed to attributing a particular mental state to natural substances. An organism's acquisition of a disposition to respond to a particular signal can be thought of in terms of a partial rewiring of its nervous system (Brown, 1958: 103); and a good deal of non-verbal signalling in both human beings and animals is perhaps plausibly accounted for in this way. The objections that will be raised here to the dispositional theory of meaning do not therefore depend upon this point of principle.

When we say that salt is soluble in water we can justify the statement by specifying both the conditions under which a particular reaction will take place and the nature of the reaction. But this is not the case with respect to more than a small part of language-behaviour. So far at least, those psychologists who subscribe to a dispositional theory of meaning have failed to prove that there is any specific disposition associated with most of the words and utterances of our everyday language-behaviour. One can of course maintain that when someone comes to learn the meaning of a word he acquires a disposition to respond to that word, not in a specific and distinctive manner on each occasion of its use, but in indefinitely many different ways according to its context. The problem here is that the term 'disposition to respond' is now being used so generally, not to say loosely, that it forfeits all its usefulness. It gives us the illusion of having provided a satisfactory theoretical account of meaning without in fact saying more than can be said, and less mis-leadingly perhaps, as follows: knowing the meaning of a word implies being able to understand it when other people use it and being able to use it appropriately oneself. It is preferable therefore that the semanticist should retain the pretheoretical term 'understanding' for what is ad-mittedly a psychological state or process standing in need of explication, rather than that he should substitute for it a term which is no more precisely defined than what it is supposed to explicate.

The upshot of our general discussion of behaviourism is that it has so far failed to provide a satisfactory general theory of meaning. It does not follow, and this point should be emphasized, that there is no merit or usefulness in the stimulus–response model of language-behaviour, but only that its limitations should be acknowledged and the terms 're-sponse' and 'disposition to respond' restricted to specific reactions under specifiable conditions. Many of the situations of everyday life are recurrent and easily identified, by the participants themselves and by the social psychologist or sociologist describing their behaviour; and in many of these situations particular utterances (of the kind that are frequently described as stereotyped or ritualistic) are more or less mandatory. There is a limited set of utterances from which we will choose when we are first introduced to someone (*How do you do?, Pleased to meet you*, etc.), when we answer the telephone, when we congratulate someone on his engagement, when we greet our friends and colleagues on first seeing them in the morning, and so on. Much of this language behaviour (which falls into the category that Malinowski called phatic*: cf. 2.4) is reasonably described as being under the control of prior behavioural or environmental stimuli. The vast majority of our utterances do not, or at least do not appear to be, under the functional control of particular stimuli in the situations in which they occur. But this should not prevent us from recognizing that language-behaviour includes, in addition to such stimulus-free* utterances, a set of stimulus-bound* utterances also, whose meaning is adequately described by saying that they are responses to prior stimuli. It is important to give due recognition to both types of utterances in the description of language; and in accepting the plausibility of a behaviouristic account of the meaning of stimulus-bound utterances, we may leave open the question whether S–R reflexes are developed upon the basis of instinct or some other innate mechanism and whether they are shaped by operant conditioning or otherwise.

We may also grant that utterances are not necessarily either wholly stimulus-free or wholly stimulus-bound. For example, if someone is asked a question, he will normally react by providing an answer. What form his utterance takes may be undetermined, or stimulus-free, in the sense that the words chosen and the way in which they are combined could not be predicted from the form of the question or the context in which it is asked; but it may be determined, or stimulus-bound, to the extent that it will have a certain grammatical structure characteristic of utterances which will serve appropriately as answers to questions of such and such a form; and it may be uttered in a certain tone of voice or style which is not only appropriate to, but determined by, the situation and the roles and status of the participants. In short, what we have distinguished as the interpersonal function of utterances might be more highly determined by prior behavioural and environmental stimuli than their propositional, or purely descriptive, aspect (cf. 2.4). Most semanticists in the past have been inclined to concentrate upon the descriptive function of language. The behaviourist theory of language may well be indaequate as a general theory of language-acquisition and language-use, but it has the merit of emphasizing the fact that in speaking a language we are engaging in a certain kind of social behaviour, which is controlled, to a considerable degree, by its success or failure in bringing about changes in the environment, including the activity or attitudes of those with whom we are interacting. At the very least, it can help us to free ourselves of the traditional tendency to treat language as nothing more than an instrument for the communication of thought (cf. 4.3). Nor should it be forgotten that even the descriptive function of language is embedded within this more general framework of social interaction. When we impart factual information to someone by means of language, we do so usually in order to influence his beliefs and behaviour (cf. 2.4). The importance of this point will become even more apparent when we come to discuss the theory of speech-acts* (cf. 16.1).

It is also possible that the reinforcement or conditioning of responses in the presence of particular stimuli, as envisaged by Skinner and other pyschologists, is not only a normal, but a necessary, element in the process of language-acquisition. It might very well be the case that children start using language by associating particular words or utterances with specific objects and situations as conditioned or reinforced responses to stimuli (cf. Quine, 1960). If this is so, however, children very soon pass beyond the stage at which all aspects of their use and understanding of language can be described in S–R terms. How they do this is not satisfactorily explained by the behaviourist. The conditioning of responses may, therefore, be but one component of a complex process; and one which, though essential, presupposes for its operation other cognitive mechanisms of a quite different kind. In short, the behaviourist theory of language may yet prove viable, if it is coupled with the acceptance of a richer set of innate and species-specific propensities for cognitive development, maturing with age in the interaction of the organism with its environment. Reference may be made once again, in this connexion, to the views of such psychologists as Piaget, according to whom there are different levels of cognitive ability in different species and progress from the lower to the higher levels is determined by innate maturational principles (3.5).[6]

---

[6] On some of these issues cf. Fodor (1968), Broadbent (1973), Greene (1972). There is a point at which, with the addition of postulated innate mechanisms, the behaviourism of a Quine seems to shade into the mentalism of a Chomsky (cf. Hook, 1969; Davidson & Hintikka, 1969).

6

Logical semantics

6.1. *The formalization of semantics*

By 'logical semantics' is here meant the study of meaning with the aid of mathematical logic. The term is commonly used by logicians in a narrower sense than this: to refer to the investigation of the meaning, or interpretation, of expressions in specially constructed logical systems. (The term 'expression' will be employed throughout this chapter in the sense in which it is customarily employed by logicians: cf. 1.5). Logical semantics in this narrower and more technical sense may be referred to, following Carnap (1942, 1956), as pure* semantics. It is a highly specialized branch of modern logic, which we shall be concerned with only in so far as it furnishes us with concepts and symbolic notation useful for the analysis of language. The present chapter is not therefore intended as an introduction to pure semantics; and it should not be treated as such by the reader. We will not discuss such questions as consistency and completeness; and no reference will be made to axiomatization or methods of proof.

Constructed logical systems are frequently referred to as languages. But we will not adopt this usage. We will refer to them, instead, as calculi*, keeping the term 'language' for natural languages. This will enable us to oppose linguistic semantics* (a branch of linguistics) to pure semantics* (a branch of logic or mathematics). Linguistic semantics, like other branches of linguistics, will have a theoretical and a descriptive section. Theoretical linguistic semantics, henceforth abbreviated as theoretical semantics*, will be concerned with the construction of a general theory of meaning for language or, alternatively and less ambitiously (as in this book), with the theoretical discussion of various aspects of meaning in language: for it is as yet uncertain whether all aspects of meaning can be brought within the scope of a comprehensive and unified theory. Descriptive linguistic semantics, henceforth abbreviated as descriptive semantics*, will have as its domain the description, or investigation, of the meaning of sentences and utterances in particular languages. (In a later chapter, we shall draw a further distinction between microlinguistic* and macrolinguistic* semantics: cf. 11.1.) The terms pure syntax*, theoretical syntax* and descriptive syntax* may be distinguished in similar fashion. A calculus whose formation rules, or syntactic rules, are specified, but for whose expressions no semantic interpretation is supplied, is an uninterpreted* calculus; a calculus for which both syntactic and semantic rules are given is an interpreted* calculus. Since we are concerned with logic solely as an aid to the more precise discussion of linguistic semantics, I have not been as careful as a logician would feel obliged to be in distinguishing, throughout the chapter, between an uninterpreted and an interpreted calculus.

Mathematical logic (or symbolic logic, as it is also called) has much the same advantages over traditional logic that the statement of a numerical problem in mathematical notation has over the statement of the same numerical problem in ordinary language. The mathematical formulation of the problem is usually much shorter as well as being clearer and less susceptible to misinterpretation. More important than this, however, is the fact that, when one is converting statements of ordinary language into some supposedly equivalent symbolic representation, one is forced to examine the ordinary language statements with more care than one might otherwise have done; and, as a consequence, instances of ambiguity or imprecision may be detected which might otherwise have passed by unnoticed.

The relationship between logic and language has long been, and still is, controversial. There are those who maintain that languages are of their nature imperfect and illogical, and therefore totally unsuited to systematic reasoning and scientific discussion: that it is hopeless and wrongheaded to attempt to correct their imperfections and that they should be replaced with logical calculi constructed especially for the purpose. Others have maintained that languages have their own internal logic, appropriate to the multifarious functions which they fulfil; that the criticisms directed against language should be turned instead against those philosophers and logicians who have failed to understand that this is so and have themselves confused language with the use, or misuse, of language; and that, in any case, the logical calculi constructed by mathematicians and logicians have been strongly influenced by the grammatical structure of particular languages and cannot therefore be regarded as independent ideal systems by reference to which language can be judged and found to be deficient.

Some of the major contributions to the development of mathematical logic have been made by scholars with a particular interest in epistemology and a commitment to empiricism (cf. 4.3). It was their view that an ideal language (to which actual languages might approximate in various degrees, but which they certainly did not realize) would directly reflect the structure of reality. Every simple expression of the language would have a single meaning and this could be described, either directly or by reduction, in terms of the relationship holding between the expression and the object or class of objects which the expression stood for, or named, in the external world. Sentences stood for facts, or states-of-affairs; and in an ideal language they would be in structural correspondence with them. For various reasons, the particularly strong form of empiricism which went under the name of logical atomism*, and with certain additional features logical positivism*, is no longer as influential as it was a generation ago. One of the main problems encountered by logical atomism was that of accommodating as part of the real world such peculiar entities as negative facts and objects of belief. Most damaging ultimately was the increasing recognition by philosophers, not only that language was used for many other purposes besides that of describing the world (whatever one might mean by 'the world'), but also that many of the other uses of language were philosophically, and indeed logically, interesting. Thus was born the movement commonly known as ordinary language philosophy (or, in a very special sense of the term, linguistic analysis). At the same time, further work in mathematical logic had made it clear that indefinitely many different calculi could be constructed, each of which may have advantages or disadvantages for some particular application. No priority or pre-eminence need therefore be attributed to those calculi which the logical atomists and logical positivists had thought of as being ideal for philosophical purposes: in particular the propositional calculus and the predicate calculus.[1]

Although they may no longer be thought of as uniquely appropriate

---

[1] Especially useful as an introduction to the background philosophical literature are such works as: Caton (1963), Feigl & Sellars (1949), Flew (1953), Lehrer & Lehrer (1970), Linsky (1952), Olshewski (1969), Parkinson (1968), Passmore (1957), Rorty (1967), Searle (1971), Stroll (1967) and Zabeeh *et al.* (1974). A classic of logical positivism in English is Ayer (1936). Some of the issues dealt with in this chapter are treated from particular, and in part conflicting points of view, by Alston (1964), Austin (1961), Cohen (1966), Harrison (1972), Putnam (1975), Quine (1953, 1960, 1970), Schaff (1960), Schiffer (1973), Strawson (1952, 1959, 1971), Ziff (1960).

for epistemological analysis, the propositional calculus and the predicate calculus are useful tools for the description of some aspects of meaning in language; and a good deal of the recent literature of philosophical and linguistic semantics presupposes a familiarity with them. It is for these reasons that a brief account of the two systems (with their standard interpretations) is included here. The reader is once again reminded that our treatment of the two systems will be relatively informal, and indeed in many respects superficial. My purpose is solely to introduce and explain the terms and notational conventions, an understanding of which is frequently taken for granted now in both theoretical and descriptive semantics.[2]

6.2. *Propositional calculus*

We shall be concerned solely with the two-valued (or non-modal) calculus of propositions in this section. This is also referred to as the deductive system of truth-functions. What is meant by these various terms will be explained below.

The term 'proposition', like 'fact', has been the subject of considerable philosophical controversy. Some authors think of propositions as purely abstract, but in some sense objective, entities; others regard them as subjective or psychological; and there are certain logicians who avoid the term entirely, because they do not wish to adopt either of these alternatives. Further difficulties are caused by the use of 'proposition' in relation to 'sentence' and 'statement': some writers identify propositions with (declarative) sentences, others identify them with statements, and others with the meanings of (declarative) sentences; and there is little consistency in the way in which 'statement' is defined. The usage that will be adopted here (without commitment as to the ontological or psychological status of the entities thus postulated) is as follows. A proposition* is what is expressed* by a declarative

---

[2] It would have been possible, and in certain respects it might have been preferable, to omit completely an account of mathematical logic, since there are many reliable textbooks available. One of the problems is that they are frequently written for intending specialists. Another is that there is a good deal of variation among logicians in the use of terms like 'sentence', 'proposition' and 'statement'. By including in this chapter three brief sections on formal logic I have been able to control the terminology and, at the risk of some oversimplification, to gear my treatment to the specific purposes of this book. In so far as I have been dependent upon specific works, these have been mainly Carnap (1958), Church (1956), Prior (1962), Reichenbach (1947), Schoenfield (1967). Had Allwood *et al.* (1977) been available at the time of writing I might well have made more direct use of it than I have been able to.

sentence when that sentence is uttered to make a statement.[3] What is meant by 'statement' will be made clear in a later chapter (cf. 16.1). There is a problem here, as will be clear from our earlier discussion of the relationship between sentences and utterances, as to whether 'sentence' should be taken to refer to text-sentences or system-sentences: we will come back to this point too (cf. 14.6). Our formulation of the relationship between sentences and propositions allows for the following possibilities: that different sentences of the same language may express the same proposition; that a sentence may express two or more propositions (so that it may be intended by the speaker, or writer, in one sense and taken by the hearer or reader, in another); and finally that not all the declarative sentences in a language will express propositions. More generally, we are postulating as a theoretical entity something that is, or may be, invariant under changes of language-system, medium, channel and even grammatical structure. At this stage we may equate 'express the same proposition' loosely with 'have the same meaning'. Double quotation-marks will therefore be used (enclosing some appropriate sentence) to refer to propositions.

Propositions may be true or false; we will use T to stand for 'true' and F to stand for 'false'. These are the two possible truth-values* that a proposition may have in the standard interpretation of the propositional calculus: it is a two-valued* system. Furthermore, it is non-modal, in the sense that it makes no use of the operators of necessity and possibility. Various many-valued* systems of modal logic have been developed; and reference will be made to some of these briefly below (6.5).

Symbols called propositional variables* are used to stand for propositions in much the same way that such symbols as x, y and z are used to stand for quantities in elementary algebra. The logician is interested primarily in proving theorems (or stating axioms) which are true independently of which particular propositions are substituted for the propositional variables. It is customary to use the letters p, q, r, ...as propositional variables.

Given that p, q, r, ...are elementary propositional formulae*, standing for simple propositions (whose internal structure does not concern us in this section), we can construct from them complex propositional formulae* (standing for complex propositions) by means of the logical connectives* (also called logical constants*). We will take each of them

---

[3] The term 'proposition' is very troublesome. There is a thorough coverage of the literature in Gochet (1972).

in turn. A formula is said to be well-formed* if it is constructed in accordance with the syntactic rules of formation.

(i) Negation. The negative* connective is the one by means of which out of any proposition, p, we can construct its negation*, not -p or $\sim p$. If p is a proposition, then, $\sim p$ is also a proposition; and if p has the value T then $\sim p$ has the value F; conversely, if p is F (we will henceforth use 'be T/F' for 'have the value T/F'), then $\sim p$ is T. This relationship we will take to be intuitively clear and undisputed: the negation of a true proposition results in a false proposition; and conversely, the negation of a false proposition results in a true proposition. It may be displayed, and indeed formally defined, by means of a truth-table* (see figure 3), in which the left hand column gives the

Negation	
p	$\sim p$
T	F
F	T

Figure 3. Truth-table for the one-place negation connective

possible truth-values of the simple proposition p and the right hand column tabulates the corresponding truth-values of $\sim p$. The closest approximation to the negation connective in more or less ordinary English is 'it is not the case that...' which converts "Anthony loved Cleopatra" to "It is not the case that Anthony loved Cleopatra".

(ii) Conjunction. In logical terminology it is not the connective itself, but the operation of conjoining and the resultant complex proposition for which the term conjunction* is employed. The conjunction of p and q by means of the conjunctive* (or conjoining*) connective is the conjunction, p-and-q or p & q. (Other commonly used symbols for the conjunctive connective are $\wedge$ and a full stop or heavy dot: $p \wedge q$ and p & q are equivalent). A conjunction is true if (and only if) the component propositions, the conjuncts*, are both true: otherwise it is false (see figure 4). It should be noted that in ordinary English clauses conjoined by means of 'and' often yield sentences in which there is understood to be some more specific connexion between the conjoined propositions such as "and consequently" or "and subsequently": cf. "He tripped and broke his leg".

		Conjunction	Inclusive disjunction	Exclusive disjunction	Implication	Equivalence
p	q	p & q	p ∨ q	p W q	p → q	p ≡ q
T	T	T	T	F	T	T
T	F	F	T	T	F	F
F	T	F	T	T	T	F
F	F	F	F	F	T	T

Figure 4. Truth-tables for the two-place connectives

(iii) Disjunction. We must distinguish between two kinds of disjunction (i.e. between two interpretations of propositions like "(Either) they have missed the bus or they have been kept late at school"): inclusive* disjunction and exclusive* disjunction. The former is symbolized as $p \lor q$. There is no equally common symbol for exclusive disjunction: we will use W. The operation of disjoining two simple propositions and the resultant complex proposition is described as a disjunction*, and the connective as disjunctive* (or disjoining*). An inclusive disjunction is defined to be true if p is true, or q is true, or both are true; and otherwise to be false. An exclusive disjunction is true if either p (but not q) or q (but not p) is true, and otherwise is false. For example, "(either) they have missed the bus or they have been kept late at school" is true under the inclusive disjunction interpretation, but false under the exclusive disjunction interpretation, if they have both missed the bus and been kept late at school. If exclusive disjunction is not explicitly indicated we will take 'disjunction' to refer to inclusive disjunction.

(iv) Implication (also called conditional*). The connective is → (⊃ is also commonly used, but we will reserve this for class inclusion). In the implication* $p \to q$ (which may be read as "p implies q" or "if p, then q") p is the antecedent* and q the consequent* (in the implication of p by q).

The terms 'imply' and 'implication' are used in a variety of distinct senses both in everyday discourse and in philosophical usage. In the standard interpretation of the propositional calculus they are used in the so called material* sense, in which there is not necessarily any connexion of meaning between the antecedent and the consequent. The meaning of the connective of material implication is defined (in a way that is often regarded as paradoxical) as follows: when the antecedent is true and the consequent is false, the implication is false; in all other cases the implication is true. Material implication, defined in this way, should not be confused with strict implication or entailment* (cf. 6.5).

(v) Equivalence (or biconditional*). An equivalence is a bilateral implication: the connective is $\equiv$ (or $\leftrightarrow$). It is defined as the conjunction of two implications: i.e. $p \equiv q$ is by definition itself equivalent to $((p \to q) \,\&\, (q \to p))$.

The definition of material equivalence that has just been given illustrates two points. First, it shows us that propositions of any degree of complexity may be built up by means of the connectives: for a complex proposition can be a component proposition in another complex proposition. Second, it illustrates the way in which other connectives can be introduced and defined in terms of more basic connectives. The reader may like to convince himself (by constructing truth tables) that both conjunction and material implication may be defined in terms of negation and disjunction:

$$(p \,\&\, q) \equiv (\sim(\sim p \vee \sim q))$$
$$(p \to q) \equiv (\sim p \vee q).$$

In other words, these equivalences are theorems which can be proved about the system on the basis of the definitions of the primitive connectives of disjunction and negation. This does not mean that there is anything epistemologicaly more basic about the connectives selected as primitive. Negation and conjunction, or negation and implication, might equally well have been chosen as primitive connectives and the others defined in terms of them. The important point to notice, as far as the standard interpretation of the propositional calculus is concerned, is that the operations of negation, conjunction, disjunction and implication are to some degree interdefinable.

So much for the system itself. Something must now be said about the notion of a truth-function, upon which the standard interpretation of the propositional calculus rests and which has been of such importance in philosophical discussions of meaning. When the truth or falsity of a complex proposition is determined solely on the basis of the truth or falsity of the component propositions and the definition of the connectives, the complex proposition is said to be a truth-function* of its component propositions; and the connectives are said to be truth-functional*. This use of 'function' is standard in mathematical terminology: a complex expression like $x+y-z$ is said to be a function* of its arguments* x, y and z, with the plus-sign and minus-sign standing for the operators* of addition and subtraction. Similarly, the logical connectives are operators and their arguments, upon which they operate, are propositions.

An alternative term for 'truth-functional' is extensional*: and the contradictory of 'extensional' is intensional*. (The reader's attention is drawn to the spelling of 'intensional': it should not be confused with 'intentional'.) Now there are many sentences of ordinary language which express what appear to be complex intensional propositions. Examples are sentences expressing propositions about someone's belief that some proposition p is true or false. For example, the truth or falsity of "Romeo thinks that Juliet is dead" is independent of the truth or falsity of "Juliet is dead". "Romeo thinks that Juliet is dead" cannot therefore be regarded as a truth-function of "Juliet is dead"; and it would normally be described as an intensional proposition. Some logicians, however, have maintained that all so called intensional propositions can, and should, be construed as extensional. According to them, "Romeo thinks that Juliet is dead" is not a truth-function of "Juliet is dead", because it is not a function of the proposition "Juliet is dead" at all. It is a function of the expression 'that Juliet is dead', which refers to something in Romeo's mind – one of his beliefs – and this is not a proposition. This might look like quibbling; but there is a very important point involved here. Regardless of whether the thesis of extensionality* is judged to be valid or not, it cannot simply be assumed that, because a sentence that operates as a clause within another more complex sentence sometimes expresses a proposition (and moreover the same proposition as it would express as an independent sentence), it always expresses a proposition when it operates as a clause in a more complex sentence. Not only what might be called belief-sentences*, but also many of the compound and complex sentences of ordinary language containing 'and' or 'if' are, prima facie at least, non-extensional, since they are taken to imply that some kind of causal, temporal or other connexion holds between the propositions expressed by the constituent clauses: "He took a dose of sleeping tablets and died"; "He had a bath and went to bed"; "If he did that, he is very brave", and so on.

Since we have been dealing with truth, it is convenient to introduce at this point the distinction between analytic and synthetic truths and the notion of tautology and contradiction. A proposition is analytic* if its truth is determined solely by its logical form and the meaning of its component elements; i.e. if it cannot but be true, or, to put it in the words of Leibniz, if it holds in all possible worlds (cf. 2.2). A proposition is synthetic* if its truth or falsity is a matter of contingent fact and cannot be determined by purely logical analysis. For example, it is generally held to be the case that "All bachelors are unmarried" is analytic, but that "All men are less than nine feet tall", whether true or false, is synthetic. The distinction between the analytic and the synthetic goes back to Kant, who, unlike many philosophers, held that it was independent of the distinction between the a priori and the a posteriori. Synthetic propositions, it should be noted, may be true or false, whereas analytic propositions (as the term 'analytic' is normally used) are necessarily true.

Complex propositional formulae which are true irrespective of what particular propositions are substituted for the propositional variables are tautologies*; and those that are false under the same conditions are contradictions*. To take the simplest cases: $p \lor \sim p$ is a tautology and $p \;\&\; \sim p$, is a contradiction. The terms 'tautology' and 'contradiction' will also be used for particular propositions, whether simple or complex, when their truth or falsity is determined solely by their logical form and the meaning of their constituent expressions. Tautologies are of course analytic.

6.3. *Predicate calculus*

This is the term that we will use for the system: others are 'calculus of functions', 'functional calculus' and, more fully, 'calculus of predicative functions'. The source and significance of these various terms will become clear as we proceed. So far we have been looking at propositions as unanalysed wholes. Predicate calculus is a system for the representation of the internal structure of simple propositions.

There are two reasons why at least a general understanding of the basic concepts and notation of predicate calculus should be of interest to the semanticist. First, it is the most widely used system for the representation of the logical structure of simple propositions. Second, it has been claimed by certain philosophers in the past (and especially by the logical atomists and other logical empiricists to whom reference was made earlier) that it correctly or accurately portrays the underlying logical form of the sentences of languages by bringing this into correspondence with the structure of facts or states-of-affairs in the external world.

Propositions are composed of terms*. This, it might be mentioned in passing, is the traditional word: a term (Latin 'terminus'), in this technical sense, is one of the terminal elements of analysis. There are two kinds of terms: names and predicates. Names* are terms which refer to individuals*. What is meant by 'individual' depends upon one's view of the world. If we adopt what might be called the metaphysics of everyday usage, we will say that particular persons, animals and discrete objects are individuals, and that places (whether understood as points or two-dimensional or three-dimensional spaces) are also to be regarded as individuals, provided that they are relatively determinate (cf. 4.3). We might be hesitant about more abstract entities such as beauty. Is this one thing which is scattered discontinuously throughout the world? Indeed, is it a thing at all? We might be doubtful, too, about the status of such things as thoughts, facts, psychological states, and so on. These are questions we will come back to (cf. 11.3). The point to be stressed here is that the predicate calculus itself is neutral with respect to what should count as individuals. For the purpose of illustration, we will assume that the persons, things and places of everyday life that we would recognize as distinct and identifiable are individuals, but not groups or collections of things, or abstractions, or psychological states, etc.

By a predicate* is meant a term which is used in combination with a name in order to give some information about the individual that the name refers to: i.e. in order to ascribe* to him some property* (cf. 4.3). We are of course concerned with propositions, and not with the grammatical structure of sentences; but, if we wish to apply the logical distinction of names and predicates to simple English sentences, we can say that proper names like 'John' or 'London' are to be identified with logical names and, not only verbs like 'eat' and adjectives like 'big', but also common nouns like 'man' or 'city', are to be identified with logical predicates.

Just as the logical connectives of the propositional calculus are to be

regarded as operators* by means of which more complex propositions
may be constructed out of less complex propositions, so predicates may
be regarded as operators by means of which simple propositions are
constructed out of names. A simple proposition is a function* of its
component name (or names): the name is an argument*. (Both 'function' and 'argument' are being employed here in the sense in which they
are normally used in mathematics: cf. 6.2.) Using the letters x, y, z as
variables for names and f, g, h as variables for predicates, we can express
the logical structure of a simple proposition as $f(x)$, $g(x)$, $f(y)$,
etc.

According to a common, but by no means universal, convention we
will employ early letters of the alphabet, lower-case, as name-constants,
$\{a, b, c, \ldots\}$, and upper-case letters, from any part of the alphabet and
with mnemonic significance, as predicate-constants. Suppose that a
stands for a particular person, John: b stands for London; T stands for
a predicate meaning "tall"; and B for a predicate meaning "big".
Then $T(a)$ would symbolize the proposition "John is tall"; $B(b)$ the
proposition "London is big"; and so on. It will be observed that there
is no means of representing present or past tense within the conventions
we have so far introduced. Propositions, for the moment, may be
regarded as tenseless (cf. 6.5).

According to the number of arguments upon which a predicate
operates, so it will be described as a one-place predicate, a two-place
predicate, a three-place predicate, and so on. Alternative terms are
'monadic', 'dyadic', 'triadic'. As a general epithet for predicates which
require two or more places to be filled with names (or name-variables)
we will use 'many-place' (alternatively 'polyadic'). It is important to
realize that the arguments are ordered*. That is to say, $f(x, y)$ is not,
in general, equivalent to $f(y, x)$; nor is $g(x, y, z)$ equivalent to $g(y, x, z)$
or $g(z, x, y)$. To illustrate informally from English: from $L(x, y)$,
"x loves y", one cannot legitimately infer $L(y, x)$, "y loves x"; from
$G(x, y, z)$, "x gives y to z", one cannot deduce $G(z, x, y)$, "z gives x to y",
or $G(y, z, x)$, "y gives z to x". We can think of transitive verbs like
'love' as two-place predicates and verbs like 'give' as three-place predicates. Of course, it may be the case for a particular pair of individuals,
that each loves the other, $L(a, b)$ and $L(b, a)$: if this is true, it is, we will
assume, synthetically true: it is a matter of contingent* fact (cf. 6.2).
It may also be the case that for a particular predicate f, $f(x, y) \equiv f(y, x)$.
For example, we might wish to say (for at least some uses of the verb
'resemble' in English), $R(x, y) \equiv R(y, x)$; that "x resembles y" and

"y resembles x" are equivalent; and that this is so is analytic*. If this is so, it will be an important property of this particular predicate; and we shall need to take account of it in describing its meaning. In general, however, the arguments which satisfy* a function are to be regarded as ordered.

We now pass on to the important topic of quantification*. Quantifiers* are operators whose effect with respect to the variables they bind* (i.e. operate upon) is similar to that of such words as 'some', 'any', 'all' and the indefinite article (in some of its uses) in English. It is possible to bind either name-variables or predicate-variables. However, by restricting quantification to name-variables we remain within the limits of what is called the lower* (or first-order*) predicate calculus.

The universal* quantifier is symbolized by prefixing to the variable that it binds an upturned letter A and putting both in parentheses: thus $(\forall x)$, which may be read as "for all x (it is the case that...)". No less commonly perhaps the upturned A is omitted; and we will adopt this convention, according to which '(x)' symbolizes the universal quantification of x. In a proposition like $(x)\,(fx)$ – the inner brackets in the propositional function $f(x)$ have been omitted and we will henceforth follow this practice whenever this is unlikely to cause ambiguity – x is bound by the universal quantifier; and the proposition may be interpreted as "for all x, it is the case that x has the property denoted by the predicate f". It should be observed that 'for all x' must not be interpreted collectively, but as "for each x taken separately": i.e. it must be interpreted distributively*.

The existential* quantifier is symbolized by prefixing to the variable that it binds a reversed E. Thus: $(\exists x)$, which may be read as "for some x (it is the case that...)". In ordinary English 'some' may be used with either a singular or a plural noun following it; and there are certain ambiguities or indeterminacies attaching to whether a specific individual, or group of individuals, is being referred to. The sense in which '$(\exists x)$' is to be interpreted in the proposition $(\exists x)\,(fx)$ is given by the paraphrase "for at least one individual (within the range of x) it is the case that the individual in question has the property denoted by the predicate f". Whether there is only one or more than one such individual is irrelevant. It is important to note, however, that, unlike the universal quantifier, the existential quantifier does carry the implication of existence: $(\exists x)\,(fx)$ is more precisely glossed as "At least one x has the property f"; or "There exists at least one x such that it has the property f".

The interpretation of the universal and existential quantifiers may be illustrated with the following propositions:

(1) $(x) (Mx \rightarrow Rx)$
(2) $(\exists x) (Mx \,\&\, Rx)$.

The first might be a representation of 'All men are rational' (i.e. "For all x, it is the case that, if x is a man, then x is rational"); the second a representation of 'Some men are rational' (i.e. "For at least one x, it is the case that x is a man and x is rational"). Three important points can now be made with reference to these examples.

(i) The ambiguity of 'Men are rational' as between the universal and the existential interpretation of 'men' (if indeed it is ambiguous in this respect in normal English), is eliminated in the symbolic representation. Neither $(Mx \rightarrow Rx)$ nor $(Mx \,\&\, Rx)$ with the variable left free* (i.e. unquantified) is a well-formed proposition.

(ii) One might argue as to whether 'Some men are rational' expresses a true proposition if one, and only one, man is rational. There can be no such argument about $(\exists x) (Mx \,\&\, Rx)$.

(iii) As interpreted here, being a man is a property denoted by a predicate; the name-variable x does not, therefore, play the same sort of role in the proposition that the noun 'men' does in what we may regard as the corresponding English sentence.

The effect of negation should be noted. The negative connective may operate upon the whole proposition, as in (3), or upon one or more of the constituent propositions, as in (4):

(3) $\sim ((x) (Mx \rightarrow Rx))$ "It is not the case that all men are rational"
(4) $(\exists x) (Mx \,\&\, \sim Rx)$ "Some men are not rational".

There are alternative interpretations of 'Some men are not rational': the symbolic representation in (4) makes precise one of them. Various theses may be proved as theorems (or taken as axiomatic) showing the interconnexions of quantifiers under negation. We shall not go into these, but it is worth noting the analogy that holds between existential quantification and disjunction, on the one hand, and between universal quantification and conjunction, on the other. Attempts have in fact been made to define the quantifiers in this way:

(5) $(x) (fx) \equiv fa \,\&\, fb \,\&\, \dots \,\&\, fe$
(6) $(\exists x) (fx) \equiv fa \vee fb \vee \dots \vee fe$.

The difficulty, from a logical point of view, is that this method of definition holds only for a finite set of individuals, $\{a, b, c, d, e\}$ let us say, all of whom we can identify; and we must know that these are all the individuals there are. For certain applications, however, we may be content to interpret $(x)\,(fx)$ and $(\exists x)\,(fx)$ in this way.

The notion of scope* may be introduced at this point. By the scope of any operator, whether it is a connective or a quantifier, is meant that part of the formula which is within its domain of operation; and this is normally indicated by brackets. For example, it is easily seen that (7) and (8) are not equivalent.

> (7) $((p\ \&\ q) \vee r)$ "Either both John came and Bill came or Henry came"
> (8) $(p\ \&\ (q \vee r))$ "Both John came and either Bill came or Henry came".

The sentence 'John came and Bill came or Henry came' can be interpreted like (7) or like (8); and, additionally, it can be given a variety of other interpretations, not all of which are truth-functional. Brackets may be dispensed with when no ambiguity will result. Thus (7) might be written as $(p\ \&\ q) \vee r$; and (8) as $p\ \&\ (q \vee r)$. And we might decide to adopt the convention that, in default of any indication to the contrary by means of overt bracketing, the scope of one operator is more extensive than that of another. For example, if we establish the convention that disjunction is more extensive than conjunction and conjunction more extensive than negation (in this sense of 'extensive'), then $p\ \&\ q \vee r$ is uniquely interpreted as $((p\ \&\ q) \vee r)$ i.e. as a disjunction, the first of whose disjuncts is a conjunction. One may compare the standard convention in simple algebra and arithmetic according to which addition is defined to be more extensive in scope than multiplication: so that $x \times y + z$ is taken as $(x \times y) + z$, and not as $x \times (y + z)$.

In many-place (or polyadic) predicative functions all the variables must be bound by a quantifier. We will call this multiple quantification*. When all the quantifiers are either universal or existential, the interpretation is straightforward enough:

> (9) $(x)\,(y)\,((Cx\ \&\ By) \rightarrow L\,(x, y))$ "All the children like all the books"
> (10) $(\exists x)\,(\exists y)\,((Cx\ \&\ By)\ \&\ L(x, y))$ "At least one child likes at least one book".

Formulae may then be abbreviated, by using a single pair of brackets for both quantifiers: i.e. by using (x, y) for $(x)\,(y)$ in (9) and $(\exists x, y)$, with only one instance of the reversed E, in (10). When the quantifiers are different – we will call this mixed quantification – the relative order of the quantifiers is significant. For, by virtue of the way in which scope is defined for quantifiers, a following quantifier comes within the scope of a preceding quantifier (and within its own scope), but not conversely. That is to say, a formula $(\exists x)(y) f((x, y)$ is to be understood as $((\exists x)((y)f(x, y)))$. The following two propositions are not therefore logically equivalent

(11) $(\exists y) (x) (By \& (Cx \rightarrow L(x, y)))$
(12) $(x) (\exists y) (Cx \rightarrow (By \& L(x, y)))$.

The first, (11), is to be understood as "It is true of at least one book that all the children like it", but (12) as "It is true of all the children that they like at least one book". More perspicuous, but equivalent, versions of (11) and (12), respectively, are:

(11a) $(\exists y) (By \& (x) (Cx \rightarrow L(x, y)))$
(12a) (x) $(Cx \rightarrow (\exists y)(By \& L(x, y)))$.

It is sometimes said that the same difference can be brought out in everyday English by using either an active or a passive sentence:

(11b) One of the books is liked by all the children
(12b) All the children like one of the books.

But there are many complexities and uncertainties attaching to the logical representation of English sentences in which words like 'some', 'any', etc., occur.

It is convenient at this point to insert a brief treatment of relations*. Many-place predicators can be regarded as relations; and the terminology developed by logicians for different kinds of relations will be useful. For simplicity we will deal only with two-place relations. The notation we will use is similar to that which we have been using for the predicate calculus. $R(x, y)$ says that a particular relation R holds between x and y. (An alternative notation for this is x R y.) The relation is said to hold in a given direction: it may or may not hold in the reverse direction. But there will always be a converse* relation, which we will symbolize as R'. (A common alternative is R^{-1}.) Thus, R' (x, y) is the converse of R (x, y). If we simultaneously permute the terms* of the relation and substitute R' for R, we obtain an equivalence. Thus: $R(x, y) \equiv R'(y, x)$. We may compare this with the equivalence which, in general, holds between corresponding active and passive sentences in English. If R stands for the relation denoted by the verb 'respect', then it is not generally the case that, if $R(x, y)$ then $R'(x, y)$ ("x respects y"

is not logically equivalent to "*x* is respected by *y*"). But it is the case that R(*x*, *y*) = R'(*y*, *x*): "*x* respects *y*" is logically equivalent to "*y* is respected by *x*".

Among the various kinds of relations recognized by logicians the following are especially important.

(i) Symmetrical* relations, where R(*x*, *y*) ≡ R'(*x*, *y*) for all values of *x* and *y*. An example is the relation denoted by the English 'be married to'. An asymmetrical* relation is one where for all values of *x* and *y* R(*x*, *y*) implies the negation of R(*y*, *x*). An example is the relation of being the father of: if *x* is the father of *y*, then *y* cannot be the father of *x*.

(ii) Transitive* relations, where, for all values of *x*, *y* and *z*, if R(*x*, *y*) and R(*y*, *z*), then R(*x*, *z*). For example if *x* is taller than *y* and *y* is taller than *z*, then *x* is taller than *z*. An example of an intransitive* relation is again being the father of.

(iii) Reflexive* relations, where, for all values of *x*, R(*x*, *x*). Examples are being the same size as or being a child of the same parents as. Being the father of or being the brother of is, however, irreflexive*, since one cannot be one's own father or one's own brother.

To be distinguished from asymmetrical, intransitive and irreflexive relations are non-symmetrical*, non-transitive* and non-reflexive* relations. A relation, R, is non-symmetrical if and only if it is not symmetrical: i.e. if for some (though not necessarily all) values of *x* and *y*, R(*x*, *y*) holds, but not R(*y*, *x*). It follows that (except for the empty relation, which is both symmetrical and asymmetrical), all asymmetrical relations are non-symmetrical, but not conversely. The terms 'non-transitive' and 'non-reflexive' are distinguished from 'intransitive' and 'irreflexive' in similar fashion. For example, loving is non-symmetrical and non-transitive (and possibly non-reflexive). Relations which are symmetrical, transitive and reflexive are said to be equivalence* relations.

We shall make considerable use of these notions in our discussions of the structure of the vocabularies of language.

6.4. *The logic of classes*

By a class*, in this context, is meant any collection of individuals* regardless of the principle by which they have been brought together for consideration as members* of that class. (We shall make no distinction between a class and a set. Some of the notation to be introduced is commonly described as belonging to set theory in mathematics.) The members of a class may be abstract as well as concrete: for example, we can just as readily talk about the class of real numbers as we can about the class of human beings at present living in a certain place. Indeed, there is nothing to prevent us from considering classes of entities, some of whose members are concrete and some of whose members are abstract. However, following our earlier decision restricting the sense of the term 'individual' (cf. 6.3), we shall be thinking primarily of classes of physical objects and relatively determinate places.

As before, we will use lower-case early letters of the alphabet to symbolize the individual members of a class, and, by virtue of the parallelism that exists, as we shall see, between logical predicates and classes, we will use capitals to symbolize classes. Thus X might be a class whose members are a, b and c. When we list the members of a class, we separate the symbols denoting them with commas and enclose them in brace brackets. Thus $\{a, b, c\}$ is the class whose members are a, b and c. Class-membership is symbolized by the Greek letter epsilon; so that '$a \epsilon X$' means "a is a member of (the class) X".

We will allow for the partial* listing of the members of the class in three significantly different ways. First, we distinguish in principle between open and closed classes: a closed* (or finite*) class is one whose members could be listed, if we had the time, space, energy, knowledge and reason to list them all; an open* (or infinite*) class (e.g., the class of natural numbers) is one whose members could not be so listed, because their number has no determinable limit. Our notational conventions will distinguish these as follows: $\{a, b, ..., c\}$ is a partially-listed closed class, but $\{a, b, c, ...\}$ is a partially-listed open class. It will be noted that both here and in the previous section we have assumed that there is an unlimited supply of letters in the alphabet to be used for various purposes: we have even assumed that there are indefinitely many early letters of the alphabet from which we can draw freely to denote every individual object and place in the universe. In other words we are regarding the alphabet, and indeed each different section of it – $\{a, b, c, ...\}$, $\{f, g, h, ...\}$, $\{p, q, r, ...\}$ and $\{x, y, z, ...\}$ – as an infinite class: and we can in fact extend it indefinitely, if necessary by using subscripts or other devices. A third kind of partial listing will be employed when we do not know whether a class is open or closed (or do not wish to commit ourselves on the point). Such classes will be called indeterminate*; and will be distinguished notationally by using 'etc.' instead of the three dots employed for open classes. Thus: $\{a, b, c, \text{etc.}\}$ is an indeterminate class.

The distinction we have drawn here between open classes and indeterminate classes is important for our purposes. Consider, for example, the class of lexemes which constitutes the vocabulary of English, or even of a single speaker of English. Is this an open or closed class? The question is probably unanswerable: certainly in the form in which it has just been put. For methodological reasons, we may decide to represent the vocabulary of English in our model of the system which underlies the language-behaviour of speakers of English as being closed (though for practical reasons unlistable). It is not difficult, however, to envisage a model in which the vocabulary is taken as open. Again, on many philosophical issues that we shall touch on in our discussion of semantics, we shall not wish to commit ourselves as to whether a certain class of entities is closed or open (e.g., the class of objects in the universe, the class of actual or conceivable states of affairs in some actual or possible world, the class of entities that a certain lexeme denotes).

Two classes are defined to be identical* (more precisely, as we shall see, extensionally identical*) if and only if they each have exactly the same members. Given that X is $\{a, b, c\}$ and Y is $\{b, a, c\}$, it follows from the definition of class-identity that $X = Y$ (where the equal-sign symbolizes identity). It may be observed in passing that the members of X and Y have been deliberately listed in a different order: this was to emphasize the important point that order of listing among the members of a class is irrelevant.

To be distinguished from class-membership is class-inclusion*. This is symbolized by a right-facing hook, ' $\supset$ ', for "includes" and a left-facing hook ' $\subset$ ', for the converse relation meaning "is included in". Inclusion is defined as follows: $X \supset Y$ (X includes Y) and $Y \subset X$ (Y is included in X; Y is a subclass* of X) both mean that every member of Y is a member of X. It should be noted that the definition of inclusion allows identity as a special case of inclusion. In fact, class-identity may be defined as symmetrical inclusion: if $X \supset Y$ and $Y \supset X$, then $X = Y$. Asymmetrical inclusion is called proper inclusion*: if X includes Y, but Y does not include X, we say that X properly* includes Y. The logic of classes admits the possibility of classes being either members or subclasses of other classes; and these two situations should not be confused. $Y \subset X$ (Y is included in X) means, as we have seen, that every member of Y is a member of X; it does not mean that the class Y is a member of the class X. On the other hand, $Y \in X$ means that the class Y (but not necessarily its members) is a member of X. It is especially important not to confuse the following two statements: (i) $x \in X$ and (ii) $\{x\} \in X$. The first asserts that x is a member of X; the second, in which '$\{x\}$' is to be read as "the class whose (sole) member is x", that the one-member class containing x is a member of X. A committee, for example, might have as its members a set of subcommittees (of varying size but each with a single vote) and one of these subcommittees might be the one-member class $\{x\}$. When x attends the meetings of the main committee and casts his vote or delivers an opinion, he will be operating constitutionally as $\{x\}$. A class contains* its members, but includes* its subclasses.

It is convenient to have a set of symbols for "is not a member of", "is not included in", "is not identical to", etc. These symbols are usually formed by putting an oblique stroke through the corresponding positive symbol. Thus, '$a \notin X$' means "a is not a member of X"; '$X \not\supset Y$' means "X does not include Y"; '$X \neq Y$' means "X is not identical to Y"; and so on. It may also be added at this point that the symbols '$\supseteq$' and '$\subseteq$' are commonly employed to make it clear that identity is allowed for as a special case of inclusion: '$X \supseteq Y$' means "X includes or is identical with Y" and '$Y \subseteq X$' means "Y is included in or identical with X".

By the union* (or sum*) of two classes, X and Y, is meant that class, $X+Y$, all of whose members are members of X or Y (or both). By the intersection* (or product*) of two classes, X and Y, is meant that class, X.Y, all of whose members are members of both X and Y. Given that X is $\{a, b, c\}$ and Y is $\{b, c, d\}$ then $X+Y$ is $\{a, b, c, d\}$ and X.Y is $\{b, c\}$.

Alternative, and equally common, symbols for the plus-sign and the dot used here are '$\cup$' and '$\cap$', respectively. Thus $X \cup Y$ symbolizes the union, and $X \cap Y$ the intersection, of X and Y. These notions are often illustrated by means of Venn diagrams, as in figure 5.

Two classes are unique and have a special status in the formalization and standard interpretation of class logic. They are the universal* class, which we will symbolize as 'U', and the empty* class (or null* class), which we will symbolize as '$\emptyset$' (i.e. zero). U is the class which contains all the individuals there are in the universe; $\emptyset$ is the class which has no members (i.e. which contains none of the individuals in the universe). What is meant by 'universe' will be dependent upon the interpretation one gives to the system and the purpose for which one uses it. Let us agree that by 'universe' we mean a universe-of-discourse*, which may be more or less restricted as we wish (cf. 6.5). The universe of discourse illustrated in figure 5 is bounded by the four straight lines and has in it just six individuals: for this universe U is $\{a, b, c, d, e, f\}$.

We can now define the complement* of a class to be that class which contains all (and only) the individuals in the universe that are not in the class in question. We will symbolize the complement of a class by means of a raised bar: $\bar{X}$ is the complement of X. In the universe illustrated in figure 5, $\bar{X}$ is {*d*, *e*, *f*}; $\bar{Y}$ is {*a*, *e*, *f*}; $\overline{X + Y}$ is the class containing all those individuals which are not members of the union of X and Y, i.e. {*e*, *f*}; and $\overline{X.Y}$ is the complement of the intersection of X and Y, i.e. {*a*, *d*, *e*, *f*}.

We have now introduced all the terms that will be needed in any reference we make subsequently to the logic of classes. More important, we have introduced a particular way of looking at things which has been very influential in twentieth-century philosophical semantics

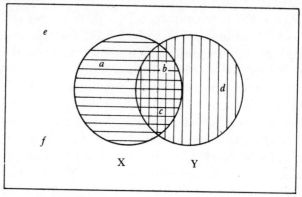

Figure 5. Venn diagrams illustrating the union and intersection of classes

(independently of its importance for the foundations of mathematics). We can now move on to consider, in a general way, some of the semantically relevant aspects of class logic.

First, how do we define, or establish, class-membership? One way of doing so, for closed classes at least, is by listing their members. This is known as extensional* definition. For, by the extension* of a term is meant the class of the things to which it is correctly applied. Alternatively, and perhaps more commonly, we can define a class on the basis of some property (or set of properties) which they have in common. Suppose, for example, we summarize the set of properties assumed to be essential for something to qualify as a dog in the word 'canine'. Then we can say that the class of dogs comprises all those objects in the universe which have this, no doubt very complex, but we will assume identifiable, set of properties. This would be an intensional* definition:

the intension* of a term is the set of essential properties which determines the applicability of the term. (Attention is again drawn to the spelling of 'intension' and 'intensional'.) Combining the class notation with the predicate-calculus notation, we can say, using 'C' for the properties we have agreed to summarize as canine and 'D' to symbolize the class of dogs

$(x) (Cx \equiv x \in D)$ "Anything that is canine is a dog".

This would be an intensional definition of the class of dogs.

One of the central, and one might say perennially controversial, issues in philosophical semantics, as we shall see, has to do with such questions as the following: Is what we are calling the property C, or 'canine', distinguishable in any way from being a member of the class D, the class to members of which we have learnt to apply the word 'dog'? Many logicians have distinguished between the extensional and intensional identity of classes, on the grounds that two classes may have exactly the same members, and yet be different classes by virtue of their intensional definition.[4] To take a traditional example (and one that has often been used by Carnap): let us assume that there are two classes X and Y. The intensional definition of X is

$(x) ((Fx \ \& \ Bx) \equiv x \in X)$

where F means "featherless" and B "biped", so that X is the class of featherless bipeds. The intensional definition of Y is

$(x) ((Rx \ \& \ Ax) \equiv x \in Y)$

where R means "rational" and A means "animal". Now let us grant, although we have not examined all the members of X and Y, that X = Y (i.e. that the two classes are extensionally identical). Do 'rational animal' and 'featherless biped' have the same meaning? Again, if two terms, let us say 'centaur' and 'unicorn', each have as their extension the empty class (for we will assume that there are no unicorns or centaurs in the universe), they can be said to have the same extension. But if they have the same extension, why do we not say that they have the same meaning? In one way or another, the distinction between intension and extension enters into the discussion of a variety of questions.

The sense in which the term 'extension' is being employed here

---

[4] A logician would say that classes are always defined extensionally: two classes are identical if and only if they contain exactly the same members. The point at issue here is whether extension is sufficient to determine and distinguish intension.

is also linked with the sense in which 'extensional' and 'truth-functional' are equivalent (cf. 6.2). Frege (1892), and following him many logicians, took the extension of a proposition to be its truth-value (and the intension of a proposition to be its meaning). The reason for this rather counter-intuitive (and controversial) view is that the truth-value of a complex proposition was held to be determined by the truth-value of its constituent propositions in much the same way as the truth-value of a simple proposition is determined by the extensions of its terms.[5] As the truth-value of $(p \,\&\, q)$ remains the same under any substitution for p or q of a proposition having the same truth-value, so the truth-value of $f(x)$ is unaffected by the substitution for x of any expression having the same extension as x. On this basis, one can define an extensional calculus to be one in which none of the propositions changes its truth-value when one expression is substituted in the proposition for another expression having the same extension. The possibility of substitution without changing the truth-value of the proposition is frequently discussed, or referred to, in philosophical semantics in connexion with Leibniz's principle of the identity of indiscernibles*; *Eadem sunt quorum unum potest substitui alteri salva veritate* ("[Two things] are the same if one can be substituted for the other without affecting truth"). The precise interpretation of Leibniz's dictum is controversial; but the Latin phrase *salva veritate* contained in it is generally understood as I have indicated ("without changing the truth-value"), and it is so frequently employed in the philosophical literature without an accompanying gloss or translation that the reader should be familiar with it.[6]

If we interpret predicative terms as names of classes we can symbolize the proposition "Alfred is a bachelor" as

$a \,\epsilon\, B$

and "Alfred is happy" as

$a \,\epsilon\, H$

It might appear that the class-logic representation is more appropriate to the first of these examples, where we use a common noun in English; and that the predicate-calculus representation is more appropriate to

---

[5] For a thorough discussion of Frege's work and its place in the philosophy of language, cf. Dummett (1973).

[6] There is a useful discussion and introduction to the literature in Zabeeh *et al.*'s (1974: 525–660) and Olshewsky's (1969: 353–457) respective chapters on the analytic and the synthetic.

the second, where we use an adjective. We will come back later to the question whether a distinction can and should be made between the predication of class-membership and the predication of properties. This has been denied by many logicians (cf. 11.3).

6.5. *Time, modality and possible worlds*

Let us suppose that we are engaged upon the description of some universe consisting of a finite number of individuals and that we have available for the description a set of predicates, each of which is either predicable* of each individual or not and, if predicable, is true of that individual or not. What is meant by 'predicable' may be explained by means of an example. Take the predicate M which, we will say, denotes the property of being married. Now M in its normal, non-metaphorical, sense cannot be predicated, we will assume, of inanimate objects (or indeed of non-human animals) and still less of places. In the description of our universe, therefore, we will say that if a refers to an inanimate individual, then $M(a)$ is not a well-formed proposition; and whether it is true or false is a question that does not arise. There are certain philosophical problems associated with the distinction between semantically ill-formed and false propositions that is invoked here. But we will assume, not only that the notion of predicability is clearly enough understood for our present purpose, but also that it is determinate and admits of no gradation. In other words, we are assuming that whether a particular predicate is predicable of a given individual is a question to which a definite answer, affirmative or negative, can always be given; and that there will never be any reason to qualify this answer in terms of more or less.

One important terminological point to be noted here is that it is predicates, and not properties, that are said to be predicable of (and, in particular propositions, predicated of) individuals; properties are ascribed* to the individuals referred to by the name or names in the proposition. For example, in saying of a particular flower that it is red, we ascribe to it the property of redness, but we predicate of it the predicate 'red'.

To return now to the universe of individuals whose description we are considering. For each individual x and for each one-place predicate f that is predicable of that individual, let there be constructed a proposition $f(x)$; for each ordered pair of individuals (x, y) and each two-place predicate g, let there be constructed a proposition $g(x, y)$; and, in general, for each ordered n-tuple of individuals $(x, y, \ldots, z)$ and each n-place predicate h, let there be constructed a proposition $h(x, y, \ldots, z)$.

Each of the resultant propositions will be described as atomic*; and any proposition which is either an atomic proposition or the negation of an atomic proposition will be called basic*. Furthermore, each pair of propositions consisting of an atomic proposition and its negation will be called a basic pair*.

We may now define a state-description* (more precisely than when we used the term earlier: 2.3) as any conjunction of basic propositions. This definition, it should be noted, allows us to distinguish between complete and partial descriptions; and also between consistent and inconsistent descriptions. A complete state-description* is one which contains at least one of each basic pair; a consistent state-description* is one that does not contain, or allow the derivation of, a contradiction (i.e. both members of a basic pair). Every distinct complete and consistent state-description will describe some possible state of the universe; and of this class of state-descriptions there will be one which describes the actual state of the universe, namely the one in which all the component basic propositions are true.

A simple example will make this point clear: we will use just two one-place predicates, F and G, and two names, *a* and *b*, each denoting a distinct individual of which F and G are predicable. Given this very simple universe of discourse, we can say that there are just sixteen possible states of the universe, as indicated in (1)–(16):

(1) SD_1: (F*a* & F*b* & G*a* & G*b*)
(2) SD_2: ($\sim$ F*a* & F*b* & G*a* & G*b*)
(3) SD_3: (F*a* & $\sim$ F*b* & G*a* & G*b*)

.
.
.

(16) SD_{16}: ($\sim$ F*a* & $\sim$ F*b* & $\sim$ G*a* & $\sim$ G*b*)

Each of these complete and consistent state-descriptions describes a possible state of the universe; and one of them, we will assume, describes the actual state of the universe. As we saw earlier (2.3), the semantic content of a proposition can be defined as the class of state-descriptions that it eliminates. Although we have made use of a very restricted universe in this example, it should be clear that the general principles are unaffected by increasing the number of individuals in the universe or the number of predicates and by introducing many-place predicates.

Instead of saying that each complete and consistent state-description describes, or defines, a possible state of the universe and that one of the set of state-descriptions defines the actual state of the universe, we might equally well say that the set of state-descriptions defines a set of possible universes, rather than a set of possible states of the same universe. Whether we talk of possible states or possible universes is irrelevant from a purely logical point of view. But the one expression rather than the other will probably be chosen with reference to the particular application that is being made of the logical framework. When we think of the physical world in everyday terms, we tend to think of it as consisting of a relatively constant set of individuals with variable properties. Between any two points of time that we select, t_1 and t_2, a certain number of new individuals will come into being and a certain number of previously existing individuals will pass away. But there will be a sufficient number of individuals identifiable as the same at both t_1 and t_2 and a sufficient number of properties also identifiable as the same, though perhaps differently distributed in relation to the individuals, for us to feel that it is appropriate to talk of one universe passing through a succession of different states. There are of course other ways of looking at the physical world; the physicist may look elsewhere for the principle of constancy in relation to which he can measure change; and some philosophers may deny that there is any constancy at all. But for our present purpose, the everyday view of the world will suffice. Let us think therefore of a universe consisting of more or less the same individuals passing through a succession of states.

As we have already seen, propositions are generally taken to be tenseless. But what does this statement mean? There are various ways in which it can be interpreted. We might say that propositions are not merely tenseless, but timeless; that, not only is there no reference within the proposition itself to the time at which it is true or false but that the notion of time is simply irrelevant to propositions; that they are themselves eternal, but may be believed or affirmed in relation to some universe or state of the universe and they will be true or false of, rather than in, that universe. Taking this point of view, we might say, for example, that the proposition Fa is true of the universe at t_1, though false of the universe at t_2 (the universe being described at time t_1 by state-description SD_1 and at t_2 by SD_2). This is the way in which many logicians and epistemologists have construed the tenselessness of propositions. Others have interpreted 'tenseless' not as "timeless", but as "of immediate temporal reference". Under this interpretation, one could believe or affirm propositions of the changing physical world as it passed through successive states, but each such proposition would have an implicit temporal reference to the immediately observed situation. All propositions would be interpreted as in the English sentence 'It is raining' under the normal conditions of utterance; that is, as meaning "It is raining at the present moment". This would not be tense, as we shall see later (cf. 15.4); for tense rests upon the possibility of opposing one point of temporal reference to another (whether as present to past and future or otherwise). Under this interpretation of the status of propositions with respect to time we might say that Fa, if uttered at t_1, would be true (not only of, but in, the universe described by SD_1), but false, if uttered at t_2. This is also a point of view which is strongly represented in the philosophical literature.

Propositions can, however, be construed as having tense. In order to represent this formally, we need to go beyond the limits of the first-order predicate calculus or the two-valued propositional calculus; and there have now been developed various systems of what we may call rather loosely tense-logic. Something will be said about these in our discussion of tense from a linguistic point of view in a later chapter (cf. 15.4).

We now turn briefly to the subject of modality*. This also is a topic that we must return to later; and we shall then see that various kinds of modality can be distinguished. Here we shall be concerned solely with the modalities of logical necessity and possibility. Logicians customarily draw a distinction, as we have seen (6.2), between analytic* propositions, which are said to be necessarily true, and synthetic* propositions, which, if true, are said to be only contingently so. The way in which the notions of logical necessity* and logical possibility* apply to these distinctions (and are interrelated in terms of negation) can be seen in the following statements: if p is necessarily T, then it is not possible that p is F; if p is possibly T, then it is not necessary that p is F. (It should be observed that under this interpretation of possibility, necessity is included as a particular case.)

How can we formalize the notions of logical necessity and possibility? One way is to draw upon the distinction between object-language and metalanguage (see 1.3). Using this method we can analyse a proposition "It is necessarily the case that p" as "The proposition 'p' is necessarily true", where p is a proposition of the object-language, 'p' is the meta-language name for p and necessary truth is predicated not of p (still less within p), but of 'p'. This is the method favoured by logicians who subscribe to the thesis of extensionality (cf. Carnap, 1958: 42). The alternative is to formalize the notions of logical necessity and logical possibility within one or other system of intensional (i.e. non-extensional), or modal, logic. There are now many different systems available (cf. Hughes & Cresswell, 1968). What may be regarded as the standard systems are based upon the two-valued propositional calculus, but extend it by introducing, in addition to the truth-functional connectives, one or more modal operators. We will here use the symbols 'nec' and 'poss' to denote the proposition-forming operators of logical necessity and logical possibility, respectively. In view of the connexion referred to above between logical necessity and possibility, the following equivalences may be taken as valid.

(17) $\text{nec } p \equiv \sim \text{poss} \sim p$
(18) $\text{poss } p \equiv \sim \text{nec} \sim p$.

And either 'nec' or 'poss' could be defined in terms of the other, leading to a distinction (however we might wish to interpret this) between a necessity-based* and a possibility-based* system of logical modality (cf. Hughes & Cresswell, 1968: 26).

A semantically important notion which we shall need to discuss more fully later is that of strict implication*, or entailment*. We will use a double-shafted arrow to symbolize this (in contrast with the single-shafted arrow used for material implication): $p \Rightarrow q$ is therefore to be understood as "p entails q" (or "q follows logically from p"). Entailment can be defined in terms of poss and material implication as follows

(19) $(p \Rightarrow q) \equiv \sim \text{poss}(p \, \& \sim q)$.

That is to say, if p entails q, then it is not logically possible for both p to be true and not-q to be true and conversely. When we say that p entails q, we shall understand this to mean that it would be inconsistent, for example, to assert p and deny q. One might say that it would be inconsistent, for example, to assert p and deny q, if p was "John is a bachelor" and q was "John is not married".

Mention was made earlier of the idea, usually attributed to Leibniz, that a proposition is necessarily true only if it is true in all possible worlds. What do we mean by the phrase 'possible world'? One way of interpreting it is in terms of the notion of state-description.[7] For, as we have seen, a state-description, provided that it is complete and consistent, may be thought of as defining either a distinct state of some

[7] Some scholars might feel that my approach to the notion of possible worlds by way of the notion of state-descriptions is rather old-fashioned. But I have found it helpful to think in such terms. An alternative approach is that of Kripke (1963) or Hintikka (1969).

universe or a distinct universe according to the viewpoint one adopts. How we use the words 'universe' or 'world' in this context is perhaps of little consequence. The former is linked with the technical term 'universe-of-discourse'; the latter with the Leibnizian phrase 'possible world'. One might argue, however, that there is some support, in colloquial usage at least, for the view that the universe (with the definite article) is more comprehensive, more enduring and even more objective than what we call the world. Let us, therefore, identify a world with a state-description of the universe or some part of the universe. A proposition will be true in some possible world, then, if it has the value T in some state-description.

Let us now assume that some omniscient external observer has accessible to him and available for consultation a set of state-descriptions descriptive of all possible states of the universe. If asked whether a certain proposition is logically possible, he can check through the state-descriptions and, finding the proposition in at least one, answer that it is: for inclusion in at least one state-description is certainly a sufficient condition of its being logically possible; and, under the assumptions we are making, it can be taken as a necessary condition also, so that exclusion from any state-description may be taken as sufficient grounds for saying that the proposition is logically impossible. Similarly for logical necessity: if a proposition occurs in all state-descriptions we can say that it is true in all possible worlds.

We have made two assumptions about our observer of all possible worlds which put him, as Leibniz of course put God, in an exceptionally favourable position for the evaluation of what is necessary and what is contingent: we have assumed, first, that he is omniscient and, second, that he is external to the worlds he is contemplating. Little need be said about the first of these assumptions. Our ability to observe other worlds is clearly very much limited by our own experience and the accumulated experience of our predecessors. We must expect, therefore, that there will be some doubt as to what is analytic and what is merely contingent in very many instances where the question arises in relation to the everyday vocabulary of a language.

The second assumption is of equal importance. For it is arguable that we are not, and cannot be, external observers of the world in which we live. At first sight, it might appear that nothing more is at issue here than a rather equivocal use of the term 'world', which is now being used differently from the sense in which we said it referred to a state-description. The point is that these two senses are perhaps inextricably bound together. For we are ourselves part of what we are describing in our state-description and our powers of observation and conceptualization are perhaps critically constrained by the conditions obtaining in the state of the universe in the region which we inhabit: by the physical make-up of our bodies, by our biologically determined drives and dispositions, by the particular culture in which we have been brought up and perhaps also by the language which we speak and which we use to construct the state-description that is our world.

Reference was made earlier to the metaphysics and everyday usage (6.3). It is, however, an important fact about our everyday use of language that there is no single metaphysical, or conceptual, framework which underlies every kind of human discourse. Statements, or propositions, which might be held to be contradictory, or absurd, in a more or less scientific discussion of the physical world may be regarded as perfectly acceptable in a mythological or religious context, in poetry, in the narration of a dream, or in science fiction. It has been pointed out already that much of the earlier work in logical semantics was carried out by philosophers whose primary concern was with the formalization of the language of scientific discourse, and many of them subscribed to the doctrine of physicalism in one form or another. It was perhaps only natural that they should think that it was possible to construct an ideal logical system within which the set of analytic propositions and contradictions would remain constant across all possible worlds and would be determined, ultimately, by the laws of physics. Nowadays, it is more generally accepted that the notion of possible worlds should be defined in relation to variable systems of beliefs and assumptions; and furthermore that rather different systems of logic might be appropriate for different kinds of discourse. This more flexible, or more relativistic, approach to the formalization of logic looks considerably more promising for the analysis of the everyday use of language.

6.6. *Model-theoretic and truth-conditional semantics*

Much of the most recent work in logical semantics, and more especially what is called model-theoretic* semantics, takes as its starting-point Tarski's (1935) definition of the notion of truth and makes this relative to actual or possible states of the universe.[8] There are several distinguishable theories of truth that have been proposed by philosophers;

---

[8] Tarski's (1944) paper is probably a better starting-point for the non-specialist. For background and further references: cf. Olshewsky (1969: 575–652) and Zabeeh *et al.* (1974: 661–74).

and they are all more or less controversial. Tarski's definition is intended to capture and make more precise the conception of truth that is embodied in the so-called correspondence theory*, according to which a proposition is true if (and only if) it denotes or refers to a state of affairs which actually exists in the world that the proposition purports to describe. An alternative way of putting this is to say that a true proposition is in correspondence with reality and that a false proposition is not. It will be observed that, under this interpretation of the term 'truth', the truth of a proposition depends upon the existence or reality of something outside the language or system in which the proposition is formulated. If the proposition $f(x)$ refers to an entity, x, and ascribes to x a certain property, f, the proposition is true if and only if x exists and has the property, f. As Tarski puts it, in his standard example:

(1) 'Snow is white' is true if and only if snow is white.

At first sight, this example looks singularly unhelpful as the basis upon which to build a formal theory of truth.

The first point that must be made, in connexion with Tarski's formalization of the notion of truth, is that it rests upon the distinction between metalanguage* and object-language* (cf. 1.3). It is Tarski's achievement to have drawn this distinction and to have worked out its consequences. The predicate 'true' belongs to the vocabulary of the metalanguage, whereas the proposition of which it is predicated is part of (or, alternatively, formulated in) the object-language. What we find exemplified in (1), therefore, is a complex metalanguage proposition, $p \equiv q$, in which p contains an expression referring to an object-language proposition, "Snow is white", and $p \equiv q$ says of this proposition that it is true if and only if a certain state of affairs obtains. It embodies a purely formal notion of truth, in that it abstracts from the empirical or epistemological question of determining whether snow is or is not white. The expression "Snow is white" refers to a proposition expressed by a sentence of the object-language, but it does so by serving as a term in the metalanguage and its function is indicated by the quotation marks (cf. 1.2). The fact that the sentence in quotation marks in Tarski's example is identical, in vocabulary and grammatical structure, with the metalanguage sentence which expresses a proposition describing a state of affairs external to both the object language and the metalanguage is, in principle, irrelevant. We might equally well use English to formalize the notion of truth for French:

(2) 'La neige est blanche' is true if and only if snow is white.

Or conversely,

(3) 'Snow is white' est vrai si, et seulement si, la neige est blanche.

More interestingly, we might use a specially constructed logical calculus with which to formalize the notion of truth for all natural languages; and this is what a number of logicians and linguists are now trying to do in model-theoretic semantics.[9] If we do this, however, we must make sure that the logical metalanguage is rich enough to enable us to refer to all the sentences of all natural languages. Since the set of grammatically, and semantically, well-formed sentences in any natural language is presumably infinite, we cannot in principle proceed by listing all the sentences in any natural language and assigning to each a metalinguistic name. The possibility of extending Tarski's formalization of truth to the semantic analysis of natural languages is clearly dependent upon the possibility of specifying the truth-value of the propositions expressed by complex declarative sentences in terms of the truth values of the propositions expressed by simple declarative sentences. This brings us to the notion of the truth-conditions* of a sentence: the conditions which must hold in any possible world in which, or of which, a sentence, rather than a proposition, is true.

So far we have restricted the application of the predicates 'true' and 'false' to propositions; and we have adopted Tarski's formulation of the correspondence theory of truth, according to which we can say that a proposition is true if and only if a particular state-of-affairs exists in the world that is being described. But Tarski and his followers apply the terms 'true' and 'false' to sentences; and they define the term 'proposition', if they make use of it at all, on the basis of their theory of the meaning of sentences. The first problem that faces us in applying the term 'true' and 'false' to the declarative sentences of natural languages is that many sentences are ambiguous. What we are concerned with, therefore, is the truth or falsity of sentences under a given interpretation. It is, in fact, the notion of truth-under-a-given-interpretation which enables us to define ambiguity. For we can say that an ambiguous declarative sentence is one that might be true under one interpretation and false under another interpretation in some possible state of the universe: i.e. in some possible world. If there is a possible world in which a sentence is both true and false, we can say that the sentence expresses two (or more) distinct propositions, and it is up to the linguist

---

[9] What is said here should not be taken to imply that Tarski's definition of truth and model-theoretic semantics are indissolubly associated.

to account for this by locating the ambiguity either in the expressions of which the sentence is composed or in its grammatical structure.

A second, and more serious, problem has to do with the fact that the vast majority of the expressions that are used in natural languages to refer to individuals are not unique in their reference. We cannot say of a sentence like 'That man over there is my father' that it expresses a true or a false proposition unless we know who has uttered it and who is the person being referred to by means of the expression 'that man over there'. And yet it would be paradoxical to describe such sentences as being ambiguous or semantically indeterminate. If we wish to take account of the fact that the truth-value of the proposition expressed may vary according to the time and place of utterance, we must have some means of indexing the objects in the world and associating these indices with the expressions that occur in sentences. What this implies, in effect, is that the interpretation of a sentence, on any given occasion of its utterance, will be determined jointly by its meaning and by what has come to be called its point-of-reference* (or index*). We will be discussing the notion of reference* in some detail later (cf. 7.2). Here we must be content with a very loose and informal account of what is meant by the term 'point-of-reference' in model-theoretic semantics.

We will begin by drawing a distinction between two kinds of worlds: an extensional world and an intensional world. An extensional world is simply a set of individuals which have certain properties, engage in certain activities, are related to one another in various ways and are located each in a certain place. An intensional world is what we have been referring to as a state-description. We can now draw a distinction between being true in a world and being true of a world.[10] If true, a proposition will be true in some intensional world and it will be true of some (actual or possible) extensional world. To say that a proposition is true in some intensional world implies that it exists in that world; to say that it is true of some extensional world implies that the state-of-affairs (process, activity, etc.) which it describes exists in that world. It will be obvious that this way of talking about truth brings out the connexion between truth and existence that is implicit in the correspondence theory and Tarski's explication of it; and we shall make use of the distinction between the two kinds of world in our discussion of tense* and modality* in a later chapter (17.3).

We have defined an intensional world as a state-description: i.e. as

---

[10] This is a somewhat idiosyncratic terminological distinction, which is not drawn in standard presentations of model-theoretic semantics.

a set of propositions. It is easy to see that we could give a psychological interpretation to this concept by identifying a particular set of propositions with the beliefs of some particular person at some time. But we are not concerned at this point with the psychological interpretation of intensional worlds; we are treating them as purely abstract logical constructs.[11]

Various logical relations can be defined in terms of intensional worlds. A logically necessary proposition is one that is true in all possible intensional worlds; a logically impossible proposition is true in none. One proposition p will entail* another proposition q (i.e. $p \Rightarrow q$) if all possible intensional worlds that contain p also contain q. Provided that the logical calculus that is used to formalize the structure of propositions is truth-functional, the truth-value of any complex proposition will be determined by the truth-value of its constituent simple propositions and the definition of such operations as negation, conjunction, disjunction, implication and quantification. The problem of specifying the truth conditions of complex propositions is therefore reduced, in principle, to that of specifying the truth-conditions of simple, atomic, propositions. To do this, we must associate with each individual in any extensional world that we wish to describe a name which uniquely identifies that individual: the individual then serves as an interpretation for the name. We must also provide an interpretation for the one-place and many-place predicates in the vocabulary of the logical calculus that we are using to describe our set of extensional worlds. A one-place predicate may be interpreted for any arbitrary extensional world as the set of all the individuals that have a particular property in that world. An n-place predicate may be interpreted as the set of all the n-tuples of individuals that are related in a particular way in any extensional world. If this is done, we can say that an atomic proposition is true of any arbitrary extensional world if and only if the n-tuple of individuals that its constituent names are interpreted as is a member of the set of n-tuples that its predicate is interpreted as. For example, the atomic proposition "Alfred is married to Beatrice" – $M(a, b)$ – will be true of any world in which 'Alfred' and 'Beatrice' are interpreted as an ordered pair of individuals in the set of all the ordered pairs which serves as the interpretation for the two-place predicate 'married'. What we have done, it will be observed, is to provide, in principle, an extensional

---

[11] Another alternative is to treat them as constructs within a computerized, or computerizable, system of information-processing: cf. Minsky (1966), Winograd (1975), Woods (1975).

interpretation for names and at least some of the predicates in the object-language.

But model-theoretic semantics takes the view that, in general, the extension of names and predicates in natural languages is not fixed, once and for all, in relation to an unchanging universe, but is determined by a particular point-of-reference*: the time and place of utterance, a variety of known and assumed facts about the extensional world that is being described, and several other factors that may be loosely described as contextual. For example, the sentence 'Alfred is married to Beatrice' might be uttered on one occasion with reference to one pair of individuals and on another occasion with reference to a quite different pair of individuals. Furthermore, the proposition expressed by the sentence might be true of the world at one time, but false at some earlier or later time: the individuals may not yet be married or they may have just got divorced. What can we say then about the truth-conditions* of a sentence (i.e. about the conditions under which it may be used to make a true statement)? In general, we can say that its constituent expressions must be interpreted not as individuals and sets of individuals in the actual world, but as their intensional correlates in some model* of the actual world. Truth then becomes a particular instance of the more general notion of truth-in-a-model. By a model, in the usage of the term, is meant a formal (but not necessarily complete) representation of a possible world. A true sentence will be one that is true in that model which (partly) represents, or describes, the actual world (at some particular time). For our purposes, we can treat the terms 'model', 'intensional world' and 'state-description' as equivalent.

To return to our example. We can understand the sentence 'Alfred is married to Beatrice' without knowing or being able to determine the actual truth-value of whatever proposition it expresses. But we cannot understand it, and therefore cannot be said to know what it means, unless we know under what conditions the proposition it expresses would be true; and we can formulate these conditions with respect to an intensional world in which 'Alfred' is interpreted as one individual concept*, 'Beatrice' as another individual concept, and the predicate 'married' as a set of ordered pairs which contains this particular pair. Under this intensional interpretation of the names and predicates, the sentence expresses a proposition that is true in the model; and it is true of at least one possible extensional world. It is true of any world in which the objects, a and b, correlated by the model with the individual concepts assigned to 'Alfred' and 'Beatrice' actually exist and the ordered pair *a*, *b* is in the extension of 'married' at a time determined by the point-of-reference as one that is simultaneous with, or contains, the time at which the sentence is uttered. What this means, in effect, is that the model will say that the sentence is true if and only if *a* and *b* as interpreted by the model are married at the time that the sentence is uttered. It is the point-of-reference that assigns 'Alfred' and 'Beatrice' to particular individuals and assigns a temporal specification to the extensional world that is being described.

It may well appear that the model-theoretic approach to defining the meaning of sentences is unnecessarily complex. But it is no more than an attempt to take account of the factors which determine our interpretation of quite ordinary utterances. It is often easy enough to state the relevant conditions informally, as we shall be doing throughout most of this book, but it is extraordinarily difficult to make them precise, and model-theoretic semantics, in its various versions, has not so far dealt satisfactorily with more than a small part of the complexity of natural languages. It can be argued, however, that model-theoretic semantics has succeeded in formalizing a notion of the underlying logical structure of sentences which can, in principle, be used to define the truth conditions, and hence the meaning, of any declarative sentence in any natural language. The problem of applying this approach in the semantic analysis of particular languages lies in constructing the most appropriate logical metalanguage for the purpose and showing in detail how particular sentences of any natural language can be interpreted in terms of the logical interpretations assigned to them in the metalanguage.

Throughout this chapter we have been concerned with formal systems constructed by logicians which can be used to formalize, or discuss more precisely, at least certain aspects of the descriptive function of language. We have said that a proposition is what is expressed by a declarative sentence when that sentence is uttered to make a statement (cf. 6.2). It is important to realize, however, there is no simple one-to-correspondence in the everyday use of language between the grammatical structure of a sentence and the kind of communicative act that is performed, in particular situations, by the utterance of that sentence (1.6). We will come back to this point again later in our discussion of Austin's (1962) notion of illocutionary force*. But it should be constantly borne in mind when one is considering the application of logical systems to the analysis of language.

7

Reference, sense and denotation

7.1. *Introductory*

In the first chapter of this book it was pointed out that the word 'meaning' had a number of distinguishable, but perhaps related, senses. Subsequently we drew a broad distinction between three kinds of meaning signalled by language: descriptive, social and expressive (2.4). In chapter 3 we saw that languages may be unique among natural semiotic systems in their capacity to transmit descriptive, as well as social and expressive, information. In this, as in the previous chapter, we shall be concerned solely with descriptive meaning.

Distinctions of the kind we shall be discussing have been drawn by many philosophers, but they have been drawn in a variety of ways. It is now customary, as we shall see, to draw a twofold distinction between what we will call sense* and reference*. Other terms used for the same, or at least a similar, contrast are: 'meaning' and 'reference' (where 'meaning' is given a narrower interpretation than it bears as an everyday pre-theoretical term); 'connotation' and 'denotation'; 'intension' and 'extension'.

No attempt will be made to compare systematically the usage of different authors. But it may be helpful to point out one or two of the terminological pitfalls for the benefit of readers who are not already familiar with the various senses in which the terms mentioned above are employed in the literature. The term 'reference', as we shall define it below, has to do with the relationship which holds between an expression and what that expression stands for on particular occasions of its utterance. What is meant by saying that an expression stands for something else we have already discussed in connexion with the notion of signification (4.1); and we shall come back to it in the next section. It should be pointed out here, however, that many authors use 'reference', and perhaps more particularly 'referential', in a way which, unless one is aware that there are two rather different senses involved, can lead to confusion.

As we have seen, Ogden and Richards (1923) employed the term 'referent' for any object or state-of-affairs in the external world that is identified by means of a word or expression (they did not, however, distinguish between forms, lexemes and expressions), and 'reference' for the concept which mediates between the word or expression and the referent. This notion of reference is consistent with the philosophical notion of reference which we shall be discussing in the next section, except that philosophers generally use the term 'reference', not for the postulated mediating concept, but for the relationship which holds between the expression and the referent. Ogden and Richards, however, went on to distinguish the reference of words and expressions from what they called their emotive* meaning – their capacity to produce a certain emotional effect upon the hearer or listener. Two words, they said, might have the same referential meaning, but differ in emotive meaning: e.g. 'horse' and 'steed'. This distinction between referential and emotive meaning (or between cognitive* and affective* meaning, to use the terms preferred by other authors) is quite different, it should be noted, from the distinction drawn by philosophers between reference and sense. The opposition between a more central, or stylistically neutral, component of meaning and a more peripheral, or subjective, component of meaning is a commonplace of discussions of synonymy; and it is not infrequently conflated with the distinction we have drawn between descriptive and social or expressive meaning (cf. 2.4). The reader should be aware that the terms 'reference' or 'referential meaning' are now fairly well established in the literature of linguistic semantics and stylistics in the sense of 'cognitive meaning' or 'descriptive meaning'. But 'reference' is now widely employed, not only by philosophers, but also by linguists, in the sense which we will give to it in the following section.

The term 'connotation' can also lead to confusion. As used by philosophers, it is generally opposed to 'denotation'; but the way in which the two terms are contrasted is by no means constant throughout the philosophical literature. It was J. S. Mill (1843) who introduced the terminological opposition itself, and a short quotation will show what kind of distinction he had in mind: "The word 'white' denotes all white things, as snow, paper, the foam of the sea, and so forth, and implies, or as it was termed by the schoolmen, connotes, the attribute whiteness". According to Mill, an expression denoted a class of individuals of which it was the name (so that denotation was subsumed under naming); but, if it was what Mill called a concrete general term, like 'white' or 'man', in addition to denoting the class or one of its members, it also implied the property or properties by virtue of which individuals were recognized as members of the class in question. The reader will see here the connexion between 'denotation' and the extension* of a term, on the one hand, and 'connotation' and the intension* of a term, on the other (cf. 6.3). In more recent philosophical writing Mill's terms 'denotation' and 'connotation' are often used for the somewhat different distinction of reference and sense, which derives from Frege (1892).

The reason why Mill chose the term 'connote' is clear enough. As he says himself, it is intended to suggest that what he calls the signification of the attributes of a subject is something additional to the signification, or denotation, of all the subjects which possess these attributes. Somewhat similar is the notion which underlies the non-philosophical use of the term 'connotation' according to which we might say, for example, that a particular word has a pleasant or desirable connotation. In this usage, the connotation of a word is thought of as a emotive or affective component additional to its central meaning. The reader should be on his guard whenever he meets the term 'connotation' in semantics. If it is explicitly contrasted with 'denotation', it will normally have its philosophical sense; but authors do not always make it clear in which of the two senses it is to be taken.

A further terminological difficulty derives from the failure, on the part of many writers, to distinguish clearly between sentences and utterances and from the looseness with which terms like 'word' and 'expression' are commonly employed. It is perhaps for this reason that, although a twofold distinction between sense and reference is common enough (in whatever terms it is drawn), the quite different distinction which we shall make between reference and denotation is only rarely to be met with in the literature. As we shall see, reference (as it will be defined below) is an utterance-dependent notion. Furthermore, unlike sense and denotation, it is not generally applicable in English to single word-forms; and it is never applicable to lexemes. This clearly distinguishes reference from what Mill meant by 'denotation'; for, as we have seen, this was a relation, not between expressions and what they stood for on particular occasions of their utterance, but between lexemes and the whole class of individuals named by these lexemes.

7.2. Reference

When we make a simple descriptive statement, it is frequently, if not always, appropriate to maintain that what we are doing involves saying, or asserting*, something about somebody or something; and we do this characteristically, though not necessarily (cf. 1.6) by uttering a declarative sentence. We can of course make statements which would not normally be construed as asserting something of a particular individual or class of individuals. For example, the sentence 'It is raining', when uttered to make a descriptive statement, does not assert of some entity that it has a certain property or that it is engaged in some process or activity. We might wish to say, it is true, that it is being used to make a descriptive statement about the weather, but not that it is ascribing* to the weather, conceived as an individual, some particular property or characteristic. Let us confine our attention, then, to utterances of which it is reasonable to say, without straining normal usage, that they are intended to tell us something about some particular entity (or entities) or group (or groups) of entities.

When a sentence like 'Napoleon is a Corsican' is uttered to make a statement, we will say that the speaker refers* to a certain individual (Napoleon) by means of the referring expression*. If the reference is successful, the referring expression will correctly identify for the hearer the individual in question: the referent*. It should be noted that, according to this conception of the relation of reference, it is the speaker who refers (by using some appropriate expression): he invests the expression with reference by the act of referring. It is terminologically convenient, however, to be able to say that an expression refers to its referent (when the expression is used on some particular occasion and satisfies the relevant conditions); and we will follow this practice.[1] It should be clearly understood, however, that, according to the view of reference adopted here, when we ask "What does the expression 'x' refer to?", we are asking the same question as we would when we ask "What is the speaker referring to by means of 'x' (in uttering such-and-such a sentence)?". There are other ways of defining the notion of reference such that it would make sense to distinguish between these two questions and allow for the possibility that an expression may have

[1] There are many authors for whom this sense of the term 'refer' is not derivative, but primary. For background and a philosophical justification of the point of view taken here: cf. Linsky (1967). Most of the references cited in note 1 to chapter 6 are relevant. So too is Linsky (1971), Quine (1966).

reference independently of the speaker's use of the expression to refer to some entity.

In the case of sentences which contain only one referring expression, the expression we use in order to refer to what we are talking about is typically the subject of the sentence, and this is combined with a predicative expression* (which is typically the grammatical predicate).[2] For example, '(be) a Corsican' is a predicative expression in 'Napoleon was a Corsican'. But sentences may contain two or more referring expressions. For example, if the sentence 'Alfred killed Bill' is uttered, with its characteristic force of making a statement, both 'Alfred' and 'Bill' would be referring expressions, their referents being the individuals identifiable by name as Alfred and Bill. Whether we maintain that, in making this statement, we are asserting something of Alfred (namely, that he killed Bill) or that we are asserting something of both Alfred and Bill (namely, that they were interconnected in a particular way in an event of killing) is a question that we may leave on one side. It is the former of these interpretations that was generally adopted in traditional logic; it is the latter that is perhaps more naturally reflected in the predicate calculus notation, $K(a, b)$.

(i) Singular definite reference. Among referring expressions we can distinguish those that refer to individuals from those that refer to classes of individuals: we will call these singular* and general* expressions, respectively. We can also distinguish those which refer to some specific individual (or class of individuals) from those which (granted that they do have reference) do not refer to a specific individual or class; and these we will call definite* and indefinite* expressions, respectively. There are problems attaching to the interpretation of general referring expressions. Sometimes we refer to a class of individuals distributively* in order to ascribe a certain property to each of its members; on other occasions we do so collectively* in order to ascribe a property to, or assert something of, the class as a whole; and there are various ways in which we can predicate an expression of a class, as distinct from its members. Indefinite reference is even more complex, and it is philosophically more controversial. We shall be concerned initially with singular definite reference. This is relatively uncontroversial and may be taken as basic.

---

[2] To say that a sentence contains a referring expression is to say that it contains an expression which, on some occasion of the utterance of the sentence, may be used to refer.

From a grammatical point of view, we may recognize three main kinds of singular definite referring expressions in English: (a) definite noun phrases, (b) proper names and (c) personal pronouns.

Definite noun phrases were classified by Russell (1905) as definite descriptions*. The term 'definite description' derives from the view that we can identify a referent, not only by naming it, but also by providing the hearer or reader with a description of it, sufficiently detailed, in the particular context of utterance, to distinguish it from all other individuals in the universe of discourse. For example, 'the tall man over there', in a given context of utterance, could be used as a definite description uniquely identifying some referent. We are deliberately using the term 'definite description', it should be noted, in a rather wider sense than the sense in which it was introduced by Russell: and we are binding it, in principle, to the context of utterance. Russell assimilated personal and demonstrative pronouns to the class of names; and his view of definite descriptions was restricted by his rather idiosyncratic distinction of naming and describing. But the term 'definite description' is now quite widely employed without commitment to Russell's theory.

Although the three kinds of singular definite expressions listed in the previous paragraph are fairly sharply distinguished from one another grammatically in English and each of them is associated with a characteristically distinct means of identifying the person or object that the speaker is referring to on a particular occasion of utterance, there are borderline cases; and in the historical development of English expressions have frequently moved from one category into another. Many place names and family names originated as definite descriptions or titles; and proper names can be regularly converted into descriptive lexemes and used as such in referring or predicative expressions. In other languages, there are even instances of honorific titles, which themselves may have been used earlier as definite descriptions, developing into personal pronouns: an example is the Spanish word 'Usted'. The fact that movement from one category to another may take place in the course of the historical development of a language suggests that the functional distinction between the three kinds of singular definite referring expressions is not absolutely clear-cut.

The grammatical differences between the kinds of expressions used for each of the three ways of identifying a singular definite referent are not as striking in all languages as they are in English. Nonetheless, it may be true that (due allowance being made for borderline cases) all

7

languages provide systematically for these three kinds of singular definite reference. Assuming that this is so, as a matter of empirical fact, it is a question of some theoretical interest to speculate whether any of the three kinds of referring expressions is more basic or essential than the others. Many philosophers have taken reference by naming to be essential to language and have even tried to subsume the whole of reference under naming (cf. 7.5). But this is surely misguided. There are times when we do not know the name of a person or place and can yet refer to this person or place quite naturally and satisfactorily by means of a definite description; and if language is to be used, as it is, for making reference to an indefinitely large range of individuals, it must provide the means for identifying these individuals other than by naming them. It is easier, in fact, to conceive of a language without proper names than it is to conceive of a language operating without some systematic means of referring by definite description. Undoubtedly, however, the combination of naming with description makes of language a more efficient and more flexible semiotic system. Whether personal pronouns are, in principle, dispensable is a question of a different order; and it may be postponed until we have introduced the notion of deixis* (15.2). We will take no further account of pronominal reference in this section.

It has been emphasized that reference is an utterance-dependent notion; and that, whenever we talk of an expression in a given sentence as having reference, we are assuming that the sentence in question has been, or could be, uttered with a particular communicative force in some appropriate context of use. In other words, whenever we say that an expression in a particular sentence refers to a certain entity or group of entities, the term 'sentence' is being employed in the sense of 'text-sentence', rather than 'system-sentence' (14.6).

It is a condition of successful reference that the speaker should select a referring expression – typically a proper name, a definite noun-phrase or a pronoun – which, when it is employed in accordance with the rules of the language-system, will enable the hearer, in the context in which the utterance is made, to pick out the actual referent from the class of potential referents. If the expression is a definite noun-phrase operating as a definite description, its descriptive content will be more or less detailed according to the circumstances; and the manner of description will often depend upon the speaker's assumption that the hearer is in possession of quite specific information about the referent. For example, in some circumstances it might be necessary for the speaker to incorporate within the noun phrase an adjective or relative clause, whose function it is to specify one particular member of a class of individuals. The clause 'who was here yesterday' might be sufficient for this purpose if it were incorporated in the noun phrase 'the man who was here yesterday': and its employment by the speaker within this definite description of the referent would be dependent upon his assumption that the hearer knew that a man had been at the place referred to by 'here' on the previous day. If they had already been talking about the person in question 'the man' (or the pronoun 'he') might well be sufficiently specific.

In many cases the use of a common noun preceded by the definite article will suffice without further description, even though the referent has not been previously mentioned, because the speaker can fairly assume, in the given situation or universe of discourse, that the hearer will know which of the potential referents satisfying* the description he is referring to. For example, if I say to my wife or children, *The cat has not been in all day*, in a context in which there has been no previous mention of any cat, I can be sure that the reference will be successful. If an Englishman uses referentially the expression 'the queen' and an American the expression 'the president', in a context in which no queen or president has already been referred to, they will normally expect to be understood as referring to the queen of England and to the president of the United States respectively. Expressions of this latter kind come very close to acquiring, in the appropriate context, the status of uniquely referring titles (like 'the Pope'); and uniquely referring titles have a tendency, as Strawson (1950) puts it, to grow capital letters and to be treated orthographically in written English as proper names. In general, titles constitute a class of expressions which "shades off into definite descriptions at one end and proper names at the other" (Searle, 1969: 81).

(ii) Reference, truth and existence. The condition that the referent must satisfy* the description has commonly been interpreted by philosophers to imply that the description must be true of the referent. If a distinction is drawn between correct reference and successful reference, one can perhaps maintain the general principle that we can refer correctly to an individual by means of a definite description only if the description is true of the individual in question. But successful reference does not depend upon the truth of the description contained in the referring expression. The speaker (and perhaps also the hearer) may mistakenly believe that some person is the postman, when he is in fact the professor of linguistics, and incorrectly, though successfully, refer to him by means of the expression 'the postman'. It is not even necessary that the speaker should believe that the description is true of the referent. He may be ironically employing a description he knows to be false or diplomatically accepting as correct a false description which his hearer believes to be true of the referent; and there are yet other possibilities. 'Satisfaction', in the sense in which it is employed by philosophers, is a technical term which presupposes or implies truth. It is arguable, however, that the more basic and more general notion governing the use of definite descriptions is that the hearer can be assumed capable of identifying the referent on the basis of the properties ascribed to it, whether correctly or not, in the description.

A classic philosophical example may be introduced at this point. The following sentence,

(1) The present King of France is bald,

was analysed by Russell (1905) as asserting that there is one, and only one, individual who currently occupies the throne of France and that this individual is bald. Russell's analysis of this sentence, or more precisely of the proposition expressed by this sentence (which we will assume is being uttered to make a statement) depends upon his theory of descriptions and his notion of logically proper names. We need not go into the details. It is sufficient to say that, according to Russell, the proposition expressed by the sentence is, not a single simple proposition, but a conjunction of three propositions: (a) that there exists a king of France; (b) that there is no more than one king of France; and (c) that there is nothing which has the property of being king of France and which does not also have the property of being bald. All three propositions are said to be asserted. Since the first of the conjuncts – the existential proposition (a) – is false, the conjunction of which it is a component is false (by virtue of the truth-functional definition of conjunction in the propositional calculus: 6.2).

Russell's analysis has been challenged by a number of scholars, notably by Strawson (1950). Strawson did not deny that Russell's sentence was meaningful. Nor did he deny that, for the sentence to be true (i.e. for it to be possible for anyone uttering the sentence to make a true assertion), the three component propositions listed above as conjuncts must each be true. What he disputed was Russell's claim that the sentence was false if the component existential proposition (a) was false. For, in Strawson's view, this proposition (as well as the uniqueness proposition listed as (b) above) is not asserted, but presupposed*, by the use of the definite description 'the (present) King of France'. If the proposition (or any one of the propositions) presupposed by the use of a definite description is in fact false, then the definite description, according to Strawson, fails to refer; and the sentence of which it is a constituent expression cannot be used to make an assertion. The sentence is meaningful; but the question whether it is true or false simply does not arise.

Strawson's criticism of Russell has engendered a considerable amount of philosophical controversy; and his notion of presupposition* has been developed and extended in different ways by linguists and logicians (cf. 14.3). Here it may simply be mentioned that Strawson himself has more recently expressed the view that the issue is not as clear-cut as he previously maintained it to be; that his own analysis and Russell's "are tailored...to emphasise different kinds of interest in statement; and each has its own merits" (Strawson, 1964). Many philosophers avoid commitment on the question and say that existential propositions are either presupposed or implied by the use of a referring expression; and we can leave it at that.

There is, however, another point. Both Russell and Strawson can be criticized for saying that the truth of the component existential and uniqueness propositions which are presupposed or implied by (the use of) a definite description with a referential function is a necessary condition for making a true assertion about a referent. Now, it is indeed the case that the speaker is (normally) committed to a belief in the existence of a referent by his use of a definite description; but, as we have seen, this does not necessarily imply that the description is true of the referent or even held to be true by the speaker. Existence is a tricky concept in any case, and we must allow for various kinds of existence pertaining to fictional and abstract referents (or, alternatively, show how these apparently diverse kinds of existence relate to the physical existence of spatiotemporally continuous and discrete objects). Furthermore, if we are to give a comprehensive account of the way in which referring expressions are used in everyday discourse, we must admit the possibility that the speaker can, on occasion, talk about things of whose existence (in any sense of 'existence') he is uncertain. The most that can be said perhaps is that the speaker, in using a singular definite referring expression commits himself, at least temporarily and provisionally, to the existence of a referent satisfying his descripton and invites the hearer to do the same.

As for the condition of uniqueness, which is commonly said to be necessary for successful reference by means of a singular definite referring expression: it is clearly not the case that this must hold in any absolute way. When I say *The cat has not been in all day*, I am by no means committed to the belief that there is only one individual that I can refer to by means of the expression 'the cat'. What I assume, presumably, is that I will be understood to be referring to a definite individual and that the description I offer will be sufficiently specific, in the given context, to identify uniquely for the hearer the referent I have in mind. It is in this rather restricted, context-dependent, sense that the condition of uniqueness is to be interpreted in linguistic semantics. Furthermore, it is not only definite descriptions whose uniqueness of reference is relative to context. Most proper names are such that they may be borne by several individuals; and their context-dependent uniqueness of reference, like that of 'the Pope', is in principle no different from that of the majority of definite descriptions.

Philosophers have naturally enough given a lot of attention to discussing the conditions under which we can be said to be committed to a belief in the truth of the existential propositions that are presupposed or implied by the referring expressions we employ in making statements. But philosophers are professionally concerned with the explication of the notions of truth, knowledge, belief and existence. The fundamental problem for the linguist, as far as reference is concerned, is to elucidate and to describe the way in which we use language to draw attention to what we are talking about. In many situations, it may be unclear, and of little consequence, whether a speaker is implicitly committed, by the words he utters, to a belief in the truth of particular existential propositions; and it is rarely the case that a speaker uses a referring expression for the purpose of ontological commitment. Philosophy and linguistics undoubtedly converge in the study of reference, and each can benefit from their joint discussion of the notions involved. But their primary concerns remain distinct; and it is only to be expected that what the one discipline considers to be crucial the other will regard as being of secondary importance, and conversely.

What has just been said is admittedly a somewhat personal assessment of the relationship between the linguistic and the philosophical treatment of reference; and it would no doubt be disputed by those linguists and philosophers who take the notion of truth to be central to the whole of semantics. It should be pointed out, however, that there is at least one group of scholars whose conception of the centrality of truth is such that there is no real conflict between their approach to the formalization of the conditions of appropriate reference in terms of truth and the notion of successful reference outlined above. If the notion of truth is relativized to that of truth-under-an-interpretation, as it is in model-theoretical* semantics, a definite description like 'the postman' may be satisfied in some possible world that is not the actual world (cf. 6.5). But model-theoretical semantics is itself controversial.

(iii) Non-referring definite noun-phrases. It should not be supposed that the sole function of definite noun phrases in English is to refer to specific individuals (or classes of individuals). A definite noun-phrase may occur as the complement of the verb 'to be' and it may then have a predicative, rather than a referential, function. This point may be illustrated by means of the following sentence:

(2) Giscard d'Estaing is the President of France.

As it stands, (2) can be understood in various ways. In particular, it might be understood to express a proposition that is comparable with such propositions as the following: that Giscard d'Estaing comes from the Auvergne, that he likes playing tennis, and so on. Under this interpretation of (2), the phrase 'the President of France' is not being used to refer to an individual; it is being used with predicative function to say something about the individual that is referred to by means of the subject-expression, 'Giscard d'Estaing'.

There is, however, another interpretation of (2), it must be added, according to which both 'Giscard d'Estaing' and 'the President of France' function as referring expressions and the copula asserts an identity between the two referents. It so happens that in English, as in many, but not all, languages, the predicative and the equative copula are identical: the verb 'to be' is used in both cases. There are nonetheless important differences between predicative and equative* sentences containing the verb 'to be' in English: if (2) is taken as an equative sentence the two referring expressions are interchangeable (as are the two terms in an equation like $3^2 = 9$) and the definite article is an obligatory component of 'the President of France'; if (2) is taken as a predicative sentence the two noun-phrases are not interchanageable and the article is optional in the predicative noun-phrase (cf. 12.2).

Donnellan (1966) has pointed out that a definite noun-phrase may also be employed non-referentially as the subject of a sentence. One of his examples is

(3) Smith's murderer is insane.

There is of course one interpretation of this sentence under which 'Smith's murderer', which is a definite noun-phrase even though it does not contain the definite article (at least in surface structure*: cf. 10.5), is understood to refer to some specific individual. But there is another interpretation which can be brought out more clearly by paraphrasing (3) as

(4) Whoever killed Smith is insane.

In particular circumstances even 'whoever killed Smith' might be construed as a referring expression (though not of course as an expression with singular definite reference). Normally, however, we might expect (4) to be uttered in situations where the speaker is not simply asserting of some individual (who might have been referred to in all sorts of other ways which make no mention of the crime) that he is insane, but where the fact of having committed the murder is being put forward as grounds for the assertion that is made. If (3) is also construed in this way, then the expression 'Smith's murderer', according to Donnellan (1966) is being used attributively; and "in the attributive use, the attribute of being the so-and-so is all important, while it is not in the referential use".

It is important to realize that sentences, which like (2) and (3), are ambiguous in various ways in the written medium, are not necessarily ambiguous in the spoken language. Linguists have recently given considerable attention to determining the role of such prosodic* features as stress and intonation with respect to presupposition* and what Austin (1962) called illocutionary force* (cf. 16.1). It is still an open question whether these prosodic features, and especially stress, should be regarded as grammatically determined properties of system-sentences. According to an alternative view, they might be described as features which are superimposed upon sentences by the speaker (when the sentences in question are uttered as spoken text-sentences) in actual contexts of use. Whether they are to be treated by the linguist in the one way or the other is perhaps more a matter of methodology than of fact. However they are described, they are undoubtedly relevant to the interpretation of spoken utterances. If it is true that "in general, whether or not a definite description is used referentially or attributively is a function of the speaker's intentions in a particular case" (Donnellan, 1966), it must also be recognized that the speaker's intentions are often reflected in the prosodic features of his utterances. This fact should be borne in mind whenever sentences are discussed under the assumption that they have been, or might be, uttered by a speaker in some particular context.

(iv) Distributive and collective general reference. So far we have dealt only with definite reference, and we have been mainly concerned with singular referring expressions. There is no need for us to go into the problems of general reference. The distinction between distributive* and collective* reference should, however, be illustrated. The following sentence is ambiguous from this point of view:

(5) Those books cost £5.

If 'those books' is to be construed as meaning "each of those books", it is being used distributively; if it means "that set of books", it is being used collectively. In a case like (5) it is legitimate to talk of ambiguity, rather than indeterminacy, since the two interpretations are so sharply distinguishable. In other cases, however, and very commonly in every-day English, it is perhaps indeterminacy, rather than ambiguity, that is involved. It should also be noted that there are different kinds of collective reference. For example, as (5) is ambiguous according to whether the subject-expression has distributive or collective reference, so is

(6) The students have the right to smoke in lectures.

The distributive interpretation, according to which each student has the right to decide for himself whether to smoke or not, is straightforward enough. But the collective interpretation might well involve reference to the students as an institutionalized body; and the rights and properties of such bodies do not derive from the rights and properties of the individuals of which, in some sense, they are composed. At the same time, even if it is clear that it is as a collectivity that the students have the right to smoke (if they so decide by majority vote or whatever), it is as individuals that they will exercise this right. This means that in the proposition expressed by (6), under the collective interpretation, 'the students' has to be given a distributive interpretation as well, in so far as it is taken as the underlying subject of 'smoke'.

(v) Specific and non-specific indefinite reference. Once we move on to consider expressions whose reference (if they are indeed rightly regarded as referring expressions) is in one way or another indefinite, we strike against a host of additional complexities; and no attempt will be made here to do more than mention one or two of the more important points.

Let us begin by establishing a terminological distinction, for English, between non-definite* and indefinite* noun-phrases. A non-definite noun-phrase is any noun-phrase which is not a definite noun-phrase; an indefinite noun-phrase is either an indefinite pronoun or a noun-phrase introduced by the indefinite article (e.g. 'a man', and also phrases like 'such a man'). All indefinite noun-phrases are non-definite, but the converse is not true.

Consider now the following sentence (which we will assume is uttered to make a statement):

(7) Every evening at six o'clock a heron flies over the chalet.

It contains an indefinite noun-phrase, 'a heron', which under one interpretation of the sentence can be understood to refer to a specific, though unidentified, individual; and this interpretation would be supported if the sentence were immediately followed, in the same context, by

(8) It nests in the grounds of the chateau.

The pronoun 'it' in (8) has the same reference as – is co-referential* with – 'a heron' in (7).[3] We will say that the indefinite noun-phrase, under this interpretation of (7), is being used with indefinite, but specific*, reference. But (7) can also be interpreted in such a way that the speaker is not taken to be referring to some specific individual. Under the first interpretation, the indefinite noun-phrase is paraphrasable by means of the expression 'a particular heron'; under the second, it can be paraphrased, though perhaps not very idiomatically or precisely, with the expression 'some heron or other'. Under the latter interpretation, we will say that the indefinite noun-phrase is being used non-specifically*. We will not say, however, that it has non-specific reference, because it is far from clear that it is correctly regarded as a referring expression. Very often, of course, we cannot tell whether an indefinite noun-phrase is being used with specific reference or not; and the speaker himself might be hard put to decide. It is a characteristic feature of the grammar of English that common nouns in the singular (except when they are used as mass nouns) must be introduced with an article (whether definite or indefinite), a demonstrative adjective, or some other determiner* (cf. 11.4). Not all languages that have what

---

[3] For a convenient summary of the way linguists have defined the notion of co-reference and of some of the problems that this has generated: cf. Fauconnier (1974).

might be described as a definite or indefinite article are like English in this respect.

Whether an indefinite noun-phrase in English is being used with specific reference or not, the speaker can go on to say something more about the referent and, in doing so, he can subsequently refer to it by means of a demonstrative or personal pronoun or a definite noun-phrase. Any information that the speaker gives the hearer about the referent when it is first referred to by means of an indefinite noun-phrase is available for both participants in the conversation to use in subsequent references. For example, if X says to Y

(9) A friend has just sent me a lovely Valentine card,

he can refer subsequently to the same individual by means of the expression 'my friend', regardless of whether he had a specific person in mind originally or not. And Y can refer to the same person by means of the expression 'your friend'. The point is that, once any information at all has been supplied about an indefinite referent, it can then be treated by the participants as an individual that is known to them both and identifiable within the universe-of-discourse by means of a definite referring expression. It is not a necessary condition of successful reference that the speaker or hearer should be able to identify the individual being referred to in any sense of 'identification' other than this.

In English, the indefinite pronouns 'someone' and 'something' can also be used specifically or non-specifically. Hence, the alleged ambiguity of such sentences as

(10) Everyone loves someone,

much discussed by logicians in connexion with the scope* of the universal and existential quantifiers (cf. 6.3). Under certain grammatically determined conditions, notably in interrogative and negative sentences, 'anyone' and 'anything' occur, rather than 'someone' and 'something', in the non-specific use of indefinite pronouns. But the conditions are complex; and there is currently considerable controversy among linguists as to whether the alternation of 'someone'/'something' with 'anyone'/'anything' is purely a matter of grammatical structure (cf. 11.4). The question is complicated further by the necessity of taking into account the operation of stress in spoken English; the indefinite pronouns may be stressed or unstressed whether they are used specifically or non-specifically; and stress, here as elsewhere, has a variety of functions. Like the indefinite pronouns, noun-phrases introduced by 'some' (which alternates with 'any' in its non-specific use) may also be employed specifically or non-specifically. The following sentence is therefore subject to the same alleged ambiguity as (10) above:

(11) Every boy loves some girl.

We will not go into the question of quantification (in the logical sense of this term) and indefinite reference.

One class of sentences containing indefinite noun-phrases which has also been much discussed recently is exemplified by

(12) John wants to marry a girl with green eyes.

The expression 'a girl with green eyes' in (12) can be construed as being used specifically or non-specifically. If it is taken as a referring expression (i.e. as having specific indefinite reference), then it pre-supposes, or implies, the existence of some individual who satisfies the description, in much the same way as would the definite noun-phrase 'the girl with the green eyes' used as a referring expression in the same context. There is no presupposition or implication of uniqueness, however; and the indefinite noun-phrase does not identify the referent for the hearer in the same way as a definite noun-phrase used referen-tially. If the indefinite noun-phrase 'a girl with green eyes' is con-strued as non-specific, there is no presupposition or implication of existence at all; and this is characteristic of descriptive noun-phrases (whether definite or non-definite) which occur after verbs denoting what Russell (1940), Quine (1960), and others have called propositional attitudes* (i.e. verbs denoting belief, doubt, intention, etc.).

It has been suggested that the two interpretations of (12) can be dis-tinguished, logically, in terms of a difference in the scope of the under-lying existential quantifier:

(12a) "$(\exists x)$ (x is a girl with green eyes and John wants to marry x)"
(12b) "John wants $(\exists x)$ (x be a girl with green eyes and John marry x)".

But this analysis, which rests upon a too ready application of the predicate-calculus theory of quantification, is surely unsatisfactory as a representation of the ambiguity of (12). (12b) suggests that the person referred to by means of 'John' wants two things, that there should exist some individual having certain properties and that he should marry this individual. Now, it is clearly a condition of being able to marry a certain individual that this individual should exist. But it surely goes against all our intuitions about the meaning of (12) to say that, when it is uttered to make a statement, it is being used to assert that John wants someone with certain properties to exist. Apart from anything else, John, like most of us at one time or another, may be subject to irrational and contradictory desires: he might resolutely maintain that he wants to marry someone that he does not want to exist.[4] In which case (12b) would be false. Nor is the distinction of assertion and presupposition of much help in this case. Neither the speaker nor John need be convinced of the present or future existence of girls with green eyes. Donnellan's (1966) distinction between the referential and attributive use of descriptive noun-phrases seems to be more to the point, although Donnellan himself introduced the distinction solely in connexion with definite noun-phrases. But the most striking difference between the two interpretations of (12) appears to reside in the contrast between the specific and non-specific use of the indefinite noun-phrase.[5]

One further point should be noted about indefinite noun-phrases used non-specifically. As we have already seen, they may establish in the universe-of-discourse entities that may be subsequently referred to by means of definite noun-phrases and they may serve as antecedents with respect to personal pronouns. For example, in the following sentence,

(13) John wants to marry a girl with green eyes and take her back to Ireland with him,

'a girl with green eyes' may be construed as either specific or non-specific, and under either interpretation the pronoun 'she' (in the form *her*) is a referring expression. The fact that, under certain circumstances, a pronoun can have an antecedent used non-referentially is troublesome for any straightforward theory of pronominalization which is based on the notion of co-referentiality. Two expressions cannot have the same reference, if one of them is not a referring expression at all. The pronoun in the second clause of (13) can perhaps be said to refer to "that unique though hypothetical entity which would be crucially involved in

---

[4] It might be argued that, if John wants to marry a girl with green eyes, having no specific girl in mind, he must nonetheless want it to be the case that there is a girl with green eyes such that he marries her and that this is what is expressed by (12b). I do not find this argument at all persuasive.

[5] In saying this, I am aware that what precisely is meant by 'specific' and 'non-specific' here is a little obscure. For some discussion of the distinction and of its semantic and syntactic implications: cf. Dahl (1970), Jackendoff (1972).

actualizing the possible world characterized in the first part of the sentence" (cf. Partee, 1972: 426), but it cannot be said to be co-referential with this hypothetical entity, since this is not an expression, but a referent; and the indefinite noun-phrase in the first clause, being non-specific, does not refer to the hypothetical entity that it establishes in the universe of discourse. If the notion of co-reference is to be salvaged in cases like this, some other referring expression must, therefore, be introduced into the deep structure* or semantic representation* of the sentence (cf. 10.5).

(vi) Referential opacity. Mention should now be made of what Quine has called referential opacity*. According to Quine (1960: 141ff) constructions, or contexts, are opaque* (as opposed to transparent*) when they fail to preserve extensionality (i.e. truth-functionality: cf. 6.2) under the substitution of co-referential singular expressions (and under certain other substitutions which do not concern us here).

The co-referential expressions in question, it should be noted, may be either definite or non-definite. Consider first the following sentence, uttered by X to inform Y of some fact:

(14) Mr Smith is looking for the Dean.

Now (14) is open to two interpretations according to whether 'the Dean' is construed referentially or attributively (in Donnellan's sense); and, under either of these interpretations, Mr Smith may or may not know who is the Dean. If 'the Dean' is referential, it gives the speaker's description, not necessarily Mr Smith's description, of the referent. Let us now suppose that Professor Brown is the Dean and that X and Y know this, although Mr Smith thinks that Professor Green is the Dean. Mr Smith may have previously informed X that he was looking for Professor Brown; in which case the proposition expressed by (14) is true, provided that 'the Dean' is construed as a purely referential expression. It is not true, however, if it is taken attributively. For Mr Smith is not looking for the person, whoever it is, who is the Dean. He is looking for a particular individual who might have been referred to by X in all sorts of referentially equivalent ways. But suppose now that Mr Smith had told X who he was looking for by means of the following sentence:

(15) I am looking for the Dean.

He might intend 'the Dean' to be understood referentially (as referring to Professor Green) or attributively. (And it may be observed in passing that the referential use, in situations like this, does not sharply exclude the attributive. For Mr Smith may be looking for Professor Brown as Dean. This is commonly the case when titles are used as definite descriptions.) If X takes 'the Dean' in (15) as referential and then utters (14), intending 'the Dean' to be understood as referring to Professor Brown, then the statement he makes by uttering (14) is false, as would be the statement made by uttering

(16) Mr Smith is looking for Professor Brown,

in which he has substituted the (for him) co-referential expression 'Professor Brown'.

We will not go through all the possibilities of misunderstanding that can result by virtue of the occurrence of definite and indefinite expressions in opaque contexts. Logicians have discussed the question primarily in relation to extensionality and the scope of quantifiers in the logical structure of distinct underlying propositions; and some linguists have analysed the deep structure of sentences like (14) in similar terms.[6] There is, however, a more general point to be emphasized, which the philosophical discussion of reference in opaque contexts has made explicit, but which holds independently of any particular formalization of the structure of language. When we report the statements made by others or describe their beliefs or intentions, we do not necessarily employ the same referring expressions as they have employed or would employ. We are free to select our own referring expressions; and the possibilities of misunderstanding and misreporting which arise when we utter sentences like (14) derive from this fact. (They are compounded by, but do not depend solely upon, the possibility of misconstruing an attributive expression as referential, or conversely.) The fact that the speaker is free to select his own referring expressions in the utterance of what are traditionally described as sentences of indirect discourse (or reported speech) should be borne in mind in any discussion of the relationship between the grammatical structure of such sentences and their meaning on particular occasions of their utterance.

(vii) Generic reference. Another problem that has been attracting the attention of both logicians and linguists recently is that of so-called generic* reference. What is meant by 'generic' (not to be confused with

---

[6] For discussion and references to the recent linguistic and philosophical literature: cf. Dik (1968), Partee (1972, 1975).

'general') may be seen by considering such sets of sentences as the following

(17) The lion is a friendly beast
(18) A lion is a friendly beast
(19) Lions are friendly beasts.

Each of these sentences may be used to assert a generic proposition: i.e. a proposition which says something, not about this or that group of lions or about any particular individual lion, but about the class of lions as such.

Generic propositions, it is important to realize, are, not only tenseless, but timeless (cf. 15.4). At first sight, this statement is immediately refuted by pointing to the possibility of uttering such sentences as

(20) The dinosaur was a friendly beast,

in order to assert what is, intuitively at least, a generic proposition. But the past tense that occurs in (20) is not part of the proposition that is expressed when (20) is used to assert a generic proposition. In such circumstances, it is inappropriate to ask when it was that dinosaurs were friendly: the past tense is employed because the speaker believes that dinosaurs are extinct, not because he thinks that they have changed their properties. Generic propositions being timeless are not only tenseless, but also aspectless* (cf. 15.6). Once again, there are certain apparent exceptions to this statement; but we need not go into them here. It will be obvious from what has been said so far, therefore, that there is a difference between general reference (which was distinguished from singular reference earlier in this section) and generic reference. General referring expressions, whether distributive or collective, can occur freely in sentences that express time-bound propositions of various kinds.

The status of generic propositions is philosophically controversial: so too is the correlated notion of generic, as distinct from general, reference. The proposition expressed by (17)–(19) under the intended interpretation of them (and let us, for the moment, assume that all three sentences express the same generic proposition), would normally be formalized within the framework of the predicate-calculus (cf. 6.3) as

(21) $(x) (Lx \rightarrow Fx)$

"For all values of x, if x is a lion, then x is friendly". It has often been pointed out, however, that formulae like (21), involving universal

quantification, do not seem to capture the meaning of generic propositions. From one point of view (21) is too strong and from another point
of view it is too weak. It is too strong, in that it is falsifiable by the
discovery of but a single unfriendly lion; and this is surely not what is
intended by anyone uttering (17)–(19). It is too weak, in that it would
represent the proposition expressed by (17)–(19) as true if it just happened to be the case, as a matter of contingent fact, that all the extant
lions were friendly; and, once again, it seems clear that this is not what
is intended. There is a difference between the truth-conditions of
(17)–(19), under the intended interpretation, and the truth-conditions of

(22) All lions (as it happens) are friendly beasts.

One might very reasonably take the proposition expressed by (22) to be
true, whilst refusing to subscribe to the truth of the proposition expressed by (17)–(19). Indeed, one might believe that every lion that has
ever existed was of a friendly disposition and that every lion that will
exist in the future will be equally friendly, without being thereby
committed to the truth of the proposition expressed by (17)–(19). In
short, universal quantification seems to be irrelevant to the formalization of the meaning of (17)–(19).

So far, we have tacitly assumed that there is only one kind of generic
proposition. It is arguable, however, that there are several different
kinds; and that they merge into one another in such a way that it is
impossible to distinguish the one from the other in particular instances.
There is one class of generic propositions – let us call them essential*
propositions – which are to be interpreted as saying that such-and-such
a property is a necessary attribute of the members of the class to which
reference is made. If (17)–(19) are construed this way their truth-
conditions are such that the proposition that they express would be
held to be true if and only if being a friendly beast is an essential attribute
of lions. Needless to say, the recognition of propositions of this kind
raises all sorts of epistemological and metaphysical problems. Whatever
might be the philosophical status of essentialism, however, there can
be no doubt that the distinction between what is essential and what is
contingent is of considerable importance in the semantic analysis of
English and other languages. It is intimately bound up with the notion
of analyticity* (cf. 6.5).

Essential propositions are perhaps the most easily definable subclass
of generic propositions. Not all generic propositions, however, are
essential propositions. Indeed, it is rather unlikely that anyone would

wish to construe (17)–(19) as expressing an essential proposition. The kind of adverbial modifier that suggests itself for insertion (either in initial position or immediately after the verb) in (17)–(19) is one that approximates in meaning to 'generally', 'typically', 'characteristically' or 'normally', rather than to 'essentially' or 'necessarily'; and it is notoriously difficult to specify the truth-conditions for propositions containing adverbs of this kind (cf. Lewis, 1975). They certainly cannot be formalized, in any straightforward fashion, in terms of either universal or existential quantification; and, so far at least, there does not seem to be available any satisfactory formalization of the truth-conditions of the vast majority of the generic propositions that we assert in our everyday use of language. This point should be borne in mind in view of the rather loose appeal that is made to the notion of generic propositions or generic reference in many recent discussions of the topic.

As there are different kinds of generic propositions, so there are different kinds of generic reference. Definite noun-phrases, like 'the lion', and indefinite noun-phrases, like 'a lion', are far from being intersubstitutable in all kinds of sentences expressing generic propositions. For example, whereas

(23) The lion is extinct,

or

(24) The lion is no longer to be seen roaming the hills of Scotland,

are perfectly normal sentences, which can be used to assert a generic proposition, neither

(25) A lion is extinct,

nor

(26) A lion is no longer to be seen roaming the hills of Scotland,

can be used to assert a generic proposition. One obvious difference between definite and indefinite noun-phrases, used generically, is that, with definite noun-phrases, both a collective and a distributive interpretation is possible, but with indefinite noun-phrases (in the singular) the collective interpretation is excluded. The fact that this is so accounts for the unacceptability of (25) and (26), under a generic interpretation of 'a lion'.

It has been suggested occasionally that sentences like (18) should be construed (under the generic interpretation) as expressing a conditional proposition in which 'a lion' is not a referring expression at all (i.e.

"If something is a lion, then it is – typically, normally, characteristically, etc. – a friendly beast"). However, in view of the obscurity or indeterminacy of the truth-conditions of non-essential generic propositions, it is very difficult to be sure that there is a constant difference between the referential potential of definite and indefinite noun-phrases in sentences expressing what appear to be very similar, if not identical, generic propositions. Indeed, generic propositions pose a very serious, and so far unsolved, problem for truth-conditional semantics (cf. 6.6); and the problem is not solved, or even rendered more amenable to solution, by the introduction of a special generic quantifier, distinct from the universal and the existential quantifier. Generic propositions, and generically referring noun-phrases, are too heterogeneous to be handled in this way.[7]

From what has been said in this section, it should be clear that some understanding of how reference operates in language-behaviour is essential for the analysis of actual texts (whether written or spoken); and furthermore that the analysis of sentences in terms of the propositional and predicate calculus is by no means as straightforward as we may have appeared to assume in the previous chapter. The linguist can contribute to the study of reference by describing the grammatical structures and processes which particular language-systems provide for referring to individuals and groups of individuals. It does not follow, however, that the linguist must be concerned with the actual reference of expressions in his analysis of the grammatical structure of system-sentences.

7.3. *Sense*

All that we have said so far about sense is that it is now customary to distinguish sense* from reference*. It is perhaps helpful to add that 'sense' is the term used by a number of philosophers for what others would describe simply as their meaning, or perhaps more narrowly as their cognitive* or descriptive* meaning. For this reason the distinction of reference and sense is sometimes formulated as a distinction of reference and meaning. As was pointed out earlier, it has also been identified with Mill's distinction of denotation and connotation (cf. 7.1).

Frege's (1892) classic example, which is frequently used in discussions of sense and reference, is

(1) The Morning Star is the Evening Star.

---

[7] See Biggs (1975), Dahl (1975), Jackendoff (1972), Lawler (1972), Smith (1975).

As Frege pointed out, the two expressions 'the Morning Star' and 'the Evening Star' had the same reference (Bedeutung), since they each referred to the same planet. But they could not be said to have the same sense (Sinn). For, if they did, (1) would be tautologous, or analytic, as is (2),

(2) The Morning Star is the Morning Star.

But (1), unlike (2), is (potentially) informative: it can make the hearer aware of some fact of which he was not previously aware and which he could not derive simply from his understanding of the meaning of the sentence (cf. 2.2). It follows that 'the Morning Star' and 'the Evening Star' are not synonymous*: i.e. they do not have the same sense. So runs the standard argument.

It may be observed in connexion with (1) and (2) that expressions such as 'the Morning Star' and 'the Evening Star' might be regarded as falling somewhere between proper names and definite descriptions; and, like many uniquely-referring titles, they have, in fact, grown capital letters (as Strawson puts it: cf. 7.2). In so far as they approximate to proper names, it is legitimate to question the assertion that they have sense; for, as we shall see, it is widely, though not universally, accepted that proper names do not have sense (cf. 7.5). On the other hand, if 'the Morning Star' and 'the Evening Star' are treated like definite descriptions, which differ in sense in a way that is obvious to any speaker of English by virtue of his knowledge of the language, there is the problem that

(3) The Morning Star is not a star (but a planet)

is, not only not contradictory, but potentially informative. Of course, as a matter of historical fact, it was known to astronomers that neither the Morning Star nor the Evening Star were fixed stars, but planets, long before it was discovered that the Morning Star and the Evening Star were identical. Nonetheless, the rather uncertain status of the two expressions 'the Morning Star' and 'the Evening Star' makes them less than ideal for the purpose for which they (or rather their German equivalents) were used by Frege. One might even argue that they differ not only in sense, but also in reference, the conditions under which the planet Venus is visible from Earth, rather than its spatiotemporal continuity, being in this case more relevant to the notion of referential identity. But we need not pursue this point. Frege's example has been introduced simply to illustrate in a general way the nature of his distinction between sense and reference. Expressions may differ in sense, but have the same reference; and 'synonymous' means "having the same sense", not "having the same reference". A rather better example than Frege's is Husserl's, 'the victor at Jena' and 'the loser at Waterloo' ('der Sieger von Jena' and 'der Besiegte von Waterloo'), both of which expressions may be used to refer to Napoleon (cf. Coseriu & Geckeler, 1974: 147).

It is, incidentally, unfortunate that Frege selected 'Bedeutung' as his technical term for what is now generally called reference in English. That he did choose the German word which in non-technical usage covers much of what is covered by the English word 'meaning' was no doubt due to the fact that he, like many philosophers, thought of reference as the basic semantic relationship. There is, however, an alternative technical distinction drawn in German between 'Bedeutung' ("meaning") and 'Bezeichnung' (often translated into English as 'designation'). This distinction is at least roughly comparable with Frege's distinction between 'Sinn' and 'Bedeutung': it is, however, Frege's 'Bedeutung' which, if anything, is identifiable with what many German writers call 'Bezeichnung', and it is his 'Sinn' that is identifiable with their 'Bedeutung'.[8] One of the advantages of using 'meaning' as a very general pre-theoretical term, as we are doing in this book (cf. 1.1), is that it enables us to avoid the kind of problem that has arisen in German. It will become apparent presently that our use of 'sense' as a theoretical term is somewhat narrower than is customary in philosophical writings.

That expressions with the same reference should not always be inter-substitutable in all contexts "salva veritate" (to use Leibniz's phrase: cf. 6.4) has been a problem for those philosophers who have attempted to construct a purely extensional theory of semantics. If the meaning of an expression is the class of entities to which it refers (or may refer), how is it that even uniquely referring expressions (and, let us grant that they are uniquely-referring expressions), such as 'the Morning Star' and 'the Evening Star', or 'Tully' and 'Cicero', or 'Pegasus' and 'Medusa' (which both refer to the same class in that they refer to the null class: cf. 6.3), are not synonymous and do not satisfy Leibniz's principle of substitutability? If x and y are two expressions which refer to the same entity, it is certainly not the case that either may be substituted for the

---

[8] The 'Bedeutung' *vs.* 'Bezeichnung' distinction is drawn differently by different authors. But Brekle (1972), for example, relates it very closely to Frege's distinction. So, too, do Coseriu & Geckeler (1974).

other, without affecting the truth-value of the proposition that is expressed, in sentences like 'He does not believe that x is y'.

As Russell pointed out in one of his later works (1940: 247), the thesis of extensionality "is sought to be maintained for several reasons. It is very convenient technically in mathematical logic, it is obviously true of the sort of statements that mathematicians want to make, it is essential to the maintenance of physicalism and behaviourism, not only as metaphysical systems, but even in the linguistic sense adopted by Carnap. None of these reasons, however, gives any ground for supposing the thesis to be true." We need not discuss the reasons given by Russell, Carnap, or other philosophers for believing that the thesis of extensionality holds within everyday discourse or, at least, can be made to hold by reinterpreting the statements of ordinary language in terms of some formal system (such as the propositional calculus or predicate calculus). The fact that the thesis of extensionality is philosophically controversial (and is nowadays even less widely accepted than it was when Russell was writing) gives us good grounds, in linguistic semantics, for not feeling obliged to accept it. And, if we do not accept it, we need not be concerned with many of the problems over which philosophers have agonized.

The distinction of reference and sense is not, however, bound to any single philosophical theory of meaning; and it holds independently of such logical considerations as extensionality and the preservation of truth under substitution. Even if it proved possible to eliminate the distinction of reference and sense, for reasons of technical convenience, in the formalization of the logical structure of the propositions expressed by sentences, the distinction is crucial once we take into account the utterance of sentences in actual contexts. It is validated in linguistic semantics by the fact that, on the one hand, what we take, pre-theoretically, to be non-synonymous expressions (like 'my father' and 'that man over there') can be used to refer to the same individual and, on the other hand, the same pre-theoretically non-ambiguous expression (like 'my father' or 'that man over there') may be employed to refer to distinct individuals. It is up to the theoretical semanticist to explicate these pre-theoretical intuitions and to do so, if he can, in a way that facilitates the analysis of meaning in the everyday use of language.

Many of the classic examples used by philosophers to illustrate the distinction of sense and reference are similar to 'The Morning Star is the Evening Star' in that they have to do with the identity or non-identity of individuals referred to by expressions on either side of the verb 'to be' in equative* sentences (cf. 7.2). But most declarative sentences in English do not have the same grammatical structure as 'The Morning Star is the Evening Star'.

The statement that John is a fool, which might be made by uttering the sentence

(4) John is a fool,

is non-equative. We are not saying of two possibly distinct individuals that they are in fact identical: we are ascribing to some person called John the property or attribute of folly: or, alternatively, we are saying that he is a member of the class of fools. (We have just used the term 'non-equative', it will be noted, with respect to utterances; and this is a more basic usage than its employment by linguists in relation to a class of sentences. Sentences of a certain kind are called equative (or non-equative) because they are characteristically employed in making equative (or non-equative) utterances.) In (4) 'John' is a referring expression, but '(be) a fool' has a purely predicative function. We may now think of these expressions as having two distinct kinds of meaning. Instead of 'John' we can employ any other expression, simple or complex (a name, a pronoun or a descriptive noun-phrase): provided that it serves to identify the same individual as 'John' does in the particular context of utterance, the descriptive meaning of the statement (including the proposition that is expressed) will be unaffected. And if we substitute for 'be a fool' some other expression which has the same sense (if there is one in the language), the descriptive meaning of the statement, once again, will be unaffected. To put it in a nutshell: the criterion for substitutability in subject position in this construction is referential identity; the criterion for substitutability in predicate position is identity of sense.

Attempts have been made by many philosophers to apply the Leibnizian principle of substitutability without change of truth-value to define both reference and sense. Two expressions would have the same reference, under this application of the principle, if they could be substituted one for the other in the subject position of all sentences without affecting the truth value of any of the statements that could be made by uttering any of the sentences (i.e. without changing the truth-conditions of the sentences: cf. 6.5); and they would have the same sense, if the substitution could be carried out in the predicate position (of non-equative sentences) without changing the truth-conditions. It is now generally recognized that, as far as statements made in everyday discourse are concerned, such attempts are doomed to failure. They break down, not only in the case of belief-statements and other such intensional statements, but also in the case of any statement in which the sense and reference of expressions in the sentences used to make these statements are in part determined by the particular context of utterance; and such statements constitute the majority of the statements that are actually made in the everyday use of language.

Our criterion for sameness and difference of sense will be made more directly dependent upon the descriptive meaning of utterances; two or more expressions will be defined to have the same sense (i.e. to be synonymous*) over a certain range of utterances if and only if they are substitutable in the utterances without affecting their descriptive meaning. If the utterances are such that they have a determinate truth-value, constancy of descriptive meaning will guarantee constancy of truth-value. The converse, however, does not hold; for the substitution of one expression for another may change the descriptive meaning of a statement without thereby altering the truth-value. Let us grant for the sake of the argument that John is both a fool and a linguist. If we substitute 'linguist' for 'fool' in (4), we obtain

(5) John is a linguist.

Now (4) and (5) – or, to be more precise, the propositions expressed in statements made by uttering these sentences – have the same truth-value. But they do not have the same descriptive meaning.

How do we know that they differ in descriptive meaning? Where the difference is as gross as this, our intuitive, or pre-theoretical, response to the question "Does (5) mean the same as (4)?" is reliable enough; and it should not be forgotten that part of what we are doing in descriptive semantics is explicating such intuitive judgements. But we cannot let the matter rest there. How can we test the validity of our intuitive judgement that (4) and (5) differ in descriptive meaning? That is the theoretically interesting question.

Two statements will be descriptively equivalent (i.e. have the same descriptive meaning) if there is nothing that is entailed* by the one that is not entailed by the other (cf. 6.5). A more recognizably philosophical way of making the point is Quine's "sentences are synonymous if and only if their biconditional (formed by joining them with 'if and only if') is analytic" (1960: 65). This formulation (though it uses the term 'sentence' rather than 'utterance' or 'statement') brings out, as it is intended to do, the interdefinability of 'synonymous' and 'analytic'.

We now meet another problem. Quine himself, in a famous article (1951), challenged the notion of analyticity as one of the "dogmas of empiricism" (without thereby intending to cast any doubts upon empiricism as such). His point was that no sharp distinction could be drawn between logical and factual truth: that we should not look for "a sweeping epistemological dichotomy between analytic truths as by-products of language and synthetic truths as reports on the world". According to Quine, what we should expect to find instead is a continuous gradation between those things that we hold to be true which occupy a more central position in our conceptual scheme and in our patterns of argument and those things that we hold to be true which occupy a less central, or peripheral, position. We are more willing to make adjustments or alterations on the periphery than we are at the centre. Among the truths which occupy a very central position in our conceptual framework are mathematical propositions, such as "$2+2 = 4$", and logical principles, such as the law of the excluded middle. Such truths have frequently been regarded by philosophers as analytic and as known to be true a priori (i.e. prior to, or independently of, experience). But Quine would seem to hold that even the most central truths such as these are in principle subject to revision in the light of experience and our interpretation of experience in terms of some new conceptual framework. After all, what is generally reckoned as scientific progress has frequently led to the abandonment of propositions which were once held to be of universal validity.

There can be little doubt that, as Quine said, no hard and fast line can be drawn between analytic and synthetic truths in everyday discussion and argument. Carnap (1952) pointed out that analyticity could be guaranteed within the framework of some particular logical system (provided that it contains, or has added to it, the requisite rules of inference) by means of what he called meaning postulates*. For example, given the meaning postulate

$(x) (Bx \rightarrow \sim Mx),$

which may be read as "No x that is a bachelor is married", we can infer

$Ba \rightarrow \sim Ma:$

("If Alfred is a bachelor, then he is not married"). Of course this does not solve the descriptive problem of deciding whether $(x) (Bx \rightarrow \sim Mx)$ should be incorporated in the system in the first place; and Carnap, at the time that he made this suggestion, was not concerned with the problems of descriptive semantics. He wanted to explicate the notion of analyticity for pure semantic systems. The important point to notice is that a meaning-postulate like $(x)\,(Bx \rightarrow\, \sim Mx)$ is of itself sufficient to establish a relation of sense between the predicate B and M and is not logically dependent upon some prior or alternative specification of what each of them means. To make the point in relation to the English words 'bachelor' and 'married': it is in principle possible to know that they are related in this way (and the meaning-postulate makes precise the nature of their relationship) without knowing anything else about their meaning. That 'bachelor' should be semantically related in this way to 'married' is part of its sense; and it is part of the sense of 'married' that it should be related in a certain way to 'bachelor'. By analysing or describing the sense of a word is to be understood its analysis in terms of the sense-relations* which it contracts with other words; and each such sense-relation can be explicated by means of what Carnap called meaning-postulates.

It has already been pointed out that, although Carnap was at first concerned solely with the syntactic and semantic structure of logical calculi, he later took the view that his work could be profitably extended to the description of natural languages also; and he came to agree with Morris that the notion of meaning-postulates was necessarily a pragmatic* notion, since it depended upon a decision as to what implications and equivalences are acceptable to users of the semiotic system that is being constructed or analysed (cf. 4.4). If this is so, it should be possible for the linguist to adopt a philosophically neutral position on the epistemological distinction of analytic and synthetic truth. He can define the sense of expressions in natural language in terms of what we will call pragmatic implication*. What is meant by pragmatic implication may be explained, in sufficient detail for our present purpose, as follows: given that U_i and U_j are both statements, an utterance U_i, pragmatically implies an utterance, U_j, if the production of U_i would normally be taken to commit the speaker not only to the truth of the proposition expressed in U_i, but also to the truth of the proposition expressed in U_j. The word 'normally' is here intended to cover certain conditions which make it reasonable for us to assume or presuppose sincerity and communicative success; i.e. that the speaker not only says what he says, but both means what he says and says what he means (cf. 16.1).

It should also be noted that the notion of truth involved here is a pragmatic concept: it is defined in terms of the speaker's belief that something is so, not in terms of either matters of fact or logical necessity. Pragmatic truth need not be either invariable or determinate: speakers of a language can change their beliefs or be uncertain, to a greater or less degree, about the semantic relationship that holds between particular words. For example, we might be uncertain as to whether a bachelor is a man (of marriageable age) who is not married or one who has never been married; and we might be uncertain as to what counts as the age from which men (or boys), other than by legal definition in different states and countries, become marriageable. Nor is it difficult to envisage circumstances in which we might be quite prepared to abandon our belief that all men must be either bachelors or married, if we have previously more or less consciously subscribed to this belief. Is a monk appropriately described as a bachelor? Is a man who lives with a woman who is not his legal wife, has children by her and supports her and the children also to be described as a bachelor? The answers to these questions might be clear enough in legal usage, since marriage is a social institution which is regulated by law and words like 'married' and 'bachelor' may be explicitly defined in law in relation to various circumstances. But it does not follow that they are so clearly defined in everyday discourse.

Different speakers may hold partly different beliefs about the meaning and applicability of words, so that the set of implications that one speaker will accept as following from a given utterance may differ, to a greater or less degree, from the set of implications that another speaker will accept as following from the same utterance. But there will commonly be a considerable overlap in these two sets; and the descriptive semanticist may generally limit himself to specifying the intersection of these sets of implications without being disturbed unduly about the indeterminate instances. Our description of language need not, and should not, be any more determinate in this respect than the language-system of which it is a model (cf. 1.6).

It should be observed that we have here formulated the notion of pragmatic implication in terms of utterances, not sentences. We can subsequently define it for sentences, if we so wish, on the assumption that the referring expressions that occur in sentences have their reference fixed in relation to some possible world and on the further assumption that the sentences are being used to make utterances of various kinds. For the present, however, it is sufficient to have introduced the notion of sense and to have given a general account of the way in which it may be defined in terms of pragmatic implication.

The notion of sense presented in this section is somewhat narrower than that which is defined or assumed in most philosophical semantics. Sense is here defined to hold between the words or expressions of a single language independently of the relationship, if any, which holds between those words or expressions and their referents* or denotata* (7.4). "What is the sense of such-and-such a word or expression?" is, therefore, a more limited question than "What is the meaning of such-and-such a word or expression?" The way in which sense, reference and denotation are interrelated will be discussed in the remaining sections of this chapter. But here it should be noted that both single vocabulary words (more precisely, lexemes*: 1.5) and expressions are said to have sense (and denotation), whereas only expressions (and a subset of them at that) have reference. The sense of an expression (e.g. 'that embittered old bachelor') is a function of the senses of its component lexemes and of their occurrence in a particular grammatical construction.

It may also be added, at this point, that, although the sense, and in the previous section the reference, of expressions has been discussed solely in relation to their occurrence in utterances used to make statements, it does not follow that the notions of sense and reference are applicable only with respect to such utterances. The sense of 'that book over there' is the same both in the question *Have you read that book over there?* and in the request or command *Bring me that book over there* as it is in the statement *I have read that book over there*. Whether the reference is the same or not will of course depend upon the particular context of utterance.

7.4. *Denotation*

It has already been pointed out that the term 'denotation' is employed by many authors for what we are calling reference; conversely, 'reference' has frequently been used (e.g. in Lyons, 1968) for what we will in this section distinguish as denotation. Part of the reason for this terminological confusion, as Geach has emphasized, is the failure of many authors to distinguish clearly "between the relations of a name to the thing named and of a predicate to what it is true of" (1962: 6). It might be argued that what Geach calls "a sad tale of confusion" has already gone too far and that, as he proposes, "so battered and defaced a coin" as 'denotation' should be "withdrawn from philosophical currency" (1962: 55). But it seems to be impossible to find an alternative which is not equally battered or defaced. The usage that we adopt

here is close to, if not absolutely identical with, that of such writers as
Lewis (1943; cf. Carnap, 1956: 45), Quine (1960: 90n), Martin (1958)
and Alston (1964; cf. Lehrer & Lehrer, 1970: 25). It should be clearly
understood, however, that the treatment of denotation given here is
intended to be philosophically neutral. No more should be read into the
term 'denotation' than it is definitely said to imply. There are, in any
case, many important differences in the ways in which 'denotation' is
defined by the various authors referred to above.

By the denotation* of a lexeme (and in the first instance we will discuss the notion of denotation in relation to lexemes) will be meant the
relationship that holds between that lexeme and persons, things, places,
properties, processes and activities external to the language-system. We
will use the term denotatum* for the class of objects, properties, etc., to
which the expression correctly applies; and, for grammatical convenience, we will construe 'denotatum' indifferently as a mass noun,
a collective noun, or a countable noun as the occasion demands. For
example, we will say that the denotatum of 'cow' is a particular class
of animals, and also that the individual animals are its 'denotata'; that
the denotatum of 'red' is a particular property (viz. the colour red),
and that its denotata are red objects or, using the plural of 'denotatum'
now quite differently, various subdivisions of the property (viz. various
shades of red). There are all sorts of important logical and philosophical
distinctions lurking behind this liberal and grammatically convenient
use of the singular and plural of 'denotatum'. The status of the relationship between denotation and reference, on the one hand, and denotation
and sense, on the other, is not, however, affected by our failure to draw
these distinctions; and we could not do so without philosophical commitment, except at the cost of introducing a further set of technical
terms.

There is just one such philosophical distinction that may be singled
out for explicit mention at this point; and this is the distinction between
the intension and extension of an expression (which was introduced in
an earlier section: cf. 6.4). Many philosophers would say, like Carnap,
(1956: 233) that the extension of 'red' is the class of all red objects and
that its intension is the property of being red. The relationship between
classes and properties (and the possibility of defining one in terms of the
other) is, as we have seen, controversial (6.4). Carnap regards his distinction of extension and intension as one among a number of possible
interpretations of Frege's distinction of reference and sense. Our use
of 'denotation', it must be emphasized, is neutral as between extension

and intension. We will normally say, for example, that 'dog' denotes the class of dogs (or perhaps some typical member, or exemplar, of the class), but that 'canine' denotes the property, if there is such a property, the possession of which is a condition of the correct application of the expression. This use of 'denotation' to cover both extension and intension allows for the adoption of a neutral position on the question whether the predicate calculus and class logic are equally appropriate for the formalization of descriptive semantics. It is compatible with, though it neither implies nor depends upon, the view that there is a fundamental semantic difference between typical adjectives like 'red' and typical common nouns like 'cow' (cf. Strawson, 1959: 168).

How does denotation differ from reference? In the previous section, it was stressed that reference is an utterance-bound relation and does not hold of lexemes as such, but of expressions in context. Denotation, on the other hand, like sense, is a relation that applies in the first instance to lexemes and holds independently of particular occasions of utterance. Consider, for example, a word like 'cow' in English. Phrases like 'the cow', 'John's cow', or 'those three cows over there' may be used to refer to individuals, whether singly or in groups, but the word 'cow' alone cannot. Furthermore, as we have already seen, the reference of expressions like 'the cow' is context-dependent. Now the reference of phrases which contain 'cow' is determined, in part, by the denotation of 'cow'. For example, the phrase 'this cow' may, in certain circumstances, be understood by the hearer to mean "the object near us which belongs to the class of objects which the lexeme 'cow' denotes". How the hearer knows that the word 'cow' denotes, or is applicable to, a particular class of objects is a separate issue; there may or may not be some unique and determinate intensional definition, of which, as a speaker of English, he is intuitively aware. We will come back to this. The point to be stressed here is that in English common nouns like 'cow' are not normally used as referring expressions; and this is true for most other lexemes in the vocabulary of English. If they have denotation, their denotation will determine their reference when they are employed in referring expressions. But they do not have reference as lexemes (i.e. as vocabulary-items: 1.5).

To say that there is a distinction between denotation and reference does not imply that they are unconnected. Whatever may be referred to in a given language is generally within the denotation of at least one, and usually several, lexemes in that language. (For example, cows may be referred to in a variety of ways; and the various classes to which they belong are denoted, not only by 'cow', but also by 'animal', 'mammal', etc.) Many would claim that whatever may be referred to in one language may be referred to in any other language; and even that it will be denoted by one or more lexemes in all languages, though in some instances perhaps only at the most general level of the vocabulary. However that may be, it is clear that reference and denotation both depend in the same way upon what has been called the axiom of existence: whatever is denoted by a lexeme must exist, just as "whatever is referred to must exist" (Searle, 1969: 77). It also seems evident that denotation and reference are closely connected in the acquisition of language. We will take up this point in the next section.

How is the denotation of a lexeme to be specified by the descriptive linguist? The short, practical answer is: in any way that is likely to be successful. Consider, for example, the following specification of the denotation of 'walrus', which is cast in the form of a typical dictionary definition: "either of two species (Odolenus rosmarus and Odolenus divergens) of large, seal-like Arctic mammals, with flippers and long tusks". Anyone reading this definition, who knows the meaning of the other words in it, would probably acquire as good an understanding of the denotation of 'walrus' as most other speakers of English; and he might therefore use the word in referring and predicative expressions, and otherwise, in such a way that we should be justified in saying that he knew its meaning. Consider, however, a similar dictionary definition of 'cow': "a mature female bovine animal (of the genus Bos)". Unless the user of the dictionary happened to be a foreign zoologist who knew the meaning of 'bovine', but not 'cow', he would probably not be very much helped by such an attempt to explain to him the denotation of 'cow'. We should be better off trying to teach the denotation of 'cow' to most non-English speakers by means of some denotational equivalent in their own language (if there is one) or by confronting them with a few specimens (or pictures of them) and perhaps drawing their attention to one or two salient features (the horns, the udders, etc.). The point being made is simply this: there may be no single correct way, in practical terms, of specifying the denotation of a lexeme.

Nor is it clear, in the present state of theoretical semantics, that there is in principle any way of handling denotation in a uniform manner. We could of course adopt the positivist approach favoured by Bloomfield and others (cf. 5.3). But this would be to introduce unnecessary and irrelevant criteria into semantics. For if there is one thing that does seem to be clear in this whole area, it is this: the denotation of lexemes is not generally determined by what Bloomfield called a "scientifically accurate" description of the denotata (1935: 139). Nor indeed is the denotation of most lexemes determined solely, or even principally, by the physical properties of their denotata. Much more important seems to be the role or function of the objects, properties, activities, processes and events in the life and culture of the society using the language. Until we have a satisfactory theory of culture, in the construction of which not only sociology, but also both cognitive and social psychology, have played their part, it is idle to speculate further about the possibility of constructing anything more than a rather ad hoc practical account of the denotation of lexemes.[9]

We have dealt with the relationship between denotation and reference, as far as we need to at present. Something should now be said about the distinction of denotation and sense. It is obvious enough that the relationship between two lexemes, like 'cow' and 'animal', is to be distinguished from the relationship that either of these lexemes bears to the class of objects which it denotes: the relationship between a linguistic entity and something outside the language-system. The question is whether one of these two kinds of relationship is derivable from the other and theoretically dispensable. As we have seen, attempts have often been made to relate sense and denotation on the basis of the traditional notion of signification* or some modern (e.g., behaviourist) version of it (4.1). But there are serious objections to making either sense or denotation basic in terms of the traditional triangle of signification.

If we assume that the relationship of denotation is logically and psychologically basic (so that, for example, we know that 'cow' and 'animal' are related in sense in a certain way because of our prior knowledge that the denotatum of 'cow' is properly included in the denotatum of 'animal') we have to face the problem of how we can know the sense of words, such as 'unicorn', which have no denotation. The fact that 'There is no such animal as a unicorn' is a perfectly normal and comprehensible sentence of English (which may be used to make what is probably a true statement), whereas 'There is no such book as a unicorn' is semantically odd, depends upon the fact that 'unicorn' and 'animal' (like 'cow' and 'animal') are related in sense, in a certain way, whereas 'unicorn' and 'book' are not; and speakers

[9] And this is what I take to be the import of Putnam's (1975) notion of stereotypes or Rosch's (1973a, b) notion of natural categories, which can be related to the traditional notion of natural kinds.

of English are aware of these sense-relations. Of course, it can be argued that, although 'unicorn' has no primary denotation, it has what might be called a secondary denotation (cf. Goodman, 1952). We can draw a picture and, pointing to the picture, say *This is a unicorn*; and speakers of English may agree or disagree that what we have said is true, as they may agree or disagree about an alleged picture of a cow. But their ability to recognize our picture of a mythical animal (if it is not directly dependent upon their having seen pictures of unicorns before) rests upon their understanding of the sense of 'unicorn', and in particular upon their knowledge of its relations with such words as 'horse', 'horn', etc., and their ability to identify the denotata of these words. It is because we know the sense of 'unicorn', that we know what kind of object it would apply to, if there were anything in the world for it to apply to.

This point holds more generally, it should be noted, and not just of words that lack denotation. To return to the definition of 'walrus' given above: we interpreted this as a definition of the denotation of walrus. But in order to apply it, we need to know the sense of many of the component lexemes in the definition; and we can learn the sense of 'walrus' (its relationship with such words as 'seal' and 'mammal') without knowing whether it has a denotation or not. Sense, then, in some cases at least is epistemologically prior to denotation.

We might therefore consider the alternative method of reduction: that of taking sense to be basic in all instances and treating denotation as a derivative relation. But there are problems here too. We first learn the use of many words in relation to the persons and objects around us; and we learn the denotation of some of these words, it seems clear, before we can relate them in sense to other words in the vocabulary. It appears to be no more correct to say that denotation is wholly dependent upon sense than it is to say that sense is wholly dependent upon denotation.

Not everyone will agree with what has been said here about the necessity of taking sense and denotation to be interdependent, but equally basic, relations. Should it prove possible, within some philosophical theory of meaning, to derive the one satisfactorily from the other or both from some more basic notion, it is at least terminologically convenient for the linguist to distinguish these two aspects of the meaning of lexemes. He can use the two terms to avoid commitment on the philosophical and psychological issues involved in the controversy between nominalism and realism (4.3).

8   LSE

One further point should be made in connexion with words which lack or may lack denotation. Much of the philosophical discussion of this question has been directed towards the analysis of the meaning of such words as 'unicorn'. The fact that 'unicorn', etc., have no extension in the actual world can be treated as irrelevant within any theory of semantics which allows for the relativization of truth and denotation to possible worlds (cf. 6.5). But it is perhaps more instructive to consider a word like 'intelligent' (or 'honest', or 'beautiful'). Does 'intelligent' denote some real property or attribute of persons (and perhaps animals or even machines) as, we may assume, 'red-haired' does? Is it not possible that the word 'intelligent' is used by speakers of English in a variety of circumstances, among which we can perhaps discern certain family resemblances (cf. Wittgenstein, 1953; Waismann, 1965: 179ff), but which have no common defining property? It is certainly the case that there are languages in which there is no satisfactory translation equivalent to the English 'intelligent'. In Plato's Greek, for example, the nearest equivalents are 'sophos' and 'eumathēs'; but the former is much wider, and the latter somewhat narrower, in application (cf. Lyons, 1963).[10] Then there are adjectives such as 'dangerous', which, regardless of whether it is readily translatable into all languages or not, can hardly be said to denote an inherent property of the objects or situations to which it is applied. The linguist, whether he is working as a theoretical or descriptive semanticist, need not be concerned to answer the question whether 'intelligent' (and a host of other lexemes) denote some identifiable property or not. But he must appreciate that there are problems involved in assuming that they do.

It would be no less of a mistake to say that no lexemes have denotation, or that denotation is irrelevant in linguistic semantics, than it is to say that all lexemes must have denotation. But denotation is just one part of a wider and more complex relationship which holds between language and the world (or between language and the set of possible worlds: cf. 6.5). We live in the world and are ourselves part of it; and we use language, not only to describe the persons, things and situations in the physical world and the world of social activity with which we interact in our daily life, but also to control and adjust to these persons,

---

[10] It may be that in other authors of the period 'sunetos' is the nearest equivalent to 'intelligent'. But 'sunetos' is very rarely used in Plato; and in contexts in which we would readily use 'intelligent', 'clever' or 'bright', the Greek words 'eumathēs' or 'sophos' tend to be employed. In saying this, I am of course making certain assumptions about the cross-cultural identification of contexts (cf. Lyons, 1963).

things and situations in a variety of ways. The descriptive function of language, important though it is, is not the sole function of language, or even the most basic (cf. 2.4). If we use the term applicability* for the admittedly rather ill-defined wider relationship that holds between language and the external world we can say that a particular lexeme (or expression, or whole utterance) is applicable* (i.e. may be correctly applied) in a certain context, situational or linguistic (cf. 14.1); and that it is applicable to individuals or properties of individuals. We may use the term 'applicability', in fact, for any relation that can be established between elements or units of language (including the prosodic* and paralinguistic* features of utterances) and entities in, or aspects of, the world in which the language operates. If we consider the applicability of a lexeme with respect to the question whether it is true of the entity to which it is applied, we are concerned with its denotation. (If we consider the applicability of an expression with respect to the question whether it is intended to identify some entity or group of entities about which something is being said, or some question is being asked, etc., on some particular occasion, we are concerned with its reference.) But words may be correctly and incorrectly applied to persons and things, and other features of the external world, for all sorts of reasons, some of which have nothing to do with their denotation.

So far we have discussed denotation solely with respect to lexemes. But the notion is also clearly relevant to certain expressions which may be substituted for single lexemes in sentences and may be denotationally equivalent to, or denotationally narrower or wider than, the lexemes for which they are substituted. For example, 'dark red' is denotationally narrower than 'red', as 'red book' is narrower in denotation than either 'red' or 'book'. 'Featherless biped' and 'rational animal' (to use a traditional example) are perhaps denotationally equivalent, and each of them is perhaps denotationally equivalent to 'human being' (or 'man' in its wider sense). 'Deciduous tree' is denotationally wider than 'oak', 'beech' or 'sycamore'. The denotation of expressions such as these can generally be accounted for in terms of the logical conjunction or disjunction of the denotations of their constituent lexemes and formalized in terms of the logic of classes (cf. 6.4). We will not go further into this topic here.

It was pointed out at the beginning of this section that the term 'denotation' has been used in various ways in the literature. We have employed it with respect to lexemes and expressions considered independently of their function in sentences or utterances. The question that now arises is whether it can be consistently and usefully extended to both predicative and referring expressions. As far as predicative expressions are concerned, this extension would seem to be straightforward. For denotation and predication are closely related notions. When we ascribe a property to an individual (or group of individuals), we do so in the simplest cases by predicating of the individual (or group) a lexeme or expression denoting the property in question. For example, when we utter the sentence 'The man drinking a martini is a crook' to make an assertion about a particular individual we are predicating of him the lexeme 'crook'; and we can just as reasonably ask what is the denotation of the expression '(be) a crook' as we can what does 'crook' denote. The answer in both cases is the same; or, if we prefer to put it this way, the denotation of '(be) a crook' is the intension of the class whose extension is the denotatum of 'crook'. Subject to the existence of the correlated property or class (under some appropriate interpretation of 'existence'), complex predicative expressions like '(be) the first man to climb Mount Everest' or 'break the bank at Monte Carlo' can also be said to have a denotation.

It is less clear that referring expressions have denotation in the sense in which we are using the term 'denotation'. Proper names, when they are employed as referring expressions, identify their referents, not by describing them in terms of some relevant property or properties which the name denotes, but by utilizing the unique and arbitrary association which holds between a name and its bearer. We could say that the denotatum of a name is the class of individuals to which the name is correctly applied. We could also say that to be called such-and-such is to have a certain property just as being of a certain size, shape, etc., or having been involved in certain processes, actions, states-of-affairs, etc., is to have a certain property (in the rather liberal sense of the term 'property' with which we are at present operating). This would enable us to account naturally for the parallelism between 'There are twelve chairs in this room' and 'There are twelve Horaces in this room'. But this would tend to obscure important differences between denotation and other kinds of applicability: a name is not true of its bearer (cf. Geach, 1962: 6). We return to this question in the next section.

Personal and demonstrative pronouns, like proper names, are used as referring expressions; they differ from proper names (and expressions like 'the Morning Star' and many titles) in that their reference, as we have seen, is more obviously utterance-dependent. But it would be rather odd to talk of the denotation of 'he' or the pronoun 'this' (and still more so of 'I' or 'you') in English as something distinct from their reference, since the conditions of correct application would be referential conditions. The class of individuals to which 'he' may be correctly applied is the class of individuals that may be referred to (whether deictically* or anaphorically: cf. 15.3) by means of 'he'; and 'he' is not true of these individuals.

The third main class of referring expressions is that of descriptive noun-phrases; and philosophers have often said that referring expressions of this kind have (or, subject to the axiom of existence, may have) a denotation. For Russell, a definite descripton was said to denote an individual if that individual fitted the description uniquely. Donnellan (1966) adopts Russell's definition of denotation (without however accepting the condition of uniqueness) and uses it to draw a distinction that Russell did not draw between reference and denotation. Donnellan maintains that an expression may be used successfully to refer to an individual even though there is no individual that fits the description, and conversely that an individual may fit a definite description and be denoted, though not necessarily referred to, by it. In standard cases, however, an expression like 'the man drinking a martini', if it is used to refer, will refer to the individual (or one of the individuals) that it denotes. Granted that the principal points made by Donnellan in terms of his distinction of reference and denotation are valid, the question remains whether the definite noun-phrase, as such, can be said to have a denotation. It seems preferable, on our interpretation of denotation, to say that it is the complex predicative expression '(be) a man drinking a martini' which has denotation (and that its denotation is a function of the denotation of the expressions '(be) a man' and '(be) drinking a martini'); and that the use of the definite noun-phrase to refer to an individual implies or presupposes that the complex predicative expression is true of the individual in question. We can choose to define 'denotation' in the one way or the other. But, if we decide to use the term as we have been doing throughout this section, we cannot consistently apply it to referring expressions. It goes without saying, however, that many philosophers, if they use the term 'denotation' at all, would probably prefer to link it more closely to 'reference'.

7.5. *Naming*

As far back as we can trace the history of linguistic speculation, the basic semantic function of words has been seen as that of naming. The story of Adam naming the animals, so that "whatsoever the man called every living creature, that was the name thereof" (Genesis 2.19), is typical of a conception of meaning that is to be found in many other sacred or mythological accounts of the origin of language. St Augustine's discussion of the acquisition of language by children, in his *Confessions*, is based on the same notion, and is quoted and criticized by Wittgenstein (1953: 1): adults point to things in the child's environment and thus direct his attention to them; simultaneously they name these things by means of the words which denote them in the child's native language; and the child comes to learn the association that holds between words and things, so that he can subsequently use those words to name things himself.

This view of meaning, which Ryle (1957) in a characteristic turn of phrase christened the 'Fido'-Fido view, has persisted throughout the centuries and, although it has come in for a good deal of criticism recently from Wittgenstein, Ryle, Austin, and other philosophers of ordinary language, it is still to be found, unquestioned, in very many works on semantics. It will be clear from our discussion of denotation in the previous section that the relation which holds between a proper name and its bearer is very different from the relation which holds between a common noun and its denotata: at least in such clear cases as 'Fido': Fido, on the one hand, and 'dog': {Fido, Bingo, Tripod, Towzer, etc.}, on the other. This is not to say that there are no unclear cases; nor that there is no connexion between naming and denotation as far as the acquisition of language is concerned. If there were no such connexion it would indeed be surprising that generations of subtle thinkers should have fallen victim to the alleged error of confusing the two, and even more surprising that ordinary folk should find it natural to talk of words as names for things. The philosophical semanticist will obviously try to make do with the minimum number of theoretical notions and is occupationally prone to what Ryle elsewhere calls category-errors (1949: 17). The ordinary speaker of English, reflecting and reporting upon his language, is not similarly bound by the dictates of theoretical or ontological parsimony. We will consider the relationship between naming and denoting in the next section. But first of all we must briefly discuss one or two important features of names and the role they play in language.

Names, as they are employed in everyday language-behaviour, have two characteristic functions: referential and vocative. Their referential function has been discussed sufficiently for the present. It is worth pointing out here, however, that names are frequently used simply to draw the hearer's attention to the presence of the person being named or to remind the hearer of the existence or relevance of the person being named. The utterance of the name may be given some paralinguistic modulation sufficient to distinguish it as a warning, a reminder, an exclamation of astonishment, etc. But there need be no precise or explicit predication. It is surely not just fanciful to think that it is this function, which one might call quasi-referential* rather than fully referential, that serves as the basis for the further development of true reference in language.

By the vocative* function of names is meant their being used to attract the attention of the person being called or summoned. Once again, this function appears to be basic in the sense that it is not reducible to any other semiotic function, though the vocative, like the quasi-referential, utterance of a name may be paralinguistically modulated to give additional, mainly indexical, information. The distinction between the referential and the vocative function of names (and perhaps more commonly of titles) is systematized in many languages as a distinction between what are called terms of reference and terms of address; and the same distinction was grammaticalized in the case-systems of the classical Indo-European languages. The use of a common noun with vocative function (e.g., the use of 'child' in *Come here, child!*), whether it is distinguished as such by its form or not, approximates, it may be observed in passing, to the use of a proper name or a title.

It is important to distinguish clearly between the referential or vocative use of names and their assignment to their bearers in what we will call appellative* utterances (e.g., *This is John, He is called John Smith*). The term 'naming' is frequently unclear in respect of this distinction. We will therefore introduce the technical term nomination* for the second of the two senses of 'naming': by saying that X nominates some person as John we shall mean that X assigns the name 'John' to that person. But 'assignment' is also ambiguous as between didactic* and performative* nomination. By didactic nomination we mean teaching someone, whether formally or informally, that a particular name is associated by an already existing convention with a particular person, object or place. The role of didactic nomination in language-acquisition is something we shall be discussing presently. It should be noticed that didactic nomination not only operates in the acquisition of language, but is a continuing and important semiotic function of language. When we introduce ourselves or others by name (*This is*

John, My name is 'Harry'), we are carrying out an act of nomination; and normally it is one of didactic nomination.

Performative nomination may be exemplified by means of one of Austin's (1958) original illustrations of his notions of performative utterances: "When I say *I name this ship the Queen Elizabeth* I do not describe the christening ceremony, I actually perform the ceremony". The class of performative utterances includes many other kinds of utterances other than nominative, and we will return to it later (cf. 16.1). At this point, however, it should be noted that performative nomination may take various forms and includes not only the assignment of personal names at baptism or some other formal ceremony, but also such semiotic acts as the definition of terms (where naming and denotation are often hard to distinguish), and so on. And each kind of performative nomination will be governed by certain conditions of appropriateness: one cannot assume the role of name-giver just when and how one pleases. This is clear enough in the case of such a highly-formalized instance as christening; but it is also true of the many other less formal, and perhaps less obvious, kinds of performative nomination (the assignment of nicknames at school or in the family, of names of endearment for the private use of lovers, and so on). Mention should also be made of the fact that in many cultures people have assigned to them a different name from that which they had previously when they pass from childhood to adulthood or when they assume a new role in society; and also of the fact that the use of names is frequently subject to taboos of various kinds. The name of a person is something that is held to be an essential part of him. Performative re-nomination may be an important part of what anthropologists have called the rites of passage (rites de passage).[11]

Of particular interest is the way in which many names appear to be created by the parents' interpretation of a child's utterance as a name being used by him in vocative or quasi-referential function and the reinforcement of this utterance as a name by the parents. Whether this phenomenon can support all the weight that is put upon it by the behaviourist semanticist is, as we have seen, doubtful (cf. 5.4). But it

---

[11] This notion of rites of passage originates with Van Gennep (1908). But it has been widely employed by anthropologists: cf. Gluckman (1962), Lévi-Strauss (1963), Turner (1969). (It has also been extended to cover the ritualization of the transitions between the various more or less distinguishable stages of an encounter: cf. Firth, 1972; Laver, 1975.) There is a tendency for philosophical treatments of proper names to underestimate the ritual, and even magical, significance of names in many cultures.

may be plausibly supposed to play some role in language-learning; and most families can probably testify, anecdotally at least, to its operation in the creation of some of the names used within the family. What is interesting from the present viewpoint is the fact that the child creates the name (though he may be imitating the form of some adult lexeme), but the parents by the interpretation they impose upon his utterance make of it an instance of performative nomination.

The linguistic status of names has long been a subject of controversy, not only amongst philosophers, but also amongst linguists (cf. Ullmann, 1962: 71–9). One of the questions that has been most hotly disputed is whether names have a sense. What is probably the most widely accepted philosophical view nowadays is that they may have reference, but not sense, and that they cannot be used predicatively purely as names; and this is also the view that we shall adopt. As we shall see (cf. 7.6), we allow for the possibility that in the learning of a language the distinction between names and common nouns may not be always clear-cut, so that there might be a time when 'chair', for example, is treated as a name which happens to be associated with several otherwise unrelated objects and, conversely, when all the people called 'Horace' are thought of as having one or more other properties by virtue of which the name 'Horace' is peculiarly appropriate. It is our assumption, however, that, apart from a relatively small number of borderline cases the distinction between names and common countable nouns in adult English is one that is readily drawn. Utterances like *There are twelve Horaces in this room* (understood as meaning "There are twelve people called Horace in this room") are to be accounted for, it is assumed, by means of a rule for using proper names which depends for its application upon the recognition that they are proper names; and rules like this may or may not be specific to particular languages. Such much discussed examples as 'He is no Cicero' or 'Edinburgh is the Athens of the north' are in this connexion irrelevant: 'Cicero' and 'Athens' are here being used predicatively, or, more precisely, within predicative expressions (in what was rather loosely classified in traditional grammar and rhetoric as one kind of synechdoche*). That names can, in a given culture or society, acquire more or less definite associations, such that the name can be said to symbolize* eloquence or architectural beauty, is an important fact; and it is this fact which accounts for the ease with which names can in the course of time become ordinary common nouns (e.g., the Italian word 'cicerone', which is now fairly well established in French, English and other languages, for "museum guide" (Ullmann, 1962: 78)).

But it does not invalidate the principle that names are without sense; and Jespersen's claim (1924: 66), in deliberate contradiction of Mill, that proper names (as actually used) "connote the greatest number of attributes" is misleading; for it trades upon an equivocation between the philosophical and the more popular sense of 'connotation' (cf. 7.1).

Using the term 'connotation' in the non-philosophical sense, as Jespersen appears to be doing, we can certainly agree that many proper names have quite specific connotations, or associations. The connotations which one person associates with a name may be different from the connotations which another person associates with the same name, even in cases where both persons would use the name to refer to or address the same individual (or set of individuals). When the bearer of the name is a historically, politically or culturally prominent place or person, the connotations of the name of this place or person may be relatively constant for members of a particular language-community sharing the same culture (cf. 'Cicero', 'Athens', 'Judas', 'Napoleon', 'Shakespeare', 'Mecca', etc.). And if they were asked to say what they knew, or believed, about the bearer of the name, they could be expected to provide a set of identifying descriptions: *Cicero was the greatest Roman orator, Cicero was the author of the Verrine orations, Cicero denounced Catiline in the Senate*, etc.

These identifying descriptions, or some disjunction of them, will provide names with what Searle (1958; 1969: 162ff) calls a descriptive backing*, such that the names in question (although they do not have sense) are "logically connected with characteristics of the objects to which they refer". The descriptive backing of a name may serve as the basis for the use of the name predicatively in such sentences as 'He is no Cicero' (where 'Cicero' symbolizes eloquence). The fact that names may have a descriptive backing also accounts for their use in certain kinds of existential statements (e.g., *Cicero never existed*) and equative statements (e.g., *Cicero was Tully* or *Cicero and Tully were one and the same person*). The sentence 'Cicero never existed', when used to make a statement, may be held to imply that (contrary to what the hearer may have supposed to be the case) there never existed any great Roman orator who was the author of the Verrine orations, and/or denounced Catiline in the Senate and/or, etc. The equative statement *Cicero was Tully* may be held to imply that the descriptive backing of both 'Cicero' and 'Tully' is true of the same individuals (cf. Searle, 1969: 171). There are considerable problems attaching to the formalization of this notion of the descriptive backing of names. In particular, it is unclear what should count as the essential characteristics of the individual to which a name refers. Nor is it obvious that all existential and identity statements can be satisfactorily analysed in this way. But there are many instances of the use of names in such statements for which an analysis in terms of their descriptive backing does seem to be appropriate.

The principle that names have no sense is not invalidated by the fact that performative nomination, whether formal or informal, may be determined by certain culturally prescribed conditions of semantic appropriateness. In some cultures there is a more or less well-defined set of institutionalized personal names ('John', 'Mary', etc.) which are assigned to children shortly after birth according to a variety of more or less strict criteria. Most English-speaking families will no doubt respect the convention that 'John' should not be assigned to girls or 'Mary' to boys (though there are some institutionalized names, e.g. 'Lesley', that they might assign happily to children of either sex): it is therefore possible to infer, with a very good chance of being right, from an utterance like *My friend John came to see me on Wednesday* that the friend who came to see me was male. But this fact of itself does not force us to say that 'John' and 'male' are semantically related in the way that 'man' or 'boy' and 'male' are. If a girl happened to be called 'John', we would have no hesitation in saying *John has just cut herself*. We might wonder why, in defiance of convention, she was given the name 'John' in the first instance; but that is a different matter. The sentence *John has just cut herself* is not only grammatically acceptable (under any reasonable explication of grammatical acceptability), but also, one might argue, semantically acceptable. Even if we admit that names such as 'John' or 'Mary' are part of the English language, as words like 'boy' or 'girl' are (and this is another controversial issue), we are by no means obliged to concede the point that they have sense.

Nor are we obliged to concede this point in the case of names which are not taken from a more or less fixed list of personal names as they are for the most part in English-speaking countries, but are taken from the ordinary vocabulary of a language and are assigned by virtue of the meaning of the expressions in question. If we trace the etymology of institutionalized names of persons and places in various languages (in that branch of semantics that is known as onomastics*), we will usually find that they had the same kind of origin. For example, 'John' comes, through Greek and Latin, from a Hebrew name, which could be interpreted in terms of the ordinary vocabulary of Hebrew as "God has been gracious". We will call this the etymological meaning* of the name; and it would seem to be appropriate to extend the coverage of this term to include the synchronically* motivated, as well as diachronically* discoverable, interpretation of names (for the distinction of synchronic and diachronic description, cf. 8.2). Very frequently, however, as the standard anthropological treatments of word-magic and taboo have shown, the symbolic meaning both of names and of other words is governed by conventions that are specific to a particular culture.

One question which has been much discussed in the literature is whether names belong to a particular language-system in the way that other words do. It has often been argued that names like 'John' or 'London' are not English words as 'man' or 'city' are and that the lexicographer should not be expected to list them in a dictionary. Ryle (1957), for example, says: "Dictionaries do not tell us what names mean – for the simple reason that they do not mean anything". Geach (1962: 27) maintains against this point of view that "it is part of the job of a lexicographer to tell us that 'Warsaw' is the English word for 'Warszawa'; and a grammarian would say that 'Warszawa' is a Polish word – a feminine noun declined like 'mowa' ". And he asks: "what is wrong with this way of speaking?" The answer is that there is nothing wrong with it, for a rather limited class of instances. But the situation with respect to the translation of proper names from one language into another is in general far more complicated than Geach's example would suggest.

As far as place names are concerned it is probably the case that, if there is a conventional translation equivalent, it will always be used. Where there is not, there can be complications. If I was translating from German into English would I put 'Danzig' or 'Gdansk' as the name of the now Polish town? It would surely depend upon what I was translating, my political sympathies, and so on. The translation of personal names is far more complex. Even when there exists a well-established translation equivalent, it is not always appropriate to use it. An Englishman named James will not normally be addressed or referred to in French as Jacques, but as James: the very Englishness of his name, as it were, is an essential part of it. As pronounced in French, however, it will probably be accommodated to the French phonological system and thus become, in that respect, a French word. And there is nothing to prevent monolingual English-speaking parents from calling their monolingual English-speaking son Jacques, rather than James. The point is that there is no clear theoretical answer to the question whether names "belong to the language in which they are embedded" (Geach, 1962: 27). For there is no single principle which determines their translation from one language into another. However, some institutionalized place names and personal names are so common in certain countries that one would expect all speakers of the language used in that country to recognize their status as names. If the question whether such names belong to the language and should be included in a dictionary is considered in purely practical terms it can be answered with Geach in the affirmative. But one would only list the well-known institutionalized names: it is, in any case, impossible to list all the names one might use when speaking English, since there is in principle no limit to this set.

There is one important difference between certain institutionalized place names and certain personal names that has not so far been mentioned. Very many institutionalized place names, when used as referring expressions by most speakers of a language, are unique in their reference, but personal names like 'James' are not. Furthermore, whereas 'James' and 'Jacques', subject to the reservations expressed in the previous paragraph, are translation equivalents, as 'London' and 'Londres' are, the conditions which determine their translation equivalence are quite different. 'Londres' will be used in French to translate 'London' only when it refers to the capital of Great Britain; and not when it refers to London, Ontario, or any of the other towns and cities that bear the name 'London'.

Enough has been said perhaps to show that the questions whether names belong to a language or not and whether they have a meaning or not do not admit of a simple and universally valid answer.[12] What has been emphasized in this section is the fact that some names at least can be said quite reasonably to have a symbolic, etymological or translational meaning. But they do not have sense, or some unique and special kind of meaning which distinguishes them as a class from common nouns. It has also been stressed that personal names may have a vocative as well as a referential or quasi-referential function in language-behaviour. There is no reason whatsoever to suppose that their vocative function is derived from, or in any way less basic than, their referential function.[13]

---

[12] For some discussion of the linguistic status of names: cf. Kuryłowicz (1960), Sørensen (1963).
[13] There are many contexts in which it is hard to separate the vocative from the referential function (e.g., in roll-calling); and there are others in which neither the vocative nor the referential function of names is involved.

7.6. *Reference, sense and denotation in language-acquisition*

In the previous sections of this chapter we have been at some pains to distinguish reference, sense, denotation and naming. We must now show how these different kinds, or aspects, of meaning are, or may be, interrelated in the acquisition of language.

There is a clear connexion in everyday English between the noun 'name' and the verb 'call'; and it is no coincidence that the verb 'call' can mean, not only "to name", but also "to address", "to summon" and "to assign a name to". First of all, it should be observed that names, as we have seen, are characteristically used to refer to or address individuals. We can say equally well *What is X called?* or *What is the name of X?* And there are occasions when the noun 'name' and the verb 'call' are employed in this way with respect to classes of individuals. If we come across an animal of unfamiliar species, we can ask *What is the name of this animal?* or *What is this animal called?* expecting to be given in reply, not the name of the individual animal (if it happens to have one), but the word which denotes all members of the species. It might be argued that our question, in either version of it, is ambiguous; and that we can eliminate the ambiguity by using the plural (substituting 'these animals' for 'this animal' and making the necessary grammatical changes: *What are these animals called?*). There is some force in this argument; but the point about ambiguity cannot be pressed too hard. For the lexeme which denotes the class can also be used to address an individual member of the class. We can say *Come here, dog* or *Come here, Fido.* One can of course insist that the former is to be analysed, semantically or logically, as "Come here, you who are a dog" and the latter as "Come here, you who are named Fido". The predicative function of the statement "It's a dog" must certainly be distinguished from the appellative function of the statement "It's Fido" in the analysis of English. It does not follow, however, that this distinction must be imposed upon vocative expressions. Nor does it follow that the distinction is clear from the start in the acquisition of language by children.

The distinction between names and common nouns like 'dog' or 'boy' is fairly clear in adult English when either is used referentially in the singular. The grammatical structure of English is such that any singular countable noun in a referring expression must be accompanied by a determiner*, quantifier* or syntactically equivalent form. One can say *The boy came yesterday* or *James came yesterday*, but not (as grammatically acceptable utterances) *Boy came yesterday* or *The James came* *yesterday*. In many other languages the grammatical distinction between proper names and common nouns with referential function is less sharp; and this is true also of the speech of very young English-speaking children. It is at least arguable, therefore, that the distinction between referring to an individual by name and referring to the same individual by means of a descriptive noun-phrase is something that the child only gradually acquires.

One might even argue the stronger claim that the distinction between naming and describing is never absolutely clear in vocative expressions; and that it would be unclear in the case of many referential expressions in English were it not for the fact that purely syntactic rules influence us to interpret countable nouns in the singular preceded by determiners or quantifiers as common nouns rather than proper names. Even so, there remain a number of borderline cases: is 'the sun' a proper name (like 'The Hague') or an expression containing a common noun? Once we use 'sun' in the plural (as in the sentence 'There may be other suns in the universe as well as our own') we may be inclined to say that it is a common noun. But a nominalist might argue that cases like this can still be analysed like sentences containing proper names in the plural ('There are other Peters in the room'). However, we are not concerned to defend a nominalist analysis of particular examples (and still less of all phrases containing common nouns), but merely to show that, although 'reference', 'denotation' and 'naming' need to be distinguished, they can coincide. And they may do so typically in the conditions in which children acquire their native language. The nominalist's account of the acquisition of reference and denotation deserves the most serious consideration (cf. Quine, 1960).

Before we proceed, it must be emphasized that, as far as the subject we are discussing is concerned, there is no necessary connexion between nominalism and empiricism, still less between nominalism and behaviourism. The way in which the child comes to re-identify individuals and group them into classes, might very well depend upon an innate faculty or mechanism, not only for classification, but for classification according to certain universal principles which have their reflexion in language. Even the behaviourist will admit the necessity of postulating some innate mechanisms (cf. Quine, 1969); what is psychologically and philosophically controversial is the nature of these mechanisms. The linguist should not feel obliged to commit himself on such issues.

Quine (1960: 80–124) distinguishes four phases in what he calls the ontogenesis of reference and denotation (using the term 'reference' to cover both). In the first phase, it is assumed that all words are used to name unique denotata; in the second phase, the child acquires the distinction between proper names and words with multiple denotation; in the third phase, he learns how to construct and use such collocations as 'tall man' and 'blue book'; and in the fourth and final phase, he masters the use of collocations like 'taller than Daddy'. We will be concerned solely with the transition between the first and the second of these four phases.

It has already been pointed out that common nouns like 'dog' can be used in English on occasion to refer to or address individuals; and we can readily imagine that a child first uses and understands such nouns in the same way that he uses and understands proper names. In addition to countable common nouns, we must also consider mass nouns like 'water' and words like 'red', which denote qualities. The first thing that must be said is that the distinction between single and multiple denotation is here far less clear than it is in the case of countable nouns; hence the convenience of allowing the term 'denotatum' itself to fluctuate between various interpretations as a countable noun, as a mass noun, or a collective noun (see 7.4). Consider such utterances as *I don't like water* or *My favourite colour is red*. What is being referred to by means of the expressions 'water' and 'red'? It is arguable that denotation and reference coincide here. And yet we should probably not wish to say that water and red are individuals. Although it is possible to think of water as an individual ("a single scattered object, the aqueous part of the world") and similarly to think of the denotatum of 'red' as an individual ("the scattered totality of red substance" (Quine, 1960: 98)), we have to make a considerable intellectual effort in order to see the world in this way.

It is worth observing at this point that in English it is usually the plural of countable nouns which corresponds to the singular of mass nouns in sentences of the kind we are considering. An utterance like *I don't like books* (in contrast with *I don't like these books*) is very similar to *I don't like water*. One is perhaps inclined to say that the reference of *books* coincides with the denotation of 'book' in the utterance of this sentence (so that it would be wrong to insist that the form *books* is ambiguous between an existentially and universally quantified interpretation: cf. 6.3). If we make another deliberate intellectual effort, we can think of all the books there are in the world as discontinuous parts of a single scattered object. But we probably feel that it is even less natural to think of books in this way than it is to think of all the lakes, pools, rivers and so on as parts of a single aqueous individual. And we should no doubt resist entirely any suggestion that we could reasonable think of human beings or animals (above a certain phyletic level) as discontinuous parts of some single scattered whole. We have either acquired or were born with some principles of classification which, on the one hand, inhibit us from categorizing rather amorphous and spatially discontinuous substances like water as individuals and, on the other hand, positively incline us towards the individuation* of persons, animals and discrete, but temporally continuous, physical objects.

It is probable that the principles of individuation are, to some considerable degree at least, universal and independent of the language we are brought up to speak as children. At the same time, it must be appreciated that neither the grammatical distinction of countable nouns and mass nouns nor the grammatical distinction of singular and plural, which in English support and strengthen our appreciation of the corresponding semantic distinctions, are by any means universal in language. Very many languages make use of what are called classifiers* for the purpose of explicit individuation and enumeration and have no distinction of singular and plural in nouns. The classifiers are comparable in syntactic function with such words as 'pool' or 'pound' in English phrases like 'two pools of water', 'that pool of water', 'three pounds of butter'. But they are used, obligatorily, not only with nouns which denote amorphous or scattered substances like water or butter but also with nouns denoting classes of individuals, so that 'three men' might be translated in a way which suggests a semantic analysis something like "three persons of man". In such languages the difference between single and multiple denotation is less sharp than it is in most English utterances. Most of the common nouns will be like 'salmon' in English, which in an utterance such as *I like salmon* can be taken as referring to a class of individuals (cf. *I like herrings*) or to a stuff or substance (cf. *I like meat*). But to say that it must refer to either the one or the other is perhaps to force an unreal and unnecessary choice upon us. Why should we not take it as indeterminate rather than ambiguous? And why should we not think of an example like this as representative of what is the normal situation in an early stage of language-acquisition?

We have seen that what eventually become lexemes which denote classes of individuals in the adult language may have been first used and understood by the child as names. At this stage, a purely nominalistic interpretation of the meaning of all expressions is, we may assume, acceptable. There is no need to distinguish between reference and denotation, because each expression will be used to refer to what it denotes and what precisely it does refer to may be somewhat indeterminate.

What now of the distinction of denotation and sense? This too is perhaps unnecessary for the analysis of language-behaviour at the very earliest stage when all expressions are interpreted as names (if this is in fact the case). For then, we may suppose, the difference between 'red' and 'green', say, may not be clearly distinct from the difference between 'boy' and 'girl', on the one hand, and 'John' and 'Peter', on the other. Once these differences are established, however, it is clear from our earlier discussion that the notion of sense comes into its own.

Sense-relations determine the limits of the denotation of particular lexemes (for lexemes that have denotation); and the sense and denotation of semantically related lexemes is learned, more or less simultaneously and presumably by a process of gradual refinement (involving both specialization* and generalization*: cf. 8.5), during the child's acquisition of a language-system. Neither sense nor denotation is psychologically or logically prior to the other. Normally, it may be assumed, the child learns or infers the denotationally relevant differences between boys and girls, between men and women, at the same time as he is learning the sense of 'boy' and 'girl', and of 'men' and 'women', and as part of the same process. Ostensive definition* (i.e. the definition of the meaning of a word by pointing to, or otherwise drawing the child's attention to, one of the denotata), in so far as it plays any role at all in language-acquisition, usually involves both the sense and the denotation of lexemes. For example, if a parent says to the child *That's a boy and this is a girl*, he is not only presenting to the child typical denotata of the two words 'boy' and 'girl', but, if he is understood by the child to be using the words in contrast, he is simultaneously teaching the child, or reinforcing the child's assumption, that there is a sense-relationship holding between 'boy' and 'girl', such that (x) $(x$ be a boy $\rightarrow x$ not be a girl) and (x) $(x$ be a girl$\rightarrow x$ not be a boy). Of course, explicit ostensive definition of this kind (despite the importance assigned to it in many empiricist theories of meaning) is relatively uncommon in the acquisition of language. The child learns the applicability of words, expressions and utterances in all sorts of situations of language-use; and his initial assumptions about the sense and denotation of the words he hears in utterances may be guided by more or less specific innate principles of categorization. Language-acquisition is a very complex process, and it is uncertain to what extent various parts of it are governed by the maturation of innate cognitive structures and mechanisms (cf. 5.4). But it is clear enough that the acquisition of the denotation of words cannot be separated from the acquisition of their sense, and that neither can be separated from learning the applicability of words and utterances in actual situations of use.[14]

[14] For references to recent work on language-acquisition, see note 13 to chapter 3.

8
Structural semantics I: semantic fields

8.1. *Structuralism*

In this section we shall be concerned with the more general principles of what is commonly known, in Europe at least, as structural linguistics*.[1] Unfortunately, the term 'structuralism' has acquired a somewhat different, and much narrower, sense in the United States, where it now tends to be employed with reference to the theoretical and methodological principles of the so called post-Bloomfieldian school, which was dominant in American linguistics in the period immediately following the Second World War. Many of the principles of post-Bloomfieldian structuralism were not only alien to, but at variance with, the principles of what we may here refer to (for reasons which will be explained below) as Saussurean* (including post-Saussurean) structuralism. We need not go into all the differences between post-Bloomfieldian and Saussurean structuralism. Most of them are irrelevant in the present context. What must be emphasized, however, in view of the polemical associations which attach to the term 'structuralism' in the works of Chomsky and other generative grammarians (cf. 10.5), is that there is, in principle, no conflict between generative grammar and Saussurean structuralism, especially when what we are calling Saussurean structuralism is combined, as it has been in certain interpretations (as we shall see below) with functionalism* and universalism*. In particular, it should be noted that Saussurean structuralists, unlike many of the post-Bloomfieldians (for whom 'structural semantics' would have been almost a contradiction in terms), never held the view that semantics should be excluded from linguistics proper. The post-Bloomfieldian version of 'structuralism' has been mentioned here in order to forestall the possibility of misunderstanding and confusion. From now on we will restrict our attention to Saussurean structuralism; and the terms 'structuralism' and 'structural linguistics' will be used in this sense throughout the book.

[1] Part of this chapter has been published in Robey (1973).

It is the Swiss scholar, F. de Saussure, who is generally regarded as the founder of modern structural linguistics: hence our use of the term 'Saussurean' to characterize the whole movement. This term should not be taken to imply that the principles of structuralism actually originated with Saussure. Some of the notions that we now think of as characteristicaly structuralist can be found in the works of Herder, W. von Humboldt and even Leibniz; and they may well go back further than this. The details of the pre-Saussurean development of structuralism, and of Saussure's indebtedness to it, are complex and obscure. But it may be mentioned here that there was a structuralist vein in post-Kantian German idealist philosophy. This was developed independently of Saussurean structuralism by such scholars as Cassirer (1923, 1945; cf. also Urban, 1939; Langer, 1942); but, together with the more specifically Saussurean version of structuralism, it exercised a powerful influence on the theories of Trier and Weisgerber, whose work we shall be discussing below (8.2).

Saussure's earliest work in linguistics, a revolutionary analysis and reconstruction of the Indo-European vowel-system (1878), whose full significance was not appreciated for some fifty years, was already deeply imbued with structuralist principles. But it was his *Cours de Linguistique Générale* (1916) which initiated the movement now known as structural linguistics; and it is from the *Cours* that much of the standard terminology of structuralism derives. The circumstances of publication were such that Saussure's *Cours* contains a number of obscurities and inconsistencies; it was not in fact written for publication by Saussure himself, and it may not faithfully represent Saussure's ideas in every respect. It is, however, the *Cours*, as published, that has been of historic importance. The main lines of Saussure's doctrine are not in doubt; and we need not be concerned here with the finer points of exegesis.[2]

What, then, is the central thesis of structuralism? To put it first in its most general form, it is this: that every language is a unique relational structure*, or system*, and that the units which we identify, or postulate as theoretical constructs, in analysing the sentence of a particular language (sounds, words, meanings, etc.) derive both their essence and

---

[2] In recent years some of Saussure's own notes have been discovered and published (cf. Godel, 1957); and they are being used, together with other sources, to establish a critical edition (cf. Saussure, 1967–71). A useful selection of key passages from Saussure (1916), with a commentary, appears in Rouler (1975); and a glossary of Saussurean terminology is to be found, quoted in context, in Engler (1968).

their existence from their relationships with other units in the same language-system. We cannot first identify the units and then, at a subsequent stage of the analysis, enquire what combinatorial or other relations hold between them: we simultaneously identify both the units and their interrelations. Linguistic units are but points in a system, or network, of relations; they are the terminals of these relations, and they have no prior and independent existence.

This general notion may be illustrated first from the phonology*, or sound-system, of English. It would be generally agreed that the word-form *pit* consists of three segments in both the spoken and the written medium (cf. 6.2), and that these are arranged in a particular sequential order (*tip* is a different word-form from *pit* – they are not tokens of the same type – and *ipt* is not a word-form of English at all). The segments of the written form are, of course, letters; the segments of the spoken form are sounds, or phonemes*. According to many linguists, the phonemes of a language are not the minimal units of the sound-system, but consist of unordered sets of components (or distinctive features*). We need not be concerned with this question.

Now the spoken form *pit*, when pronounced, is a continuous burst of sound, which the phonetician can analyse into a fairly large number of overlapping acoustic components; and these can be correlated with continuously varying states of the speech-organs which determine the shape of the vocal tract, the free or obstructed passage of air through the mouth and nose, the rate of vibration of the vocal cords, and so on. The correlation between the variable states of the speech-organs and the variable properties of the vocal signals produced by the selection of different values of the articulatory variables is quite complex (and not yet fully understood). But one thing is clear: neither the utterance-act nor the utterance-signal is composed of a sequence of discrete physical units. Furthermore, every pronunciation of a word-form like *pit* (as part of a complete utterance) is somewhat different from every other pronunciation of the same word-form by different speakers and by the same speaker on different occasions. How then do we identify these physically different forms as tokens of the same type? What is the nature of the identity or constancy which underlies this diversity of physical manifestation? The structuralist will say that it is an identity of pattern or structure.

Every acceptable pronunciation of *pit* is kept distinct from every acceptable pronunciation of such forms as *bit*, *fit*, *kit*, etc. (in the same dialect*: cf. 14.5) by a variety of acoustic differences clustering around, or having their focal point at, the beginning of the continuous burst of sound; from every acceptable pronunciation of such forms as *pet, pat*, etc. by differences in the middle of the bursts; and from every acceptable pronunciation of such forms as *pick, pin*, etc. by differences at the end of the bursts. We say that there is a *p*-phoneme, a *b*-phoneme, an *f*-phoneme, etc. in English because *pit, bit, fit*, etc. and *cop, cob, cough*, etc. operate as distinct forms in English. They realize different morpho-syntactic words. Each of the morphosyntactic words, in the examples given, is associated with a different lexeme. This is not a necessary con-dition for phonemic difference: *men* and *man* realize different morpho-syntactic words associated with the same lexeme 'man'. What we can describe in very loose phonetic terms as a *p*-sound, a *b*-sound, an *f*-sound, etc. are functional*, or linguistically relevant, in English. But there are many languages in which this is not the case. There are languages in which a *p*-sound and a *b*-sound (or a *p*-sound and an *f*-sound) are in free variation*, in the sense that the substitution of the one for the other in the same phonetic environment preserves the type-token identity of the resultant forms. In such languages we would not say that there is a *p*-phoneme and a *b*-phoneme: but rather, that there is one phoneme (label it what you will for convenience of reference) which may be realized as either a *p*-sound or a *b*-sound. There are also languages in which what we can identify phonetically in the bursts of sound as a *p*-sound occurs only at the end of forms and what we can identify phonetically as a *b*-sound occurs only at the beginning. In this case they will be regarded, not as free variants, but as positionally determined variants (allophones*, to use the technical term) of the same phoneme: i.e. as realizations of the same phoneme.

What counts, then, in establishing the inventory of phonemes in any language is whether the bits of the phonetic complex correlated with them stand in a relationship of functional contrast* or not. Every lan-guage draws a more or less different, and in principle unique, set of distinctions in the continuum of sound and makes them functional by utilizing them to keep distinct the tokens of different word-types and utterance-types. We said earlier that a linguistic unit was a point in a relational structure and that it derived both its essence and existence from its relations with other units in the same language-system. What is meant by this admittedly rather abstract statement should now be some-what clearer, as far as phonology is concerned. A phoneme is an abstract, theoretical construct which is postulated as the locus of functional contrasts and equivalences holding among sets of forms. Each phoneme is associated with a set of positionally determined phonetic variants (and a range of permissible variation within each phonetic variant). But it is not itself a physically identifiable unit. Furthermore, we cannot go about the business of establishing the phonemic inventory of a language piecemeal: first deciding that there is a *p*-phoneme, then that there is a *b*-phoneme, and so on. We say that there is a *p*-phoneme and a *b*-phoneme, because there is a relationship of functional contrast between pairs of forms; and we postulate two distinct phonemes as terms in this functional relationship. In the analysis of language, relations of contrast and equivalence in language-behaviour are methodologically prior to the units which the linguist postulates as the terminals of these relations in his descriptive model of the language-system. This is one of the cardinal principles of structuralism.

Before proceeding with the exposition, we should perhaps forestall a possible misunderstanding on one point. When the structuralist says that each language draws a unique set of distinctions in the continuum of sound and makes them functional, this does not necessarily imply that there are no general, or even universal, selectional principles governing the phonological structure of languages. Many structuralists, it is true, have expressed the view that the selection of a particular set of phonological distinctions by particular languages is completely arbitrary. But this view, which may be characterized as relativism* (in contrast with stronger or weaker versions of universalism*: see below) is not essential to structuralism. It is undoubtedly the case that certain phonetic distinctions are more commonly made functional in the languages of the world than are others, as also are certain grammatical and semantic distinctions. Whatever may have been the historical association between relativism and at least certain versions of structuralism, the principles of structural linguistics as they are presented here are compatible with, though they do not imply, at least some kind of universalism.

As with the phonological system of a language, so with its grammatical structure. Each term in a grammatical category (e.g. past in the English category of tense, or plural in the category of number) is in contrast with other terms in the same category. Different languages make a different selection, as it were, from the set of possible distinctions that could be made and grammaticalize* them (i.e. make them grammatically functional) in terms of such categories as tense, number, gender, case, person, proximity, visibility, shape, animacy, etc., and group words into classes of the kind we refer to traditionally as parts of speech. These categories and parts of speech are combined to form sentences according to rules or principles which vary, within certain limits, from one language to another. As we shall see in a later chapter (10.2), there are certain problems attaching to the notion of grammaticalization* invoked here: problems which derive from different conceptions of the scope of grammar. But the general point being made in this section is unaffected by current controversies in linguistics about such questions. The units of grammatical description derive their linguistic validity from the place they occupy in a network of functional relations and cannot be identified independently of these interrelations.

The point that has already been made in relation to phonology and grammar may also be made with respect to the lexical* structure of languages (i.e. the structure of their vocabularies). The naive monolingual speaker of English (or of any other language) might be tempted to think that the meanings of lexemes (their sense and denotation) are independent of the language that he happens to speak and that translation from one language to another is simply a matter of finding the lexemes which have the same meaning in the other language, selecting the grammatically appropriate forms and putting them together in the right order. But this is not the case, as anyone who has any practical experience of translation is well aware.[3] First of all, there is the obvious problem that two or more meanings may be associated with homonymous* lexemes in the one language, but not in the other (cf. 13.4). We might not be able to translate a particular sentence because we do not know which of the homonyms was encoded in the signal and transmitted by the speaker. For example, the French sentence 'Je vais prendre ma serviette' is translatable into English as 'I'll go and get my towel' or 'I'll go and get my brief-case' (or 'I'll go and get my napkin', and in various other ways) by virtue of the homonymy which holds between 'serviette$_1$' and 'serviette$_2$'. (Actually, it is not clear whether this is a case of homonymy or polysemy*, since the criteria for distinguishing pre-theoretically between homonymy and polysemy are uncertain: cf. 13.4. But this is irrelevant to the point being made here.) Problems of translation which arise as a result of homonymy (or polysemy) speak neither for nor against structuralism in semantics. If the ambiguity is resolved by the context in which the sentence is uttered, it can be correctly interpreted by the hearer and, in principle, correctly translated into another language.

Of greater theoretical interest is the fact that one language may

---

[3] On translation: cf. Beckman & Callow (1974), Brower (1959), Catford (1965), Mounin (1963), Nida (1964), Nida & Taber (1969), Steiner (1975).

lexicalize* (i.e. provide a word for) a meaning that is not lexicalized in the other. In the most trivial instances, this may be simply because the language which lacks a lexeme for a particular meaning is spoken in a part of the world in which a particular object or class of objects does not exist. It would not be surprising, for example, to discover that there was no word for "snow" in a language of equatorial Africa. Less trivial than an example like this, but of essentially the same character, are cases where one language gives lexical recognition to some artefact, social institution or abstract concept for which, for culturally explicable reasons, there is no equivalent lexeme in another language. There are many languages, for example, in which one would be hard put to translate 'piano', 'sacrament', 'justice' or even 'family'. In cases like this also, we can say that the language lacks a word for a particular meaning, because the world in which the language normally operates (in a somewhat extended sense of 'world') does not contain anything to which the word would apply. Throughout history and pre-history languages have made good their lexical deficiency in this respect, as one culture came under the influence of another and imported from it goods of various kinds, social institutions, religious and legal concepts, and so on, by borrowing words from other languages (cf. 'restaurant', 'potato', 'vodka', etc.) or, less commonly, by associating a new meaning with an already existing lexeme. The fact that one language may lexicalize a meaning that another language does not for the reasons mentioned in this paragraph has been known and discussed by scholars for centuries; and, of itself, like the kind of ambiguity which is caused by homonymy and polysemy, it is compatible with either a structuralist or a non-structuralist theory of meaning.

There is, however, a theoretically more interesting reason why what is loosely called word-for-word translation is generally unsatisfactory and frequently impossible; and this is that the boundaries between the meanings of what at first sight appear to be semantically equivalent words in different languages may be, and very often are, incongruent*. The whole question of what constitutes semantic equivalence between lexemes from different languages is complex and controversial; it depends ultimately upon the cultural equivalence of objects, institutions and situations. Bilingual speakers who are sufficiently familiar with the cultural context in which two languages operate will often, if not always, be in agreement about the semantic equivalence or non-equivalence of lexemes. Their judgements of semantic equivalence are in most cases purely intuitive; but, in so far as they are intersubjectively consistent and reliable, they can be taken as part of the data to be accounted for in descriptive and theoretical semantics (cf. 1.6). If a lexeme from Language A (in one of its senses) is judged to have (roughly) the same meaning as a lexeme from Language B (in one of its senses) by bilingual speakers of the two languages, we can say that the two lexemes (in their relevant senses) are (roughly) equivalent in applicability*: they can be applied to the same things or in the same situations (cf. 7.4). Since denotation is included in applicability, we can consider the denotational equivalence or non-equivalence of lexemes across languages to be a part of their equivalence or non-equivalence in applicability. But denotational equivalence is relatively independent of the cultural context; it is therefore more amenable to experimental verification than other aspects of applicability and can be discussed, satisfactorily enough for our present purpose, without prejudging controversial questions about the cultural equivalence of objects, institutions and situations. In talking about the semantic equivalence of lexemes across languages in this section we will restrict our attention to denotational equivalence.

Let us take just one example, for the moment, of the difficulties which arise in translating from one language to another by virtue of the denotational non-equivalence of lexemes in the two languages. Suppose that we were asked to translate into French the sentence 'The cat sat on the mat'. We are not concerned now with the problems which derive from differences in the grammatical structure of English and French; and still less with the difficulty of preserving the rhythm and internal rhyme (between *cat* and *mat*). But it may be noted in passing that French obligatorily grammaticalizes the distinction between being seated and taking up a sitting position (so that 'être assis' and 's'asseoir' would be distinct predicative expressions); and differences in the category of tense in the two languages might cause us to hesitate (for standard literary French) between *s'assit*, *s'est assis(e)* and *s'asseyait*. But how do we translate the expression 'the cat'? As 'le chat', knowing that the animal being referred to was male or being ignorant of or unconcerned with its sex? Or as 'la chatte' knowing that it was female? (We will assume that 'the cat' in the English sentence refers to a member of the species felis domestica: there are of course other possible interpretations.) The fact that French will use 'chatte' in reference to a female cat, known to be female, whereas English will not necessarily use a phrase like 'tabby cat' in the same circumstances means that 'cat' and 'chat' are denotationally non-equivalent. This is a relatively trivial example of denotational non-equivalence. But it is typical of many such differences between the denotation of roughly equivalent words in English and French. The translation of 'the mat' is more interesting. Is it a door-mat that is being referred to ('paillasson'), or a bedside mat ('descente de lit'), or a small rug ('tapis') – not to mention various other possibilities? There is a set of lexemes in English, 'mat', 'rug', 'carpet', etc., and a set of lexemes in French 'tapis', 'paillasson', 'carpette', etc.; and none of the French words has the same denotation as any one of the English lexemes. Each set of lexemes divides, or categorizes, a certain part of the universe of domestic furnishings in a different way; and the two systems of categorization are incommensurate. It does not follow of course that in practice we cannot translate satisfactorily enough into French words like 'mat'. For what we do when we translate is to determine, as best we can from the context, how the objects being referred to would be categorized in terms of a more or less similar, but frequently incongruent, system of distinctions; and very often it is of little consequence that, in default of any information in the context which would decide the question one way or the other, we are forced to decide arbitrarily between alternatives.

It is only too easy to be aware of the difficulties of translating from one language into another and yet to underestimate, or miss completely, the theoretical implications of the facts which give rise to these difficulties. As we saw in the previous chapter, the denotation of a lexeme is limited by the relations of sense which hold between it and other lexemes in the same language (cf. 7.6). The denotation of 'mat' is limited by its contrast in sense with 'rug' and 'carpet'; the denotation of 'paillasson' in French is limited by its contrast in sense with 'tapis' and other lexemes. We could not reasonably say that 'mat' has two meanings because it is translatable into French by means of two non-synonymous lexemes, 'tapis' and 'paillasson'; or that 'tapis' has three meanings because it can be translated into English with three non-synonymous lexemes, 'rug', 'carpet', and 'mat'. The meanings of words (their sense and denotation) are internal to the language to which they belong. This, as far as the vocabulary of languages is concerned, is what is meant by saying that each language has its own semantic structure, just as it has its own grammatical and phonological structure.

8.2. *The Saussurean dichotomies*

We shall return to the structuralist conception of vocabulary in later sections. At this point it will be convenient to introduce four Saussurean distinctions which have been of great importance in the development of structuralism.

The first is the distinction of langue* and parole*. Little need be said about this, since essentially the same distinction has already been drawn in terms of language-behaviour (parole) and the language-system (langue) which underlies the language-behaviour of a particular language-community (cf. 1.6). There are no generally accepted equivalents for Saussure's 'langue' and 'parole': we will continue to employ the terms language-system* and language-behaviour*. Saussure's doctrine of the language-system is in certain respects unclear; and the precise nature of the distinction he wished to draw has been the subject of considerable controversy.[4] He emphasized the supra-individual and social character of the language-system (in terms which owed much to Durkheim); and yet he also insisted that it had some psychological validity, being stored in the brain of every member of the language-community. We need not go into these details here. Linguists will argue about the degree of abstraction and idealization involved in the postulation of an underlying relatively uniform, language-system; and many of them will deny that the system they postulate is internalized, as such, in the brains of the native speakers of the languages they are describing. But most linguists do nowadays draw some kind of distinction between language-behaviour and the system of units and relations underlying that behaviour.

The second Saussurean distinction is that of substance* and form*. In view of the fact that 'form' is widely employed in linguistics in other senses (cf. 1.5) we will substitute for it in this discussion the alternative term structure*. The Saussurean notion of substance is very close to the Aristotelian and scholastic concept of matter. ('Substance' has a quite different sense in the philosophical tradition which stems from Aristotle, but it is now well established in linguistics in the Saussurean sense.) In modern scientific and colloquial usage 'matter' denotes something with spatiotemporal extension. We must abstract from this more particular implication of the term in our interpretation of the Saussurean concept of substance. To take a traditional example: when a sculptor carves a statue out of a block of marble he takes something

---

[4] Coseriu (1952) distinguishes between system and norm, whilst Hjelmslev (1953) abstracts from the socio-psychological implications of Saussure's view of the language-system. Chomsky's (1965) distinction of 'competence' and 'performance' is, in certain respects, comparable with Saussure's distinction of 'langue' and 'parole' (cf. 1.6).

which, for the present purpose, we may think of as being shapeless and internally undifferentiated and gives to it, by the process of sculpting, a definite and distinctive shape, so that it becomes, for example, a statue of Apollo or Pegasus. The marble, considered as substance, is potentially many things, but in actuality it is none; it becomes one thing rather than another by the imposition of one structure rather than another on the undifferentiated substratum.

So it is, says Saussure, with language. But languages result from the imposition of structure on two kinds of substance: sound and thought. The phonological composition of a word-form is a complex of phonemes, each of which, as we have seen, derives its essence and its existence from the structure imposed by the language-system upon the continuum (i.e. substance) of sound. The meaning of a lexeme derives from the imposition of structure on the otherwise nebulous and inchoate continuum of thought.

The distinction of substance and structure is crucial in Saussurean structuralism. Not all structuralists, however, have conceived of the substance of meaning as Saussure did. Many scholars have described meaning in language in terms of the categorization of reality or of the external world, rather than in terms of the imposition of structure upon some conceptual substance. Structuralism can be associated with either phenomenalism or idealism or indeed explicitly dissociated from both.[5] We will not go into these various interpretations of the substratum of meaning. Here it may simply be noted that the validity of the distinction of substance and structure in semantics is far more controversial than it is in phonology.

The third of Saussure's dichotomies has to do with the relationships which hold between units in the language-system. These relationships are of two kinds: paradigmatic* and syntagmatic*. The syntagmatic* relations which a unit contracts are those which it contracts by virtue of its combination (in a syntagm*, or construction) with other units of the same level*. For example, the lexeme 'old' is syntagmatically related with the definite article 'the' and the noun 'man' in the expression 'the old man'; the letter i is syntagmatically related with p and t in

---

[5] Spang-Hanssen (1954) gives a useful summary of various earlier theories of meaning from a structuralist point of view. I take Whorf (1956) to be a phenomenalist (though his philosophical position is perhaps not entirely clear: cf. Black, 1959); Cassirer (1923) to be an idealist; and Hjelmslev (1953) to be neutral. The question is discussed from a materialist (and, more specifically, Marxist) point of view by Schaff (1960, 1964: cf. Olshewsky, 1969: 101–11, 736).

the written word-form *pit*. It is important to note that, although syntagmatic relations are actualized, as it were, in language-behaviour, they are nonetheless part of the language-system. The fact that *the old man* can occur in English utterances as a grammatically correct phrase (as a form of the expression 'the old man') depends upon the fact that the constituent lexemes belong to parts of speech whose combinatorial possibilities are determined in the underlying language-system. The form *the old man* is one of a whole set of forms, *the young man, the tall man, the young woman*, etc., all of which can be described as Noun-Phrases with the internal structure Article+Adjective+Noun. The fact that the expression 'the old man' is a semantically acceptable collocation* in English (whereas 'the cylindrical cube', for example, is not) depends upon the meaning associated with the constituent lexemes in the language-system. We shall have more to say about syntagmatic relations in grammar and semantics later.

The paradigmatic* relations contracted by units are those which hold between a particular unit in a given syntagm and other units which are substitutable for it in the syntagm. For example, 'old' is paradigmatically related with 'young', 'tall', etc. in expressions like 'the old man', 'the young man', 'the tall man', etc., as 'man' is paradigmatically related with 'woman', 'dog', etc. in expressions like 'the old man', 'the old woman', 'the old dog', etc. Similarly, the letters *i, e* and *a* are intersubstitutable for one another in the word-forms *pit, pet* and *pat*.

All this is obvious enough, once it is made explicit. The theoretically important point is that the structure of the language-system depends at every level upon the complementary principles of selection and combination. The set of paradigmatically related, or intersubstitutable, units that can occur in one position is typically different from the set of units that can occur in another position. We identify units by virtue of their potentiality of occurrence in certain syntagms; and the selection of one element rather than another produces a different resultant syntagm. To describe a language-system is to specify both the membership of the paradigmatic sets and the possibilities of combination of one set with another in well-formed syntagms. Looked at from this point of view, languages can be seen, at each level of analysis, as having two dimensions, or axes, of structure; and every unit has its place at one or more points in the two-dimensional structure.

The selection of one unit rather than another from a set of paradigmatically related units is relevant to the notion of information* (whether signal-information* or semantic information*) discussed in a previous chapter (2.3). As far as semantic information is concerned, the possibility of selecting one unit rather than another (and in most cases combining it, according to the rules of the signalling-system, with other meaningful units) is a precondition of being able to transmit different messages within the signalling-system in question. Paradigmatically related units are not necessarily different in meaning, however; the selection of one lexeme rather than another may have no effect upon the message that is transmitted. In this case, we can say that the inter-substitutable lexemes are completely synonymous*. The selection of one rather than another may change the social or expressive meaning of the utterance, but hold constant its descriptive meaning (if it has descriptive meaning): in which case, we can say that the inter-substitutable lexemes are descriptively synonymous* (i.e. that they have the same sense). Paradigmatically related lexemes which differ in sense may be semantically unrelated (e.g. 'old' and 'tall' in such syntagms as 'the old man' and 'the tall man'); or they may be semantically related in various ways. They may be incompatible* in sense (e.g. 'blue' and 'green'); or, not merely incompatible, but antonymous* (e.g. 'old' and 'young', in certain syntagms, and 'old' and 'new', in others). The one may be a hyponym* of the other (e.g. 'cat' and 'animal') or the converse* of the other (e.g. 'parent' and 'child'). These and other paradigmatic relations of sense will be discussed in some detail in chapter 9. The informal exemplification given here should be sufficient to indicate what is meant by paradigmatic relations of sense in the lexical structure of a language.

One further point should be stressed here with reference to lexical structure. When we consider the distinctions of meaning that are lexicalized in particular language-systems, we see that it is frequently the case that one language will pack into a single lexical item (i.e. will make paradigmatic) information which in another language must be conveyed, if it can be conveyed at all in the system, by means of a collocation (i.e. by syntagmatic modification). For example, in Turkish there is no word meaning "brother" and no word meaning "sister"; the lexeme 'kardeş' covers both, and it must be combined with another lexeme in order to draw the distinction (which in English is lexicalized) between "brother" and "sister". On the other hand, there are languages in which the distinction between "elder brother" and "younger brother" is lexicalized. It is well-known that Eskimo has no word for "snow", but a number of different lexemes denoting different kinds of snow; and that Arabic has no single lexeme meaning "camel", but once again

a variety of words for different kinds of camel. Rather extravagant speculations about differences in the mentality of speakers of different languages have sometimes been based on differences of lexical structure
such as these. They may be safely discounted. It does seem to be the case,
however, that particular languages tend to lexicalize those distinctions
of meaning which are important and most frequently drawn in the
cultures in which the languages in question operate; and this is hardly
surprising. What should be noted, in the present context, is that lexicalization has the effect of transferring information from the syntagmatic to the paradigmatic dimension.

Little need be said at this stage about the fourth Saussurean distinction: between the synchronic* and the diachronic* investigation of
languages. By the synchronic analysis of a language is meant the investigation of the language as it is, or was, at a certain time; by the diachronic analysis of a language is to be understood the study of changes
in the language between two given points in time. If we apply strictly
the distinction of the diachronic and the synchronic, we will say that the
notion of one language (e.g. English) existing over the centuries (from
the time of Shakespeare to the present day, shall we say) is fallacious.
What we have underlying the language-behaviour of people living at
different periods are distinct language-systems; each of these systems
can be studied, synchronically, independently of the other; and diachronic linguistics can investigate how an earlier system was transformed
into a later system. As we shall see later, language-change is but one
aspect of language-variation; and the dimensions of language-variation
are geographical and social, as well as temporal (cf. 14.5). When we
talk of a language-community existing in a particular place at a point in
time, we are not using the term 'point in time' in a literal sense. It
would be absurd to think of languages changing overnight, or even
from one year to the next (except for the acquisition of a small number
of lexemes denoting newly invented or imported objects and institutions).
The synchronic language-system is a theoretical construct of the linguist; and it rests upon the more or less deliberate, and to some degree
arbitrary, discounting of variations in the language-behaviour of those
who are held, pre-theoretically, to speak the same language. If pressed,
we have to admit that there is a somewhat different language-system
(a different idiolect*) underlying the language-behaviour of every
individual, and that this too changes through time. What we would
generally regard as two dialects of the same language spoken at the
same time may differ from one another more significantly than two

9

diachronically distinct states of what we would consider to be the same language or dialect. The distinction of the synchronic and the diachronic dimensions in language-variation can only be sensibly applied with respect to periods relatively well separated in time. In linguistics, as in other sciences, we must be careful not to be misled by the models and metaphors which we employ in order to systematize and describe the data. In particular, we should not think that in taking smaller and smaller intervals of time between successive synchronic states of a language, we come closer and closer to giving a faithful account of the Heraclitean flux of language-change.

Within certain limits, however, the distinction of the diachronic and the synchronic dimension in language is not only defensible, but methodologically essential. All too often in the past, grammarians and lexicographers have taken texts from widely separated periods and treated them as samples of the same language. A particular manifestation of the failure to respect the distinction of the diachronic and the synchronic in semantics (coupled with a failure to keep distinct the descriptive and prescriptive point of view in the discussion of language) is what might be called the etymological fallacy*: the common belief that the meaning of words can be determined by investigating their origins. The etymology of a lexeme is, in principle, synchronically irrelevant. The fact that the word 'curious', for example, can be traced back to the Latin 'curiosus' meaning "careful" or "fastidious" (and that it also had this meaning in earlier stages of English) does not imply that this, rather than "inquisitive", is its true or correct meaning in present-day standard English. Again, purists may object to the use of the word 'disinterested' to mean "indifferent" (rather than "impartial") by many speakers of English today; and the linguist, in his non-professional capacity, might well share their distaste for this usage. But, if this is the meaning associated with the word in the language-community whose language he is describing, this is the meaning that he must assign to it in his model of the language-system.

We shall not be concerned with diachronic (or historical*) semantics as such in this book, except incidentally. In a later chapter, however, we shall see that the diachronic dimension of language, together with other dimensions of language-variation (social, geographical and personal) is of considerable stylistic* importance; and, to this extent, since social and expressive meaning, if not descriptive meaning, is intimately bound up with style*, synchronic semantics cannot but be concerned with diachronic variation in language. When we come to discuss this question, however, it will be important not to confuse the investigation of the synchronic relevance of past changes in a language with the diachronic comparison of distinct language-systems (cf. 14.5).

8.3. *Relativism and functionalism*

The four Saussurean dichotomies that we have briefly discussed in the previous section have been taken up by many different schools of linguists, and developed and qualified in different ways, over the last fifty years. We need not go into the various points of agreement and disagreement. But there is one further notion that should be introduced, which, though it is not to be found in Saussure, has been associated with at least two of the major European schools of post-Saussurean structuralism, the Prague School and the Copenhagen School. This is the notion that the phonemes and the meanings of words in all languages can be analysed into yet smaller components* (or distinctive features*) and that, although the complexes of components (i.e. the phonemes and word-meanings) and the paradigmatic and syntagmatic interrelations of these complexes are unique to particular languages, the ultimate components of sound and meaning are language-neutral. According to this view, neither the substance of sound nor the substance of meaning is an undifferentiated continuum within which languages draw purely arbitrary distinctions. What we have in each case, it is maintained, is a set of potential distinctions, a subset of which are actualized by each language.

This thesis, as it has just been presented, is empirically indistinguishable from the Saussurean thesis of the continuity of substance. Granted a universal inventory of potential distinctions of sound and meaning, every language might yet make its own unique selection from this inventory, so that no single distinction was actualized in all languages. The thesis becomes more interesting, however, as an alternative to the Saussurean notion of substance, when it is coupled with the further proposition that certain distinctions of sound and meaning are more readily actualized than others. For this proposition is undoubtedly in conflict with what has been, historically, one of the most characteristic and most challenging aspects of structuralism in linguistics: its insistence that the actualization of particular phonological, grammatical and semantic distinctions in different language-systems is completely arbitrary. This can be referred to as the doctrine of linguistic relativism*. Since its best known proponent, in recent times, was Whorf (1956), it is commonly known as Whorfianism, or the Whorfian hypothesis (cf. Gipper, 1972).

The doctrine of linguistic relativism has been the subject of considerable controversy over the last fifteen or twenty years. It has recently been challenged, in a particularly interesting way, with respect to the vocabulary of colour by Berlin and Kay (1969); and their hypothesis has since been extended to other areas of the vocabulary by other scholars.[6] Now, it is a well-established fact that word-for-word translation of colour terms across languages is frequently impossible; some languages have only two basic colour terms, others have three or four, whereas others, including English, have as many as eleven; and the denotational boundaries between roughly equivalent colour terms in different language are often incongruent. The situation with respect to the vocabulary of colour is therefore typical of what was said to hold for the vocabulary as a whole earlier in this section; and the vocabulary of colour has often been used by semanticists to illustrate the notion of lexical structure.

What Berlin and Kay maintain is that there are eleven psycho-physically definable focal points, or areas, within the continuum of colour and there is a natural hierarchy among at least six of these focal areas which determines their lexicalization in any language: all languages with only two basic colour terms have words whose focal point is in the area of black and white (rather than, say, in yellow and purple); all languages with only three basic colour terms have words for black, white and red; all languages with only four basic colour terms have words for black, white, red and either green or yellow; all languages with only five basic colour terms have words for black, white, red, green and yellow; and all languages with only six basic colour terms have words for black, white, red, green, yellow and blue. It is also hypothesized, though somewhat tentatively, that children learn the denotation of colour terms in an order which reflects the same natural hierarchy, first mastering the distinction of black and white, then learning red, afterwards green or yellow, and so on.

The details of the hypothesis are open to question.[7] Let us assume, however, for the sake of the argument that it is essentially correct. What conclusions follow?

The first point to be made, and it is of the greatest importance, is that

---

[6] Notably by E. R. Heider (= E. H. Rosch): cf. Rosch (1973a, b)

[7] McNeill (1972) is very critical; Conklin (1973) is more constructively critical and sets the Berlin and Kay work in a more general framework; Kay (1975) brings the hypothesis up to date and introduces amendments. Harrison (1973) makes some interesting philosophical points about the acquisition of colour vocabulary.

a distinction may be drawn between the central, or focal, denotation, of a lexeme and its total denotation. Two languages might well differ with respect to the boundaries that they draw in a denotational continuum and yet be in agreement with respect to what is central, or focal, in the denotation of roughly equivalent words. It is undeniable that, in the past, structuralists have overemphasized the importance of determining the denotational boundaries of words. Furthermore, it should not be forgotten that most of the phenomenal world, as we perceive it, is not an undifferentiated continuum; and the way in which it is categorized conceptually and linguistically might very well depend upon our recognition of certain focal types of colour, shape, texture, biological and social function, etc. The vocabulary of colour has no doubt so often been used by structuralists to illustrate what is meant by the imposition of structure upon the substance of meaning, because the notion of an a priori undifferentiated denotational continuum is in this area of the vocabulary (unlike many others) readily interpretable. But the continuity of colour is nonetheless a very sophisticated concept. The world created by modern technology, with its profusion of colours of all shades in dress, furnishings, paintings, cars, book-jackets, and other artefacts, is very untypical of the world in which man has lived throughout most of his history. The natural environment leaves much of the colour space unfilled. If there are indeed a limited number of universal psycho-physical focal colour areas, it seems plausible that these will correlate with the characteristic colours of the salient* objects in man's physical and cultural habitat.

We may use the notion of salience*, which has just been introduced, to modify the essentially Saussurean version of structuralism developed earlier in this section, and more particularly the doctrine of the substance of meaning. All men, wherever they are born and in whatever culture they are reared, are genetically endowed, we may assume, with the same perceptual and conceptual predispositions, at least to the extent that these genetic predispositions determine the acquisition of linguistically pertinent distinctions of sound and meaning. The evidence at present available would suggest that any child, whatever his parentage might be, is capable of learning any language at all, provided that he is brought up in an environment in which the language is used for all the multifarious activities of everyday life. By virtue of his perceptual and conceptual predispositions the child will notice certain aspects of his environment rather than others. These may be described as biologically salient*; and it is within the province of neurophysiology and cognitive psychology to determine how and why they are salient. It is possible, as has been hypothesized, that there is a biologically fixed maturational sequence in the acquisition of certain perceptual and conceptual distinctions; and, if this is so, this could be at least one factor responsible for the natural hierarchy in distinctions of sound and meaning that is said to be found in the languages of the world. For example, the greater salience of variations in luminosity (coupled with the biological importance of the succession of day and night in human life) could account for the universal lexicalization of the distinction of black and white; the neurophysiological basis of the distinction of reddish and greenish hues (i.e. the fact that there are particular cells in the retina that react to these hues) might account for the almost universal lexicalization of these focal areas in the vocabulary of colour; and so on. The maturation of the biologically determined perceptual and conceptual framework will be conditional, of course, upon the presence in the environment of objects having the appropriate properties; and, as we have seen, the child's association of a lexeme with its denotatum (or, more generally, with the objects and situations to which it is applicable) may also depend upon the behavioural reinforcement of responses to the salient environmental stimuli (cf. 5.4).

Superimposed upon the biologically determined hierarchy of perceptual and conceptual distinctions, there would seem to be another kind of salience, which depends upon and extends it. This is what may be called cultural salience*. Every language is integrated with the culture in which it operates; and its lexical structure (as well as at least part of its grammatical structure) reflects those distinctions which are (or have been) important in the culture. (The qualification suggested by the parenthetical "or have been" in the previous sentence is intended to cover the possibility that languages may preserve, and perhaps for a considerable time, lexical and grammatical distinctions which no longer correlate with cultural distinctions, although they once did. The vocabulary of kinship affords many examples of this.) By being brought up in a certain culture, and as part of this process of acculturation, the child becomes aware of the culturally salient features of his environment; and, once again, he may well do so in a hierarchically determined manner. Many anthropologists have maintained that there are universals of culture, just as there are biologically determined universals of cognition. Indeed, it may be impossible, in many cases, to draw a distinction between biological and cultural universals.

When due allowance has been made for the influence of biological and cultural universals in determining the structure of language, there still remains a considerable part of the structure of particular languages which, on present evidence, does not appear to be so determined. The structuralist thesis, that every language-system is unique, is not invalidated by the possibility that every language-system has a universal infrastructure*. Nor is it affected by the possibility that the universals of language-structure are determined, not by general biological and cultural factors of the kind referred to above, but by a species-specific human capacity for the acquisition of language as such. Structuralism, then, is compatible with various kinds of universalism*; it does not necessarily imply an acceptance of the doctrine of linguistic relativism.

Structuralism has frequently been associated with functionalism* in twentieth-century linguistics, especially in the work of the Prague School. By 'functionalism' is meant (in the present context and throughout this book) the view that the structure of every language-system is determined by the particular functions that it has to perform. Since certain human and social needs are universal, there are certain functions that all languages are called upon to fulfil; and these will tend to be reflected in their grammatical and lexical structure. For example, in all societies, we may assume, there are occasions when it is necessary to make descriptive statements, to ask questions and to issue commands; it is not surprising therefore that most languages, if not all, should distinguish grammatically between declarative, interrogative and imperative sentences. All languages must provide the means of referring to objects and persons in the situation of utterance; hence the existence in all languages of a set of grammaticalized and lexicalized deictic* distinctions interrelating sentences with features of the situation-of-utterance (cf. 14.1). These are but two illustrations of what is meant by the determination of structure by function. Much of what is common to the structure of different language-systems (as well as their more general design features: cf. 3.4) can be accounted for in terms of the general conditions which govern language-behaviour and the functions which languages are regularly called upon to perform as signalling-systems.

In so far as the more specific semiotic needs of one society differ from those of another, languages will tend to differ one from another in their grammatical and lexical structure. At its most trivial (to return to a point made earlier), this implies that a language will not provide a lexeme denoting any object or class of objects which the society using the language never has occasion to refer to. More generally, it means (and this point also has been made earlier), that the grammatical and lexical structure of different languages will tend to reflect the specific interests and attitudes of the cultures in which they operate. What it does not mean, however, is that every grammatical and lexical distinction must be correlated with some important difference in the patterns of thought of the society using the language. One cannot legitimately draw inferences about differences of world-view solely on the basis of differences of linguistic structure: the cultural and linguistic differences must be independently identifiable before they can be correlated.

8.4. *Semantic fields*

What has now come to be known as the theory of semantic fields* (or field-theory*) was first put forward as such by a number of German and Swiss scholars in the 1920s and 1930s: notably Ipsen (1924), Jolles (1934), Porzig (1934), Trier (1934). Its origins, however, can be traced back at least to the middle of the nineteenth century (cf. Geckeler, 1971: 86ff) and, in a more general way, to the ideas of Humboldt (1836) and Herder (1772). There can be no question of attempting here a comprehensive treatment of field-theory, still less of reviewing the very considerable body of descriptive work based on the theory which has appeared in the last forty years. This task has been more than adequately performed by others (cf. Öhman, 1951; Ullmann, 1957; Oksaar, 1958; Kühlwein, 1967; Seiffert, 1968; Geckeler, 1971). We will restrict our attention for the most part to Trier's version of field-theory, which, despite the criticisms that can be directed against it, is widely and rightly judged to have "opened a new phase in the history of semantics" (Ullmann, 1962: 7). It should be pointed out, however, that Trier published nothing on field-theory after 1938 (cf. Malkiel, 1974). His ideas were further developed by his students, and also by L. Weisgerber, who associated himself with Trier in the 1930s and continued to elaborate and refine his own theory of semantic fields after the Second World War. Weisgerber (1954) explicitly related his ideas to those of Trier in his contribution to a collection of articles celebrating Trier's work. Subsequently, he became the acknowledged leader of the Sprache und Gemeinschaft (Language and Society) movement, which has been responsible for some of the major publications in what by now might be called the Trier–Weisgerber theory (cf. Coseriu & Geckeler, 1974: 118ff).

But first a word of warning about terminology. Trier himself, in different works and in different parts of the same work, employs a variety of terms, and it is not always clear in what sense he is employing them. As Geckeler justly remarks in his critical, but generally sympathetic, discussion of the subject: "The definition of his terms is not exactly Trier's strong point" (1971: 107). In particular, it is uncertain whether 'area' ('Bezirk') is synonymous with 'field' ('Feld') and how, if at all, 'lexical field' ('Wortfeld') is to be distinguished from 'conceptual field' ('Sinnfeld'). Trier himself avoids the term 'semantic field' ('Bedeutungsfeld'), used by Ipsen, Jolles and Porzig. We will draw our own distinctions between these several terms in the exposition of field-theory given below; and this is a rather different set of distinctions, it should be noted, from those drawn by Weisgerber. For the present we shall be concerned solely with lexical structure – i.e. the structure of the vocabulary – as Trier and most structural semanticists have been; but lexical structure, as we shall see later, is but one part of semantic structure.

There is the further difficulty that Trier does not explain what he means by 'sense' ('Sinn') and what he means by 'meaning' (Bedeutung'), and how each of these is to be distinguished from the obviously Saussurean 'value' ('Geltung'). It is therefore very difficult to interpret such key passages as the following (1934: 6): "The value [Geltung] of a word can only be determined by defining it in relation to the value of neighbouring and contrasting words. It is only as a part of the whole that it has sense [Sinn]; for it is only in the field that there is meaning [Bedeutung]". What is clear is that the German terms 'Sinn' and 'Bedeutung' are not to be taken here (or in any of the work that derives from Trier) in the technical sense that Frege gave to them (i.e. "sense" and "reference": cf. 7.1). Nor does Trier's distinction between 'sense' and 'meaning', if any distinction is in fact intended, seem to correlate with the distinction frequently drawn in German work on semantics between 'designation' ('Bezeichnung') and 'meaning' ('Bedeutung') (cf. 7.2). This latter distinction is explained in various ways (cf. Kronasser, 1952: 60ff; Ullmann, 1957: 160ff; Geckeler, 1971: 78ff, 189ff; Brekle, 1972: 54ff). But commonly it is held to depend upon whether one takes the lexemes of a particular language as one's starting point or the objects, properties and relations external to language: in the former case one is concerned with meaning (what meaning does such-and-such a lexeme have vis-à-vis other lexemes in the same system?); in the latter, with designation (by what lexeme is such-and-such an entity or class of entities designated in a given language). This distinction between meaning and designation plays an important role in

Weisgerber's development of field-theory, which he links, more closely than Trier himself has done, with the Humboldtian notion that languages determine the patterns of thought, or world-view, of the societies which use them (cf. Weisgerber, 1939, 1950). We shall take no further account of the notion of designation in our discussion of field-theory. It is unclear how it relates to denotation and reference, as we have defined them (see chapter 7); and it is doubtful whether it covers anything that cannot be satisfactorily referred to (in discussing the problems of translation, for example) by means of the terminology that we have already established. We will cast the whole of our exposition and criticism of field-theory, as far as this is possible, within the terminological framework that we have constructed in earlier sections of this book. In particular, we will assume that field-theory is concerned with the analysis of sense.

Trier looks upon the vocabulary of a language as an integrated system of lexemes interrelated in sense. The system is in constant flux. Not only do we find previously existing lexemes disappearing and new lexemes coming into being throughout the history of a language; the relations of sense which hold between a given lexeme and neighbouring lexemes in the system are continually changing through time. Any broadening in the sense of one lexeme involves a corresponding narrowing in the sense of one or more of its neighbours. According to Trier, it is one of the major failings of traditional diachronic semantics that it sets out to catalogue the history of changes in the meanings of individual lexemes atomistically, or one by one, instead of investigating changes in the whole structure of the vocabulary as it has developed through time. Both diachronic and synchronic linguistics must deal with systems of interrelated elements; and diachronic linguistics presupposes, and is dependent upon, synchronic linguistics. For what one must do when one describes the historical development of a language is to compare a set of successive synchronic language-systems. So far, what Trier has to say about the methodology of diachronic linguistics is what any post-Saussurean structuralist might say (though perhaps not Saussure himself); and, subject to the reservations expressed above about applying the synchronic–diachronic distinction with respect to successive periods that are very close in time (cf. 8.2), it can be accepted.

The procedure followed by Trier in diachronic semantics is not one of comparing successive states of the total vocabulary (which would be hardly practicable, even if it were theoretically feasible). What he does is to compare the structure of a lexical field* at time t_1 with the structure of a lexical field at time t_2. They are comparable because, although they are different lexical fields (and necessarily so, since they belong to different synchronic language-systems), they cover the same conceptual field*. (We are at this point introducing a distinction between 'lexical field' and 'conceptual field' which may not be Trier's. But it is convenient to draw the distinction in this way, and it seems to be compatible with his usage of the two terms.) The part-whole relationship which holds between individual lexemes and the lexical field within which they are interpreted is identical with, or at least similar to, the part-whole relationship which holds between the lexical fields and the totality of the vocabulary. As Trier puts it in a much-quoted passage (cf. Ullmann, 1957: 157; Oksaar, 1958: 13–14; Geckeler, 1972: 105): "Fields are living realities intermediate between individual words and the totality of the vocabulary; as parts of a whole they share with words the property of being integrated in a larger structure (sich ergliedern) and with the vocabulary the property of being structured in terms of smaller units (sich ausgliedern)". As Ullmann points out (1957: 157), the German terms 'ergliedern' and 'ausgliedern' are difficult to translate satisfactorily into English, which cannot bring out so nearly the two correlative aspects of "organic and interdependent articulateness"; articulateness, or structural integration (Gliederung), is a key concept for Trier, as it was for Humboldt and Saussure.

For our first example of what is meant by a conceptual field, we may take once again the continuum of colour, prior to its determination by particular languages. It has already been pointed out (8.1) that colour terminology provides a particularly good illustration of differences in the lexical structure of different language-systems. Actually, there are problems attaching to the recognition of a conceptual, and in this case psycho-physically definable, field of colour, neutral with respect to different systems of categorization. But let us accept for the moment that it is reasonable to think of the continuum, or substance*, of colour in this manner. As we have already seen, different languages and different synchronic states of what may be regarded, diachronically, as the same language evolving through time, can be compared in respect of the way in which they give structure to, or articulate (gliedern), the continuum by lexicalizing certain conceptual (or psycho-physical) distinctions and thus giving lexical recognition to greater or less areas* within it. Considered as a continuum, the substance of colour is (in our distinction of 'area' and 'field') a conceptual area (Sinnbezirk); it

becomes a conceptual field (Sinnfeld) by virtue of its structural organization, or articulation, by particular language-systems. The set of
lexemes in any one language-system which cover the conceptual area
and, by means of the relations of sense which hold between them, give
structure to it is a lexical field (Wortfeld); and each lexeme will cover a
certain conceptual area, which may in turn be structured as a field by
another set of lexemes (as the area covered by 'red' in English is structured by 'scarlet', 'crimson', 'vermillion', etc.). The sense of a lexeme
is therefore a conceptual area within a conceptual field; and any
conceptual area that is associated with a lexeme, as its sense, is a
concept.

Let us now consider the application of this model to diachronic
semantics. Apparently, the lexeme 'braun' covered a wider area of the
conceptual field of colour in eighteenth-century German than it does in
present-day German, where it is in contrast with 'violett' (cf. Öhman,
1953: 133). Instead of saying that 'braun' in the earlier period had two
distinct senses ("brown" and "violet"), one of which it lost to
'violett', when this lexeme came into the language from French, as a
traditional lexicographer or semanticist might be inclined to say, the
field-theorist would maintain that the internal structure of the conceptual field (as articulated by the two different lexical fields) had
changed between the two periods. 'Braun' had only one sense, but a
different sense, in each of the two language-systems.

But why, it might be asked, do we say that 'braun' at time t_1 is the
same lexeme as 'braun' at time t_2, if they belong to different language-
systems? This is a question which arises, not only in the diachronic
comparison of language-systems, but also in the synchronic comparison
of dialects; and the answer depends, ultimately, on the same considerations. What are generally considered to be different dialects of the same
language may differ, often quite considerably, in phonology and grammar; and in this respect they are different language-systems. But there
will be a greater or less degree of regular correspondence between the
forms of one dialect and the forms of another; and it is by virtue of the
recognition of this correspondence that speakers of different dialects
can understand one another (to the extent that they can) and will say
that they use many of the same words, but pronounce them differently.

For example, the form that, as pronounced by a speaker of various
dialects of Scottish English, is conventionally written *hoose* is readily
identifiable, in this way, as a form of the lexeme 'house' by speakers of
other dialects of English. The vowel-systems of Scottish English are

quite different from the vowel-system of standard English in its so-called Received Pronunciation (and different again from the vowel-systems underlying other dialects and accents); and it is not possible to map the forms of the one onto the forms of the other by means of a one-to-one phonetic transformation of the vowels. But there are certain regular phonetic correspondences; and it is on the basis of these that we can identify forms, and hence lexemes, across dialects. And it is by virtue of regular correspondences of the same kind (which are traditionally accounted for in terms of sound laws) that we can say that two forms from different language-systems are, from a diachronic point of view, identifiable as corresponding forms of the same lexeme. The lexeme whose citation form in present-day German is *braun* can thus be identified diachronically, not only with the lexeme whose written citation form in eighteenth-century German was also *braun*, but also, going back seven or eight centuries beyond that, with the lexeme whose citation form in Old High German was *brūn*. There are considerable problems of detail, when it comes to demonstrating diachronic lexical identity in particular cases; for changes in the grammatical system (especially in morphology), as well as in the phonological system, must be taken into account. But in principle the diachronic identity of lexemes from different language-systems can be established (and the branch of linguistics known as etymology* depends upon it). Let us grant, then, that lexemes can endure over long periods of time, even though the language-systems in which they are incorporated are constantly changing and both the forms of a lexeme and its meaning may change as a consequence.

If we were to compare two diachronically distinct lexical fields which cover the same conceptual field we might find: (i) that there has been no change either in the set of lexemes belonging to the two fields or in their sense-relations; (ii) that one of the lexemes has been replaced with a new lexeme (or each of a subset of the lexemes has been replaced) without, however, any change in the internal structure of the conceptual field; (iii) that there has been no change in the set of lexemes, but there has been a change of some kind in the internal structure of the conceptual field; (iv) that one (or more) of the lexemes has been replaced and the internal structure of the conceptual field has also changed; (v) that one (or more) of the lexemes has been added or lost with (of necessity, if we discount for the moment the possibility of synonymy in the earlier or later system) some consequential change in the internal structure of the conceptual field. These various possibilities are diagrammed in figure 6. The first is of little interest; the two diachronically distinct systems are isomorphic and lexically identical. The second is also of little interest to the structural semanticist; the two systems are still isomorphic, though they differ lexically. It is the remaining three situations which field-theory is adapted to handle, and which traditional atomistic theories of semantic change are likely to misinterpret. The change in the structure of the conceptual field resulting from the addition of 'violett' to the vocabulary of German is, we will assume,

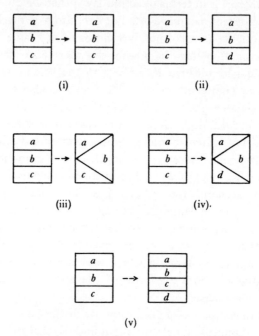

Figure 6. Various kinds of diachronic change

an instance of (v). Let us now look briefly at one of Trier's own most famous examples as an illustration of (iv).

According to Trier, there was a change in the conceptual field of knowledge and understanding (der Sinnbezirk des Verstandes), as structured by the vocabulary of Middle High German, between the beginning and the end of the thirteenth century. About AD 1200 this conceptual field was covered by a lexical field containing the three nouns 'wîsheit', 'kunst' and 'list'; a hundred years later it was covered by a lexical field containing the nouns 'wîsheit', 'kunst' and 'wizzen'. (All four of these lexemes are identifiable as diachronically the same in Modern German: 'Weisheit' ("wisdom"), 'Kunst' ("art"), 'List' ("cunning"), 'Wissen' ("knowledge"). But no two of them are interrelated in sense in the same way as they were either in AD 1200 or 1300.) By AD 1300 'list' had moved into a lexical field covering another conceptual field; and 'wizzen' had moved into the same lexical field as 'wîsheit' and 'kunst'. But this was not simply a matter of 'wizzen' taking the place occupied previously by 'list' and covering the same conceptual area. In the earlier period, 'kunst' covered "roughly speaking, the higher or courtly range of knowledge, including social behaviour" and 'list' covered "the lower, more technical range of knowledge and skill, devoid of courtly distinction", while 'wîsheit' was "not only an alternative for the other two, in most of their applications, but also for their synthesis, viewing man as a whole, and merging intellectual, moral, courtly, aesthetic and religious elements into an indissoluble unity" (Ullmann, 1957: 166). In the later period, 'wîsheit' could not be used as an alternative for 'kunst' and 'wizzen' (i.e. they were not related to it in terms of hyponymy: cf. 9.4); each of the three lexemes now covered a different conceptual area in the field of knowledge and understanding. These three areas can be characterized, roughly, as differing with respect to the depth of insight and learning upon which they are based; 'wîsheit' covers the deepest kind of knowledge (and is used typically for religious and mystical apprehension) and 'wizzen' the shallowest, or most ordinary, kind of knowledge, while 'kunst' covers the area between the other two. Trier associates the change which took place in the field of knowledge and understanding between the two periods with the social changes which occurred at this time and the breakdown in the medieval synthesis of what we would now distinguish as science, philosophy and theology.

Now there is much that can be criticized (and has been criticized) in Trier's work on the vocabulary of earlier stages of German, from both a theoretical and a methodological point of view. The texts upon which he based his analysis of the underlying language-systems are stylistically very restricted: they can hardly be taken as representative of the language as a whole. Furthermore, they are generally translations of, or commentaries upon, Latin texts; and this introduces two further methodological problems. First, the selection of German lexemes may have been determined by a somewhat slavish attempt to represent the distinctions of sense associated with particular Latin lexemes in the originals by treating the German lexemes as translation equivalents. So-called literal, or faithful, translations are notoriously unsatisfactory as translations; the Italian slogan, 'Traduttore, traditore' ("The translator is a betrayer"), which itself can hardly be translated satisfactorily into English, is relevant in more ways than one to the whole question of faithful translation (cf. Jakobson, 1959). The translator may be unfaithful to his own language, as well as to the text whose content and style he is attempting to reproduce. The second problem is that the linguist working on Middle High German texts of the kind used by Trier must often of necessity interpret the German in the light of the accompanying Latin. On purely methodological grounds, therefore, we should be justified in questioning the results of Trier's analysis. And it has been justly remarked that "research carried out by Trier's pupils according to his methods deals almost exclusively with abstract fields and invariably with fields from the earlier periods of a language" (Oksaar, 1958: 15).

We will now take up the additional point mentioned in this quotation, relating to the "abstractness" of such fields as the field of knowledge and understanding. But first it should be observed that some work has now been done, from a field-theory point of view, on modern languages, where the data are more abundant and easier to check; and the results, though they do not invalidate the theory in all its details, are certainly less readily summarized in a few broad generalizations than are the results obtained from the sparse and perhaps unrepresentative texts of earlier periods.

As we have seen, it is, according to Trier, the same conceptual field that is structured by different lexical fields at different periods. But how do we know that this is so? Even more important than the methodological problem of verifying that this is or is not the case in particular instances is the theoretical question of deciding what, if anything, is meant by saying that it is or is not the same conceptual field. No explanation is given of this identity; and yet this is the constant, in relation to which changes in the sense of lexemes in diachronically distinct lexical fields are determined. In the case of colour terms, each colour recognized by a particular language can be associated with an area in the psycho-physical continuum of colour (its denotatum); and the limits of this area can be established, approximately but well enough for the purpose (due account being taken of the difference between the focal and peripheral areas: cf. 8.3), in a neutral metalanguage. But this obviously cannot be done with what may be loosely described as abstract words such as 'knowledge' and 'understanding' (to take a pair of English lexemes). It is doubtful whether 'knowledge' and 'understanding' have identifiable denotata (cf. 7.4); if they do, the relation of denotation is much more complex than the relation which holds between 'red' or 'blue' and their denotata.

It has sometimes been suggested by critics that field-theory is valid only for the analysis of abstract words. But no evidence has been offered in support of this suggestion. In so far as one can draw a distinction between abstract and concrete fields (in this rather loose usage of the terms 'abstract' and 'concrete'), Trier's own model is in fact more obviously applicable to concrete conceptual fields, where the lexemes have identifiable denotata, than it is to abstract fields, where they do not. Trier's critics have been right to point out the methodological danger of developing a whole theory on the basis of the analysis of lexemes relating to "concepts [Begriffskomplexe] from the higher sphere of the abstract (intelligence, understanding, beauty)" (Quadri, 1952: 153). The danger, however, is not that abstract lexemes are inherently more clearly distinct from one another in sense than are concrete lexemes, but rather that it is much easier to make unverifiable generalizations about the meaning of abstract lexemes like 'beauty' or 'intelligence' in a conceptualist framework than it is about concrete lexemes such as 'red' or 'table' (cf. 4.3). If these generalizations are taken at face-value, they may well give the impression that the abstract part of the vocabulary of a language is more neatly structured and tidier, as it were, than the concrete part. But this is surely an illusion bred of methodological vagueness and subjectivism. The truth of the matter seems to be that the determining principles of lexical structure apply equally to both abstract and concrete words. If field-theory is reformulated within a non-conceptualist framework we can agree with Geckeler: "as far as its application is concerned, field-theory need not be restricted to particular sections of the vocabulary" (1971: 162). It is arguable, moreover, that our intuitive understanding of the determining principles of lexical structure as they apply to abstract words is rooted in our prior understanding and control of these principles with respect to more concrete lexemes (i.e. lexemes with observable denotata).

Trier's theory of conceptual and lexical fields appears to be based upon the assumption that, underlying the vocabularies of all languages, there is an a priori unstructured substance of meaning (which, like many other structural semanticists, he refers to by means of the philosophically loaded term 'reality'): "Every language articulates reality [gliedert das Sein] in its own way, thereby creating its own particular view of reality [ihr besonderes Seinbild] and establishing its own unique concepts [ihre, dieser einen Sprache eigentümlichen, Inhalte]" (Trier, 1934: 429). This notion of the substance of meaning (or substance of the content-plane, as Hjelmslev and his followers would say: cf. Hjelmslev, 1953: 29ff; Spang-Hanssen, 1954: 129ff; Uldall, 1957: 26ff) is open to three different lines of criticism. Since these points have already been made above in more general terms, it will be sufficient merely to repeat them briefly here. First, it is difficult to give any clear interpretation to the notion of conceptual substance; and if the notion of substance is restricted to denotational continua in the phenomenal world (where it can be applied in a relatively non-controversial manner), there will be many lexical fields that are left without any area of substance to articulate. Second, it is obviously wrong to say that reality (in the intended sense) is invariant through time and over different regions of the earth. If the natural and cultural habitat of a particular society does not present instances of certain flora and fauna, of certain climatic conditions, of certain social institutions or artefacts, etc., these things simply do not exist for that society. And finally, we must grant that reality (in the intended sense) has a structure which is to a considerable degree independent of the lexical structure of particular languages. The external world, or reality, is not just an undifferentiated continuum: on the one hand, it contains many objects which are perceived and treated behaviourally as individuals; and, on the other, it contains many classes of individuals which, most notably in the case of biological species, are distinguished by their behaviour and appearance (and in the case of biological species by their capacity to interbreed and reproduce) as members of the same natural kinds (to use the traditional term). This is not to say, of course, that lexical structure does no more than reflect the structure of reality. We have already seen that this is not so (8.3). The point being made here is simply that, although there are certain perceptual continua in the external world, there are also certain more or less clearly distinct objects and classes of objects. The notion of a denotational continuum must not be pushed too far.

Many other more specific criticisms have been made of Trier's theory of semantic fields, which we need not go into here: its reliance upon the metaphor, or analogy, of a two-dimensional mosaic; its refusal to countenance the possibility of there being any gaps or overlaps in a lexical field; its insistence that the whole vocabulary is a single integrated and fully articulated system (cf. Geckeler, 1971: 115–67). Trier has also been criticized for his concentration upon paradigmatic relations of sense to the exclusion of syntagmatic relations; and this point merits rather more extensive discussion.[8]

8.5. *Syntagmatic lexical relations*

It has already been mentioned that other theories of semantic fields besides Trier's (and Weisgerber's) were put forward in the 1920s and 1930s. In contrast with Trier and about the same time, Porzig (1934) developed a notion of semantic fields (Bedeutungsfelder) which was founded upon the relations of sense holding between pairs of syntagmatically connected lexemes; and there ensued a lively controversy as to which of the two theories was more fruitful and illuminating. There can no longer be any doubt that both Trier's paradigmatic relations and Porzig's syntagmatic relations must be incorporated in any satisfactory theory of lexical structure; and Trier and Porzig came to accept that their originally sharply opposed views were complementary, rather than being necessarily in conflict (cf. Kühlwein, 1967: 49).

Porzig bases his theory on the relationships holding within bipartite syntagms (or collocations*: cf. 14.4) composed (typically) of a noun and a verb or a noun and an adjective. The two lexemes in each such syntagm are bound together by what he calls an essential meaning-relation (wesenhafte Bedeutungsbeziehung). A quotation from one of his more recent works will illustrate the general nature of these relations: "What does one bite with? With the teeth, of course. What does one lick with? With the tongue, obviously. What is it that barks? A dog. What does one fell? Trees. What is it that is blond? Human hair. The fact that is here illustrated by means of a few examples is so banal [alltäglich] that we are inclined to overlook it and above all to underestimate its importance" (1950: 68).

Now there are a number of points that arise in connexion with syntagmatically related pairs of lexemes such as 'lick':'tongue', 'blond': 'hair', 'dog':'bark', etc. The first, and perhaps the most obvious point, is that lexemes vary enormously with respect to the freedom with which they can be combined in syntagms with other lexemes. At one extreme, we have adjectives like 'good' or 'bad' in English which can be used in

---

[8] It is not customary to link Whorf with Trier. But, in my view, there is a very striking similarity in the way they express themselves. Indeed, some of the criticisms directed here against Trier's theory of lexical fields would seem to be valid against many other versions of structural semantics. In addition to the references cited in the text the following may be found helpful: Ader (1964), Baldinger (1970), Elwert (1968), Gipper (1959, 1963), Lehrer (1974), Leisi (1953), Wotkjak (1971).

collocation* with almost any noun; at the other extreme, we find an adjective like 'rancid', which may be predicated of butter and little else. Porzig is drawing attention to this fact, and more particularly to the impossibility of describing the meaning of collocationally restricted lexemes without taking into account the set of lexemes with which they are syntagmatically connected, whether explicitly in texts or implicitly in the language-system, by means of an essential meaning-relation. One could hardly hope to explain the meaning of the verb 'bark' without mentioning dogs or of 'blond' without mentioning hair.

But what is the theoretical significance of these collocational restrictions? First of all, it should be noted (as was pointed out above: 8.2) that there are many distinctions of sense that can be made either by the syntagmatic modification of a more general lexeme or by the use of a more specific single lexeme. For example, we can use the syntagm 'unmarried man' (with 'man' modified by 'unmarried') or the single lexeme 'bachelor', in many contexts at least, as having the same sense. In many cases, one language will use a syntagm where another language employs a single lexeme with roughly the same meaning. For instance, the verbs 'kick' and 'punch' are in paradigmatic contrast in English; their most common translation equivalents in French are 'donner un coup de pied' and 'donner un coup de poing' ("to strike with the foot" and "to strike with the fist"). There is what Porzig would call an essential meaning-relation between 'kick' and 'foot', and between 'punch' and 'fist'. Let us refer to the lexicalization of this syntagmatic modifying component (for want of a better term) as encapsulation*. The sense of 'with the foot' is encapsulated* in the sense of 'kick', as the sense of 'with the teeth' is encapsulated in the sense of 'bite'.

So far we have talked about encapsulation in terms of the creation of a single more specific lexeme to do the work, as it were, of a syntagm. This would imply some kind of priority of the general over the more specific; and many structural semanticists, including Trier, have conceived of lexical structure in this way. They have suggested that the vocabulary of a language is articulated in terms of successively more specific distinctions. But Porzig put it the other way round. In his view, all words get their original meaning by virtue of their application to persons, objects, qualities, activities, processes and relations in highly specific situations. Their original meaning is correspondingly specific, and concrete (sachlich): "for every word there is some usage proper to it [eine eigentliche Verwendung], in which it has its concrete meaning [seine sachliche Bedeutung]". Some words preserve their original concrete meaning without extending or generalizing it to any appreciable degree; these are the words which in any synchronic language-system enter into a highly restricted set of collocations. But most lexemes, though they may still preserve their original meaning (as their nuclear or central meaning), will come to be applied, in the course of time, to a wider range of things and in a wider range of situations. For example, according to Porzig, the German verb 'reiten' ("ride") was originally restricted in denotation, or applicability, to riding on horseback; and this is still identifiable as its central meaning. But now it can also be used to denote such activities as sitting astride a beam ('auf einem Balken reiten'). The similarity in the two different states-of-affairs describable by means of the verb 'reiten' is self-evident; and the broadening of the meaning of 'reiten' which results from its application to sitting astride a beam, rather than a horse, can be classified as an instance of what is traditionally called metaphorical* extension.

It may be mentioned, in connexion with Porzig's example 'reiten', that the English verb 'ride' (which is diachronically related to it), has been generalized in a somewhat different direction. Whether its central meaning in modern English is still determined by its syntagmatic relation with the phrase 'on a horse' is debatable. In present-day English, the verb 'ride' can be applied, not only to the activity of managing a horse whilst one is seated upon and being conveyed by it, but also to the activity of managing a bicycle whilst one is seated upon and being conveyed by it. This rather clumsy and verbose description of the nature of the activity involved is intended to bring out three points of similarity between riding a horse and riding a bicycle: (i) being in control, (ii) being conveyed by it and (iii) being in a certain posture (in relation to the conveyance). There are, of course, indefinitely many points of similarity, as there are indefinitely many points of difference, between any two activities. But these three at least seem to be relevant to what we are taking, for the purpose of illustration, to be the central meaning of 'ride' (and the German 'reiten'). In German one would not normally use the verb 'reiten', but 'fahren', of riding a bicycle: 'fahren' *vs.* 'gehen' (like the Russian 'ezditj' *vs.* 'xoditj') lexicalizes the distinction between locomotion on foot and being conveyed. Conversely, one would not normally apply the English verb 'ride' to being seated astride a beam: the condition of being conveyed appears to be criterial. The English verb 'ride' is also used in a number of other situations where German would employ 'fahren': of riding in a carriage (where all but the condition of being conveyed has disappeared) and, in American English at least, of travelling as a passenger in a car or train (though not in a ship or aeroplane).

The main purpose of this brief and informal comparison of some of the applications of 'reiten' and 'ride' (both of which have many other applications) has been to illustrate what Porzig means by extension from an original highly specific to a subsequent more general meaning. The principles upon which extensions of this kind depend – generalization* and abstraction* – have long been recognized in diachronic semantics (cf. Bréal, 1897) and in traditional discussions of metaphor*, on the one hand, and in studies of the acquisition of language on the other: and we have had occasion to mention them, from the latter point of view, in our account of behaviourist semantics (cf. 5.3). It is to Porzig, however, that the credit must go for emphasizing the fact that abstraction and generalization depend upon the relaxation of syntagmatic relations between lexemes and for insisting that syntagmatic relations, no less than paradigmatic relations of sense, determine the structure of a lexical field.

The comparison of 'ride' and 'reiten', sketchy and unsystematic though it has been, will also serve to illustrate two additional points. First, it is obvious that the relationship between what is assumed to be the central meaning of a lexeme and its subsequent more general meaning or meanings is motivated* (rather than arbitrary*: cf. 4.2). It does not follow, however, that it should be possible, even in principle, to predict the direction or directions in which the meaning of a lexeme will be generalized: we have seen that 'ride' and 'reiten' were generalized in different ways from what is plausibly assumed to be the same originally restricted application. We cannot here go into the whole question of semantic change, of which generalization is one aspect. The literature of diachronic semantics is full of examples which would suggest that both external and internal factors may be relevant: by external factors is here meant changes in the natural or cultural environment in which a language operates; and by internal factors, structural pressures in the language-system, deriving from the totality of syntagmatic and paradigmatic relations in a particular lexical field, which might inhibit certain changes of meaning whilst promoting, or at least permitting, others. So far, however, there is no convincing evidence to support any kind of deterministic theory of semantic change. The causal factors may vary from one instance to another; and in many instances they may be beyond the scope of empirical research (cf. Ullmann, 1957: 183ff). To say that it must be possible in principle to predict the direction of semantic change is as idle as it was for Bloomfield to suggest that we could in principle foretell whether a certain environmental stimulus would cause a speaker to produce a certain utterance (cf. 5.3).

The second point that should be made in connexion with the example of 'reiten' and 'ride' is the general structuralist point, that we cannot say, without qualification, that they have or have not the same meaning. There is no reason to deny that they have the same meaning when they are applied to the activity of riding a horse; and 'ride' in 'ride a bicycle' can be plausibly said to have the same meaning as it has in 'ride a horse'; and yet 'reiten' cannot be used in the translation of this expression. This fact cannot be inferred from any general analysis of the concept of riding in terms of the three relevant conditions, or components, listed earlier. As speakers of a language we must know, and as descriptive linguists we must discover, that there is, for many lexemes at least, a set of syntagms in which they can be employed and another set of syntagms in which they cannot. At the same time, it must be recognized that the native speaker of a language is able to use most lexemes in syntagms that he has not previously encountered, and that he will usually be judged by his fellows to have used them correctly. In so far as this is a matter of productivity*, rather than creativity* (cf. 3.4), theoretical and descriptive semantics must take account of it. We must not go from the one extreme of saying that the collocations of a lexeme are determined by its meaning or meanings (where meaning is defined independently of syntagmatic considerations) to the other extreme of defining the meaning of a lexeme to be no more than the set of its collocations.

In our presentation and development of Porzig's notion of syntagmatic relations between lexemes (which linguists in the post-Bloomfieldian tradition discuss in terms of selection restrictions*), we have tacitly accepted his view that all lexemes are originally applied, phylogenetically and ontogenetically, in very specific and concrete situations and that they are correspondingly restricted syntagmatically. We can do no more than speculate (and to little purpose) about the ultimate origins of language (cf. 3.5); and diachronic semantics will only take us so far in the history of any language or family of languages. But the diachronic evidence that we do have would suggest that in all periods semantic change has proceeded not only by way of generalization and abstraction, but also by means of the converse process of specialization*. Every example of generalization in the classic works on diachronic semantics (e.g. Sturtevant, 1917; Kronasser, 1952; Ullmann, 1957; Hoenigswald, 1960) and etymological dictionaries can be matched with an example of specialization: e.g. the generalization of the Latin 'panarium' ("bread basket") to the French 'panier' ("basket") with the specialization of the old English 'mete' ("food") to the Modern English 'meat'.

Evidence from work on the acquisition of language would seem to suggest that children normally proceed by way of specialization from a wider to a narrower sense in learning the meaning of words (cf. E. V. Clark, 1973). For example, a child may first apply the word 'daddy' to all men that he meets and only later adjust his understanding and use of the word to the more restricted sense it bears in adult English. Unfortunately, it is, for methodological reasons, more difficult to identify cases of progressive generalization in the acquisition of language. If the child uses the word 'animal' in referring to cats, let us say, and does so at first under the impression that it denotes just cats, the fact that he is restricting the sense of 'animal' in this way will not result in his producing utterances which will strike his parents as semantically anomalous. We should perhaps allow that both specialization and generalization play a part in language-acquisition. This question has already been touched on in connexion with the child's acquisition of denotation (cf. 7.6).

Here we are concerned to point out the relevance of syntagmatic considerations to the discussion of specialization. If a lexeme is frequently used in collocation with a restricted set of syntagmatically modifying lexemes or phrases, it may come to encapsulate their sense. This has happened, for example, in the case of 'drive'. Its frequent collocation with 'car' has resulted in the encapsulation of "a/the car" (in sentences like 'Will you drive or shall I?') or "by car" (in 'He's driving up to London'). The verb 'drive' is still used, of course, in a variety of other collocations where it has a more general meaning; and it also has a number of other specialized meanings, which encapsulate the sense of other lexemes (e.g., *He drove off* might be said of a golfer striking the ball) and can be explained as having arisen as a result of its frequent collocation with these lexemes.

8.6. *General evaluation of the theory of semantic fields*

There is much else that would need to be discussed in a fuller treatment of the theory of semantic fields; and a number of other points will be made in later sections of the book. Although we have concentrated in this chapter upon the apparently opposed, but in fact complementary, views of Trier and Porzig, it should be mentioned that important contributions have been made to what, in a very general way, may be described as field-theory by many other scholars. Independently of Trier and his followers (though inspired indirectly, through Boas and Sapir, by Humboldt), a number of American anthropologists have investigated the vocabulary of kinship, plants, disease, and other culturally important and variable systems of classification and have described their results in similar terms to the field-theorists (cf. Hymes, 1964: 385ff). Structural semantics in France has been developed in a characteristically different direction. On the one hand, there has been with Matoré (1953) and his followers a tendency to concentrate upon those fields in the vocabulary of a language which are subject to rapid change and expansion and reflect important political, social and economic developments. On the other hand, such scholars as Greimas (1965) and Barthes (1964) have sought to extend the Saussurean notion of lexical structure defined in terms of syntagmatic and paradigmatic relations to the stylistic analysis of texts and to other semiotic systems than languages. As far as Porzig's emphasis on syntagmatic relations is concerned, this can be related, as we shall see later, to a variety of topics that have been treated in the more recent literature: to Kuryłowicz's (1936) proposals for the analysis of derived* lexemes (cf. 13.2); to Firth's contextual theory of meaning (cf. 14.4); and to the work of such scholars as Meljčuk (1974) and Apresjan (1974) on the interrelation between syntax and semantics (cf. 12.3).

There has been no dearth of research within the framework of field-theory, though much of it, as was mentioned earlier, has been directed to the investigation of older texts. What is lacking so far, as most field-theorists would probably admit, is a more explicit formulation of the criteria which define a lexical field than has yet been provided. Most authors who have written recently on the subject of semantic fields have conceded that the majority of lexical fields are not so neatly structured or as clearly separated one from another as Trier originally suggested; and this concession of a point that has been constantly urged against field-theory by its critics may be held to detract from its value as a general theory of semantic structure, for it necessarily makes the theory more difficult to formalize. On the other hand, vaguely formulated though it has been, field-theory has proved its worth as a general guide for research in descriptive semantics over the last forty years; and it has undoubtedly increased our understanding of the way the lexemes of a language are interrelated in sense. The fact that it has not been, and perhaps cannot be, formalized would be a more damaging criticism, if there were available some alternative theory of the structure of vocabulary which had been formalized and which had been tested against an equal amount of empirical evidence; and this is not yet the case.

Before continuing with a more detailed discussion of different sense-relations, let us attempt to make precise the notion of a lexical field. As we have seen, the Saussurean (and post-Saussurean) structural semanticist takes the view that the meaning of any linguistic unit is determined by the paradigmatic* and syntagmatic* relations which hold between that unit and other linguistic units in a language-system (cf. 8.2). Lexemes and other units that are semantically related, whether paradigmatically or syntagmatically, within a given language-system can be said to belong to, or to be members of, the same (semantic) field*; and a field whose members are lexemes is a lexical field*. A lexical field is therefore a paradigmatically and syntagmatically structured subset of the vocabulary (or lexicon*: cf. 13.1).

In what might be described as the strongest version of field-theory, it is held that the vocabulary, V, of a language is a closed set of lexemes, $V = \{l_1\ l_2\ l_3,\ \ldots,\ l_n\}$, which can be partitioned into a set of lexical fields $\{LF_1,\ LF_2,\ LF_3,\ \ldots,\ LF_m\}$: i.e. divided into subsets, such that (i) the intersection of any two distinct fields is empty (no lexeme is a member of more than one field), (ii) the union of all the fields in V is equal to V (there is no lexeme which does not belong to some field). In view of the criticisms of Trier's theory mentioned above, it would seem to be more prudent not to accept that either of these two conditions necessarily holds in every, or indeed any, language-system. Both of them can of course be made to hold by definition.

There are other assumptions explicit or implied in what we have called the strongest version of field-theory which we do not wish to be committed to. The first is that both the vocabulary and each of the fields in the vocabulary are closed sets of lexemes: we will leave open the possibility that they are either open* or indeterminate* (i.e $V = l_1,\ l_2,\ l_3,\ \ldots$ or $V = \{l_1,\ l_2,\ l_3,\ \text{etc.}\}$ and $LF_i = \{l_{i_1},\ l_{i_2},\ l_{i_3},\ \ldots\}$ or $LF_i = \{l_{i_1},\ l_{i_2},\ l_{i_3},\ \ldots\}$: cf. 7.4). The second is the assumption that the whole vocabulary is a field, structured (in terms of the relations holding between the lexical fields which it includes) in the same way as are the lexical fields themselves. Neither of these assumptions appears to be theoretically essential; and descriptive semantics can get along quite well without them.

To conclude this section, two further theoretical and methodological points may be emphasized, which have emerged in recent work in field-theory semantics and upon which there is fairly widespread agreement. The first is the necessity of taking into account the context in which words occur. The second is the impossibility of studying the vocabulary of a language independently of its grammatical structure. In the next chapter we will deal with some of the more important paradigmatic relations of sense which determine the structure of lexical fields. We will also say something about the componential analysis of meaning which, though it was first developed independently of field-theory, has many affinities with it and has in fact been adopted in some of the more recent work in the theory of semantic fields.

9

Structural semantics II: sense relations

9.1. *Opposition and contrast*

The notion of sense* (as distinct from denotation* and reference*) has already been introduced (chapter 7).[1] Our purpose in this chapter is to develop and reformulate what seem to be the basic principles of the theory of semantic fields in terms of sense-relations* (i.e. relations of sense holding within sets of lexemes) without postulating any underlying conceptual or perceptual substance (cf. 8.4). The treatment will be relatively informal and at times somewhat speculative. We begin by discussing the notion of paradigmatic opposition.

From its very beginnings structural semantics (and indeed structural linguistics in general) has emphasized the importance of relations of paradigmatic opposition*. Trier himself opens his major work (1931) with the challenging statement, that every word that is pronounced calls forth its opposite (seinen Gegenteil) in the consciousness of the speaker and hearer; and this statement can be matched with similar assertions by other structural semanticists. Trier, it will be noted, claims, as others have done, that the opposite is in some way present in the mind of the speaker and hearer during an act of utterance. Whether this is true or not is a psychological question, and one that is more relevant to the construction of a theory of language-behaviour than it is to the analysis of a language-system (cf. 1.6). In what follows we make no assumptions about what goes on in the mind of the speaker and hearer during an utterance. Trier's statement also appears to imply that every word in the vocabulary has an opposite, and only one opposite. Whether this is true or not, is a question with which we shall be concerned in this section.

The standard technical term for oppositeness of meaning between

[1] Much of what appears here in chapter 9 is an expansion of chapter 10 of Lyons (1968). The reader is reminded, however, that there are certain terminological differences. In particular, the term 'denotation' was not used in Lyons (1968).

lexemes is antonymy*. But this is hardly more precise in the usage of most authors than the word 'oppositeness' which it replaces, and dictionaries will classify as antonyms* pairs of lexemes which, as we shall see, are related in a variety of ways ('high':'low', 'buy':'sell', 'male':'female', 'arrive':'depart', 'left':'right', 'front':'back', etc.). What all these examples have in common, it should be noted, is their dependence upon dichotomization. We can leave to others to enquire whether the tendency to think in opposites, to categorize experience in terms of binary contrasts, is a universal human tendency which is but secondarily reflected in language, as cause producing effect, or whether it is the pre-existence of a large number of opposed pairs of lexemes in our native language which causes us to dichotomize, or polarize, our judgements and experiences. It is, however, a fact, of which the linguist must take cognizance, that binary opposition is one of the most important principles governing the structure of languages; and the most evident manifestation of this principle, as far as the vocabulary is concerned, is antonymy.

But lexical opposites, as we have already said, are of several different kinds; and it is a moot point just how many dichotomous relations should be held to fall within the scope of 'antonymy'. Let us begin by drawing a distinction between gradable* and ungradable* opposites (cf. Sapir, 1944). Grading* involves comparison. When we compare two or more objects with respect to their possession of a certain property (this property being denoted typically in English by an adjective), it is usually, though not always, appropriate to enquire whether they have this property to the same degree or not. For example, we might ask *Is X as hot as Y?* The fact that we can say *X is as hot as Y* or *X is hotter than Y* depends upon the gradability of 'hot'. A lexeme like 'female' (unlike 'feminine'), on the other hand, is ungradable: we would not normally say *X is as female as Y* or *X is more female than Y* (though *X is not as feminine as Y* is a perfectly acceptable utterance). Each of these lexemes is paired in the vocabulary with what would generally be described as its opposite: 'cold' and 'male', respectively. Now the fact that 'hot' and 'cold' are gradable lexemes, whereas 'female' and 'male' are ungradable, is bound up with an important logical difference between the two pairs.

Ungradable opposites, when they are employed as predicative expressions, divide the universe-of-discourse (i.e. the objects of which they are predicable: cf. 6.3) into two complementary* subsets. It follows from this, not only that the predication of either one of the pair implies the predication of the negation of the other, but also that the predication of the negation of either implies the predication of the other. For example, the proposition "X is female" implies "X is not male"; and "X is not female" (provided that 'male' and 'female' are predicable of X) implies "X is male".

With gradable opposites, however, the situation is different. The predication of the one implies the predication of the negation of the other: the proposition "X is hot" implies "X is not cold"; and "X is cold" implies "X is not hot". But "X is not hot" does not generally imply "X is cold" (though on occasions it may be interpreted in this way, and we will come back to this point).

What has been said so far about the distinction of ungradable and gradable opposites might, at first sight, appear to be covered satisfactorily enough by the traditional logical distinction of contradictories* and contraries*. A proposition *p* is the contradictory* of another proposition *q*, if *p* and *q* cannot both be true or both false; e.g. "This is a male cat": "This is a female cat" (as well as such corresponding affirmative and negative propositions as "The coffee is cold": "The coffee is not cold"). A proposition *p* is the contrary* of another proposition *q*, if *p* and *q* cannot both be true (though both may be false); e.g., "The coffee is hot": "The coffee is cold" (as well as such pairs as "All men are bald": "No men are bald").[2] Applying this distinction to the sentences which express such propositions and then derivatively, in an obvious way, to the lexemes used as predicative expressions in them, we could say that 'male' and 'female' are contradictories and that 'hot' and 'cold' are contraries; and this is correct. But there are many contraries that would not generally be regarded as opposites (e.g., 'red': 'blue', not to mention innumerable other pairs such as 'tree':'dog', 'square':'abstract', etc.): they are not dichotomously opposed to one another.[3] The distinction of contradictories and contraries corresponds to the distinction of ungradable and gradable lexemes within the class of lexical opposites in a language, but it applies more widely; and the fact that gradable antonyms can generally be taken as contraries, rather than contradictories, is a consequence of gradability, not its cause.

[2] This statement about contraries is not intended to do more than point out one important and relevant difference between contraries and contradictories. As it stands, it would allow as contraries such pairs as "This coffee here is hot" and "There is no coffee here"; and not everyone would wish to accept this consequence.

[3] Such lexemes are regarded as antonyms by Katz (1964, 1966). But this is an unusually broad interpretation of the term 'antonymy'.

Grading is made explicit in comparative sentences such as 'Our house is as big as yours' and 'Our house is bigger than yours'. In English, there are alternative, though less common, kinds of comparative sentences, employing the verbs 'equal', 'differ' and 'exceed' ('Our house equals/differs from/exceeds yours in size'), the adjectives 'same' and 'different' ('Our house is the same as/different from yours in size'), as well as the correlative and antonymous adverbs of degree 'more' and 'less' ('Our house is more/less comfortable than yours'); and there are various other constructions possible, some of them more acceptable than others in particular instances. But there is considerable variation across languages in the way in which grading is grammaticalized in sentences which may be identified, in terms of their grammatical structure, as comparative. It is by no means the case that all languages with adjectives are explicitly graded in the most common kinds of comparative sentences by means of the adverbs of degree corresponding to 'more' and 'most' (correlative with 'less' and 'least' respectively). In what follows, we will assume that the grammatical constructions available for explicit grading, and their equivalence in what can be regarded as paraphrases of particular sentences, can be satisfactorily accounted for as part of the grammatical analysis of any language whose vocabulary we are investigating; and we will illustrate the points being made here about gradable antonyms by means of a limited set of English comparative sentences.

The first point to be noted is that the propositions expressed by comparative sentences like 'Our house is bigger than yours' or 'X's proof (of the theorem) is simpler than Y's' imply, and are implied by, the propositions expressed by sentences like (a) 'Your house is smaller than ours', 'Y's proof is more complex than X's' or (b) 'Your house is less big than ours', 'Y's proof is less simple than X's'. The relationship between sentences like 'Our house is bigger than yours' and 'Your house is smaller than ours' can be handled in terms of the converseness* of their predicates (cf. 6.3), as can corresponding active and passive sentences like 'John killed Bill' and 'Bill was killed by John': we will come back to this. The point to be noted here is that the substitution of one of a pair of gradable antonyms for the other and the transposition of the relevant nominal expressions within a comparative sentence results in a semantically equivalent sentence. This is obvious enough.

Rather less obvious is the fact that the use of a gradable antonym always involves grading, implicitly if not explicitly. This was stressed by Sapir (1944), who seems to have been the first linguist to employ the term 'grading' in this sense.[4] When we say, for example, *Our house is big* (i.e. when we utter the sentence 'Our house is big' in order to assert the proposition "Our house is big") we are not ascribing the property bigness, or size, to the referent of 'our house', as we are ascribing the property redness to the referent of 'that' when we say *That's a red book.* We are implicitly comparing the house with something else and asserting that it is bigger. The standard of comparison may have been explicitly introduced in the context in which the sentence is uttered. Commonly, however, it will be some generally accepted norm. *Our house is big* might therefore be understood as meaning something like "Our house is bigger than the normal house" or "Our house is big for a house"; and the norm will be variable across different languages (or cultures) and across different groups within the same society. Failure to recognize the logical properties of gradable antonyms has given rise to a number of pseudo-problems. Plato, for example, was puzzled by the apparent possibility of opposite qualities (e.g. tallness and shortness) co-existing in the same object: if we can say *X is taller than Y and shorter than Z* we appear to be ascribing both tallness and shortness to X. More recently, logicians and linguists have discussed such obviously fallacious deductions as "This is a small elephant, therefore it is a small animal" (in contrast with "This is a red book, therefore it is a red object").[5] As Sapir puts it: "such contrasts as 'small' and 'large', 'little' and 'much', 'few' and 'many' give us a deceptive feeling of absolute values within the field of quantity comparable to such qualitative differences as 'red' and 'green' within the field of color perception. This feeling is an illusion, however, which is largely due to the linguistic fact that the grading which is implicit in these terms is not formally indicated, whereas it is made explicit in such judgments as "There were fewer people there than here" or "He has more milk than I" " (1944: 93).

Grading may also be semi-explicit. By semi-explicit grading is here meant the use of some comparative construction without explicit mention of the standard of comparison. For example, 'Our house is bigger' is graded semi-explicitly, and the standard of comparison will usually have been previously introduced in the context. So too is 'Our

---

[4] The point Sapir was making is well known to logicians and goes back at least as far as Aristotle (cf. *Categories* 56).

[5] Katz (1972: 254) draws a distinction between relative and absolute adjectives in this connexion. Kamp (1975) brings out clearly the logical problems that arise if relative adjectives are treated, semantically, like ordinary, one-place predicates. See also: Bierwisch (1967), Cruse (1976), Givón (1970), Ljung (1974).

house is too big' (the equivalent of which in certain languages is not distinguished from the equivalent of 'Our house is bigger', as the equivalent of 'Our house is the biggest' may not be distinguished from the equivalent of 'Our house is very big'): the standard of comparison is here more complex, since it brings in the notion of purpose and a whole range of possible criteria which may or may not be made explicit ("...too big for us to maintain", "...too big for its site", etc.). In so far as a proposition must have some determinate truth-value (cf. 6.2), we cannot say what proposition is expressed by sentences of this kind unless we can establish, from the context or otherwise, the relevant standard of comparison.

In many languages, including English, the most commonly used opposites tend to be morphologically unrelated (e.g. 'good':'bad', 'high': 'low', 'beautiful':'ugly', 'big':'small', 'old':'young'). But these are outnumbered in the vocabulary by such morphologically related pairs as 'married':'unmarried', 'friendly':'unfriendly', 'formal':'informal', 'legitimate':'illegitimate', etc. In each case the base-form* of one member of the pair is derived* from the base-form of the other by the addition of the negative prefixes *un-* or *in-* (cf. 13.2). By virtue of this morphological correspondence, words like 'unfriendly', 'informal', etc., may be described as morphologically negative* with respect to the corresponding morphologically positive* words 'friendly', 'formal', etc. Now the first point to notice is that, although most morphologically unrelated opposites, in English at least, are gradable and many morphologically related opposites are ungradable, the distinction between morphologically related and unrelated opposites is independent of, and does not correlate absolutely with, the semantic distinction of ungradable and gradable opposites: 'married':'single', like 'married':'unmarried', is ungradable, whereas 'friendly':'unfriendly', like 'friendly': 'hostile', is gradable. These examples have been deliberately chosen to illustrate the further point that the same lexeme may be paired with both a morphologically related and a morphologically unrelated word in the vocabulary.

What is perhaps more important is that even morphologically unrelated opposites, like 'good' or 'bad', can be distinguished syntactically and semantically in terms of their positive or negative polarity*. We tend to say that small things lack size, that what is required is less height, and so on, rather than that large things lack smallness and that what is required is more lowness. 'How good is it?' can be used without any presupposition or implication that the referent of 'it' is good rather than bad; but 'How bad is it?' carries with it the presupposition that the referent of 'it' is bad rather than good (in relation to some relevant norm). The positive opposite tends to precede the negative when opposites are co-ordinated in what Malkiel (1959) calls irreversible binomials*: cf. 'good and bad', 'high and low', 'great or small'. This principle of preferred sequence is in fact of much wider application. It enables us to distinguish a positive and a negative member in such contrasting pairs as: 'man' and 'woman', 'parent' and 'child', 'north' and 'south', 'heaven' and 'earth', 'food' and 'drink', 'buy' and 'sell', etc. As Malkiel points out, it seems to correlate quite well with what, on other grounds too, we might describe as a hierarchy of semantic preference.

Sapir discusses the polarity of antonyms in terms of "the tendency to slip kinaesthetic implications into speech [which] so often renders a purely logical analysis of speech insufficient or even misleading" (1944: 104). Lehrer observes that "it is the negative case which approaches some limit or zero point, while this is not true of the positive cases. A thing can be so narrow or so short or so small that it approaches zero in extension, but there is no corresponding limit to how large, wide or tall something can be" (1973: 27; cf. also H. Clark, 1973). If we add to Lehrer's observation the fact that most morphologically negative gradable antonyms are also semantically negative (or marked), we can perhaps account for Sapir's feeling that gradable antonymy is suffused with kinaesthetic implications. The notion of a limit is relevant to only a subset of the antonymous pairs in a language, and most obviously to lexemes having to do with spatial and temporal extension; morphological relationship again is relevant to only a subset of the antonymous pairs; approximation to the limit or zero point and the prefixation of *un-* or *in-* are independent of one another, but they correlate with negative polarity, which is relevant in all instances of gradable antonymy; and it is for this reason perhaps that we interpret as negative all the lexemes which function syntactically like 'small' or 'narrow' and like 'unfriendly' or 'informal'.

It requires but a moment's reflexion to see that there is no logical necessity for languages to have morphologically unrelated opposites (regardless of whether the languages in question are such that they can be said to have a level of morphological structure or not: cf. 10.1). English would be just as efficient a semiotic system, one might think, if we had such pairs as 'good':'ungood', 'wide':'unwide', 'far':'unfar', etc. Indeed, there is no logical necessity for languages to have lexical opposites at all. Suppose we were to amend the grammatical structure of English slightly, so that "X is not good", "X is bad", "X is very bad" were expressed by means of the sentences 'X not is good' (or 'X does not be good'), 'X is not good', 'X is very not good'. The language would serve just as well for making distinctions of descriptive meaning as it does at present with a larger vocabulary.[6] What then is the reason for the existence of lexical opposites, and more particularly morphologically unrelated gradable opposites?

We have already noted that antonymy reflects or determines what appears to be a general human tendency to categorize experience in terms of dichotomous contrasts. Now it seems clear that the lexicalization of polarity in two morphologically unrelated gradable antonyms (which adds to the arbitrariness and discreteness of the system: cf. 3.4) enhances in some way the distinctness, or separation, of the two poles, so that, as Sapir suggests: "contrasting qualities are felt as of a relatively absolute nature, so to speak, and 'good' and 'bad', for instance, and even 'far' and 'near', have as true a psychological specificity as 'green' and 'yellow'. Hence the logical norm between them is not felt as a true norm, but rather as a blend area in which qualities graded in opposite directions meet. To the naive, every person is either good or bad; if he cannot be easily placed, he is rather part good and part bad than just humanly normal or neither good nor bad" (1944: 101). It is perhaps for this reason that most of the common gradable antonyms in English and other languages are morphologically unrelated: it reflects a more complete lexicalization of polarized contrasts. In fact, it can be argued that complete lexicalization necessarily implies morphological unrelatedness. Morphological relatedness between lexemes (or derivation*) is traditionally regarded by linguists as falling midway between grammaticalization and lexicalization: 'good' and 'bad' are more obviously different lexemes than are 'friendly' and 'unfriendly'. But this is a more general point; and we will take it up in a later chapter: 13.2.

Although gradable and ungradable opposites may be distinguished

---

6 It is interesting to note that C. K. Ogden, the inventor of Basic English – he was also the author of a short, but important, book on the notion of opposition (cf. Ogden, 1932) – saw fit to include among the 850 lexemes of Basic English 50 pairs of morphologically unrelated opposites. He also allowed for the formation within the system of a further 50 opposites by prefixing *un-* to what he called the name of the quality, though he advised the learner to make use of 'not' (cf. Ogden, 1968: 131). Whatever other criticisms one might make of Basic English, one must surely concede that Ogden's instinct or judgement was right in this respect.

in terms of their logical properties, it must also be borne in mind that gradable antonyms are frequently employed in everyday language-behaviour as contradictories rather than contraries. If we are asked *Is X a good chess-player?* and we reply *No*, we may well be held by the questioner to have committed ourselves implicitly to the proposition that *X* is a bad chess-player. This fact is perhaps best handled, like many others, by appealing to a certain number of general semiotic principles which govern the normal use of language. (Some of these have been codified and discussed recently by Grice as what he calls conversational implicatures*: cf. 14.3.) For most practical purposes we can usually get along quite well by describing things, in a first approximation as it were, in terms of a yes/no classification, according to which things are either good or bad, big or small, etc. (relative to some relevant norm). If we deny that something is good or assert that it is not good without qualifying our statements in any way or supplying any further information relevant to this dichotomous yes/no classification, it is reasonable for the other participants to assume that we are satisfied with a first approximation in terms of which gradable antonyms are interpretable as contradictories. The proposition "*X* is not good" obviously does not of itself imply "*X* is bad", but under the operation of this principle it may be held to do so on particular occasions of the utterance of a sentence expressing it. If the speaker did not wish to be committed to the implication, he could have been expected to make it clear that a first approximation was insufficiently precise, by saying, for example, *X is not good, but he's not bad either: he's fair/pretty good/just about average.*

It is also a fact of normal language-behaviour that ungradable opposites can, on occasion, be explicitly graded. But the explanation of this fact is usually of a different order. If someone says to us *Is X still alive then?* and we reply *Very much so* or *And how!*, we are not thereby challenging the ungradability of 'dead':'alive' in the language-system. What we are grading, presumably, are various secondary implications, or connotations* (cf. 7.1), of 'alive'. So too, if we say *X is more of a bachelor than Y*, we are probably comparing *X* and *Y* in terms of certain more or less generally accepted connotations of 'bachelor'. But there are other occasions when we will grade a pair of normally ungradable antonyms, because we do reject their interpretation as contradictories. 'Male' and 'female' are obvious examples. We normally operate under the assumption that any arbitrarily selected human being will be either male or female (rather than neither male nor female, or both male and female), but we may well recognize that certain people cannot be satis-factorily classified in terms of this yes/no opposition of 'male' and 'female'. We can say, for example, *X is not completely male* or *X is more male than female*. But in cases like this, we are modifying the language-system, if only temporally. Recognition of the possibility of grading normally ungradable antonyms, in either of the two ways mentioned here, does not imply that there is not a sharp distinction to be drawn between gradable and ungradable antonyms in a language-system.

So far we have been using the terms 'antonymy' and 'opposition', more or less equivalently, for various kinds of contrasts between lexemes; and we have not explicitly distinguished between oppositions and contrasts. Opinions will differ about the advisability of drawing a terminological distinction in one way rather than another. But the following classification appears to be workable and convenient; and we will henceforth follow it. Contrast* will be taken as the most general term, carrying no implications as to the number of elements in the set of paradigmatically contrasting elements. Opposition* will be restricted to dichotomous, or binary, contrasts; and antonymy* will be restricted still further, to gradable opposites, such as 'big':'small', 'high':'low', etc. The reason for this deliberate restriction in the scope of the terms 'antonymy' and 'antonym' lies in the fact that, as we have seen, gradable opposites manifest the property of polarity more strikingly than do other opposites. Ungradable opposites like 'male' and 'female' will be termed, for reasons which should now be clear, complementa-ries*. This leaves the terms 'contradictory' and 'contrary' free for employment in the sense in which they have been defined by logicians.

Cutting across the distinction of antonyms and complementaries is the distinction that many structural semanticists, following Trubetzkoy (1939), draw between privative* and equipollent* opposites. This dis-tinction (which has been exemplified above in our discussion of polarity) has been drawn, though not necessarily in the same terms, in many general treatments of opposition and contrast (e.g., Ogden, 1932). A privative opposition is a contrastive relation between two lexemes, one of which denotes some positive property and the other of which denotes the absence of that property: e.g., 'animate':'inanimate'. An equipollent opposition (or, more generally, an equipollent contrast) is a relation in which each of the contrasting lexemes denotes a positive property: e.g., 'male':'female'.

To be distinguished from antonymy and complementarity is con-verseness*, exemplified by pairs like 'husband':'wife' (which may be

regarded as two-place predicates). The sentence 'X is the husband of
Y' expresses a proposition whose converse is expressed by 'X is the wife
of Y' (cf. 6.3). As was noted above, the comparative forms of explicitly
graded antonyms (*bigger*:*smaller*, etc.) and corresponding active and
passive forms of transitive verbs (*killed*:*was killed*) also operate within
sentences as do lexical converses: '*X* killed *Y*' expresses a proposition
which is the converse of the proposition expressed by '*X* was killed by
Y'. Now, by virtue of the definition of the logical relation of converseness, if *R* is a two-place relation and *R'* is its converse, we can
substitute *R'* for *R* and simultaneously transpose the terms in the
relation to obtain an equivalence: $R(x, y) = R'(y, x)$. Provided that the
appropriate grammatical changes are carried out under the transposition of the nominal expressions, we can do the same for pairs of sentences containing converse lexemes or expressions and the propositions
expressed by the two members of each pair of sentences will be equivalent: "*X* is bigger than *Y*" $\equiv$ "*Y* is smaller than *X*", "*X* precedes
Y" $\equiv$ "*Y* follows *X*", "*X* killed *Y*" $\equiv$ "*Y* was killed by *X*". Converse relations between lexemes which may be used as two-place
predicative expressions are especially common in areas of the vocabulary
having to do with reciprocal social roles ('doctor':'patient', 'master'/
'mistress':'servant', etc.) and kinship relations ('father'/'mother':
'son'/'daughter', etc.), on the one hand, and temporal and spatial
relations ('above':'below', 'in front of':'behind', 'before':'after',
etc.), on the other.

The situation with respect to lexemes like 'buy' and 'sell' is rather
more complex. If we treat them as three-place predicates and correlate
the order of the terms in the symbolic representation of the relations
$R(x, y, z)$ and $R(x, y, z)$ with such grammatical functions as subject,
direct object, indirect object, etc., in the sentences containing 'buy', we
can say that 'buy' is the 1–3 converse of 'sell' (cf. Bar-Hillel, 1967a).
Knowing that it is the first and third of the nominal expressions that
must be transposed in 'buy' $(x, y, z) \equiv$ 'sell' (z, y, x) and knowing also
what grammatical changes must be made in sentences containing 'buy'
and 'sell', we can relate such pairs of sentences as '*X* bought *Y* from *Z*':
'*Z* sold *Y* to *X*' in terms of the equivalence of the propositions expressed
by them. It is possible, however, that the semantic relation which holds
between many-place converses can in all cases be analysed as the
product of two or more simpler relations (cf. 12.4).

9.2. *Directional, orthogonal and antipodal opposition*

So far we have recognized three kinds of lexical opposition: antonymy (narrowly defined in terms of gradability), complementarity and converseness. There is yet a fourth type, with various subtypes, which, though it cannot always be distinguished from these three, is sufficiently important in language to be given a separate label. We will call it directional* opposition. It is seen most clearly in the relationship which holds between 'up':'down', 'arrive':'depart', and 'come':'go'. What these pairs have in common, in what might be regarded as their most typical usage, is an implication of motion in one of two opposed directions with respect to a given place, *P*. But there are important differences between them. If we compare 'up':'down' with 'come':'go', we can see immediately that, whereas 'come':'go' is based upon an opposition between motion towards *P* and motion away from *P* (as also is 'arrive':'depart'), 'up':'down' is based upon an opposition drawn within motion away from *P*. 'Right':'left' and 'front':'back', when they are employed in directional or orientational expressions, are like 'up':'down' in this respect. But the directionality of 'up':'down' (i.e. in the vertical dimension) is absolute, in a way that the directionality of 'right':'left' and 'front':'back' is not. This is an important point; and we will come back to it (cf. 15.5).

If 'come':'go' is compared with 'arrive':'depart', it will be seen that there are various differences. The most important, from a theoretical point of view, has to do with the fact that the opposition between 'come' and 'go', like the opposition of 'here' and 'there' and many other pairs, involves deixis* (cf. 15.1), whereas the opposition between 'arrive' and 'depart' does not. We can say "*X* arrived in Paris last night", regardless of whether we are ourselves in Paris at the time of the utterance, or were in Paris at the time of the event being described.

Directional opposition cannot be discussed satisfactorily except within a more general framework which analyses location as being in a certain state and motion as some kind of change of state. Looked at from this point of view arriving in Paris stands in the same relation to being in Paris, as getting married to being married, or acquiring wealth to having wealth; and departing from or leaving Paris is in the same relation to being in Paris as dying is to living or forgetting is to knowing. It would be difficult to exaggerate the importance of directional opposition, both deictic and non-deictic, as a structural relation. It is all-pervasive in both the grammatical and the lexical structure of languages:

it is central to the analysis of the grammatical categories of tense, aspect and case and the personal and demonstrative pronouns, and it is the basis of much that we might think of as metaphorical in the use of particular lexemes and expressions. Furthermore, it may well be that our understanding, not only of directional opposition, but of opposition in general, is based upon some kind of analogical extension of distinctions which we first learn to apply with respect to our own orientation and the location or locomotion of other objects in the external world. This is the thesis of localism*, to which we will return (cf. 15.7).

Motion from a place P results in being at not-P (or not being at P); and motion to P results in being at P. This gives rise to two possible relations of consequence* based on directionality, which may be distinguished as positive or negative, according to whether the resultant location is P or not-P. Positive consequence is exemplified in the implicational relation which holds between the proposition expressed by 'X has come/gone to P' and the proposition expressed by 'X is (now) at P'; negative consequence in the relation which holds between the proposition expressed by 'X has come/gone from P' and the proposition expressed by 'X is not/no longer at P'. Positive or negative consequence is relevant to the analysis of the sense of pairs of lexical opposites in many different areas of the vocabulary. 'Learn' and 'know' (in certain contexts) are related by means of the implication that holds between such pairs of propositions as "X has learned Y" → "X (now) knows Y" (i.e. X has gone from not knowing Y to knowing Y); and 'forget' and 'know' by means of the implication "X has forgotten Y" → "X does not/no longer knows Y" (i.e. X has gone from knowing to not knowing Y). Similarly for the positively related 'get' ("acquire"): 'have' ("possess"), on the one hand, and the negatively related 'lose': 'have', 'die':'(be) alive', '(get) divorced':'(be) married', on the other. By virtue of these relations of consequence, 'learn':'forget' (as well as 'remember':'forget' in other contexts and with somewhat different implications), 'get married':'get divorced', etc., may be regarded as directional opposites, like 'to':'from'.

Let us now draw another distinction between orthogonal* and antipodal* opposites. If we consider the oppositions which hold within the set {'north', 'south', 'east', 'west'} we see that they are of two kinds. Each of the four members of the set is opposed orthogonally (i.e. perpendicularly) to two others ('north' is opposed in this way to 'east' and 'west', 'east' is opposed to 'south' and 'north', etc.) and antipodally (i.e. diametrically) to one other ('north' is thus opposed to 'south' and 'east' to 'west'). The antipodal oppositions are dominant in this set of four lexemes in the sense that native speakers of English will undoubtedly say that 'north' and 'south' or 'east' and 'west' are opposites rather than 'north' and 'east' or 'north' and 'west'. When the antipodal opposites are employed as two-place predicative expressions (or within such two-place predicative expressions as 'to the south of') they are of course converses. But the more special relationship that holds between 'north' and 'south' and between 'east' and 'west' derives from the fact that all four lexemes belong to the same field and each lexeme is diametrically opposed to its converse in a two-dimensional space. Similarly, 'above' is diametrically opposed to 'below', 'in front of' to 'behind' and 'left' to 'right' in a three-dimensional space. We will use the term 'antipodal' for this kind of opposition.

The examples that have just been given illustrate the nature of antipodal opposition in a relatively straightforward and intuitively obvious manner. But antipodal opposition is by no means confined to areas of the vocabulary having to do with location or orientation in physical space. It is arguable that it operates, to some degree at least, in the area of colour. Any native speaker of English would probably agree, without hesitation, that 'black' and 'white' are opposites. Some speakers, though perhaps a minority, would claim that 'green' is similarly opposed to 'red' and 'blue' to 'yellow'.[7] Now it is interesting to note that the focal areas denoted by these words are just those areas which are given lexical recognition in languages with a six-term colour system, according to the hypothesis put forward by Berlin and Kay (cf. 8.3), and also that they can be arranged as paired antipodal opposites in a three-dimensional space.[8] The fact that most speakers of English treat 'black' and 'white' as opposites, but not (except in certain special contexts) 'red' and 'green', and still less 'blue' and 'yellow', would suggest that the principle of antipodal opposition, in English at least, is given only partial recognition in the vocabulary of colour, though it may play some role in the acquisition of colour terms by children.

[7] These three pairs are in fact treated as opposites in Basic English, though few English speakers would think that the contrast between 'blue' and 'yellow', or even between 'green' and 'red', is of the same order as the contrast between 'black' and 'white'. According to Ogden (1932: 88) "The sensitive colourist ... will be emphatic that red and green provide the typical and indubitable case of opposition. They pull him apart, as it were, emotionally, and the fact that they neutralize one another as complementaries is merely a corollary of their fundamental opposition".

[8] There is at least one theory of colour which would seem to account for these antipodal relations: namely Hering's (1874) theory (cf. Zollinger, 1973).

Kinship vocabulary in many languages also manifests the principle of antipodal opposition in various ways. Let us consider, for simplicity, just a two-dimensional space structured in terms of the symmetrical relations being-married-to (being-the-spouse-of) and being-born-of-the-same-parents-as (being-the-sibling-of). Suppose that a is the spouse of b, that c is the sibling of a, and d the sibling of b. This can be symbolized as: spouse $(a, b) \equiv$ spouse (b, a); sibling $(a, c) \equiv$ sibling (c, a); sibling $(b, d) \equiv$ sibling (d, b). We can arrange the four members of the set a, b, c, d in a rectangular space as we can arrange the cardinal points of the compass, such that a is orthogonal* (i.e. perpendicular) to b, c to a and d to b. Now the complex relation being-the-sibling-of-the spouse-of, which may be symbolized as sibling-$\times$-spouse (x, y) is an antipodal opposition which is the product of the two orthogonal relations sibling (x, z) and spouse (z, y). The converse antipodal relation, spouse-$\times$-sibling (y, x), is a product of spouse (y, z) and sibling (z, x). These antipodal relations, holding between b and c and between a and d in the present example, may be referred to as in-law relations. We cannot know in advance, of course, that they will be lexicalized in any given language, even though the language operates in a society which institutionalizes monogamous marriage and structures its kinship system in terms of it. But let us just briefly compare two languages that do lexicalize these in-law relations: English and (nineteenth-century) Russian.

In English, being the sibling of the husband is identified lexically with being the sibling of the wife ('brother/sister-in-law'). Furthermore, sibling-$\times$-spouse (x, y) is identified with spouse-$\times$-sibling (x, y). There is, however, in standard English no lexeme 'sibling-in-law' (or any single lexeme that is synonymous with this). We must choose between 'brother-in-law' and 'sister-in-law' according to the sex of the person being referred to. What we find identified lexically in English, therefore, are "brother-of-spouse" and "husband-of-sibling" (as well as "husband-of-sibling-of-spouse") by means of 'brother-in-law' and "sister-of-spouse" and "wife-of-sibling" (as well as "wife-of-sibling-of-spouse") by means of 'sister-in-law'. In other words, a brother-in-law is a male sibling-in-law and a sister-in-law is a female sibling-in-law.

In the Russian system, there are six lexemes to be considered. As in English, the sex of the person being referred to is in all cases relevant. But being the sibling of the husband is distinguished lexically from being the sibling of the wife: and both relations are asymmetrical. Given that a is the husband of b, then the relation between b and c ("brother's wife") is lexicalized as 'nevestka' and the relation between *d* and *a* ("sister's husband") as 'zjatj'. The converse of 'nevestka' (*b*, *c*) is lexicalized in the disjunction of 'deverj' ("husband's brother") and 'zolovka' ("husband's sister"); and that of 'zjatj' (*d*, *a*), in the disjunction of 'shurin' ("wife's brother") and 'svojačinica' ("wife's sister"). It will be obvious that the sense of these Russian lexemes (as it has been represented so far) is more readily accounted for than is the sense of 'brother-in-law' and 'sister-in-law' in English as the product of the senses of an ordered pair of asymmetrical relations taken from a set meaning {"husband", "wife", "brother", "sister"}, each of which is in fact lexicalized in Russian, as in English. The fact that two of the products ("sister's wife" and "brother's husband") are not lexicalized requires no explanation. But it would have been quite conceivable, a priori, that there should be a distinct converse for 'shurin' and 'svojačenica', on the one hand, and for 'deverj' and 'zolovka', on the other, just as it is quite conceivable, a priori, that "male sibling of male" and "male sibling of female" should be distinguished lexically. Both the Russian and the English systems are internally consistent and isomorphic as far as the orthogonal relations are concerned, but they differ with respect to the lexicalization of the antipodal oppositions.[9]

The distinction between orthogonal and antipodal opposites that has just been illustrated is not restricted, in principle, to converses. 'Man' is opposed to its complementary 'woman', on one dimension, and to its complementary 'boy', on another dimension, as 'girl' is opposed orthogonally to 'boy' and 'woman'. By virtue of this fact, 'man':'girl' and 'woman':'boy' are antipodal opposites, though, presumably for non-linguistic reasons, they are less commonly opposed in use. But it is important to realize that there is not necessarily a single answer to the question "What is the opposite of such-and-such a lexeme?" The

[9] There are also other differences between the two systems which we would need to take account of in a more detailed analysis. "Wife's sister's husband" is given separate lexical recognition in Russian, though none of the other three possibilities under "spouse-of-sibling-of-spouse" is. Wives of brothers are symmetrically related to one another in the "nevestka"-relationship. Husbands of sisters do not stand in any lexically recognized relationship. Furthermore, it is not just "sister's husband", but also "daughter's husband", that is lexicalized as 'zjatj'; and "son's wife" is included in the sense of 'nevestka'. Since "husband's father" and "wife's father" are distinguished lexically, as also are "husband's father" and "wife's mother", the statement of the various converse relations between pairs of lexemes is quite complex: it is, however, internally consistent, as the reader can verify for himself. The nineteenth-century Russian system described here has now been replaced with a simpler one. This does not affect the points made in the text.

orthogonal oppositions are dominant in the set {'man', 'woman', 'boy', 'girl'}, as the antipodal oppositions are dominant in the set {'north', 'south', 'east' and 'west'}. In '{spring', 'summer', 'autumn', 'winter'}, 'winter' is more strongly opposed to its antipodal opposite 'summer' than it is to its orthogonal opposites 'spring' and 'autumn', but 'spring' is no more strongly opposed to its antipode 'autumn' than it is to 'summer' and 'winter'. Nor is the distinction between orthogonal and antipodal opposition always as clear in the vocabulary as might appear to be the case from the perhaps rather special instances that have been mentioned; and the interpretation of some of these might well be challenged. We are less conerned at this point to defend the distinction in particular instances than we are to elucidate various aspects of the notion of lexical opposition.

The term 'antonymy' was coined in the nineteenth century to describe a phenomenon, oppositeness of meaning, which was itself conceived as being the opposite of synonymy; and there has been a lot of confusion in semantics caused by the common practice of treating the terms 'synonym' and 'antonym' themselves as opposites. 'Antonymy' (in the broader sense of "oppositeness of meaning") has often been thought of as referring to the opposite extreme from identity of meaning: i.e. to the maximum degree of difference in meaning. But this is obviously wrong, in so far as most of the examples of antonymy cited in dictionaries and handbooks of semantics are concerned. When we compare and contrast two objects with respect to their possession or lack of one or more properties, we do so generally on the basis of their similarity in other respects. We can say that X is married and Y is single, but in all other respects similar. Moreover, we cannot predicate the word 'married' and 'single' of X and Y, unless a certain number of other words are also predicable of X and Y. This holds for most, if not all, lexical opposites. Oppositions are drawn along some dimension of similarity.

Now some semanticists have proposed, as we shall see in our treatment of componential analysis, that the sense of all lexemes in the vocabulary should be describable in terms of a set of binary contrasts (cf. 9.9). This implies that every lexeme can be compared with every other lexeme in the vocabulary in a multidimensional space structured in terms of oppositions. Within this space there will be numerous instances of orthogonal opposition (holding between lexemes which are in opposition on a single dimension); and within various subspaces there will be instances of antipodal opposition of the kind mentioned above. But antipodal opposites like 'north' and 'south' in a two-dimensional subspace and 'red' and 'green' in a three-dimensional subspace (if indeed they are to be analysed in this way) will of course be identical with respect to the possession or lack of all the other components of meaning defined within the total space. Suppose, however, that there were certain pairs of lexemes which differed on every dimension. These might then be described as being maximally different in meaning or absolute opposites (within the vocabulary taken as a whole lexical system); and they would be in a maximal antipodal opposition. Given such a classification of lexemes, it would also be possible (if there seemed to be any point in doing so) to pose such questions as the following: "Is 'man' more similar in meaning to 'ashtray' than it is to 'beauty'?" Now there are many proposals that have been made for measuring similarity of meaning (along a scale going from identity to maximal difference) which would, in principle, answer such questions. But none of them, in so far as they have been applied, has yielded any useful results; and it is doubtful whether there is any validity in the notion of a scale of similarity and difference of meaning applied to the vocabulary as a whole and having as its theoretical end-points synonymy and absolute antipodal opposition.

However that may be, the distinction between antipodal and orthogonal opposition seems to be applicable, and usefully so, in the analysis of particular lexical fields (such as the field of kinship); and the recognition of antipodal oppositions within multidimensional fields might bring the analysis of certain cyclically ordered sets of lexemes such as {'north', 'south', 'east', 'west'} within the scope of componential semantics, and even such sets as 'black', 'white', 'red', 'green', 'yellow', 'blue', which is partly cyclical.

9.3. Non-binary contrasts

Less need be said about non-binary contrasts of sense than about opposition. It seems clear that there are such contrasts, even if many apparently non-binary contrasts (for example, the contrasts which hold between each of the set of colour words and every other member of the set) ultimately prove to be analysable in terms of several binary distinctions. It is hard to imagine that {'Sunday', 'Monday', ..., 'Saturday'}, {'January', 'February', ..., 'December'} or even {'rose', 'peony', 'tulip', 'delphinium', etc.} will be satisfactorily analysable in this way. Nor does there appear to be any good reason for believing that many-member lexical sets like this necessarily belong to some specialized

technical or scientific subvocabulary rather than to the general vocabulary of a language. The most that can be said perhaps is that the elabora-
tion of many-member lexical sets (e.g., the words denoting the elements
in chemistry or different species in botany) is more typical of specialized
taxonomies than it is of language in general; and it is noteworthy that
specialized taxonomies, even when they make use of everyday words,
will often tend to impose upon lexical sets in the taxonomy a more
rigid structure than is characteristic of the vocabulary of everyday
usage.

  The relationship of sense which holds between lexemes in many-
member sets such as {'Sunday', 'Monday', ..., 'Saturday'} may be
described as incompatibility*. This notion is difficult to make as precise
as the notion of opposition. It has been pointed out, for example, that
a definition of incompatibility in terms of contradictoriness runs into
problems: "X is a rose" implies "X is not a peony/tulip/delphinium/
etc."; but "X went there on Saturday" does not imply "X did not go
there on Sunday/.../Friday" and "Bill punched Mary" does not
imply "Bill did not kick/slap Mary" (cf. Lehrer, 1974: 25). This is
true; and yet it is evident that there is a relationship of incompatibility
holding within the lexical sets in question. Given that X went on only
one day (or that we are enquiring about one occasion of his going), if
we say *It was on Saturday that X went there* we will normally be held
to have said something which implies "X did not go there on Sunday".
Similarly, given that Bill struck or hit Mary in one way rather than
another, if we say *Bill púnched Mary* (with heavy stress on the verb,
marked here with an acute accent) we will normally be held to have said
something which implies "Bill did not kick/slap Mary". X's going on
Saturday is incompatible with his going on Sunday or any other day, not
in the sense that he could not have gone both on Saturday and also on
Sunday, but that he could not have gone on both-Saturday-and-Sun-
day. There is the further difficulty that incompatibility, as a structural
relation, is not always clearly distinguishable, pre-theoretically at least,
from what we would be inclined to describe as unrelatedness of meaning. But we will not go further into this question here. The important
point is that incompatibility as a lexical relation, like opposition, is
based on contrast within similarity: 'rose' and 'pig' are contraries,
but there is little point in discussing their status as incompatibles, since
the one denotes a flower and the other an animal; and the sense of the
one can hardly be said to delimit the sense of the other.

  Various kinds of ordering are found in many-member sets of incompatibles: by a many-member set, in this context, is meant a set which contains more than two lexemes. Such sets may be serially* or cyclically* ordered. In a serially ordered set there are two outermost members (if the set is determinate), and all other lexemes in the set are ordered between two others; in a cyclically ordered set every lexeme is ordered between two others. Among serially ordered sets, scales* may be distinguished from ranks* according to whether the constituent lexemes are gradable or not (cf. Lehrer, 1974: 29). The ordering in scales in terms of incompatibility is characteristically less strict than it is in ranks. Consider, for example, the set {'excellent', 'good', 'fair', 'poor', 'bad', 'atrocious'}. First of all, it is somewhat indeterminate: should we add to it 'superb', 'awful', etc.? Secondly, although we would probably agree that they can be arranged on a scale in the order in which they have just been listed, it is only when two or more of them are explicitly contrasted in some particular context (cf. *She's not (just) good – she's excellent*) that they are taken as incompatible. Furthermore, within the set we can identify the antonymous pair 'good':'bad' as being stylistically more neutral and perhaps more general in applicability than the others; and this is typical of lexical scales. What are frequently regarded as stylistically less neutral, more emotive, lexemes, e.g., 'excellent' or 'atrocious', are perhaps descriptively equivalent to explicitly graded exressions like 'very good' or 'very bad'. The scale {'hot', 'warm', 'cool', 'cold'} is rather unusual in English in that it contains an outer and an inner pair of antonyms, 'hot':'cold' and 'warm':'cool'. However, as Lehrer points out, when they are implicitly graded with respect to some temperature norm for food or weather they "contrast in a way similar to incompatible terms" (1973: 28). The outermost members of a scale (e.g., 'freezing' and 'boiling' in the set {'boiling', 'hot', 'warm', 'cool', 'cold', 'freezing'}) may be described as scalar opposites.

Ranks exhibit the principle of serial ordering in a stricter form; but they are less characteristic of the non-technical use of language. One of Trier's examples of a lexical field falls into this category: sets of lexemes used for grouping examination candidates according to their performance. If the convention accepted by the examiners is that every candidate will be classified in terms of the rank {'excellent', 'good', 'average', 'fair', 'poor'}, these lexemes will be construed as a serially ordered set of incompatible and ungradable terms; and the sense of any lexeme will be determined by its position in the rank. The set of lexemes used to describe differences of military rank provides another example:

within the set {'field marshal', 'general', ..., 'corporal', 'private'},
as they are applied with respect to the British army, the outermost
members 'field marshal' (a phrasal lexeme) and 'private' are rank
opposites. Numerals, in English {'one', 'two', ..., 'twelve', ...,
'hundred', 'thousand', 'million', 'billion', ...}, also constitute a rank,
which has the interesting property that it has its own subgrammar
according to which an infinite set of lexically complex expressions may
be constructed. It may be mentioned in passing that there are interesting
formal differences in the subgrammars of numerals found in different
languages; and these have been attracting the attention of linguists
recently (cf. Hurford, 1975).

   The most obvious examples of cyclical sets, or cycles*, are to be
found among words that denote units or periods of time: {'spring',
'summer', 'autumn', 'winter'}; {'January', ..., 'December'}; {'Sunday', ..., 'Saturday'}. These are all ordered in terms of successivity:
hence the analyticity* of "spring immediately precedes summer",
"Saturday immediately follows Friday", "October is between Septem-
ber and November" (cf. Leech, 1969: 116). Unlike scales and ranks,
cycles do not have outermost members, or extremes: every member of
the set is ordered between two others. The fact that there is a conventional first and last member in many of these sets (that January is the
first month of the year, Saturday the last day of the week, etc.) does not
detract from their cyclicality: "John came on Saturday and Peter came
on the following day" implies "Peter came on Sunday", and "John
came on Monday, but Peter came on the preceding day" also implies
"Peter came on Sunday". On the other hand, it must be recognized
that alternative interpretations of phrases like 'next Friday', 'last
Thursday' ("Friday of next week":"the next Friday following to-day";
"Thursday of last week":"the most recent Thursday"), which,
according to the day of the week on which they are uttered, may differ
in reference, rest upon a potential conflict between taking the set as
a cycle and taking it as a series.

   Finally, in this brief discussion of serial and cyclical sets of lexemes,
it may be observed that both principles may be operative within the
same lexical field. Within the set of basic colour words in English
{'black', 'grey', 'white'} constitute a scale; and {'red', 'yellow',
'green', 'blue', 'purple'} a cycle. It has already been mentioned that
both 'black':'white' (at the extremities of a scale) and 'red':'green',
'yellow':'blue' (within a cycle) can perhaps be regarded as antipodal
opposites.

9.4. *Hyponymy*

No less important than opposition and contrast as a paradigmatic relation of sense is the relation which holds between a more specific, or
subordinate, lexeme and a more general, or superordinate, lexeme, as
exemplified by such pairs as 'cow':'animal', 'rose':'flower', 'honesty':
'virtue', 'buy':'get', 'crimson':'red'. There is no generally accepted
term for this relation (or its converse). Recently, however, the term
hyponymy* (coined by analogy with 'antonymy' and 'synonymy') has
been gaining currency; and it would seem to be more appropriate than
such alternatives as 'inclusion' or 'subordination', which are also used
in other senses in linguistics and logic. Let us say, then, that 'cow' is
a hyponym* of 'animal', 'rose' is a hyponym of 'flower', and so on;
and further, that 'rose', 'tulip', 'daffodil', etc., since each is a hyponym
of 'flower', are co-hyponyms* (of the same lexeme). The obvious
Greek-based correlative term for the converse relation, 'hyperonymy'
(cf. Mulder & Hervey, 1972), is unfortunately too similar in form to
'hyponymy' and likely to cause confusion. We will use instead super-
ordination*, which, unlike 'subordination', is not widely employed as
a technical term in linguistics with a conflicting sense.

Hyponymy is frequently discussed by logicians in terms of class-
inclusion* (cf. 6.4); and, up to a point, this is satisfactory enough. For
example, if X is the class of flowers and Y is the class of tulips, then it
is in fact the case that X properly includes Y ($X \supset Y$ & $Y \not\supset X$). But
there are problems attaching to the definition of hyponymy in terms of
the logic of classes. First of all, it is unclear whether we should say that
a hyponym is included in its superordinate or a superordinate in its
hyponym(s). If we consider the extension* of lexemes, we would say
that the superordinate lexeme is more inclusive; but as far as the intension* of lexemes is concerned the hyponym is more inclusive (tulips
have all the defining properties of flowers, and certain additional properties which distinguish them from roses, daffodils, etc.). This fact,
in itself, is not particularly troublesome; it is indeed axiomatic in logic
that extension and intension should be related in this way under inclusion. More serious, however, is the problem that class-logic does not
seem to be suitable for the formalization of semantics, unless we make
rather controversial assumptions about the interdefinability of denotation and sense: saying, for example, that the denotatum of 'flower' is
a class of objects and its sense is the defining properties of the class.
This is the approach followed by such scholars as Carnap (1956). But

we are using the term 'denotation' for the relation which holds between lexemes and either classes of individuals or properties, activities, processes and relations, as seems appropriate in particular cases (cf. 7.4); and we have rejected the assumption that, if a lexeme has sense, it must also have denotation.

Hyponymy is definable in terms of unilateral implication. For example, 'crimson' is established as a hyponym of 'red' and 'buy' as a hyponym of 'get' by virtue of the implications "She was wearing a crimson dress" → "She was wearing a red dress", "I bought it from a friend"→ "I got it from a friend" (i.e. between the propositions expressed by the sentences 'She was wearing a crimson dress' and 'She was wearing a red dress', etc., when these sentences are uttered to make an assertion). The definition of hyponymy in terms of unilateral implication enables us to define synonymy* as bilateral, or symmetrical, hyponymy: if x is a hyponym of y and y is a hyponym of x, then x and y are synonymous. If hyponymy is defined as non-symmetrical (as it must be if synonymy is treated as symmetrical hyponymy), then proper hyponymy* may be distinguished from synonymy as being asymmetrical (for the distinction between non-symmetrical and asymmetrical relations, cf. 6.3). This distinction of asymmetrical hyponymy as a special case of non-symmetrical hyponymy is analogous with the standard distinction of proper inclusion from inclusion in the logic of classes (cf. 6.4). Throughout this section we shall be concerned primarily with proper hyponymy, and we will use the term 'hyponymy' without qualification in this sense.

Hyponymy is a transitive relation. If x is a hyponym of y and y is a hyponym of z, then x is a hyponym of z (cf. 6.3). For example, 'cow' is a hyponym of 'mammal' and 'mammal' is a hyponym of 'animal'; therefore 'cow' is a hyponym of 'animal'.

Generally speaking, in English, when the relation of hyponymy holds between nouns, it is possible to insert syntactically appropriate expressions containing them in place of x and y in the following formula 'x is a kind of y' (where x is a hyponym of y) and this will yield a sentence which expresses a metalinguistic or reflexive proposition which (to the degree that any metalinguistic proposition relating to natural languages is analytic) is analytic (cf. 6.5). Thus: the proposition expressed by 'A cow is a kind of animal', 'A tulip is a kind of flower', etc., may be taken to be analytic. Under more restricted conditions, 'sort' and 'type' may be substituted for 'kind' in colloquial English: 'A cow is a sort of animal', 'A tulip is a type of flower'. There are many other more specific lexemes (which are themselves hyponyms of 'kind') which may be employed, for certain values of x and y: e.g., 'shade' in 'Crimson is a shade of red', 'make' in 'An Aston Martin is a make of car', and so on. When a noun x is superordinate to more than one hyponym, y, z, etc., such expressions as the following will be accepted as meaningful: 'cows and other (kinds of) animals', 'tulips and other (kinds of) flowers', which may be contrasted with the semantically anomalous 'cows and other (kinds of) flowers' and 'tulips and other (kinds of) animals'. It may be assumed that the frequent occurrence of such expressions plays an important part in the establishment of hyponymy and co-hyponymy in language-acquisition; and it is important to note that one can learn, in this way, that one lexeme is a hyponym of another or that two lexemes are co-hyponyms without in principle knowing anything more of their meaning. Indeed, much of our knowledge of the meaning of words in our native language may be of this kind. We might know, for example, that 'banyan' is a hyponym of 'tree' or 'osprey' of 'bird' and yet be unable to say how banyans differ from other trees or ospreys from other birds.

Now it is also to be observed that a question like *What kind of animal was it?* (put, shall we say, by a parent to a child after a visit to the zoo) may be answered appropriately with either *An elephant* or *A big one* (where 'one' may be thought of as a pronominal substitute for 'animal'). This would suggest that, in many cases at least, a hyponym encapsulates* the sense of some adjectival modifier and combines it with the sense of the superordinate lexeme (cf. 8.5). This does not mean that the hyponym is always equivalent to, or synonymous with, a phrase in which the superordinate lexeme is modified by means of one or more adjectives. In some instances this may be so: 'tyrant' is a hyponym of 'ruler', and 'despotic ruler' or 'cruel ruler' is perhaps equivalent (in many contexts) to 'tyrant'; and it may well be that the sense of 'tyrant' is often learned by virtue of its equivalence to one or other of these phrases, the sense of 'cruel' or 'despotic' and of 'ruler' being known in advance. But the sense of a word like 'cow' is surely not learned on the basis of its equivalence to a phrase like 'bovine animal'. The process is much more likely to be the reverse. Our understanding of 'bovine' will be dependent upon our prior knowledge of what kind of animals cows are. The point that is being made here is simply that, for many nouns at least, the sense of a hyponym can be regarded as the product of the sense of a superordinate noun and of some actual or potential adjectival modifier. The appropriateness of

A tyrant or *A cruel one* in reply to the qestion *What kind of ruler was x?* reflects this fact.

Verbs, adjectives, adverbs and other parts of speech cannot be inserted into the formula '*x* is a kind of *y*' without prior nominalization* (cf. 10.3), and even then the resultant sentence is generally rather unnatural, if not absolutely unacceptable (e.g. 'Buying is a kind of getting'). But there are other words and phrases which serve to structure the vocabulary in terms of hyponymy for the other parts of speech, as 'what kind of...' does for nouns. Comparable with the questions *What kind of animal was it?*, and *Was it a cow or some other kind of animal?* are *How did he get it – by buying it or stealing it?* and *Did he buy it or get it in some other way?* Similarly for adjectives like 'friendly' and 'nice': *When you say he's nice, do you mean that he is friendly or nice in some other way?* As we can say *A cow is an animal of a certain kind,* so we can say though perhaps less idiomatically, *To buy something is to get it in a certain way* and *To be friendly (to someone) is to be nice (to someone) in a certain way.*

In general as adjectival modification is to nouns, so adverbial modification is to verbs and adjectives; and as 'what kind of...' is answered by an adjectivally modified noun or a hyponymous noun, so 'how' or 'in what way' is answered by an adverbially modified or hyponymous verb or adjective. There are, however, many different subclasses of adverbs; and 'how' or 'in what way' is not always appropriate to the type of adverbial modification that is involved. It would be tedious, even if it were feasible, to attempt to list here all the ways in which hyponymy is manifest for the different parts of speech, and subclasses of them, by the use of interrogative words and phrases and of phrases containing 'some other' or 'a certain' (comparable with 'some other kind' and 'of a certain kind'); and the function and distribution of these words and phrases could not be satisfactorily accounted for except within the framework of a comprehensive grammatical description of the language. We will assume, however, that the general principle is clear. Hyponymy is a paradigmatic relation of sense which rests upon the encapsulation in the hyponym of some syntagmatic modification of the sense of the superordinate lexeme.

Generally speaking, co-hyponyms of the same superordinate will contrast in sense (we will temporarily disregard the possibility of non-contrasting, synonymous co-hyponyms); and the nature of the contrast can be explicated in terms of a difference in the encapsulated syntagmatic modification of the superordinate. For example, 'buy' and 'steal' are in contrast, as co-hyponyms of 'get', in such sentences as 'x bought the book from y' and 'x stole the book from y'.

Having established that two lexemes are co-hyponyms of the same superordinate and that they are in contrast, we can go on to determine the nature of their contrast by specifying the relations which hold between them and other lexemes under implication. In some cases, but not all, their contrast in sense can be associated with a contrast between two syntagmatic modifiers of the superordinate lexeme. For example, 'buy' is in contrast with 'steal' as a hyponym of 'get' and the contrast between the two co-hyponyms can be associated with the contrast between the adverbial phrases 'by purchase' and 'by theft' used as syntagmatic modifiers of 'get'. But the sense of the nouns 'purchase'

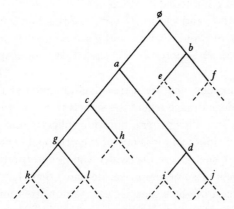

Figure 7. A model of a hierarchically organized vocabulary

and 'theft' could hardly be analysed satisfactorily except in terms of 'buy'/'sell' and 'steal'; and it seems that there is no single pair of contrasting expressions in English which could serve as syntagmatic modifiers of 'get' in a non-circular metalinguistic gloss on 'buy' and 'steal'. This is by no means untypical. The expressions 'by purchase' and 'by theft', when they are employed in this way, are best thought of as summarizing a whole set of more particular modifications of the sense of 'get' encapsulated in 'buy' and 'steal'.

9.5. *Hierarchical structure in the vocabulary*

The relation of hyponymy imposes a hierarchical structure upon the vocabulary and upon particular fields within the vocabulary; and the hierarchical ordering of lexemes can be represented formally as a tree-diagram, as illustrated schematically in figure 7. In the diagram,

$a, b, c, \ldots, k, l$, etc. stand for individual lexemes; and the point of origin, or root, of the tree is labelled with zero ($\emptyset$). Two branches are shown issuing from each node; but this is of course appropriate only for co-hyponyms related by opposition (cf. 8.3). The broken lines indicate further branches on the tree. As we have seen, hyponymy is transitive; so that any lexeme is a hyponym of any other lexeme that dominates* it on the tree (i.e. that is higher on the tree and connected by a path consisting solely of descending branches). For example, in terms of figure 7, $H(f, b)$, $H(l, a)$, $H(l, c)$, $H(g, a)$, and so on (where 'H' stands for the relation of hyponymy). If we now introduce the notion of direct, or immediate, domination (being connected by just a single descending branch), we can say that a immediately* dominates both c and d, but not g, h, l, etc.; that c immediately dominates g and h; that b immediately dominates e and f; and so on. By virtue of this fact a is the immediate superordinate of c and d, and c and d are immediate hyponyms of a: there is no (proper) hyponym of a such that c or d is a (proper) hyponym of it.

We may now consider whether a tree-diagram such as the one presented in figure 7 does in fact reflect the structure of the vocabulary, or parts of the vocabulary. This general question splits up into a number of more particular questions; and it is one of the principal heuristic advantages of constructing such diagrams (which can be interpreted as simple mathematical models of some empirical domain) that they force us to consider points which might otherwise escape our attention.

One such point may be mentioned and dismissed without a great deal of discussion. It would be natural, looking at figure 7, to enquire whether the sense-relation which holds between g and h is necessarily or ever the same as that which holds between i and j; more generally, if (i) y and z are immediate co-hyponyms of x, (ii) q and r are immediate co-hyponyms of p, and (iii) x and p are immediate co-hyponyms of n, is it always or ever the case that $R_i(y, z) = R_j(q, r)$? The answer seems to be that sometimes it is and sometimes it is not. For example, in everyday English (in which such words as 'mammal', 'vertebrate', etc. would not be used) 'horse' (x) and 'sheep' (p) are immediate co-hyponyms of 'animal' (n); 'stallion' (y) and 'mare' (z) are immediate co-hyponyms of 'horse', and 'ram' (q) and 'ewe' (r) are immediate co-hyponyms of 'sheep'; and the sense-relation holding between 'stallion' and 'mare' is the same, we may assume, as the relation between 'ram' and 'ewe'. On the other hand, 'bird' and 'fish' (as well as 'animal' and perhaps 'person') are immediate co-hyponyms of 'creature'; but the contrasts within the set {'eagle', 'thrush', 'starling', 'curlew', 'tern', 'oyster-catcher', etc.} and {'cat', 'horse', 'sheep', 'cow', 'wolf', 'elephant', etc.} are heterogeneous and idiosyncratic. At best, we might be able to find various kinds of scalar opposites within each set, based on such criteria as size, friendliness or utility to man, and so on. But it would be hopeless to attempt a complete analysis of the sense of the members of each set in terms of contrasts relevant to both sets. The theoretical significance of this will become clearer when we move on to consider the problems of componential analysis. The reader is meanwhile invited to consider various sets of co-hyponyms in English and other languages in the light of the point raised in this paragraph.

In figure 7, we have put a zero rather than a letter standing for some actual lexeme at the root of the tree. This is intended to suggest that the vocabulary, and indeed any particular part of it, may be structured hierarchically from a point which itself is not associated with an actual lexeme. In so far as figure 7 represents the hierarchical structure of the vocabulary as a whole, it seems clear that there will be no lexeme at the point of origin. The fact that lexemes, in most languages at least, fall into a number of distinct parts of speech would of itself preclude the hierarchical ordering of the vocabulary in terms of hyponymy under a single lexeme. For a lexeme belonging to one part of speech cannot be a hyponym of a lexeme belonging to another part of speech. If figure 7 represents the structure of the vocabulary as a whole, then, *a* and *b* are superordinates which are not hyponyms of any other lexeme; and the branches descending to them from the root of the tree must be eliminated.[10]

But is it the case that the vocabulary of a language is structured hierarchically in terms of hyponymy under several different points of origin, each one associated with a particular part of speech or some major subclass of one of the parts of speech? This is, at first sight at least, a more plausible notion; and it relates to the Aristotelian doctrine of the categories of predication and subsequent developments of it. Let us first of all consider the nouns in English. There is no lexeme in English which is superordinate to all nouns. Even the more or less technical word

[10] Anthropologists have paid a good deal of attention to the notion of hierarchical structure in the vocabulary especially in connexion with the study of so-called folk-taxonomies* (cf. Berlin, Breedlove & Raven, 1966, 1974; Conklin, 1962, 1972; Frake, 1962; Sturtevant, 1964). One point that seems to be well established is that folk-taxonomies, unlike modern scientific taxonomies, are not exhaustive of the domain that they classify: nor do they reach the same degree of specificity in all areas.

'entity' fails in this respect, since it covers only countable nouns; and its nearest equivalents in everyday English, 'thing' and 'object', are still more restricted. There is no lexeme which is superordinate to all abstract nouns, or all concrete nouns, or all mass nouns, or all the members of any of the major subclasses of nouns that are customarily recognized for English (cf. 11.3). What we find instead is a set of very general lexemes – 'person' (or 'human being'), 'animal', 'fish', 'bird', 'insect', 'thing', 'place', 'stuff', 'material', 'quality', 'property', 'state', etc. – which are superordinate to larger or smaller subsets of these subclasses of nouns.[11] The traditional definition of nouns, it may be observed, as words which denote persons, places and things is deficient (apart from its other inadequacies) in that it makes no mention of animals, fishes and birds, on the one hand, and of qualities, states, feelings, etc., on the other. It is also important to note that 'animal' in ordinary English is, not superordinate to, but in contrast both with 'person' and with 'fish', 'bird' and 'insect' and that, although 'creature' is superordinate to all five lexemes, it is stylistically restricted in various ways. There is no support in the lexical structure of English, therefore, for the view that all nouns denoting animate beings are hierarchically ordered, in terms of hyponymy, as a single class.

It is even more strikingly the case for other parts of speech than it is for nouns that they are not hierarchically organized under a single superordinate lexeme. There are certain very general verbs like 'act', 'move', 'become', 'make', 'get' and 'be', which have large numbers of hyponyms. We have already seen, for example, that 'get' has as hyponyms 'buy' and 'steal', and to these we may add 'borrow', 'win', 'earn', 'catch', 'find', 'grasp', etc. But no one of the most general verbs in English is superordinate to all the transitive or intransitive verbs, to all the verbs of state or verbs of activity, to all the verbs of motion, or to all the members of any of the traditionally recognized subclasses of verbs. If we take the most common adjectives in English we will see that there are no superordinate adjectives at all of which particular subsets are hyponyms. There are no lexemes of which adjectives, denoting differences of colour are all hyponyms. We do not say *Was it red or coloured in some other way?*; but rather *Was it red or (of) some other colour?* Similarly for subclasses of adjectives denoting differences of shape, texture, taste, sound, age, size, state of mind, etc.

---

[11] In many languages, some of the most general nouns, comparable semantically with English 'person', 'animal', 'thing', etc., function syntactically as classifiers (cf. 11. 4).

There is no paradigmatic superordinate of which 'round', 'square', 'oblong', etc. are hyponyms: what we find instead is what might be called a quasi-paradigmatic relation between these more specific adjectives and the more general abstract noun 'shape' (cf. *What shape was it, round or square?*). Adjectives like 'sweet', 'sour' and 'bitter' stand in a similar kind of quasi-paradigmatic relation with the superordinate verb 'taste' (cf. *What does it taste like?*), and derivatively with the corresponding noun 'taste' (cf. *What kind of taste has it got?*). Furthermore, the nouns 'shape', 'size' and 'colour' are in quasi-paradigmatic relation with the verb 'look (like)', as it is employed in such sentences as *What does it look like?* and in paradigmatic relation with the corresponding noun 'appearance' (cf. *Describe its appearance – what colour and shape was it, red and square, or green and round?*).

The sense in which the term 'quasi-paradigmatic' is being used here should be clear enough from the examples; and it can easily be made precise within the framework of a reasonably comprehensive transformational* grammar of English (cf. 10.3). We may describe the relationship between, for example, 'round' and 'shape' or 'sweet' and 'taste' as being one of quasi-hyponymy*. If we include quasi-hyponymy with hyponymy as a relation in terms of which vocabularies are structured hierarchically, the hypothesis that the vocabulary in all languages is structured hierarchically under a relatively small set of lexemes of very general sense is rather more plausible. It is a hypothesis, however, which is difficult to evaluate on the basis of the evidence that is at present available.

Conventional dictionaries, in which lexemes (in their citation form) are listed in alphabetical order and their principal senses defined and exemplified with quotations (usually from written sources), will frequently append to some, though not all, of their entries a list of so called synonyms and antonyms. The better and more comprehensive alphabetical dictionaries will give some indication of the contexts in which roughly equivalent lexemes are interchangeable and will draw attention to differences in their connotations or emotive import; but no dictionary systematically distinguishes the different kinds of lexical opposition found in language (cf. 8.3). As far as relations of hyponymy and antonymy are concerned, these are rarely made explicit; and they cannot always be inferred from the definitions.

There is, however, another kind of dictionary, which is commonly described as being conceptual, rather than alphabetical (cf. Ullmann, 1957: 313ff; 1962: 254ff). The best known of these, and the earliest in modern times, is *Roget's Thesaurus of English Words and Phrases* (1852). The principle underlying a conceptual dictionary, or thesaurus* (to employ a distinctive term and one which does not presuppose any commitment to conceptualism* in semantics: cf. 4.3) is, as Roget himself put it in his introduction to the first edition, to classify "the words and phrases of the language, not according to their sound or their orthography, but strictly according to their signification". Although Roget's work was designed primarily "to facilitate the expression of ideas and to assist in literary composition", it was strongly influenced by seventeenth-century philosophical speculation (deriving from ideas of Francis Bacon, Descartes and Leibniz) about the possibility of constructing an ideal language for the systematization and development of scientific knowledge and more particularly by the famous *Essay* on this subject (1668) by John Wilkins (cf. Robins, 1967: 112ff; Salmon, 1966). Thesauri comparable with Roget's for English, but drawing upon advances made in descriptive semantics in the intervening period, also exist for German (Dornseiff, 1933) and Spanish (Casares, 1942); and there is an outline thesaurus for French, overtly modelled on Roget, in the appendix to Bally (1909). Also to be mentioned in this connexion is Buck's *Dictionary of Selected Synonyms in the Principal Indo-European Languages* (1949). None of these works, however, valuable though they are, provides the information we would need in order to resolve the question whether the vocabularies of the languages they deal with are organized on strictly hierarchical principles.

The most ambitious scheme for the construction of a thesaurus in terms of an allegedly universal framework of semantic categories and subcategories that has so far been produced is Hallig and Wartburg's (1952) so-called conceptual system (Begriffssystem). Despite its claim to be an empirically based and universally applicable classificatory system, which reflects "the intelligent average person's picture of the world [Weltbild] as this is determined by the pre-scientific general concepts established in language [durch die sprachlich bedingten vorwissenschaftlichen Allgemeinbegriffe bestimmt]", it is open to the criticism that it is as much an a priori system as Roget's and probably biased, in so far as it is grounded in descriptive semantics, in favour of the naive realism of speakers of what Whorf (1956) called Standard Average European. It can also be criticized on other grounds (cf. Ullmann, 1957: 314f; Geckeler, 1971: 99f). It is difficult to justify, for English at least, even the highest-level tripartite division of the vocabulary into lexemes relating to the universe, to man, and to man and the universe;

as it is difficult to justify, in terms of hyponymy and quasi-hyponymy, Roget's six main classes of lexemes, (i) abstract relations; (ii) space; (iii) matter; (iv) intellect; (v) volition; (vi) sentient and moral powers.

So far relatively little is known about the lexical structure of the vast majority of the world's languages; and, as we have seen, it is as yet impossible to evaluate, even for well studied and easily accessible European languages, the hypothesis that the vocabulary is hierarchically ordered, as a whole, in terms of hyponymy and quasi-hyponymy. The theoretical semanticist should be correspondingly cautious about putting forward general hypotheses of this kind. It is undeniable, however, that there is some degree of hierarchical organization in all areas of the vocabularies of languages that have been investigated. Indeed, it is hard to conceive of any language operating satisfactorily in any culture without its vocabulary being structured in terms of the complementary principles of hyponymy and contrast; and the descriptive work that has been done on various areas of the vocabulary in particular languages appears to support this conclusion.

9.6. *Lexical gaps*

Let us now interpret figure 7, not as a representation of the hierarchical organization of the whole vocabulary of a language, but of particular lexical fields within a vocabulary (cf. 8.2). One of the questions which arises in this connexion is whether there can be what have been called lexical gaps*. We are not concerned here with the absence of a lexeme denoting an object which happens not to exist in the culture in which a language operates; still less with the absence of lexemes which would encapsulate the sense of contradictory syntagmatic modifiers (e.g. the non-existence of a lexeme meaning "married bachelor" or "square circle"). By a lexical gap is here meant what structuralists often describe, metaphorically, as a hole in the pattern: that is to say, the absence of a lexeme at a particular place in the structure of a lexical field. It will be recalled that, according to Trier, this is theoretically inconceivable; but the assumptions which determine his rejection of the possibility of lexical gaps are questionable (cf. 8.2). Lexical gaps of the kind that concern us here fall into the category of what Lehrer (1974: 97) calls matrix gaps. As she says "a matrix gap shows up when related lexical items are analysed into semantic features and placed on a chart or matrix". We will discuss the question, however, with particular reference to hierarchical structure. Looked at from this point of view it resolves itself into two more specific questions: (i) Can we have cohyponymy without an existing superordinate lexeme? (ii) Can we ever say that there is a lexical gap at a place in the hierarchical structure where we would expect a hyponym of an existing superordinate to be?

The answer to the first question, in the terms in which it has just been put, is decided in advance by our definition of hyponymy and consequently of co-hyponymy. But it can be reformulated in the following way: Is it ever the case that two or more lexemes are in contrast without there being any superordinate lexeme of which they are immediate hyponyms? We have already looked at a number of examples of lexical gaps of this kind. If figure 7 represented the field of colour adjectives in English, there would be no lexeme at the root of the tree. On the other hand, if we grouped together in the field lexemes belonging to different parts of speech (assuming some satisfactory integration of grammatical and lexical structure) we could say that the noun 'colour' is immediately superordinate to {'red', 'green', ...}. Under this interpretation of hierarchical structure the number of lexical gaps among superordinates will be much reduced. But it will not disappear entirely. There is no immediate superordinate for 'go' and 'come' in English; for 'teacher' and 'pupil'; for 'buy' and 'sell'; or for many other pairs of opposites in English. The non-existence of certain superordinates (and the relative infrequency or restricted application of others: e.g., 'spouse' superordinate to 'husband': 'wife', 'parent' superordinate to 'father':'mother', etc.) is related to the important notion of codability (cf. Brown, 1958: 235ff).

The second question is rather more difficult to answer in general terms. To take one of Chomsky's examples (1965: 231; cf. Lehrer, 1974: 97): in English there is a word 'corpse' meaning roughly "body of a dead human being" and a word 'carcass' meaning "body of a dead animal", but no word which is applied to dead plants. But this example is not as straightforward as it might appear at first sight. First of all, it should be noted that the sense of 'corpse' and 'carcass' is not a simple product of the sense of 'dead' and 'person', on the one hand, and of 'dead' and 'animal', on the other. 'Corpse' is not a hyponym of 'person', and 'carcass' is not a hyponym of 'animal'. Once we include the sense of 'body' in the gloss, then the alleged parallelism between 'corpse', 'carcass' and a potential, but unactualized, lexeme applicable to dead plants is destroyed. Furthermore, it might be argued that 'corpse' and 'carcass' do not contrast in the way suggested by the glosses that we have attached to them. If cannibalism were institutionalized in English-speaking countries and human beings were slaughtered with sheep, cattle and pigs for food, it is predictable that 'carcass' would be applied to the dead bodies of human beings delivered to the butcher's shop. On the other hand, if Mary's little lamb dies and, being very fond of it, she decides to inter it in the garden and perhaps to read the burial service over it during the ceremony of interment, she will certainly not describe what she is doing as burying its carcass: it will be the body, or corpse, of the lamb that is interred.

It is not a frivolous or facetious point that is being made in connexion with this example. Nor can it be dismissed with an appeal to the difference between the cognitive meaning and the emotive meaning of words. It simply is not clear that 'corpse' and 'carcass' are related in cognitive meaning, or sense, in the way that has been suggested. The point is that our dealings with dead human beings and dead animals are characteristically different and these are institutionalized in funerals and inquests, on the one hand, and in slaughterhouses, butchers' shops and the preparation of food, on the other; and it is in relation to such cultural institutions that the distinction between 'corpse' and 'carcass' is lexicalized. The fact that we do not have a word meaning "dead plant" is presumably to be accounted for by the fact that dead plants, as a class of objects have no culturally recognized role in the societies in which English has evolved. Lehrer's (1974) discussion of the vocabulary of cooking in various languages shows both the importance of cultural considerations and the difficulty of deciding what is and what is not a structurally definable lexical gap under a common superordinate.

Let us now take another example. As we saw above (cf. 9.2), there are separate words in Russian for "wife's brother", "husband's brother", "wife's sister", "husband's sister", "brother's wife" and "sister's husband", but (not surprisingly) no words for "brother's husband" and "sister's wife". There are undoubtedly two holes in the pattern at these points; but there are not two corresponding lexical gaps in English, since the in-law vocabulary of English, as we have seen, is structured in terms of different oppositions. One might be inclined to say that there couldn't possibly be words in any language meaning "brother's husband" or "sister's wife". But this is surely not so. Suppose it became more common, and more socially acceptable than it is at present, for two people of the same sex to enter into a permanent relationship, involving not only cohabitation, but an overtly recognizable distinction of roles comparable with the distinction of roles that exists in a conventional marriage. Such a relationship might well be initiated with a wedding ceremony and the exchange of vows; and the couple in question might describe themselves, and be described by others, as being married, one being the husband and the other the wife. What effect would this have on the lexical structure? The products of the senses of 'sister' and 'wife' and of 'brother' and 'husband' resulting in "sister's wife" and "brother's husband" are readily interpretable under the circumstances that we have envisaged. So the lexical gaps in the structure of the Russian vocabulary of kinship would correspond to potential, but non-existent, lexemes. If the gaps were filled by new words, the lexical structure of the language would be, to this extent, unaffected. The senses of the at present non-existent words are already there, as it were, ready to be lexicalized. Suppose, however, that they were not filled by new words, but that instead two of the existing in-law lexemes were extended in sense to fill the gaps: possibly, 'zjatj' and 'nevestka', the former coming to mean "sibling's (or child's) husband", and the latter "sibling's (or child's) wife". This would be a structural change; and it would skew the current pattern of relations that hold in this lexical field. As far as English is concerned, however, there are no gaps that need to be filled, whether by creating new words or extending the sense of already existing words. One's brother's husband is presumably the male spouse of one's sibling and is therefore readily referred to by means of the term 'brother-in-law'. Alternatively, if the sex of the referent were not held to be decisive, but rather the social role that he/she is playing, the male spouse of one's brother might be referred to by means of 'brother-in-law' or 'sister-in-law' according to whether he is the husband or the wife in the relationship.

The example discussed in the previous paragraph may seem rather fanciful: but changes do take place in social institutions and practices; and languages can adapt, along the lines suggested above, to changed circumstances. Anthropological discussions of kinship should serve to warn us against assuming in advance that even so universal a feature as biological sex must necessarily be reflected and be dominant in this area of the vocabulary. The main reason for introducing this hypothetical example at this point, however, was to illustrate the notion of lexical gaps within the framework of structural semantics and, at the same time, to give some indication of the difficulties which arise when we begin to consider seriously the difference between possible and impossible lexemes. The expressions 'female husband' and 'male wife' would probably be regarded as semantically unacceptable (like 'square circle') by most speakers of English. But, as we have seen, it does not require much imagination to envisage a world in which such expressions would not be held to be contradictory. Even in the world as we know it, the propositions expressed by such sentences as 'She is the father of five children' or 'She still loves her wife' are in no way semantically anomalous. The journalist James Morris, for example, did not cease to be the father of his children when he became a woman (and took the name 'Jan Morris': cf. Morris, 1974). The technique of envisaging possible worlds other than our own and then considering the applicability of existing lexemes, or collocations of existing lexemes, in relation to them is a technique that is fraught with difficulties. It is easy enough to submit a questionnaire to a group of native speakers, asking them what they would say in such-and-such circumstances (and it is even easier for the linguist to consult his own intuition). But the interpretation of the results obtained by such methods is always subject to Austin's caveat: "ordinary language breaks down in extraordinary cases" (1970: 68).

There are some clear cases of lexical gaps in languages which, unlike the examples discussed here at some length, present no problems with respect to the possibility of there being circumstances in which one might use a word with a particular sense. In French, as in English and other languages, there are many pairs of antipodal opposites used in the description of spatial extension or location: e.g. 'haut':'bas' ("high":"low"), 'long':'court' ("long":"short"). There is a lexeme 'profond', meaning "deep", but it has no antipodal opposite (cf. 'shallow' in English); either 'profond' is negated or the expression 'peu profond' ("deep to a small degree") is used to fill the lexical gap. If French lacked such lexemes as 'bas', 'court', etc. and regularly made use of the expressions 'peu haut', 'peu long', etc., we would not of course talk of lexical gaps: as we have seen antonymy is theoretically dispensable (cf. 9.1).

9.7. *Marked and unmarked terms*

Marking* (or markedness*), which derives from the work of the Prague School (cf. Vachek, 1964, 1966), is an extremely important concept in structural linguistics. Unfortunately, however, it is a concept which covers a number of disparate and independent phenomena. In what follows, we shall be concerned with marking only in so far as it is relevant to the analysis of lexical structure; and we shall distinguish three senses in which lexemes may be described as marked* or unmarked*.

We will begin with what may be called formal marking*. The words

'host':'hostess', 'count':'countess', 'lion':'lioness', etc., are morphologically, or formally, related complementaries (cf. 9.1). The forms of
the second member of each pair (e.g. *hostess, hostesses*) contain a suffix,
-ess, which the forms of the first member (*host, hosts*) lack. This suffix
is the formal mark of the opposition, as the prefixes *un-, in-, dis-* are the
formal marks of the opposition in 'friendly':'unfriendly', 'consistent':
'inconsistent', 'respectful':'disrespectful', etc. (cf. "one member of
the pair of opposites is characterized by the presence and the other by
the absence of a mark [Merkmal]" (Trubetzkoy, 1939: 67)). In cases
like this, the notion of marking is based on the presence or absence of
some particular element of form; and the lexemes whose forms contain
this element are said to be (formally) marked for the opposition, in
contrast with the unmarked members of each pair, which lack the element
in question. Not all of these oppositions, it should be noted, are such
that the formally marked term would be described as negative on
semantic grounds. Nor is it the case that in formally related opposites
one must be formally marked and the other formally unmarked: cf.
'useful':'useless', 'fruitful':'fruitless'.

Now formal marking commonly, though not invariably, correlates
with a difference in distribution*: the formally marked member of the
opposition tends to be more restricted in its distribution (i.e. in the range
of contexts in which it occurs) than the formally unmarked member.
But this criterion of distributional restriction is independent of formal
marking as such and may be applied equally well to formally unrelated
lexemes. As we have seen (9.1), what may be regarded as the negative
members of such oppositions as 'high':'low', 'good':'bad', 'happy':
'unhappy', etc., do not normally occur in such sentences as 'How...
was *X*?'. In contexts of this kind the opposition is said to be suspended
or neutralized*. It is an important fact about the structure of languages,
at all levels, that, when an opposition is characterized by formal marking,
it is the formally marked member that is excluded from the neutralizing
contexts; and recognition of this general correlation between formal
marking and distribution has been responsible for the extension of the
terms 'marked' and 'unmarked' on purely distributional grounds to
pairs of formally unrelated lexemes. But it must be emphasized that
two distinguishable properties are involved here, and the use of the
term 'marking' for both can lead to confusion.

Let us consider the pairs 'count':'countess' and 'lion':'lioness'.
In each case, the second member is formally marked and the first
member is formally unmarked. But the two pairs differ with respect to

the criterion of distributional restriction or neutralization. 'Lion' has a wider distribution than 'lioness': 'male lion' and 'female lion' are acceptable collocations, but 'male lioness' and 'female lioness' are not (the one being contradictory and the other tautological). The opposition between 'count' and 'countess' (or between 'prince' and 'princess'), however, is not neutralized in similar contexts: the collocations 'female count' and 'male countess' are contradictory, whereas 'male count' and 'female countess' are tautological. We can draw a distinction, therefore, between formal marking and distributional marking. When both kinds of marking are relevant, they tend to coincide (as with 'lion':'lioness', 'happy':'unhappy', etc.). But there are many formally marked lexemes that are not distributionally marked (e.g. 'countess' in relation to 'count'). And there are many distributionally marked lexemes that are not formally marked: notably, the negative members of such formally unrelated antonymous pairs as 'good':'bad', 'high':'low', etc.

Distributional marking correlates with, and in many cases can be plausibly explained as being determined by, semantic marking*; and, once again, this principle is independent of formal marking. A semantically marked lexeme is one that is more specific in sense than the corresponding semantically unmarked lexeme. 'Lioness' is more specific in sense than 'lion', as 'bitch' is more specific in sense than the formally unrelated 'dog'. For 'lioness' and 'bitch' denote only females whereas 'lion' and 'dog' can be applied, in many contexts, to either males or females; and it is for this reason that the collocations 'male lion' and 'female lion', and 'male dog' and 'female dog', are equally acceptable. In such contexts the semantic contrast between 'lion' and 'lioness' and between 'dog' and 'bitch' is neutralized. In other contexts, however, and most obviously when the opposites are employed in a disjunctive question (*Is it a dog or a bitch?*) or a statement in which one is predicated and the other negated (*It's a dog, not a bitch*), the unmarked lexeme assumes a more specific sense which is incompatible with the inherently specific sense of the marked lexeme. It should be noted, however, that, whereas all semantically marked lexemes are (by virtue of their more specific sense) distributionally marked, the converse does not hold. *X has a dog* can be uttered to make a true statement whether the animal referred to is male or female. But the proposition expressed by uttering *X has bought a big house* would be generally regarded as false if the house was in fact small rather than large in relation to the relevant norm.

So far we have discussed hyponymy (and quasi-hyponymy) under the assumption that it is necessarily an irreflexive relation (cf. 9.4). But this assumption is questionable in the light of what has now been said about semantic marking: that the unmarked member of the opposition has both a more general and a more specific sense according to context. Since 'dog' is sometimes in contrast with 'bitch' and sometimes superordinate to it, it follows that in certain circumstances 'dog' can be a hyponym of itself. "Is that dog a dog or bitch?" is a meaningful, though perhaps rather odd, sentence. If this were an isolated phenomenon in language, one might be inclined to say that 'dog' had two distinct senses "dog_1" and "dog_2", and that in one sense, "dog_1", it was superordinate to 'bitch' and in the other sense, "dog_2", co-hyponymous with it. But the phenomenon is widespread throughout the vocabulary of English and other languages. It is a direct consequence of semantic marking and should not be treated as an instance of polysemy* (cf. 13.4). As far as the relationship between 'dog' and 'bitch' is concerned, it is as if the lexical structure of English does not expect us to be concerned about the sex of dogs unless they are female, and then not always.

It is worth emphasizing that, when there are two lexemes for a particular species of animal, one lexeme being semantically marked and other unmarked for sex, it is not always the lexeme which denotes the female which is marked, as it is in English for 'lion':'lioness', 'tiger':'tigress', 'deer':'doe', and in general for all pairs of semantically marked words denoting non-domesticated animals and birds. The word 'bull' is marked in relation to 'cow', 'cock' (or 'rooster') in relation to 'hen' and (for those speakers who would not normally employ the word 'ewe') 'ram' in relation to 'sheep'. The reason for this would seem to be that males of these species are normally kept in smaller numbers by farmers than females, and purely for breeding: the main stock is female, and this is treated by the lexical structure of English as the unmarked norm. Whatever the reason, the theoretically important point is that, in the lexicalization of a distinction of sex, for some species it is the lexeme denoting males, and for other species the lexeme denoting females, that is semantically marked. The implication for componential analysis is that a single two-valued feature of plus-or-minus male or plus-or-minus female cannot be generalized over the vocabulary as a whole (cf. 9.9).

More careful consideration of these and other examples shows that whether a lexeme is semantically unmarked or not is a matter of degree. 'Dog', for many speakers of English at least, is completely unmarked semantically with respect to 'bitch' in that it can function without restriction as a superordinate in relation to its marked hyponym. 'Cow' is less unmarked than 'dog'; and the same is true of 'hen' (or 'chicken'), and perhaps also of 'sheep'. One might very well refer to a group of animals by means of an expression like 'those cows (over there)' without thereby implying that the group contained no bulls. But the same expression would probably not be used to refer to a group consisting solely of bulls. Again, one might well employ the expression 'male cow' as a reflexive or metalinguistic gloss for 'bull'; but 'male cow' (unlike 'female dog') is not an acceptable collocation in non-reflexive uses of the expression (though it was apparently used in the nineteenth century as a euphemism for 'bull'). It is self-contradictory, just as 'female bull' is. Nor can one say correctly *That cow is a bull* (as one can say *That dog is a bitch*), except of course in situations in which 'that cow' is to be construed as meaning something like "that animal which you have (incorrectly) described as a cow".

Even less unmarked than 'cow' in relation to 'bull' is 'man' in relation to 'woman'. 'Man' and 'woman' are unique among countable common nouns in English in that they can be used in the singular, without a determiner, as generic* referring expressions (cf. 7.2); and 'man' is more commonly used in this way than 'woman'. Now 'man' when it is employed in the singular in a generic referring expression is unmarked: cf. *It is man that is responsible for environmental pollution*, in which the reference of the expression 'man' may be construed as including or excluding women. Similarly, for the plural of 'man' as a generic referring expression: cf. *Men have lived on this island for ten thousand years*. But in most, if not all, other kinds of expressions, whether referential or predicative, 'man' is not held to be superordinate to 'woman'. Not only can one not say correctly *That man is a woman* (except under the circumstances noted above for 'That cow is a bull'), but one would not normally employ the expression 'those men (over there)', but 'those people (over there)', in referring to a group containing one or more women. If 'man' is said to be unmarked in relation to 'woman', it must be recognized that this is so only in highly restricted circumstances.

As we have seen, the sense of a hyponym can generally be analysed as the product of the sense of its superordinate and of some syntagmatic modifier of the superordinate. Languages provide the means of constructing an indefinitely large set of hyponymous expressions by explicit syntagmatic modification ('book', 'large book', 'large red book', etc.); that languages enable us to do this, and to be as specific and as precise in describing persons, objects, activities, etc., as the circumstances demand, depends upon the design feature of productivity* (cf. 3.4). Many of these phrases, by virtue of their frequent employment in contexts which neutralize, or render inapplicable, certain of their implications can, in the course of time, acquire a more specialized sense, as can single words under the same conditions. When this happens they are well on the way to achieving the status of phrasal lexemes or even word-lexemes. We will discuss this question more fully later (13.2). Here we are concerned to relate it to the phenomenon of semantic marking.

Our examples will be 'nurse', 'female nurse' and 'male nurse', on the one hand, and 'student', 'male student' and 'female student', on the other. The relationship between the lexeme 'student' and the hyponymous expressions 'male student' and 'female student', constructed from it by syntagmatic modification according to the productive rules of the language-system, is straightforward enough. From a statement like *My cousin is a student* nothing can be inferred about the sex of the referent of 'my cousin'; and there is no reason for us to think of 'male student' or 'female student' as single phrasal lexemes. From the statement *My cousin is a nurse*, however, most speakers of English will infer that the person being referred to is female. Is this inference based upon an implication which belongs to the sense of 'nurse'? And, if so, does 'nurse' imply 'female' in the way that 'cow' does, by virtue of being semantically unmarked in the language-system in relation to 'male nurse'? Or is the inference probabilistic, being determined by our knowledge that most nurses, like most secretaries and most students of domestic science or speech therapy, happen to be female?

It is arguable that 'nurse', by virtue of its sense in the language-system at the present time, implies 'female' (or the disjunction of 'girl' and 'woman') and that it is unmarked in relation to 'male nurse'. First of all, it should be noted that *My cousin is a male nurse* is a perfectly normal utterance (whereas *My cousin is a female nurse* is decidedly odd). Furthermore, not only is the phrase 'male nurse' of comparatively frequent occurrence in everyday discourse, but, when it is used as a predicative expression in spoken English, each of its constituent words is given equal stress. This of itself is an indication that 'male' is not being used to modify 'nurse' as a straightforward attributive adjective in implicit contrast with 'female'. The roles of nurses and male nurses in a hospital are, to some extent, distinct. To say that someone is a male nurse (when 'male nurse' is stressed in the normal way) is not to imply that he is a nurse who happens to be male. As we envisaged a change in the implications of 'husband' and 'wife' consequential upon the possible institutionalization of homosexual marriage with the distinction of the husband's role and the wife's role held more or less constant (cf. 8.3), so we can envisage a change in the implications of 'nurse' and 'male nurse' such that persons fulfilling one role would be described as nurses and persons fulfilling the other role would be described as male nurses, regardless of their sex. At the present time, however, 'nurse' and 'male nurse' should perhaps be regarded as lexemes which are related in sense as the unmarked and marked member of an opposition in the vocabulary; and they are more like 'cow' and 'bull' than 'dog' and 'bitch' in terms of semantic marking. It may be pointed out, in this connexion, that at the turn of the century in Britain the expression 'lady typist' was quite commonly employed in contexts (e.g., in advertisements) in which 'typist' would now be used.

In our discussion of semantic marking we have done little more than point out some of the distinctions that would need to be drawn in a fuller treatment of what is a complex and controversial subject. Some of the statements that have been made about particular examples might be challenged on factual grounds. There can be no doubt, however, that semantic marking is a matter of degree; and that it is an important feature of the lexical structure of languages. The fact that all the examples used above have had to do with the lexicalization of the distinction of sex in human beings and animals should not be taken to imply that semantic marking is peculiar to this distinction. We have concentrated upon this distinction partly because it is relatively straightforward and partly because it is so often invoked in discussions of semantic marking. It is rare for authors to discuss differences of degree in semantic marking; and a considerable amount of descriptive work on various languages will be required before anything like a comprehensive treatment of the subject can be written.

9.8. *Part–whole relations*

Mention should now be made of a somewhat different hierarchical relationship from hyponymy: the part–whole* relationship. This is exemplified by 'arm':'body', 'wheel':'bicycle', etc. In cases like this the distinction between hyponymy and part–whole relations is clear enough. An arm is not a kind of body but a part of a body; and phrases like 'arms and other kinds of body' are nonsensical. As a number of authors have pointed out (cf. Bierwisch, 1965; Kiefer, 1966), part–whole relations between lexemes are bound up with a particular sub-class of possessive constructions, exemplified by such semantically, and perhaps grammatically, related phrases and sentences as 'John's right arm' and 'John has a right arm'. Possessive constructions of this kind are in many languages, though not in English, distinguished grammatically from such phrases and sentences as 'John's book' and 'John has a book', the former being described as inalienable* and the latter as alienable* possessives.

Part–whole lexical relations are at least as diverse as the various kinds of hyponymy found in language, and we will not attempt to discuss them in detail. One question that has been debated in several recent treatments of the subject is whether the part–whole relation, like hyponymy, is transitive. The fact that different authors disagree about this point is perhaps an indication that here are various kinds of part–whole relations in language and that the logical differences between them are greater than the differences between various kinds of hyponymy (and quasi-hyponymy). It may also be a reflexion of a failure to maintain a consistent distinction between the part–whole relation as it holds between the referents of expressions (i.e. as a relation which holds between the separate or separable components of a thing and the whole thing of which they are components) and a structural relation of sense in the vocabularies of languages. The part–whole relationship which holds between physically discrete referents is clearly transitive: if some thing x is a part of some thing y which is a part of some thing z, then x is always describable as a part of z. Transitivity also holds, due allowance being made for a certain degree of indeterminacy in the reference of expressions in such cases, when the referents in question are not physical objects, but points or regions in physical space (or space-time). If x is a point or region which is part of a region y which is part of a region z, then x is a part of z.

The fact that one entity may be described as a part of another entity does not imply, however, that there is a part–whole relation holding in the vocabulary between the lexemes used in expressions which refer to these entities. For example, a certain object x may be referred to as 'the handle' and be a part of another object y, which may be referred to as 'the door' and be a part of a third object z, which may be referred to as 'the house'. x is a part of z (by virtue of the transitivity of the part–whole relationship holding between physical entities). But sentences like 'The house has a/no handle' or 'There's a/no handle on this house' are, to say the least, peculiar; and such phrases as 'the house-handle' or 'the handle of the house' are definitely unacceptable. Such phrases as 'the door-handle' and 'the handle of the door', as well as the sentence 'The door has a/no handle' are perfectly acceptable. So too are 'the door of the house' (and possibly 'the house-door') and 'The house has a/no door'. We might therefore be inclined to set up a part–whole relationship of sense between 'handle' and 'door' and between 'door' and 'house', but not between 'handle' and 'house'.

There are, however, many problems attaching to the notion of part–whole relations holding between lexemes. If we say that they are by definition intransitive, we shall be forced to recognize an enormous number of part–whole lexical pairs, many of which could be eliminated in the analysis of the vocabulary by means of general redundancy rules* based on transitivity, as suggested by Bierwisch (1965). For example, 'cuff':'sleeve' and 'sleeve':'jacket' are part–whole pairs, so too is 'cuff':'jacket': cf. 'These sleeves have no cuffs', 'The sleeves of this jacket have no cuffs', 'This jacket has no cuffs'. In order to account systematically for the acceptability of these three sentences and for their semantic relatedness, it would seem to be essential to invoke the notion of transitivity. For the part–whole relation holding between 'cuff' and 'jacket' is surely to be regarded as the product of the part–whole relations holding between 'cuff' and 'sleeve' and between 'sleeve' and 'jacket'. The problem, then, is that we have examples like 'handle': 'door':'house', on the one hand, and 'cuff':'sleeve':'jacket', on the other. The reader is invited to construct and consider other examples of both kinds for himself. If he does this, he will soon get some idea of the nature of the problem. To say that part–whole lexical relations are non-transitive, rather than being all transitive or intransitive, is true enough; but it hardly advances our understanding of the structure of the vocabularies of languages. What is required, if it can be found, is some general principle which would enable us to decide, with reference to the sense of particular sets of lexemes, whether they constitute what Bierwisch (1965) calls part–whole chains (Teil-von-Ketten) in the vocabulary, without specifying for each lexeme, as part of its sense, the place it occupies in a part–whole chain. None of the recent treatments of the subject, illuminating though they may have been in their discussion of particular sets of lexemes, has revealed any viable general principles of the kind required.

It could be argued that the whole question is irrelevant for linguistic semantics: that it is all a matter of our general knowledge of the relations which hold between entities in the external world. But this will not do.

We might well say, for example, and plausibly enough it might appear, that 'door' has a particular meaning and 'house' a particular meaning (analysable in terms of sense and denotation) and that the part–whole relation which was assigned above to the lexical pair 'door':'house' should be attributed instead to our knowledge of the purely contingent fact that all houses (or all normal houses) have doors. There are, however, numerous lexemes in the vocabularies of languages whose meaning cannot be specified independently of some part–whole relation of sense. How could we hope to analyse the meaning of 'sleeve' or 'lapel' without invoking a part–whole relation between these lexemes and 'coat', 'jacket', 'garment', etc. (as well as the different relation which holds between 'sleeve' and 'arm')? Even more convincing are sets of words like 'second', 'minute', 'hour', 'day', 'week', etc. The meaning of 'day', 'month' and 'year' (and perhaps 'week') could be explained, at least partly, without mentioning any part–whole relations holding within the set; and it could be regarded as a matter of contingent fact that there are approximately thirty days in a lunar month and between twelve and thirteen (lunar) months in a year. But it is in principle impossible to explain the meaning of 'second', 'minute' and 'hour' without specifying the part–whole relations holding within the set; and we could not distinguish between solar months (or calendar months) and lunar months without mentioning the part–whole relations within this set of lexemes.

The difference between hyponymy and part–whole relations, it was said, is clear enough in cases like 'arm':'body', 'wheel':'bicycle'; i.e. when the lexemes in question are nouns denoting discrete physical objects. Most of the discussion of part–whole lexical relations by linguists has been restricted to such cases. It is arguable, however, that other parts of speech besides concrete nouns denoting discrete physical objects may stand in a part–whole relation; and the distinction between the two relations in such cases is often far from obvious. For example, gold is both a kind of matter and a part of matter. We can say equally well *This substance has gold in it* or *This substance consists of/is composed of gold (and other metals)* and *This substance is gold*. We cannot sensibly say *This animal consists of a cow (and other mammals)* or *This body is an arm*. Abstract nouns, like concrete mass nouns, with which they have a certain logical affinity (cf. 11.3), may also be related both as hyponyms to a superordinate and as parts to a whole. Honesty may be regarded as a kind of virtue and also a part of virtue. So too for many verbs denoting activities. For example, the proposition "X can sew" may be held to imply a conjunction of "X can tack", "X can hem", "X can baste", etc. Each of the verbs in the set {'tack', 'hem', 'baste', etc.} is a hyponym of 'sew' and may yet be said to denote an activity which is part of the activity denoted by 'sew'. These few examples will serve to illustrate the way in which the hierarchical relationship between lexemes may, for lexemes other than countable nouns denoting discrete objects, be treated by language as hyponymy or a part–whole relation; or perhaps as a relation which is intermediate between them and shares certain characteristics with them both. Further complexities and interrelationships emerge when we consider particular types of part–whole relations such as that of being-a-temporal-slice-of (cf. the part–whole relation between 'childhood' and 'life' and the hyponymous relation which holds between 'child' and 'person'). We will not discuss these.

Mention should also be made in this section of various kinds of collectives*, such as 'cattle', 'clergy', 'furniture', 'herd', 'flock', 'family', 'library'. Collective nouns may be defined, semantically, as lexemes which denote collections or groups, of persons or objects. In English, they fall into a number of different grammatical classes. 'Cattle' and 'clergy', for example, are treated as plural, but 'furniture' as singular (cf. 'These cattle are...':'This furniture is...'). Others are singular with respect to concord within the noun-phrase, but (in British English at least) may be construed as either singular or plural for the purpose of concord with the verb or verb-phrase in the sentence (cf. 'this family': 'The family has decided...' or 'The family have decided...'). The grammatical ambivalence of many collectives with respect to the distinction of singular and plural is to be explained of course by the fact that a collection of objects may be regarded from one point of view as a single entity, but from another point of view, or for other purposes, as a plurality. We have already mentioned that plural noun-phrases (e.g. 'those men') functioning as general referring expressions are sometimes employed in order to ascribe a certain property to each of the members of a class, but that they may also be used to assert something of the class as a whole (cf. 7.2). Noun-phrases containing collectives are like plural noun-phrases in this respect; and it is interesting to note than when such noun-phrases refer to groups of human beings distributively, they necessarily select the relative pronoun 'who' (rather than 'which') and plural concord. Both of the following are possible (in British English), the former with distributive and the latter with collective reference to the Government: 'The Government, who have..., are...'; 'The Government, which has..., is...' But neither 'The Government,

who has..., is...' nor 'The Government, which have..., are...'
is grammatically acceptable.

We are here concerned with the place occupied by collectives in the
structure of the vocabulary. Many of them serve as superordinates in
relation to a set of quasi-hyponyms. It is, however, quasi-hyponymy
of a different kind from that noted above in connexion with such
examples as 'round':'shape' or 'blue':'colour'. For example, 'cattle'
is superordinate to {'cow', 'bull', 'steer', etc.}, as is shown by the
regular use of such expressions as 'cows, bulls and other cattle'; and
'clergy' is superordinate to {'bishop', 'priest', etc.}. But there are
differences between these two examples. Although 'priest' and 'bishop'
are quasi-hyponyms of 'clergy', as 'cow' and 'bull' are of 'cattle' (or
'man' and 'woman' of 'people'), 'priest' and 'bishop' also stand in
a particular kind of part–whole relation with respect to 'clergy': cf.
'priests, bishops and other members of the clergy'. 'Furniture' differs
from 'clergy' grammatically, but it is semantically parallel with it:
cf. 'tables, chairs and other kinds/items of furniture'. There are many
such collectives in the vocabulary of English and other languages which
are superordinate to sets of lexemes in a hierarchical relationship that is
ambivalent with respect to the distinction of hyponymy and the part–
whole relation. The fact that there is ambivalence of this kind correlates
with the fact that such collectives, whether they are grammatically
singular or plural, are very similar, semantically, to mass nouns; and
we have already seen that the distinction between hyponymy and the
part–whole relation is less clear-cut with superordinate mass nouns than
it is with superordinate countable nouns denoting discrete physical
objects. It should also be noted that the function of such words as 'kind',
'part', 'member', 'item', etc. (in expressions like 'kinds of animals',
'members of the clergy', 'parts of the body', 'items of furniture') is
comparable with that of the so-called classifiers* in languages which
draw no grammatical distinction between singular and plural (cf. 11.4).

Another kind of collective is exemplified by 'flock', 'herd', 'library'
and 'forest'. The relationship between 'sheep' and 'flock', 'cow' and
'herd', etc., is clearly not one of hyponymy: such phrases as 'sheep
and other kinds of flock' are nonsensical. Nor is it a part–whole relationship of the same type as that holding between 'arm' and 'body'.
Collectives like 'flock' serve much the same individuating function as
words like 'pool' or 'pound' in 'two pools of water' or 'three pounds
of butter' (cf. 7.6). There is a difference of course: 'water' and 'butter'
are mass nouns, whereas 'sheep' is a countable noun. Each sheep in

the flock is an individual. What a collective like 'flock' does is to individuate a set of undifferentiated individuals in the way that 'pool' or 'pound' individuates a quantity of water or butter. A flock may be composed of sheep and lambs, as the clergy is composed of bishops, priests, etc., and a body is composed of arms, legs, etc. Flocks, the clergy and bodies may all be considered, from this point of view, as collections of entities. But 'the flock of sheep', unlike 'the clergy of priests' and 'the body of legs', is an acceptable phrase. 'Flock', 'herd', 'forest', 'library', etc. are like the more general words 'set', 'collection', 'group', etc., except that they are syntagmatically restricted (and this also is characteristic of many, but not all, of the classifiers* in various languages: cf. 11.4). Being syntagmatically restricted, they may encapsulate* the sense of the lexemes which denote members of the collections in question (cf. 8.2). The phrases 'a herd of cattle' and 'a suite of furniture' illustrate the difference between the two different types of collectives.

9.9. *Componential analysis*

It is probably true to say that the majority of structural semanticists subscribe nowadays to some version or other of componential analysis*. This approach to the description of the meaning of words and phrases rests upon the thesis that the sense of every lexeme can be analysed in terms of a set of more general sense-components* (or semantic features*), some or all of which will be common to several different lexemes in the vocabulary. In so far as componential analysis is associated with conceptualism (cf. 4.3), the sense-components (for which there is so far no generally accepted term) may be thought of as atomic, and the senses of particular lexemes as molecular, concepts. For example, the sense of 'man' (construed as the complementary of 'woman': cf. 9.1) might be held to combine (in the molecular concept "man") the atomic concepts "male", "adult" and "human"; and the sense of 'woman' (viz. "woman") might be held to differ from that of 'man' solely in that it combines "female" (or "not-male"), rather than "male", with "adult" and "human". Componential analysis, interpreted in this way, can be related to the ideas of Leibniz and Wilkins which, as we saw earlier, served as an inspiration to Roget in the compilation of his thesaurus (cf. 9.1).

The earliest and most influential proponents of componential analysis in the post-Saussurean structuralist tradition were Hjelmslev and Jakobson. Their views are not identical, but they are similar enough as far as their advocacy of componential analysis is concerned: they both believed that the principles that Trubetzkoy (1939) had introduced into phonology could, and should, be extended into both grammar and semantics. Foremost among the representatives of this characteristically European version of componential analysis are Greimas (1965, 1970), Pottier (1974), Prieto (1964, 1966) and Coseriu (cf. Coseriu & Geckeler, 1974). Componential analysis in America appears to have developed independently. It was first proposed, not by linguists, as a general theory of semantic structure, but by anthropologists as a technique for describing and comparing the vocabulary of kinship in various languages (cf. Goodenough, 1956; Lounsbury, 1956; Wallace & Atkins, 1960). Only some years later was it taken up and generalized by such scholars as Lamb (1964), Nida (1964, 1975) and Weinreich (1963, 1966), as well as by Katz and Fodor (1963), in their seminal paper, which led to the integration of semantics and syntax within the framework of transformational grammar* (cf. 10.5).

We will not deal systematically with the similarities and differences between the several versions of componential analysis mentioned in the previous paragraph. We will concentrate instead upon some of the more general theoretical and methodological questions that any version of componential analysis must face; and we will begin by introducing a notational convention which will enable us to formulate these questions more clearly. Our convention will be to use small capitals for the representation of sense-components. Instead of saying that "man" is the product of "male", "adult" and "human", we will say that "man" (the meaning, or more precisely the sense, of the lexeme 'man': cf. 7.3) is the product of MALE, ADULT and HUMAN. What is meant by 'product' here is one of the questions that we must discuss. Another is the relationship between MALE and "male", between ADULT and "adult", between HUMAN and "human", and so on. For, as "man" is the meaning of the English lexeme 'man', so "male" is the meaning of the English lexeme 'male' and "human" is the meaning of the English lexeme 'human'.

One answer to the question whether MALE is to be identified with "male", ADULT with "adult", and so on, is that there is a sharp distinction to be drawn, in principle, between the meanings of lexemes and the atomic concepts, or sense-components, into which these meanings can be factorized; and that, consequently, MALE and ADULT are not to be identified with "male" and "adult". MALE, ADULT, etc., are held to belong to a set of universal atomic concepts which may or may not be lexicalized* in particular languages; and lexicalization is held to consist in providing a lexeme whose meaning contains at least one of these atomic sense-components. It follows that different languages will not necessarily lexicalize the same sense-components and, in so far as they do lexicalize the same sense-components, that they will not necessarily combine them in the same way. We will provisionally accept this point of view, which, as we have already seen, enables the structural semanticist to avoid the more extreme kind of relativism (cf. 8.3).

We must now ask what is meant by the term 'product' when it is said, for example, that "man" is the product of MALE, ADULT and HUMAN. In this case, it is plausible to interpret 'product' in terms of the conjunction of sense-components: the extension of 'man' (construed as the complementary of 'woman') is the intersection of the classes M, A and H, whose intensions are the atomic concepts MALE, ADULT and HUMAN, respectively (cf. 6.4). It is this interpretation of product (though it is rarely made explicit) which seems to underlie most of the earliest work on componential analysis, both European and American. For example, Pottier's (1964) well-known analysis of the French lexemes 'chaise', 'fauteuil', 'canapé' and 'tabouret' (roughly equivalent to English 'chair', 'arm-chair', 'sofa' and 'stool') in terms of the sense-components FOR SITTING UPON, WITH LEGS, WITH A BACK, WITH ARMS and FOR ONE PERSON is presumably to be understood in this way. So too is Hjelmslev's (1959) analysis of 'ram', 'ewe', 'man', 'woman', 'boy', 'girl', 'stallion', 'mare', and Katz and Fodor's (1963) analysis of what they took to be the four distinct senses of 'bachelor'.

Analyses of kinship vocabulary, on the other hand, typically allow for both the disjunction and the conjunction of sense-components. For example, on the assumption that this is in fact the correct analysis and that, not only MALE, but also the two-place relational predicates SPOUSE (x, y) and SIBLING (x, y), are atomic concepts, the sense of 'brother-in-law' might be represented (in part at least) as MALE (x) & (SPOUSE-OF-SIBLING-OF (x, y) $\lor$ SIBLING-OF-SPOUSE-OF (x, y)). As this example shows, once we combine both conjunction and disjunction we must introduce into the representation of the sense of lexemes (by means of brackets or otherwise: cf. 6.4) a distinction between such classes as $(X.(Y+Z))$ and $((X.Y)+Z)$. For $(X.(Y+Z))$, but not $((X.Y)+Z)$, is extensionally identical with $(X.Y)+(X.Z)$: e.g., if x is y's brother-in-law, then x is either both male and the spouse of the sibling of y or both male and the sibling of the spouse of y. Our example also shows: (i) that, if relational predicates like SPOUSE (x, y) and SIBLING (x, y) are admitted into the stock of atomic concepts, there must be some way (whether by using variables like x and y or otherwise) of indicating the directionality of the relation; and (ii) that, if complex relations like SPOUSE-OF-SIBLING-OF (x, y) and SIBLING-OF-SPOUSE-OF (x, y) are employed, they must be defined in such a way that they are not necessarily equivalent. It will not do, therefore, to say that the sense of a lexeme is an unstructured set of sense-components: that "brother-in-law", for instance, is the product of MALE, SPOUSE and SIBLING. As we have already seen (in our brief consideration our English and Russian: cf. 9.2) SIBLING-OF-SPOUSE-OF and SPOUSE-OF-SIBLING-OF may or may not be lexicalized by means of the same lexeme; and the sex of y, instead of or in addition to the sex of x, may be criterial. MALE (x) & MALE (y) & SIBLING-OF-SPOUSE-OF (x, y), MALE (x) & FEMALE (y) & SIBLING-OF-SPOUSE-OF (x, y), MALE (x) & MALE (y) & SPOUSE-OF-SIBLING-OF (x, y) and MALE (x) & FEMALE (y) & SPOUSE-OF-SIBLING-OF (x, y) are all, in principle, lexically distinguishable; and whether they are distinguished or not in different languages is a matter of contingent fact.

Indeed, it requires but a moment's reflexion to see that certain more complex combinations of SPOUSE and SIBLING are possible and that whether, and how, they are lexicalized in particular languages is also a matter of contingent fact. Many speakers of English (though apparently not all) subsume SPOUSE-OF-SIBLING-OF-SPOUSE-OF (x, y), but not SIBLING-OF-SPOUSE-OF-SIBLING-OF (x, y), or SPOUSE-OF-SIBLING-OF-SPOUSE-OF-SIBLING-OF (x, y), or SIBLING-OF-SPOUSE-OF-SIBLING-OF-SPOUSE-OF (x, y), etc., under 'brother-in-law' and 'sister-in-law'. All of these relations are lexicalizable; and it must be possible to specify which of them are grouped together in the same lexeme and which are not. It must also be possible, in principle, to handle certain recursive* combinations of SPOUSE (x, y) and SIBLING (x, y). One's sibling's sibling is either oneself or one's sibling. But in a non-monogamous society one's spouse's spouse is not necessarily oneself. It follows that a simple relation like SPOUSE (x, y) is infinitely recursive, and, unlike the much more obviously recursive (and presumably non-atomic) relation of being the ancestor of, it is non-transitive (cf. 6.4). None of the kinship terms of English (apart from 'ancestor' and 'descendant') would seem to involve recursion. There are other languages, however, in which the recursive application of the same atomic relation is fundamental to the componential analysis of the vocabulary of kinship (cf. Lounsbury, 1964). As far as English is concerned, we must specify which of the infinitely many products of such putative atomic relations as SPOUSE (*x*, *y*) and SIBLING (*x*, *y*) are lexicalized and which of them are not; and, as we have seen, this cannot be done simply by listing the sense-components that are combined. Not every relation containing both SPOUSE (*x*, *y*) and SIBLING (*x*, *y*) is lexicalized as 'brother'in-law' or 'sister-in-law'.

It is arguable that the notion of product with which we operate when we say that the sense of a lexeme is the product of a set of atomic concepts must be even richer than the one that we have elaborated so far. According to Weinreich (1966), lexemes have an internal structure which mirrors the syntactic structure of sentences and phrases; and this point of view has been adopted by the so-called generative semanticists* (cf. 10.5). For example, McCawley (1971) has suggested that the sense of the verb 'kill' can be analysed into CAUSE, BECOME, NOT and ALIVE and that those elements are not simply conjoined (as, let us say, MALE, ADULT and HUMAN are conjoined in the sense of 'man'), but are combined in a hierarchical structure, which may be represented here (with the omission of certain variables) as (CAUSE (BECOME (NOT (ALIVE)))). Associated with this analysis is the further proposal that, in this case, English lexicalizes not only the whole complex, but each of the constituent combinations: that ALIVE is lexicalized in 'alive', (NOT ALIVE) as 'dead', and (BECOME (NOT ALIVE)) as 'die'.

We will not here go into the details of this analysis. It is sufficient for the present purpose to point out that, on the assumption that CAUSE, BECOME, NOT and ALIVE combine to yield as their product the sense of the verb 'kill', they must be combined in a hierarchical structure of the kind that is manifest in the complex expression 'cause to become not alive', rather than that which is manifest in, let us say, 'cause not to become alive' or 'not (to) cause to become alive'. As we shall see later, a somewhat different view of the internal structure of lexemes is taken by those scholars who base their theory of grammar on the notion of valency* (cf. 12.2). But they too would argue that the principles or operations by means of which sense-components are combined in lexemes in the process of lexicalization are essentially the same as the principles or operations whereby words and expressions are combined in syntactically well-formed sentences.

Enough has been said to show that matrices of the kind that are often employed in lists of sense-components must be supplemented, for some lexemes at least, with a specification of the way in which the sense-components are combined; and furthermore that their combination cannot in all instances be accounted for in terms of the simple operations of

conjunction and disjunction (with or without recursion). We may now
take up a number of other points.

The first has to do with the question of binarism* and the use of
feature-notation* (which is commonly though not necessarily associated
with binarism). As we have seen, the principle of dichotomous contrast
is of considerable importance in the lexical structure of languages:
many pairs of lexemes can be described as antonyms or complementaries (cf. 9.1). Furthermore, many of the oppositions that hold between
antonyms and complementaries can be regarded as having a marked and
an unmarked member (cf. 9.7). The thesis of binarism*, as we shall
interpret the term, says that all lexical contrasts are both dichotomous
and privative. As the phonemes /p/ and /b/ in French stand in opposition
to one another on the phonological dimension of voice, so do 'man' and
'woman', 'boy' and 'girl', etc., on the semantic dimension of sex (cf.
Greimas, 1965: 20ff; Pottier, 1974: 61ff), and as /b/ can be said to contain the phonological feature of voice, which /p/ lacks, so (it might be
argued) "man" and "boy" contain the sense-component MALE, which
"woman" and "girl" lack.

But why, it may now be asked, do we say that "woman" and "girl"
lack the component MALE, rather than that "man" and "boy" lack the
component FEMALE? As we have seen, it is 'man' rather than 'woman'
that is the unmarked member of the opposition, though 'man' is by
no means as completely unmarked as 'dog' is in relation to 'bitch'
(cf. 9.7). If we apply to semantics the same kind of considerations that
Trubetzkoy (1939) introduced into phonology, it is clearly preferable
to say that the sense-component whose presence or absence distinguishes "woman" from "man" and "bitch" from "dog" is
FEMALE. But there is no such reason to say that 'boy' is semantically
unmarked in relation to 'girl', 'ram' in relation to 'ewe' or 'stallion'
in relation to 'mare'. It is equally appropriate to say that "boy" and
"ram" contain MALE, which is lacking in "girl" and "ewe", as it is to
say that "girl" and "ewe" contain FEMALE, which is lacking in "boy"
and "ram". This would not be a problem, perhaps, if it were not for
the fact that in other pairs of complementaries, like 'cow':'bull' and
'duck':'drake', it is the one denoting the male that is semantically
marked.

If we take the view that there is a universal set of atomic concepts
which are lexicalized in particular languages, the fact that, as far as the
distinction of sex is concerned, it is sometimes MALE and sometimes
FEMALE that appears to be present in the meaning of the marked member

of a pair of complementaries confronts us with a dilemma. We can arbitrarily select either MALE or FEMALE as a putative universal atomic concept and define the other negatively in terms of it (i.e. we can operate either with +FEMALE and −FEMALE or with +MALE and −MALE); and, as we have just seen, this will lead to the unsatisfactory analysis of certain pairs of complementaries. Alternatively, we can allow that both MALE and FEMALE are atomic concepts; but this would run counter to the whole spirit of binarism, since it would leave +MALE and +FEMALE as theoretically unrelated, and potentially co-existent, components and (in default of some supplementary statement or rule to the effect that +MALE implies −FEMALE and that +FEMALE implies −MALE) it would not contribute in any way to an explication of the relationship of entailment which holds between such propositions as "That horse is a stallion" and "That horse is not a mare".

We have just introduced a further notational convention. This is the use of a plus-sign or a minus-sign to distinguish between the positive and the negative values of what is referred to technically, in linguistics, as a feature*. The term 'feature', it may be added, is also employed with respect to the values of the variable: i.e. not only is the variable ±MALE (or ±FEMALE) described as a feature, but so also are its two values, +MALE and −MALE (or +FEMALE and −FEMALE). We will continue to use the term 'component' for the values, reserving 'feature' for the variable of which they are values.

The use of feature-notation raises a further question. If −MALE is held to represent, not a component equivalent to FEMALE, but the absence of +MALE, how do we capture the difference between "horse" and "mare"? For "horse" also lacks the component +MALE (on the assumption that the feature in terms of which "stallion" and "mare" are distinguished is ±MALE, rather than ±FEMALE), and at this point it may be added that it is not uncommon for the term 'unmarked' to be used by linguists in a way that obscures the difference between 'dog' or 'duck', on the one hand, and 'horse' or 'child', on the other. The words 'horse' and 'child', in this usage of the term 'unmarked', are said to be unmarked for the feature ±MALE (or ±FEMALE). But 'horse' and 'child' are not the unmarked members of a privative opposition, as 'dog' and 'duck' are. We must be careful, therefore, to draw a distinction between the minus-value and the zero-value of a feature: i.e. between −MALE (cf. "duck" and ØMALE (cf. "horse" or "child") and between −FEMALE (cf. "dog") and ØMALE (cf. "horse" or "child"). Unless this distinction is drawn, a proposition like "That's a horse over there" will be wrongly held to be equivalent to either "That's a stallion over there" or "That's a mare over there", according to whether $\pm$FEMALE or $\pm$MALE is selected as the feature whose values distinguish "stallion" and "mare".

Indeed, there is yet a further distinction that one might wish to draw: between those lexemes whose meaning is compatible with both the negative and the positive value of a binary feature and those lexemes whose meaning is compatible with neither the negative nor the positive value. For example, "horse" is compatible with both $+$MALE and $-$MALE (or both $+$FEMALE and $-$FEMALE), whereas "house", it might be argued, is compatible with neither. If the distinction between the minus-value and the zero-value of a binary feature is accepted, the further distinction between the zero-valued 'horse' and the non-valued 'house' is readily represented by saying that, whereas the meaning of 'horse' contains ØMALE (or ØFEMALE) as a component, the meaning of 'house' contains no value of $\pm$MALE (or $\pm$FEMALE). But by adopting this way of representing the distinction between "horse" and "house" with respect to the feature $\pm$MALE (or $\pm$FEMALE) we are obviously making the feature in question three-valued rather than binary. An alternative is to reject the distinction between zero-valued and non-valued lexemes and to say that neither 'horse' nor 'house' is specified for any value of $\pm$MALE (or $\pm$FEMALE). This is more in keeping with the spirit of binarism; and it is arguable that it is sufficient for the purpose of componential analysis to distinguish between minus-valued and un-specified. The fact that both 'male horse' and 'female horse' are normal and readily interpretable expressions whereas 'male house' and 'female house' are not (on the assumption that this is to be accounted for in terms of the meaning of 'horse' and 'house') is explicable in terms of the presence in "horse" of a component like $+$ANIMATE and its absence from "house". Only animate entities may be male or female; and the fact that there are some species of sexless or hermaphroditic creatures is perhaps reasonably held to be a matter of contingency, rather than of logical necessity, and to be irrelevant to the description of English or any other language.

There are, of course, many lexical contrasts which do not appear to be dichotomous (cf. 9.3); and, as we have seen both here and earlier, even an apparently straightforward dichotomous contrast such as that which holds between 'man' and 'woman', 'ram' and 'ewe', 'stallion' and 'mare', etc., presents the analyst with various problems if he wishes to treat it as a privative opposition, comparable with the phonological opposition that holds between the phonemes /b/ and /p/, /d/ and /t/, etc.

A further difficulty with feature-notation is that it cannot naturally represent the distinction between complementarity and antonymy without failing to represent the similarity between these two kinds of dichotomous contrast (cf. 9.1). Bierwisch (1969), for example, draws a distinction between what he calls singular markers like HUMAN, whose logical negation, NON-HUMAN, is simply its contradictory and does not denote a positive property, and what he refers to as antonymous n-tuples (in an unusually broad sense of the term 'antonymous' deriving from Katz, 1964, 1966). Examples of these so-called antonymous n-tuples are {MALE, FEMALE} and {BLACK, WHITE, RED, GREEN, ...}; and it is suggested that each member of the set is a positive value of an n-valued feature (where $n = Z$). Thus, MALE would be one of the two possible equipollent values of the feature SEX; BLACK would be one of the possible values of the feature COLOUR; and so on. (More precisely, what we have just represented as MALE and BLACK would be bipartite sense-components consisting of (i) a superordinate marker taken from the set $M =$ {SEX, COLOUR, AGE, SPECIES, ...} and (ii) a subordinate marker, μ, specifying which particular location within the domain denoted by the superordinate marker is denoted by the subordinate marker. But we need not go into the details of Bierwisch's formalism in the present connexion.) Within this framework, it is easy enough to formulate a general rule accounting for the relationship that holds between complementary equipollent values of a two-valued feature, since two-member n-tuples are merely a particular case of n-valued n-tuples. Any logical relationship that is defined to hold between an arbitrary member of an n-member set and either the conjunction or the disjunction of the remaining n-1 members of the set will hold between each member of a two-member set and the remaining single member. But the importance of dichotomous lexical opposition in language is such that it is counter-intuitive, to say the least, to treat complementarity as being no different in kind from multiple equipollent contrast, even though it may be satisfactory enough from a purely formal point of view to do this. Furthermore, antonymy (in the narrower sense that we have given to the term: cf. 9.1) cannot be handled within this framework without introducing some supplementary notational convention or some additional component (such as the positive value of the two-valued feature $\pm$POLAR or the two-place relational component GREATER (x, y): cf. Bierwisch, 1967, 1970) to distinguish antonyms from complementaries.

We will make no further use of feature-notation in this section; and we will say no more about binarism and the formal, or notational, problems that it gives rise to. There are various more general points to be made about componential analysis.

Componential analysis can be seen as an extension of field-theory and, more particularly, as an attempt to put field-theory on a sounder theoretical and methodological footing (cf. 8.4); and this is the way that componential analysis is commonly presented by European structuralists (cf. Geckeler, 1971). That it should be so interpreted is natural enough. It is important to realize, however, that it neither presupposes field-theory nor is it presupposed by it. On the one hand, it is possible to hold the view that certain subsets of the totality of lexemes in a language constitute a field and contract a variety of sense-relations with one another and at the same time to reject componential analysis as a method of identifying the field and stating the sense-relations holding among the members of the field. On the other hand, one might equally well adopt componential analysis as a means of stating the sense-relations that hold among sets of lexemes, but refuse to recognize that the notion of a lexical field has any role to play.

Only one aspect of what some scholars see as the interdependence of field-theory and componential analysis need concern us here; and this is the distinction that has been drawn on the basis of this alleged interdependence between two kinds of semantic components: between semes* and classemes* (cf. Pottier, 1974; Coseriu, 1967). According to Coseriu, semes are the minimal distinctive features of meaning that are operative within a single lexical field, and they serve to structure the field in terms of various kinds of opposition (cf. Coseriu & Geckeler, 1974: 149). Examples of semes would be the sense-components that Pottier recognizes as being distinctive in the lexical field consisting of 'chaise', 'fauteuil', etc. Classemes, in contrast with semes, are very general sense-components that are common to lexemes belonging to several different lexical fields; and they tend to be, not only lexicalized, but also grammaticalized (cf. Coseriu & Geckeler, 1974: 152). Examples of classemes would be ANIMATE/INANIMATE, MALE/FEMALE and possibly CAUSE and HAVE. Hjelmslev's analysis of the meaning of 'man', 'woman', 'stallion', 'mare', etc. would presumably involve both semes and classemes.

The distinction between semes and classemes has been mentioned here because in certain respects it corresponds, at least roughly, with the equally controversial, but more familiar, distinction between distinguishers* and markers*, which, as it was originally drawn by Katz and Fodor (1963), was held to reflect the distinction between what was systematic for the language in the meaning of a lexeme and what was not. The part of the meaning of a lexeme that was systematic was to be represented by a set of markers and the residue by a distinguisher. The necessary and sufficient conditions for deciding whether a particular component is a marker or a distinguisher were not precisely specified in Katz and Fodor (1963); and the whole basis of the distinction between the two kinds of components was challenged by Bolinger (1965), Weinreich (1966), Bierwisch (1969) and others. What concerns us here is the similarity between the seme/classeme distinction drawn by certain European structuralists and the distinguisher/marker distinction that has been postulated by some transformational grammarians and rejected by others.

At first sight, these two distinctions would appear to have nothing in common: the one is overtly based on the prior delimitation of lexical fields; the other is totally independent of field-theory and is held to rest primarily on the notion of systematicity within the language. But there is a similarity between the European structuralists' conception of classemes and Katz's conception of markers. When Katz says that his markers are systematic for the language (that MALE, for example, is systematic for English), what he has in mind is the role that the markers play, according to his theory, in the statement of selection restrictions* (cf. 10.5). For example, the anomaly of a sentence like 'That man is pregnant' (on the assumption that it is semantically anomalous) could be accounted for by ensuring that 'pregnant' cannot combine with any noun whose meaning contains the component MALE; and this implies that MALE is systematic for English. Similarly, when Pottier and Coseriu divide semantic components into semes and classemes, they emphasize that it is the classemes that determine the semantically based syntagmatic interdependences between nouns and adjectives or nouns and verbs: that it is the classeme MALE, for example, that determines the selection of Italian 'ammogliarsi' (rather than 'maritarsi'), Rumanian 'a se însura' (rather than 'a se mărita'), Russian 'ženitsja' (rather than 'vyxoditj zamuž') in sentences corresponding to English sentences containing the verb 'marry'. There is perhaps less similarity between 'semes' and 'distinguishers', since the former are held to depend upon minimal functional oppositions (whether privative or equipollent), whereas the latter are merely the residue of lexical meaning that is not accounted for in terms of markers. At the same time, it is evident that such components as Pottier's FOR SITTING UPON (which he classifies as a seme) would be treated as distinguishers by Katz.

Now, systematicity within the language, as Katz construes this notion, tends to correlate with several other characteristics. The semantic distinctions and equivalences between lexemes that are accounted for in terms of classemes or markers, in the examples that are given by the authors who operate with two kinds of semantic components, are such that: (i) they are readily identifiable across languages and are less obviously language-dependent or culture-dependent than are the distinctions and equivalences accounted for in terms of semes or distinguishers; (ii) they are syntactically relevant and may be grammaticalized as well as lexicalized; (iii) they are not restricted to a few lexemes, but are widely distributed throughout the vocabulary. All these criteria are independent of one another. It follows that, if any one of them was made definitive (on the assumption that it could be specified precisely enough for the purpose), it might be in conflict with the others. For example, MALE is not syntactically relevant in Turkish (there are no distinctions of gender, the personal pronouns are not distinguished with respect to the sex of the referent, etc.): but it seems to be as widely distributed throughout the vocabulary as it does in English, French, Russian, etc.; and it is, of course, an especially plausible case of what might be held to be a language-independent and culture-independent atomic concept.

This discussion of the seme/classeme distinction, on the one hand, and of the distinguisher/marker distinction, on the other, has not only served to emphasize the fact that there are difficulties involved in making these distinctions precise. It has had the more positive purpose of relating the notion of componential analysis to the discussion of universalism and relativism in the previous chapter (8.3). So far, in our exposition of componential analysis we have not explicitly called into question the assumption that sense-components must be universal atomic concepts. But this assumption can be challenged.

As far as the conceptual status of sense-components is concerned, it must be emphasized that there is no necessary connexion between componential analysis and conceptualism* in the sense that we have given to this term (cf. 4.3). It would be quite possible to factorize the sense-relations that hold between lexemes and to treat these factors as theoretical constructs, whose postulation simplifies the description of the language, but does not commit the linguist to the existence of any corresponding mental entities. For example, as we can extract from the arithmetical proportion $21:14::15:10$ the factors 7, 5, 3 and 2, since $(7 \times 3):(7 \times 2)::(5 \times 3):(5 \times 2)$, so we can extract from the semantic proportion 'man':'woman'::'stallion':'mare' the factors a, b, c, d (however these factors might be labelled or symbolized in the linguist's model of the language-system). The factors would derive their linguistic significance from the fact that each of them enables the linguist to account for the semantic acceptability or unacceptability of sets of sentences: the presence of a in "man" would account for the acceptability of 'That man cuts his own hair' and the unacceptability of 'That man cuts her own hair' or 'That man is pregnant'; the presence of both b and d in "mare" (and of d, in combination with one or more specified components in "foal") would account for the acceptability of 'That mare has just given birth to a beautiful little foal' and the presence of either a or c (or both) in "man", "woman" and "stallion" would account for the unacceptability of 'That man/woman/stallion has just given birth to a beautiful little foal'. Whether these sentences are in fact semantically anomalous or not is, of course, a separate question (cf. 10.5). The point is that the extraction of sense-components can be carried out on the basis of such proportions as 'man':'woman'::'stallion':'mare'; and the validity of the factors stands or falls by their explanatory power in relation to the use of language.

Most proponents of componential analysis, it is true, would not be content to say that sense-components are to be defined solely in terms of the acceptability of sentences and the relations of equivalence and implication that hold between sentences within a single language. (But this, it may be observed, was Hjelmslev's view; and, to this extent, our presentation of his analysis of 'man':'woman', 'stallion':'mare', etc., was rather misleading.) They would wish to say that the labels chosen to identify the components have more content than our algebraic factors a, b, c and d; and they would wish to relate at least some of the factors to the external world in terms of the relation of denotation, saying that MALE (our a) denotes the class of all entities that have such-and-such a property, that HUMAN (our c) denotes the class of all entities that have a different (but compatible) property, and so on. There can be no quarrel with this. It is obvious, however, that, unless one provides some extensional definition of MALE, HUMAN, etc., or some intensional definition that does not make metalinguistic use of the English words 'male', 'human', etc. (or the French words 'mâle', 'humain', etc.; or the Russian words 'mužkoj', 'čelovečeskij'; or the words of some other natural language), no explanation has been given of the meaning of 'male', 'human' or of the sense-components in the meaning of 'man' that adds anything to an analysis that makes use of purely algebraic symbols (cf. Lewis, 1972). Furthermore, in view of the looseness with which the term 'concept' tends to be employed by semanticists and the criticisms that have been directed against conceptualism by both philosophers and psychologists, it must be emphasized that the extensional or intensional definition of MALE, HUMAN, etc. does not necessarily involve the postulation of any correlated mental entities.

Let us now turn to the question of atomicity. Ever since Leibniz put forward his proposals for the construction of a universal symbolic language the principle of atomicity has been prominent in philosophical discussions of the way in which the meanings of words might be analysed into smaller, and presumably more basic, components. By 'basic', in this context, it is implied that the components in question constitute the points of attachment between language and the external world: i.e. that they can be defined by relating them directly to entities outside language. It was Leibniz's intention that the symbols in his universal language should express simple (i.e. atomic) ideas; and this has generally been held to imply, in the empiricist tradition at least, that they should be acquired by virtue of immediate sensory experience. Whatever the philosophical merits of the empiricist principle of atomicity, it is obvious that most of the sense-components that have been postulated by linguists (e.g., MALE, ALIVE, FOR SITTING UPON) are not atomic in this sense.

It may be that there are certain lexemes whose denotation can be accounted for in terms of perceptual distinctions that are physiologically atomic in that they can be shown to depend upon an all-or-nothing response to a sensory stimulus. For example, the recognition of a reddish or greenish hue might be physiologically atomic: it appears to be the case that there are specific cells in the retina that either respond or fail to respond to a stimulus according to whether it is or is not of the hue to which the cells are tuned; and we have already seen how this fact might be relevant to the hypothesis of Berlin and Kay (cf. 8.3). As far as most sense-components are concerned, however, it is hard to see how one might decide, even in principle, whether they are atomic or non-atomic. The notion of perceptual atomicity seems irrelevant to them (e.g., SPOUSE, SIBLING); and there is no other notion of atomicity that is not open to the criticism that its validity is unverifiable. But atomism, like conceptualism, is clearly not an essential ingredient of componential analysis. We need say no more about it.

The connexion between componential analysis and universalism is rather more complex, since there are several versions of universalism; and much of the attraction of componential analysis undoubtedly derives from its association, whether this is contingent or essential, with one or other of these versions. The most extreme form of the thesis of universalism would combine at least the following three distinguishable sub-theses: (i) that there is a fixed set of semantic components, which are universal in that they are lexicalized in all languages; (ii) that the formal principles by which these sense-components are combined to yield as their products the meanings of lexemes are universal (and presumably innate); and (iii) that the sense of all lexemes in all languages is decomposable, without residue, into variable combinations of (homogeneous) sense-components. The distinction between (i) and (ii) has to do with the distinction that Chomsky (1965) draws between substantive and formal universals. Let us therefore refer to (i) and (ii) as the theses of substantive and formal universality, respectively; and to (iii) as the without-residue thesis.

As we have seen, Katz does not subscribe to the composite thesis of extreme universalism: he does not hold to the without-residue part; and his view of substantive universals is not that all languages must lexicalize (or grammaticalize) them, but rather that all the sense-components (other than distinguishers) which are lexicalized in any language are taken from a fixed inventory (the knowledge of which is innate). This is the view that Chomsky and all his followers take of all substantive universals, semantic, syntactic and phonological. It is certainly Bierwisch's view, who criticizes Katz's notion of distinguishers on the ground that they can be analysed into more basic elements and in doing so explicitly declares his adherence to what at first sight looks like extreme universalism; and this would also seem to be the view of the so-called generative semanticists* (cf. 10.5). The Chomskyan form of the thesis of substantive universality is therefore much weaker than what we have presented above as (i).

None of the European structuralists have been or are extreme universalists. Hjelmslev maintained his own, relatively weak, version of the thesis of formal universality, but explicitly rejected the thesis of substantive universality in any form whatsoever. More recent writers in the same post-Saussurean tradition (notably Pottier, Coseriu, Greimas) have also made it clear that they reject at least the strong form of the thesis of substantive universality; and their adherence to the without-residue thesis is weakened partly by their methodological principle that the analysis should not be carried beyond the point at which every lexeme is distinguished from every other non-synonymous lexeme and partly by their recognition of two kinds of sense-components – classemes and semes. Although some of the semes might be universal, and even atomic (e.g., the semes which distinguish "red" from "green"), most of them are patently non-universal; and some of them are complex and residual in the way that Katz's distinguishers are. Finally, it might be mentioned that Russian scholars like Meljčuk, Žolkovskij, Apresjan, whose work will be referred to later (cf. 12.6) would not appear to sub-scribe to the thesis of extreme universalism, despite their interest in the construction of a universal semantic metalanguage, whose vocabulary (like that of Leibniz's symbolic language: cf. Apresjan, 1974: 38) is to be composed of atomic sense-components; nor would Leech (cf. 1974: 231–62), or Lehrer (1974), or Wierzbicka (1972), who has devoted a whole book to the establishment of an inventory of universal sense-components and to an exemplification of how such sense-components are lexicalized. In short, it is not clear that there is any representative of extreme universalism to be found among linguists who currently advo-cate or practise componential analysis.

On present evidence, the most plausible version of the universalist thesis would seem to be the one that was outlined above in our discussion of the hypothesis put forward by Berlin and Kay (cf. 8.1). If some (but by no means all) of the semantic distinctions drawn in languages are determined by a genetically transmitted disposition to respond to biologically and culturally salient stimuli, languages will tend to lexicalize (and perhaps also to grammaticalize) these semantic distinctions: e.g., the difference between what is vertically extended and what is not, between what is solid and what is not, between what is animate and what is not. Consequently, the analysis of many, if not all, language-systems will reveal that there are sense-relations holding in many areas of the vocabulary which can be accounted for by postulating such components as VERTICAL, SOLID, ANIMATE; and these sense-components (whose distribution throughout the languages of the world will pre-sumably vary in proportion with the relative salience of the distinctions they encode) will be such that they would be treated as markers (rather than distinguishers) by Katz. In so far as the marker/distinguisher distinction corresponds with the classeme/seme distinction (and neither of these two distinctions, as we have seen, has yet been made precise), they would also be classemes (rather than semes): for they would tend to be syntactically relevant and operative in several lexical fields. Not all the markers or classemes recognized in the analysis of particular languages, however, would be substantive universals, since there is nothing to prevent a language from lexicalizing a non-universal distinction and making it syntactically relevant. It follows (i) that the distinction between classemes and semes, on the one hand, and between markers and distinguishers, on the other, cannot be expected to correspond, other than approximately, with the distinction between universal and non-universal sense-components and (ii) that the inventory of sense-components in terms of which the vocabulary of any particular language is described might contain both universal and non-universal sense-components.

We have now completed our exposition of the general principles of componential analysis. The recent literature of linguistic semantics is full of programmatic statements to the effect that the meaning of all lexemes in all languages can, and must, be accounted for in terms of the combination of allegedly more basic, and possibly universal, sense-components. So far, however, the analyses that have been published are incomplete and, for the most part, unconvincing; and they have been confined to relatively few areas of the vocabulary in relatively few languages. For this reason alone one should be cautious about accepting as valid the claims that are made on behalf of componential analysis by its more enthusiastic advocates. But there are other reasons too.

It is now widely recognized that in certain areas of the vocabulary in which componential analysis has been practised, and most notably in the field of kinship vocabulary (cf. Romney & D'Andrade, 1964), it is possible to provide several equally plausible analyses for the same set of lexemes. Given that this is so, how do we decide that one analysis is correct and that the others are not? So far this question remains unanswered. Indeed, it is not even clear that it is answerable. For it has yet to be demonstrated that sense-components of the kind that linguists have tended to invoke in their analysis of the meaning of lexemes play any part whatsoever in the production and interpretation of language-utterances; and, if the allegedly more basic sense-components cannot be shown to have any psychological validity, much of the initial attraction of componential analysis disappears.

The psychological reality of sense-components has often been called into doubt. So too has their universality. What is not usually mentioned, however, in general discussions of the merits of componential analysis is the fact that, even in those areas in which it looks relatively convincing, it leaves unexplained at least as much as it succeeds in explaining. For example, if the meaning of the lexemes 'man', 'woman', 'adult', 'girl', 'boy' and 'child' are analysed in terms of the sense-components HUMAN, ADULT and FEMALE, we can readily explain the fact that phrases like 'adult child' or 'male girl' are semantically anomalous. In doing so, we must assume (and it is more often assumed than stated explicitly in treatments of componential analysis) that "male" (i.e. the sense of the English lexeme 'male') contains and is exhausted by the sense-component ⟨—FEMALE, that "adult" contains and is exhausted by ADULT, and so on. On this assumption, however, 'male child' should be synonymous with 'boy'. But it is not. An eighteen-year old boy is certainly not a child. Furthermore, if "boy" differs from "girl" solely in that it contains —FEMALE, rather than FEMALE, how do we account for the fact that the lexemes 'boy' and 'girl' simply are not used in such a way that the allegedly common —ADULT can be given a unitary interpretation? By any of the most obvious criteria (sexual maturity, etc.), girls reach what would normally be described as adulthood earlier, rather than later than, boys; and yet they are described as girls far longer than boys are described as boys. The proposition "*X* is now a man" may well imply "*X* is no longer a boy"; but "*X* is now a woman" does not imply "*X* is no longer a girl". It might be argued, of course, that this difference in the use of the lexemes 'boy', 'girl' and 'child', according to which the allegedly common component —ADULT is given a different interpretation in the three cases, involves something over and above their literal meaning. But what is this additional ingredient? It is easy enough to save any hypothesis by postulating unidentified additional elements or by invoking too swiftly the distinction between literal and non-literal meaning. Since componential analysis promotes the search for generalization (i.e. for the identification of the same sense-components over the largest number of lexemes) it is always liable to fall victim to rather facile over-generalizations. Whenever we appeal to such allegedly common sense-components as HUMAN, ADULT and FEMALE, we must ask ourselves what their cross-lexemic status is, how they are to be identified and what their explanatory power is.

It is important also to keep constantly in mind the difference between a lexeme, the meaning of a lexeme and some hypothetical sense-component which is in correspondence with the meaning of a lexeme (e.g., between 'human', "human" and HUMAN). There is no reason, in principle, why the citation-forms of lexemes from English or any other language should be used to label the sense-components that one postulates in the semantic analysis of English; and if some other system of identification were adopted (e.g. a numerical system according to the sense-component's position in some standardized master list), there would be less likelihood of our assuming that, because we know the meaning of, let us say, 'human', we also know the meaning of HUMAN. Since the meaning of 'human' is supposed to be explained in terms of the postulated theoretical entity HUMAN (i.e. "human" is held to contain and be exhausted by HUMAN), the theoretical entity itself must be defined otherwise than in terms of 'human'. Unless this is done, componential analysis is reduced, not only in practice, but also in principle, to the highly questionable procedure of treating as basic sense-components in the analysis of any language that the linguist is describing the meanings of certain lexemes, like 'human', 'adult' or 'female' from his own native language or from some other language that is commonly employed as a metalanguage in theoretical and descriptive linguistics.

Bibliography

Abercrombie, D. (1965). *Studies in Phonetics and Linguistics*. London: Oxford University Press.

Abercrombie, D. (1967). *Elements of Phonetics*. Edinburgh: Edinburgh University Press.

Abercrombie, D. (1968). 'Paralanguage'. *British Journal of Disorders of Communication* 3. 55–9.

Abraham, S. & Kiefer, F. (1966). *A Theory of Structural Semantics*. The Hague: Mouton.

Adams, P. (ed.) (1972). *Language in Thinking*. Harmondsworth: Penguin.

Ader, D. (1964). 'Verzeichnis der Schriften Jost Triers'. In W. Foerste & K. H. Borck (eds.) *Festschrift für Jost Trier zum 70. Geburtstag*. Köln & Graz: Böhlen.

Al, B. P. F. (1974). *La Notion de Grammaticalité en Grammaire Générative-Transformationelle*. Leyde: Presse Universitaire de Leyde.

Alston, W. P. (1964). *Philosophy of Language*. Englewood Cliffs, N.J.: Prentice-Hall.

Allwood, J. *et al*. (1977). *Logic in Linguistics*. Cambridge & New York: Cambridge University Press.

Antal, L. (1963). *Questions of Meaning*. The Hague: Mouton.

Antal, L. (1964). *Content, Meaning and Understanding*. The Hague: Mouton.

Apresjan, J. D. (1974). *Leksičeskaja Semantika*. Moskva: Izd. 'Nauka'.

Argyle, M. (1967). *The Psychology of Interpersonal Behaviour*. Harmondsworth: Penguin Books.

Argyle, M. (1969). *Social Interaction*. London: Methuen.

Argyle, M. (1972). 'Non-verbal communication in human social interaction'. In Hinde (1972).

Argyle, M. (ed.) (1973). *Social Encounters*. Harmondsworth: Penguin Books.

Argyle, M. (1974). *Bodily Communication*. London: Methuen.

Austin, J. L. (1958). 'Performatif-Constatif': paper presented at Royaumont Conference. English translation in Caton (1963).

Austin, J. L. (1961). *Philosophical Papers*. London: Oxford University Press. (2nd edition, 1970).

Austin, J. L. (1962). *How To Do Things With Words*. Oxford: Clarendon Press.

Ayer, A. J. (1936). *Language, Truth and Logic*. London: Gollancz. (2nd edition, 1946.)

Baldinger, K. (1957). *Die Semasiologie: Versuch eines Überblicks*. Berlin: Deutsche Akad. der Wissensch. zu Berlin.

Baldinger, K. (1970). *Teoría Semantica: Hacia una Semántica Moderna.* Coleción Romania, 12. Madrid: Alcala.

Bally, C. (1909). *Traité de Stylistique Française.* Paris: Leroux.

Bar-Hillel, Y. (1954a). 'Logical syntax and semantics'. *Language* 30. 230–7. (Reprinted in Bar-Hillel, 1964.)

Bar-Hillel, Y. (1954b). 'Indexical expressions'. *Mind* 63. 359–76. (Reprinted in Bar-Hillel, 1964.)

Bar-Hillel, Y. (1964). *Language and Information.* Reading, Mass.: Addison-Wesley.

Bar-Hillel, Y. (1967a). 'Dictionaries and meaning-rules'. *Foundations of Language* 3. 409–14. (Reprinted in Bar-Hillel, 1970: 347–53.)

Bar-Hillel, Y. (1967b). Review of Fodor & Katz (1964). In *Language* 43. 526–50. (Reprinted in Bar-Hillel, 1970.)

Bar-Hillel, Y. (1970). *Aspects of Language.* Jerusalem: Magnes.

Bar-Hillel, Y. (ed.) (1971). *Pragmatics of Natural Language.* Dordrecht–Holland: Reidel.

Bar-Hillel, Y. & Carnap, R. (1952). 'An outline of a theory of semantic information'. Technical Report, 257. Cambridge, Mass.: MIT Research Laboratory of Electronics. (Reprinted in Bar-Hillel, 1964: 221–74.)

Barthes, R. (1964). *Eléments de Sémiologie.* Paris: Seuil. English version: *Elements of Semiology.* London: Cape, 1967.

Barthes, R. (1967). *Système de la Mode.* Paris: Seuil.

Bartsch, R. & Vennemann, T. (1972). *Semantic Structures.* Frankfurt: Athenäum.

Bates, E. (1976). *Language in Context: The Acquisition of Pragmatics.* New York: Academic Press.

Bateson, P. P. G. & Klopfer, P. (eds.) (1974). *Perspectives in Ethology.* New York: Plenum.

Bazell, C. E. (1958). 'Linguistic Typology'. In Strevens (1966: 29–49).

Bazell, C. E. *et al.* (eds.) (1966). *In Memory of J. R. Firth.* London: Longmans.

Beckman, J. & Callow, J. (1974). *Translating the Word of God.* Grand Rapids, Michigan: Zondervan.

Bendix, E. M. (1966). *Componential Analysis of General Vocabulary.* The Hague: Mouton. (Also published as pt 2 of *International Journal of American Linguistics*, 32: 2, and publication 41 of Indiana University Research Center in Anthropology, Folklore and Linguistics.)

Bennet, J. (1976). *Linguistic Behaviour.* Cambridge: Cambridge University Press.

Benveniste, E. (1939). 'Nature du signe linguistique'. *Acta Linguistica* 1. 23–9. (Reprinted in Benveniste, 1966: 49–55. Also in Hamp *et al.*, 1966: 104–8.)

Benveniste, E. (1966). *Problèmes de Linguistique Générale.* Paris: Gallimard.

Berlin, B., Breedlove, D. E. & Raven, P. H. (1966). 'Folk taxonomies and biological classification'. *Science* 154. 273–5. (Reprinted in Tyler, 1969.)

Berlin, B., Breedlove, D. E. & Raven, P. H. (1974). *Principles of Tzeltal Plant Classification.* New York & London: Academic Press.

Berlin, B. & Kay, P. (1969). *Basic Color Terms.* Berkeley: University of California Press.

338 *Bibliography*

Bierwisch, M. (1965). 'Eine Hierarchie syntaktisch-semantischer
Merkmale'. *Studia Grammatica* 5. 29–86. (3rd edition, revised, Berlin:
Akademie-Verlag, 1970.)

Bierwisch, M. (1967). 'Some semantic universals of German adjectivals'.
Foundations of Language 3. 1–36.

Bierwisch, M. (1969). 'On certain problems of semantic representation'.
Foundations of Language 5. 153–84.

Bierwisch, M. (1970). 'On classifying semantic features'. In Bierwisch &
Heidolph (1970).

Bierwisch, M. & Heidolph, K. E. (1970). *Progress in Linguistics*. The Hague:
Mouton.

Biggs, C. (1975). 'Quantifiers, definite descriptions and reference'. In Keenan
(1975: 112–20).

Birdwhistell, R. L. (1954). *Introduction to Kinesics*. Louisville, Ky.:
University of Louisville Press.

Birdwhistell, R. L. (1970). *Kinesics and Context*. Philadelphia: University of
Pennsylvania Press & Harmondsworth: Penguin Books.

Black, M. (1959). 'Linguistic relativity: the views of Benjamin Lee Whorf'.
Philosophical Review 68. 228–38.

Black, M. (1968). *The Labyrinth of Language*. New York: Praeger.
(Published in Great Britain; London: Pall Mall, 1970 & Harmondsworth:
Penguin Books, 1972.)

Bloom, L. (1973). *One Word at a Time*. The Hague: Mouton.

Bloomfield, L. (1914). *Introduction to the Study of Language*. New York: Holt.

Bloomfield, L. (1926). 'A set of postulates for the science of language'.
Language 2. 153–64. (Reprinted in Joos, 1957: 26–31.)

Bloomfield, L. (1935). *Language*. London: Allen & Unwin. (American edition
New York: Holt, Rinehart & Winston, 1933.)

Bloomfield, L. 'Meaning'. *Monatshefte für Deutschen Unterricht* 35. 101–6.

Bobrow, D. G. & Collins, A. (eds.) (1975). *Representation and Understanding*.
New York, San Francisco & London: Academic Press.

Bolinger, D. W. (1946). 'Visual morphemes'. *Language* 22. 333–40.

Bolinger, D. (1961). *Generality, Gradience and the All-or-None*. The Hague:
Mouton.

Bolinger, D. (1965). 'The atomization of meaning'. *Language* 41. 555–73.

Bolinger, D. (1968). *Aspects of Language*. New York: Harcourt Brace & World.

Bolinger, D. (ed.) (1972). *Intonation*. Harmondsworth: Penguin.

Bononi, A. *Le Vie del Riferimento*. Milano: Bompiani.

Bower, T. G. R. (1974). *Development in Infancy*. San Francisco: Freeman.

Bréal, M. (1897). *Essai de Sémantique*. Paris. English translation: *Semantics:
Studies in the Science of Meaning*. London, 1900.

Brekle, H. E. (1972). *Semantik*. München: Fink.

Broadbent, D. E. (1958). *Perception and Communication*. London & New York:
Pergamon.

Broadbent, D. (1973). *In Defence of Empirical Psychology*. London: Methuen.

Brower, R. A. (ed.) (1959). *On Translation*. London: Oxford University Press.
(Republished New York: Oxford University Press (Galaxy Books), 1966.)

Brown, J. C. (1966). *Loglan: A Logical Language*. Gainsville, Fla.: Loglan
Institute.

Brown, R. W. (1958). *Words and Things*. Glencoe, Ill.: Free Press.

Brown, R. W. (1970). *Psycholinguistics: Selected Papers*. New York:
Free Press.

Brown, R. W. (1973). *A First Language*. London: Allen & Unwin.

Buck, C. D. (1949). *A Dictionary of Selected Synonyms in the Principal
Indo-European Languages*. Chicago: University of Chicago Press.

Bühler, K. (1934). *Sprachtheorie*. Jena: Fischer. (Reprinted Stuttgart: Fischer,
1965.)

Burling, R. (1964). 'Cognition and componential analysis: God's truth or
hocus-pocus?' *American Anthropologist*. 66. 20–8.

Burling, R. (1970). *Man's Many Voices*. New York: Holt, Rinehart & Winston.

Buyssens, E. (1943). *Les Langages et le Discours*. Bruxelles: Lebègue.

Caplan, D. & Marshall, J. C. (1975). 'Generative grammar and aphasic
disorders': review of Whitaker (1971). *Foundations of Language* 12. 583–97.

Carnap, R. (1942). *Introduction to Semantics*. Cambridge, Mass. M.I.T. Press.

Carnap, R. (1950). *The Logical Foundations of Probability*. Chicago:
University of Chicago Press.

Carnap, R. (1952). 'Meaning postulates'. *Philosophical Studies* 3. 65–73.
(Reprinted in Carnap, 1956b.)

Carnap, R. (1956a). 'The methodological character of theoretical concepts'.
In H. Feigl & M. Scriven (eds.) *Minnesota Studies in the Philosophy of
Science*, vol. 1. Minneapolis: University of Minnesota Press.
(Reprinted in Zabeeh *et al.*, 1974: 33–76.)

Carnap, R. (1956b). *Meaning and Necessity*, 2nd edition. Chicago.

Carnap, R. (1958). *Introduction to Symbolic Logic*. New York: Dover.
(Translation, with revisions, of *Einführung in die Symbolische Logik*.
Wien: Springer, 1954.)

Carroll, J. (1953). *The Study of Language*. Cambridge, Mass.: Harvard
University Press.

Casares, J. (1942). *Diccionario Ideológico de la Lengua Española*. Barcelona:
G.G.

Cassirer, E. (1923). *Philosophie der Symbolischen Formen*, vol. 1. Berlin.
English translation: *The Philosophy of Symbolic Forms*. New Haven, Conn.:
Yale University Press, 1953.

Cassirer, E. (1945). 'Structuralism in modern linguistics'. *Word* 1. 99–120.

Castañeda, H-N. (1967). 'On the logic of self-knowledge'. *Nous* 1. 9—22.

Catford, J. C. (1965). *A Linguistic Theory of Translation*. London: Oxford
University Press.

Caton, C. E. (ed.) (1963). *Philosophy and Ordinary Language*. Urbana, Ill.:
University of Illinois Press.

Chafe, W. L. (1970). *Meaning and the Structure of Language*. Chicago &
London: University of Chicago Press.

Chappell, V. C. (ed.) (1964). *Ordinary Language*. Englewood Cliffs, N.J.:
Prentice-Hall.

Chase, S. (1938). *The Tyranny of Words*. New York: Harcourt, Brace.

Cherry, C. (1957). *On Human Communication*. Cambridge, Mass.: M.I.T. Press. (Reprinted New York: Science Editions, 1959.)

Cherry, C. (ed.) (1974). *Pragmatic Aspects of Communication*. Dordrecht: Reidel, 1974.

Chomsky, N. (1957). *Syntactic Structures*. The Hague: Mouton.

Chomsky, N. (1965). *Aspects of the Theory of Syntax*. Cambridge, Mass.: M.I.T. Press.

Chomsky, N. (1968). *Language and Mind*. New York: Harcourt, Brace & World. (Enlarged edition, 1972.)

Chomsky, N. (1976). *Reflections on Language*. London: Temple Smith.

Chomsky, N. & Halle, M. (1968). *The Sound Pattern of English*. New York: Harper & Row.

Church, A. (1956). *Introduction to Mathematical Logic*. Princeton: Princeton University Press.

Clark, E. V. (1973). 'What's in a word? On the child's acquisition of semantics in his first language'. In Moore (1973: 65–110).

Clark, H. H. (1973). 'Space, time, semantics and the child'. In Moore (1973: 28–64).

Clark, H. H. & Clark, E. V. (1977). *Psychology and Language*. New York: Harcourt Brace Jovanovich.

Cohen, L. J. (1966). *The Diversity of Meaning*, 2nd edition. London: Methuen.

Conklin, H. C. (1955). 'Hanunoo color categories'. *Southwestern Journal of Anthropology* 11. 339–44. (Reprinted in Hymes, 1964: 189–92.)

Conklin, H. C. (1962). 'Lexicographical treatment of folk taxonomies'. In Householder & Saporta (1962: 119–41). (Reprinted in Tyler, 1969: 41–59.)

Conklin, H. C. (1972). *Folk Classification: A Topically Arranged Bibliography of Contemporary and Background References Through 1971*. New Haven: Department of Anthropology, Yale University.

Conklin, H. (1973). 'Color categorization': Review of Berlin & Kay, 1969. *American Anthropologist* 75. 931–42.

Cooper, David, E. (1973). *Philosophy and the Nature of Language*. London: Longmans.

Copleston, F. (1953). *A History of Philosophy*, vol. 2. London: Burns Oates & Washbourne.

Coseriu, E. (1952). 'Sistema, norma y habla'. In Coseriu (1962: 11–113).

Coseriu, E. (1962). *Teoría del Lenguaje y Lingüística General*. Madrid: Gredos. German translation: *Sprachtheorie und Sprachwissenschaft*. München: Fink, 1975.

Coseriu, E. (1967). 'Lexicalische Solidaritäten'. *Poetica* 1. 293–303.

Coseriu, E. & Geckeler, H. (1974). 'Linguistics and semantics'. In Sebeok (1974: 103–71).

Croce, B. (1902). *Estetica Come Scienza dell'Espressione e Linguistica Generale*. Palermo: Sandron. (3rd and subsequent editions, Bari: Laterza.) English translation: *Aesthetics as Science of Expression and General Linguistics*. London: Macmillan, 1922.

Cruse, D. A. (1976). 'Three classes of antonyms in English'. *Lingua* 38. 281–92.

Crystal, D. (1969). *Prosodic Systems and Intonation in English*. London & New York: Cambridge University Press.

Crystal, D. (1975). *The English Tone of Voice*. London: Arnold.

Dahl, Ö. (1970). 'Some notes on indefinites'. *Language* 46. 33–41.

Dahl, Ö. (1975). 'On generics'. In Keenan (1975: 99–111).

Dalgarno, G. (1661). *Ars Signorum*. London.

Davidson, D. & Hintikka, J. (eds.) (1969). *Words and Objections: Essays on the Work of W. V. Quine*. Dordrecht: Reidel.

Davidson, D. & Harman, G. (eds.) (1972). *Semantics of Natural Language*. Dordrecht: Reidel.

Dean, J. D. (1977). *Semantics: Theories of Meaning in Generative Linguistics*. New York: Crowell.

Deese, J. (1965). *The Structure of Associations in Language and Thought*. Baltimore: Johns Hopkins Press.

Deese, J. (1970). *Psycholinguistics*. Boston: Allyn & Bacon.

De Laguna, G. (1927). *Speech*. New Haven, Conn.: Yale University Press. (Reprinted, Bloomington, Ind.: Indiana University Press.)

De Mauro, T. (1965). *Introduzione alla Semantica*. Bari: Laterza.

De Mauro, T. (1967). *Ludwig Wittgenstein*. Dordrecht: Reidel.

Dik, S. C. (1968). 'Referential identity'. *Lingua* 21. 70–97.

Dimond, S. J. & Beaumont, J. G. (1974). *Hemisphere Function in the Human Brain*. London: Elek Science.

Dixon, R. M. W. (1971). 'A method of semantic description'. In Steinberg & Jakobovits (1971).

Dixon, R. M. W. (1973). 'The semantics of giving'. In Gross *et al.* (1973: 205–23).

Donnellan, K. (1966). 'Reference and descriptions'. *Philosophical Review* 75. 281–304. (Reprinted in Steinberg & Jakobovits, 1971.)

Dornseiff, F. (1933). *Der Deutsche Wortschatz nach Sachgruppen*. Berlin: De Gruyter.

Ducrot, O. & Todorov, T. (1972). *Dictionnaire Encyclopédique des Sciences du Langage*. Paris: Seuil.

Dummett, M. (1973). *Frege: Philosophy of Language*. London: Duckworth.

Eco, U. (1971). *Le Forme del Contenuto*. Milano: Bompiani.

Eco, U. (1972). 'Introduction to a semiotics of iconic signs'. *Versus* 2. 1–15.

Elwert, W. T. (ed.) (1968). *Probleme der Semantik*. Wiesbaden: Steiner.

Engler, R. (1968). *Lexique de la Terminologie Saussurienne*. Utrecht & Anvers: Spectrum.

Erdmann, K. O. (1925). *Die Bedeutung des Wortes*, 4th edition. Leipzig.

Esper, E. A. (1968). *Mentalism and Objectivism in Linguistics*. New York: American Elsevier.

Fauconnier, G. (1974). *La Coréférénce: Syntaxe ou Sémantique?* Paris: Seuil.

Feibleman, J. K. (1946). *An Introduction to Peirce's Philosophy*. New York: Harper.

Feigl, H. & Sellars, W. (eds.) (1949). *Readings in Philosophical Analysis*. New York: Appleton-Century-Crofts.

Ferguson, C. & Slobin, D. (eds.) (1973). *Studies in Child Language Development*. New York: Holt, Rinehart & Winston.

Fillmore, C. (1971). 'Types of lexical information'. In Steinberg & Jakobovits (1971).

Fillmore, C. & Langendoen, T. (eds.) (1971). *Linguistic Universals*. New York: Holt, Rinehart & Winston.

Firth, J. R. (1935). 'The technique of semantics'. In *Transactions of the Philological Society*. (Reprinted in Firth, 1957.)

Firth, J. R. (1937). *The Tongues of Men*. London: Watt.

Firth, J. R. (1950). 'Personality and language in society'. *The Sociological Review* 42. 37–52. (Reprinted in Firth, 1957a.)

Firth, J. R. (1957a). *Papers in Linguistics, 1934–1951*. London: Oxford University Press.

Firth, J. R. (1957b). 'Ethnographic analysis and language with reference to Malinowski's views'. In Raymond Firth (ed.) *Man and Culture*. London: Routledge. (Reprinted in Palmer, 1968.)

Firth, R. (1972). 'Verbal and bodily rituals of greeting and parting'. In J. S. La Fontaine (ed.) *The Interpretation of Ritual*. London: Tavistock Publications.

Flew, A. (ed.) (1953). *Logic and Language*, first series. Oxford: Clarendon Press.

Flores D'Arcais, G. & Levelt, W. J. M. (eds.) (1970). *Advances in Psycholinguistics*. Amsterdam: North-Holland.

Fodor, J. A. (1968). *Psychological Explanation*. New York: Random House.

Fodor, J. A. & Katz, J. J. (1964). *The Structure of Language: Readings in the Philosophy of Language*. Englewood Cliffs, N.J.: Prentice-Hall.

Fodor, J. D. (1977). *Semantics*. New York: Crowell.

Frake, C. O. (1962). 'The ethnographic study of cognitive systems'. In Gladwin & Sturtevant (1962: 72–85). (Reprinted in Tyler, 1969: 28–41.)

Frege, G. (1892). 'Über Sinn und Bedeutung'. *Zeitschr. f. Philosophie und philosoph. Kritik* 100. 25–50. English translation: 'On sense and reference'. In Geach & Black (1960: 56–78). Reprinted in Zabeeh *et al.*, 1974: 118–40; Feigl & Sellars, 1949: 82–102; etc.

Gallie, W. B. (1952). *Peirce and Pragmatism*, revised edition. London: Penguin Books & New York: Dover Publications, 1966.

Gardiner, A. H. (1932). *The Theory of Speech and Language*. Oxford: Clarendon Press.

Gardner, B. T. & Gardner, R. A. (1971). 'Two-way communication with an infant chimpanzee'. In A. Schrier & F. Stollnitz (eds.) *Behavior of Non-Human Primates*, vol. 4. New York: Academic Press.

Garver, N. (1965). 'Varieties of use and mention'. *Philosophy and Phenomenological Research* 26. 230–8. (Reprinted in Zadeeh *et al.*, 1964: 96–104.)

Garvin, P. L. (1955). *A Prague School Reader in Aesthetics*. Bloomington, Ind.: Indiana University Press.

Geach, P. & Black, M. (eds.) (1960). *Translations from the Philosophical Writings of Gottlob Frege*. Oxford: Blackwell.

Geach, P. T. (1962). *Reference and Generality*. Ithaca, N.Y.: Cornell University Press. (Amended edition, 1968.)

Geckeler, H. (1971). *Strukturelle Semantik und Wortfeldtheorie*. München: Fink.

Gelb, I. J. (1963). *A Study of Writing*, 2nd edition. Chicago: University of Chicago Press.

Gipper, H. (ed.) (1959). *Sprache, Schlüssel zur Welt: Festschrift fur Leo Weisgerber*. Düsseldorf: Schwann.

Gipper, H. (1963). *Bausteine zur Sprachinhaltsforschung*. Düsseldorf: Schwann.

Gipper, H. (1972). *Gibt es ein Sprachliches Relativitätsprinzip?: Untersuchungen zur Sapir-Whorf Hypothese*. Frankfurt: Fischer.

Givón, T. (1970). 'Notes on the semantic structure of English adjectives'. *Language* 46. 816–37.

Gladwin, T. & Sturtevant, W. C. (eds.) (1962). *Anthropology and Human Behavior*. Washington, D.C.: Anthropological Society of Washington.

Gluckman, M. (ed.) (1962). *Essays on the Ritual of Social Relations*. Manchester: Manchester University Press.

Gochet, P. (1972). *Esquisse d'une Théorie Nominaliste de la Proposition*. Paris: Colin.

Godel, R. (1957). *Les Sources Manuscrites du Cours de Linguistique Générale de Ferdinand de Saussure*. Genève & Paris: Droz.

Goffman, E. (1956). *The Presentation of Self in Everyday Life*. Edinburgh: Edinburgh University Press.

Goffman, E. (1971). *Relations in Public*. Harmondsworth: Penguin.

Goodenough, W. H. (1956). 'Componential analysis and the study of meaning'. *Language* 32. 195–216.

Goodman, N. (1952). 'On likeness of meaning'. In Linsky (1952). (Reprinted in Olshewsky, 1969: 537–42.)

Greene, J. (1972). *Psycholinguistics*. Harmondsworth: Penguin.

Greenfield, P. & Smith, J. (1974). *Communication and the Beginning of Language*. New York & London: Academic.

Greimas, A. (1965). *La Sémantique Structurale*. Paris: Larousse.

Greimas, A. J. (1970). *Du Sens: Essais Sémiotiques*. Paris: Seuil.

Greimas, A. J. *et al.* (ed.) (1970). *Sign, Language, Culture*. The Hague: Mouton.

Grice, H. P. (1957). 'Meaning'. *Philosophical Review* 67. (Reprinted in Zabeeh *et al.*, 1974.)

Grice, H. P. (1957). 'Meaning'. *Philosophical Review* 66. 377–88. (Reprinted in P. F. Strawson (ed.) *Philosophical Logic*. Oxford: Oxford University Press, 1971. Also in Steinberg & Jakobovits, 1971.)

Grice, H. P. (1968). 'Utterer's meaning, sentence-meaning, and word-meaning'. *Foundations of Language* 4. 1–18. (Reprinted in Searle, 1971.)

Gross, M., Halle, M. & Schützenberger, M. P. (1973). *The Formal Analysis of Natural Languages*. The Hague: Mouton.

Guiraud, P. (1971). *La Sémiologie*. Paris: Presses Universitaires de France. English translation: *Semiology*. London: Routledge & Kegan Paul, 1975.

Hall, E. T. (1959). *The Silent Language*. New York: Doubleday.

Hall, E. T. (1966). *The Hidden Dimension*. New York: Doubleday & London: Bodley Head.

Halliday, M. A. K. (1970). 'Functional diversity in language'. *Foundations of Language* 6. 322–61.

Halliday, M. A. K. (1973). *Explorations in the Functions of Language*. London: Arnold.

Hallig, R. & Wartburg, W. von (1952). *Begriffssystem als Grundlage für die Lexikographie. Versuch eines Ordnungsschemas*. Berlin: Akademie-Verlag.

Hammel, E. A. (ed.) (1965). *Formal Semantic Analysis*. Special publication of *American Anthropologist* 67: 5, pt 2.

Hamp, E. P., Householder, F. W. & Austerlitz, R. (eds.) (1966). *Readings in Linguistics II*. Chicago & London: University of Chicago Press.

Harman, G. (ed.) (1974). *On Noam Chomsky*. New York: Doubleday.

Harris, Z. (1951). *Methods in Structural Linguistics*. Chicago: University of Chicago Press. (Reprinted as *Structural Linguistics*, 1961.)

Harrison, B. (1972). *Meaning and Structure: An Essay in the Philosophy of Language*. New York: Harper & Row.

Harrison, B. (1973). *Form and Content*. Oxford: Basil Blackwell.

Hayakawa, S. I. (1949). *Language in Thought and Action*. New York: Harcourt, Brace.

Hayden, D. E. & Alworth, E. P. (eds.) (1965). *Classics in Semantics*. London: Vision.

Hayes, J. R. (ed.) (1970). *Cognition and the Development of Language*. New York: Wiley.

Hayes, K. J. & Hayes, C. (1955). 'Intellectual development of a home-raised chimpanzee'. *Proceedings of the American Philosophical Society* 95. 105–9.

Heider, E. R. (=Rosch, E. H.) (1971). ' "Focal" color areas and the development of color names'. *Developmental Psychology*. 4. 447–55.

Heider, E. R. (1972). 'Universals in color naming and memory'. *Journal of Experimental Psychology*. 3. 337–54.

Heider, E. R. & Olivier, D. C. (1972). 'The structure of the color-space in naming and memory for two languages'. *Cognitive Psychology* 3. 337–54.

Hempel, C. G. (1965). *Aspects of Scientific Explanation*. New York: Free Press.

Henle, P. (ed.) (1958). *Language, Thought and Culture*. Ann Arbor: University of Michigan Press.

Herder, J. G. (1772). 'Abhandlung über den Ursprung der Sprache'. In B. Suphan (ed.), *Herder's Sämmtliche Werke*, vol. 2. Berlin, 1877.

Hering, E. (1874). 'Grundrisse einer Theorie des Farbensinnes'. *Sitz. Ber. Öst. Akad. Wiss, Math.-Naturwiss. Kl., Abt.* 3. 70. 169–204.

Herriot, P. (1970). *An Introduction to the Psychology of Language*. London: Methuen.

Hewes, G. W. (1973). 'Primate communication and the gestural origin of language'. *Current Anthropology* 14. 5–32.

Hinde, R. A. (ed.) (1972). *Non-Verbal Communication*. London & New York: Cambridge University Press.

Hintikka, J. (1969). 'Semantics for propositional attitudes'. In J. W. Davis *et al.* (eds.) *Philosophical Logic.* Dordrecht: Reidel. (Reprinted in Linsky, 1971: 145–67).

Hjelmslev, L. (1953). *Prolegomena to a Theory of Language.* (Translated from the Danish, 1943, by F. J. Whitfield.) Bloomington, Ind.; Indiana University.

Hjelmslev, L. (1959). 'Pour une sémantique structurale'. In *Essais Linguistiques.* Copenhague: Cercle Linguistique de Copenhague, 1959.

Hockett, C. F. (1953). Review of Shannon & Weaver (1949). In *Language* 29. 69–93.

Hockett, C. F. (1958). *A Course in Modern Linguistics.* New York: Macmillan.

Hockett, C. F. (1960). 'The origin of speech'. *Scientific American* 203. 89–96.

Hockett, C. F. & Altmann, S. (1968). 'A note on design features'. In Sebeok (1968: 61–72).

Hoenigswald, H. M. (1960). *Language Change and Linguistic Reconstruction.* Chicago: University of Chicago Press.

Hook, S. (ed.) (1969). *Language and Philosophy: A Symposium.* New York: New York University Press.

Höpp, G. (1970). *Evolution der Sprache und Vernunft.* Berlin, Heidelberg & New York: Springer.

Householder, F. W. (1971). *Linguistic Speculations.* London & New York: Cambridge University Press.

Householder, F. W. & Saporta, S. (eds.) (1962). *Problems in Lexicography.* Publications of Indiana University Research Center in Anthropology, Folklore and Linguistics, 21. (Supplement to *International Journal of American Linguistics,* 28.) Baltimore: Waverley Press.

Hughes, G. E. & Cresswell, M. J. (1968). *An Introduction to Modal Logic.* London: Methuen.

Humboldt, W. von (1836). *Über die Verschiedenheit des Menschlichen Sprachbaues.* Berlin. (Reprinted Darmstadt: Claasen & Roether, 1949.)

Hurford, J. R. (1975). *The Linguistic Theory of Numerals.* London, New York & Melbourne: Cambridge University Press.

Huxley, R. & Ingram, E. (eds.) (1972). *Language Acquisition: Models and Methods.* New York: Academic Press.

Hymes, D. (ed.) (1964). *Language in Culture and Society.* New York: Harper & Row.

Ipsen, G. (1924). 'Der alte Orient und die Indogermanen'. In *Festschrift...* *Streitberg.* Heidelberg: Winter.

Itkonen, E. (1974). *Linguistics and Metascience.* Studia Philosophica Turkuensia, 2. Kökemäki: Societas Philosophica et Phaenomenologica Finlandiae/ Risteen Kirjapaino.

Jackendoff, R. (1972). *Semantic Interpretation in Generative Grammar.* Cambridge, Mass.: M.I.T. Press.

Jakobson, R. (1936). 'Beitrag zur allgemeinen Kasuslehre'. *Travaux du Cercle Linguistique de Prague* 6. 240–88. (Reprinted in Hamp *et al.,* 1966.)

Jakobson, R. (1959). 'On linguistic aspects of translation'. In Brower (1959: 232–9).

Jakobson, R. (1960). 'Linguistics and poetics'. In Sebeok (1960).

Jakobson, R. (1971). *Selected Writings*, vol. 2: *Word and Language*. The Hague: Mouton.

Jakobson, R. & Halle, M. (1956). *Fundamentals of Language*. The Hague: Mouton.

Jespersen, O. (1924). *The Philosophy of Grammar*. London: Allen & Unwin.

Jespersen, O. (1909–49). *A Modern English Grammar on Historical Principles*. Copenhagen: Munksgaard. Reprinted, London: Allen & Unwin, 1954.

Jolles, A. (1934). 'Antike Bedeutungsfelder'. *Beiträge zur Deutschen Sprache und Literatur* 58. 97–109.

Joos, M. (ed.) (1957). *Readings in Linguistics*. Washington, D.C.: American Council of Learned Societies. (Republished as *Readings in Linguistics I*. Chicago & London: Chicago University Press.)

Kamp, J. A. W. (1975). 'Two theories about adjectives'. In Keenan (1975: 123–55).

Kasher, A. (1972). 'Sentences and utterances reconsidered'. *Foundations of Language* 8. 313–45.

Katz, J. J. (1964). 'Analyticity and contradiction in natural language'. In Fodor & Katz (1964: 519–43).

Katz, J. J. (1966). *The Philosophy of Language*. New York: Harper & Row.

Katz, J. J. (1972). *Semantic Theory*. New York: Harper & Row.

Katz, J. J. & Fodor, J. A. (1963). 'The structure of a semantic theory'. *Language* 39. 170–210. (Reprinted in Fodor & Katz, 1964: 479–518.)

Kay, P. (1975). 'Synchronic variability and diachronic change in basic color terms'. *Language and Society* 4. 257–70.

Keenan, E. L. (ed.) (1975). *Formal Semantics of Natural Language*. London & New York: Cambridge University Press.

Key, M. R. (1975). *Paralanguage and Kinesics*. Metuchen, N.J.; Scarecrow.

Kiefer, F. (1966). 'Some semantic relations in natural language'. *Foundations of Language* 2. 228–40.

Kiefer, F. (ed.) (1969). *Studies in Syntax and Semantics*. Dordrecht: Reidel.

Koerner, E. F. K. (1973). *Contribution au Débat Post-Saussurien sur le Signe Linguistique*. The Hague: Mouton.

Korzybski, A. (1933). *Science and Sanity*. Lancaster, Pa.: International Non-Aristotelian Library.

Koziol, H. (1967). *Grundzüge der Englischen Semantik*. Wien & Stuttgart: Braumüller.

Kripke, S. A. (1963). 'Semantical considerations on modal logic'. *Acta Philosophica Fennica* 16. 83–94. (Reprinted in Linsky, 1971: 63–72.)

Kronasser, H. (1952). *Handbuch der Semasiologie*. Heidelberg: Winter.

Kühlwein, W. (1967). *Die Verwendung der Feindseligkeitsbezeichnungen in der Altenglischen Dichtersprache*. Neumünster: Karl Wachholtz.

Kunjunni Raja, K. (1963). *Indian Theories of Meaning*. Madras: Adyar Library and Research Centre.

Kuryłowicz, J. (1936). 'Dérivation lexicale et dérivation syntaxique'. *Bulletin de la Société de Linguistique de Paris* 37. 79–92. (Reprinted in Hamp *et al.*, 1966: 42–50.)

Kuryłowicz, J. (1960). 'La position linguistique du nom propre'. In *Esquisses Linguistiques*, pp. 182–92. Wrocław-Krakow: Wydawnictwo Polskieij Akademii Nauk. (Reprinted in Hamp *et al.*, 1966: 362–70.)

Ladefoged, P. (1971). *Preliminaries to Linguistic Phonetics*. Chicago: University of Chicago Press.

Lamb, S. M. (1964). 'The sememic approach to structural semantics'. In Romney & D'Andrade (1964: 57–78).

Langer, S. K. (1942). *Philosophy in a New Key*. Cambridge, Mass.: Harvard University Press.

Latacz, J. (1967). *Zum Wortfeld 'Freude' in der Sprach Homers*. Heidelberg: Winter.

Laver, J. (1968). 'Voice quality and indexical information'. *British Journal of Disorders of Communication* 3. 43–54.

Laver, J. (1970). 'The production of speech'. In Lyons (1970).

Laver, J. (1975). 'Communicative functions of phatic communion'. In A. Kendon *et al.* (eds.) *The Organization of Behavior in Face-to-Face Communication*. The Hague: Mouton.

Laver, J. (1976). 'Language and nonverbal communication'. In E. C. Carterette & M. P. Friedman (eds.) *Language and Speech* (vol. 7 of *Handbook of Perception*). New York: Academic Press.

Laver, J. (1977). *The Phonetic Description of Voice Quality*. London & New York: Cambridge University Press.

Laver, J. & Hutcheson, S. (eds.) (1972). *Face to Face Communication*. Harmondsworth: Penguin.

Lawler, J. (1972). 'Generic to a fault'. In *Papers from the Eighth Regional Meeting Chicago Linguistic Society*. Chicago: Chicago Linguistic Society.

Leech, G. N. (1969). *Towards a Semantic Description of English*. London: Longmans.

Leech, G. N. (1974). *Semantics*. Harmondsworth: Penguin.

Lehrer, A. (1974). *Semantic Fields and Lexical Structure*. Amsterdam & London: North Holland & New York: American Elsevier.

Lehrer, A. & Lehrer, K. (eds.) (1970). *Theory of Meaning*. Englewood Cliffs, N.J.: Prentice-Hall.

Leibniz, G. W. von (1704). 'Table de définitions'. In Louis Couturat (ed.) *Opuscules et Fragments Inédits de Leibniz*, pp. 437–510. Paris, 1903.

Leisi, E. (1953). *Der Wortinhalt*. Heidelberg: Winter. (3rd edition 1967).

Lenneberg, E. H. (1967). *The Biological Foundations of Language*. New York: Wiley.

Leontjev, A. A. (ed.) (1971). *Semantičeskaja Strucktura Slova*. Moskva: Izd. 'Nauka'.

Lepschy, G. C. (1966). *La Linguistica Strutturale*. Torino: Einaudi. English edition: *A Survey of Structural Linguistics*. London: Faber, 1970.

Lévi-Strauss, C. (1963). *Anthropologie Structurale*. Paris: Plon. English translation: *Structural Anthropology*. London & New York: Basic Books, 1963.

Lewis, C. I. (1943). 'The modes of meaning'. *Philosophy and Phenomenological Research* 4. 236–50. (Reprinted in Linsky, 1952.)

Lewis, D. (1969). *Convention.* Cambridge, Mass.: Harvard University Press.

Lewis, D. (1972). 'General Semantics'. In Davidson & Harman (1972: 169–218).

Lewis, D. (1975). 'Adverbs of quantification'. In Keenan (1975: 3–15).

Lieberman, P. (1974/5). 'On the evolution of language: a unified view'. *Cognition* 2. 3–94.

Linsky, L. (1950). 'On using inverted commas'. *Methodos* 2. 232–36. (Reprinted in Zabeeh *et al.*, 1974: 106–16.)

Linsky, L. (ed.) (1952). *Semantics and the Philosophy of Language.* Urbana, Ill.: University of Illinois Press.

Linsky, L. (1967). *Referring.* London: Routledge & Kegan Paul.

Linsky, L. (ed.) (1971). *Reference and Modality.* London: Oxford University Press.

Ljung, M. (1974). 'Some remarks on antonymy'. *Language* 50. 74–88.

Lounsbury, F. G. (1956). 'A semantic analysis of the Pawnee kinship system'. *Language* 32. 158–94.

Lounsbury, F. G. (1964). 'The structural analysis of kinship semantics'. In H. G. Lunt (ed.) *Proceedings of the Ninth International Congress of Linguists* pp. 1073–93. The Hague: Mouton.

Lyas, C. (ed.) (1971). *Philosophy and Linguistics.* London: Macmillan.

Lyons, J. (1963). *Structural Semantics.* Oxford: Blackwell.

Lyons, J. (1968). *Introduction to Theoretical Linguistics.* London & New York: Cambridge University Press.

Lyons, J. (ed.) (1970). *New Horizons in Linguistics.* Harmondsworth: Penguin.

Lyons, J. (1972). 'Human language'. In Hinde (1972: 49–85).

McCawley, J. (1971). 'Prelexical syntax'. In R. J. O'Brien (ed.) *Report of the Twenty-Second Annual Round Table Meeting on Linguistics and Language Studies.* Washington, D.C.: Georgetown University. (Reprinted in Seuren, 1974: 29–42.)

McIntosh, A. (1961). 'Patterns and ranges'. *Language* 37. 325–37.

McNeill, D. (1970). *The Acquisition of Language.* New York: Harper & Row.

McNeill, N. B. (1972). 'Colour and colour terminology': review of Berlin & Kay (1969). *Journal of Linguistics* 8. 21–34.

Malinowski, B. (1930). 'The problem of meaning in primitive languages'. In second and subsequent editions of Ogden & Richards, *The Meaning of Meaning.*

Malinowski, B. (1935). *Coral Gardens and Their Magic,* vol. 2. London: Allen & Unwin. (Reprinted Bloomington, Ind.: Indiana University Press, 1965.)

Malkiel, Y. (1959). 'Studies in irreversible binomials'. *Lingua* 8. 113–60. (Reprinted in Malkiel, 1968: 311–55.)

Malkiel, Y. (1968). *Essays on Linguistic Themes.* Oxford: Blackwell.

Malkiel, Y. (1974). Review of H. Geckeler *Zur Wortfelddiskussion* (1971). In *Foundations of Language* 12. 271–85.

Malmberg, B. (1972). *Readings in Modern Linguistics.* The Hague: Mouton.

Martin, R. M. (1958). *Truth and Denotation.* Chicago: University of Chicago Press.

Martinet, A. (1957). 'Arbitraire linguistique et double articulation'. *Cahiers Ferdinand de Saussure* 15. 105–16. (Reprinted in Hamp *et al.*, 1966: 371–8.)

Martinet, A. (1949). 'La double articulation linguistique'. *Travaux du Cercle Linguistique de Copenhague* 5. 30–7.

Martinet, A. (1960). *Eléments de Linguistique Générale.* Paris: Colin.

Matoré, G. (1953). *La Méthode en Lexicologie.* Paris: Didier.

Matthews, P. H. (1972). *Inflexional Morphology.* Cambridge: Cambridge University Press.

Matthews, P. H. (1974). *Morphology.* London: Cambridge University Press.

Matthews, P. H. (1975). Review of Brown (1973). *Journal of Linguistics* 11. 322–43.

Meljčuk, I. A. (1974). *Opyt Teorii Lingvističeskikh Modelej "Smysl↔Tekst".* Moskva: 'Nauka'.

Mill, J. S. (1843). *A System of Logic.* London: Longmans.

Miller, G. A. (1951). *Language and Communication.* New York: McGraw Hill.

Miller, G. A. (ed.) (1968). *Psychology of Communication.* Harmondsworth: Penguin.

Miller, G. A. (1972). 'English verbs of motion: a case-study in semantics and lexical memory'. In Melton, A. W. & Martin, E. (eds.) *Coding Processes in Human Memory.* Washington: Winston.

Miller, G. A. & Johnson-Laird, P. N. (1976). *Perception and Language.* Cambridge, Mass.: Harvard University Press & London: Cambridge University Press.

Minsky, M. (ed.) (1966). *Semantic Information Processing.* Cambridge, Mass.: M.I.T. Press.

Mohrmann, C., Sommerfelt, A., & Whatmough, J. (eds.) (1961). *Trends in European and American Linguistics 1930–1960.* Utrecht & Antwerp: Spectrum.

Moore, T. E. (ed.) (1973). *Cognitive Development and the Acquisition of Language.* New York & London: Academic Press.

Morris, C. W. (1938). *Foundations of the Theory of Signs.* In Neurath *et al.* (1939). (Reprinted in Morris, 1971.)

Morris, C. W. (1946). *Signs, Language and Behaviour.* Englewood Cliffs, N.J.: Prentice Hall. (Reprinted in Morris, 1971).

Morris, C. W. (1964). *Signification and Significance.* Cambridge, Mass.: M.I.T. Press. (Chapter 1 reprinted in Morris, 1971.)

Morris, C. W. (1971). *Writings on the General Theory of Signs.* The Hague: Mouton.

Morris, Jan (= James) (1974). *Conundrum.* London: Faber.

Morton, J. (ed.) (1971). *Biological and Social Factors in Psycholinguistics.* London: Logos.

Mounin, G. (1963). *Problèmes Théoriques de la Traduction.* Paris: Gallimard.

Mounin, G. (1970). *Introduction à la Sémiologie.* Paris: Éditions de Minuit.

Mounin, G. (1974). Review of Hinde (1972). *Journal of Linguistics* 10. 201–6.

Mulder, J. & Hervey, S. (1972). *Theory of the Linguistic Sign.* The Hague: Mouton.

Nash, W. (1971). *Our Experience of Language.* London: Batsford.

Neurath, O., Carnap, R. & Morris, C. (eds.) (1939). *International Encyclopaedia of Unified Science*. Chicago: University of Chicago Press.

Nida, E. A. (1951). 'A system for the description of semantic elements'. *Word* 7. 1–14.

Nida, E. (1964). *Towards a Science of Translating*. Leiden: Brill.

Nida, E. (1975). *Exploring Semantic Structures*. Munich: Fink.

Nida, E. A. & Taber, C. R. (1969). *The Theory and Practice of Translation*. Leiden: Brill.

Nöth, W. (1975). *Semiotik: Eine Einführung mit Beispielen für Reklameanalysen*. Tübingen: Niemeyer.

Ogden, C. K. (1932). *Opposition*. London. (Reprinted, with a new introduction by I. A. Richards, Bloomington, Ind.: Indiana University Press, 1968.)

Ogden, C. K. (1968). *Basic English: International Second Language*. (A revised and expanded edition of *The System of Basic English*, prepared by E. C. Graham.) New York: Harcourt Brace.

Ogden, C. K. & Richards, I. A. (1923). *The Meaning of Meaning*. London: Routledge & Kegan Paul.

Öhman, S. (1951). *Wortinhalt und Wortbild*. Stockholm: Almqvist & Wiksell.

Öhman, S. (1953). 'Theories of the linguistic field'. *Word* 9. 123–34.

Oksaar, E. (1958). *Semantische Studien im Sinnbereich der Schnelligkeit*. Stockholm: Almqvist & Wiksell.

Oldfield, R. C. & Marshall, J. C. (eds.) (1968). *Language*. Harmondsworth: Penguin.

Olshewsky, T. M. (ed.) (1969). *Problems in the Philosophy of Language*. New York: Holt, Rinehart & Winston.

Orr, J. (1962). *Three Studies on Homonymics*. Edinburgh: Edinburgh University Press.

Osgood, C. E. (1953). *Method and Theory in Experimental Psychology*. London & New York: Oxford University Press.

Osgood, C. & Sebeok, T. (eds.) (1954). *Psycholinguistics*. Bloomington: Indiana University Press.

Osgood, C. E., Suci, G. J. & Tannenbaum, P. H. (1957). *The Measurement of Meaning*. Urbana, Ill.: University of Illinois Press.

Palmer, F. R. (ed.) (1968). *Selected Papers of F. R. Firth, 1952–59*. London: Longmans & Bloomington, Ind.: Indiana University Press.

Palmer, F. R. (ed.) (1970). *Prosodic Analysis*. London: Oxford University Press.

Palmer, F. R. (1976). *Semantics: A New Outline*. Cambridge: Cambridge University Press.

Parisi, D. (1972). *Il Linguaggio Come Processo Cognitivo*. Torino: Boringhieri.

Parkinson, G. H. R. (ed.) (1968). *The Theory of Meaning*. London: Oxford University Press.

Partee, B. (Hall). (1972). 'Opacity, reference and pronouns'. In Davidson & Harman (1972: 415–41).

Partee, B. (Hall). (1975). 'Deletion and variable binding'. In Keenan (1975: 16–34).

Passmore, J. (1957). *A Hundred Years of Philosophy*. London: Duckworth & New York: Basic Books, 1966.

Pedersen, H. (1931). *Linguistic Science in the Nineteenth Century*. (Translated from the Danish.) Cambridge, Mass.: Harvard University Press. (Republished as *The Discovery of Language*. Bloomington, Ind.: Indiana University Press, 1959.)

Peirce, C. S. (1931–58). *Collected Papers*, vols. 1–8, edited by C. Hartshorne & P. Weiss. Cambridge, Mass.: Harvard University Press.

Peirce, C. S. (1940). *The Philosophy of Peirce: Selected Writings*, edited by J. Buchler. London.

Piaget, J. (1923). *Le Langage et la Pensée chez l'Enfant*. Neufchâtel & Paris.

Pike, K. (1948). *Tone Languages*. Ann Arbor: University of Michigan.

Pike, K. L. (1967). *Language in Relation to a Unified Theory of the Structure of Human Behaviour*. The Hague: Mouton.

Popper, K. (1968). *The Logic of Scientific Discovery*, 2nd revised edition. New York: Harper & Row.

Porzig, W. (1934). 'Wesenhafte Bedeutungsbeziehungen'. *Beiträge zur deutschen Sprache und Literatur* 58. 70–97.

Porzig, W. (1950). *Das Wunder der Sprache*. Bern: Francke.

Pottier, B. (1964). 'Vers une semantique moderne'. *Travaux de linguistique et de literature* 2. 107–37.

Pottier, B. (1974). *Linguistique Générale*. Paris: Klincksieck.

Premack, D. (1970). 'Language in a chimpanzee?' *Science* 172. 808–22.

Premack, A. (1974). *Chimps who can Read*. New York: Harper & Row.

Prieto, L. (1964). *Principes de la Noologie*. The Hague: Mouton.

Prieto, L. J. (1966). *Messages et Signaux*. Paris: Presses Universitaires de France. (2nd edition 1970.)

Prior, A. N. (1962). *Formal Logic*, 2nd edition. Oxford: Clarendon Press.

Putnam, H. (1975). *Mind, Language & Reality*. London & New York: Cambridge University Press.

Quadri, B. (1952). *Aufgaben und Methoden der Onomasiologischen Forschung*. Romanica Helvetica, 37. Bern.

Quillian, M. R. (1966). 'Semantic memory'. In Minsky (1966).

Quine, W. V. O. (1940). *Mathematical Logic*. Cambridge, Mass.: Harvard University Press.

Quine, W. V. (1951). 'Two dogmas of empiricism'. *Philosophical Review* 60. 20–43. (Reprinted in Quine, 1953: 20–46; Olshewsky, 1969: 398–417; Zabeeh *et al.*, 1974: 584–610.)

Quine, W. V. (1953). *From a Logical Point of View*. Cambridge, Mass.: Harvard University Press.

Quine, W. V. (1960). *Word and Object*. Cambridge, Mass.: M.I.T. Press.

Quine, W. V. (1966). *The Ways of Paradox*. New York: Random House.

Quine, W. V. (1969). 'Reply to Chomsky'. In Davidson & Hintikka (1969: 302–11).

Quine, W. V. (1970). *Philosophy of Logic*. Englewood Cliffs, N.J.: Prentice Hall.

Quirk, R. & Svartvik, J. (1966). *Investigating Linguistic Acceptability*. The Hague: Mouton.

Reichenbach, H. (1947). *Elements of Symbolic Logic*. London & New York: Macmillan.

Robey, D. (ed.) (1973). *Structuralism: An Introduction*. Oxford: Clarendon Press.

Robins, R. H. (1967). *A Short History of Linguistics*. London: Longmans.

Roget, P. M. (1852). *Thesaurus of English Words and Phrases*. London. (Abridged and revised, with additions by J. L. Roget & S. R. Roget, Harmondsworth, Middlesex: Penguin, 1953.)

Romney, A. K. & D'Anrade, R. G. (eds.) (1964). *Transcultural Studies in Cognition*. (Special publication of *American Anthropologist* 66, no. 3, pt 2.)

Rorty, R. (ed.) (1967). *The Linguistic Turn*. Chicago: University of Chicago Press.

Rosch, E. H. (=Heider, E. R.) (1973a). 'On the internal structure of perceptual and semantic categories'. In Moore (1973: 114–44).

Rosch, E. H. (1973b). 'Natural categories'. *Cognitive Psychology*. 4. 328–50.

Rossi, I. (ed.) (1974). *The Unconscious in Culture: The Structuralism of Lévi-Strauss in Perspective*. New York: Dutton.

Roulet, E. (1975). *F. de Saussure: Cours de Linguistique Générale*. Paris: Hatier.

Russell, B. (1905). 'On denoting'. *Mind* 14. 479–93. (Reprinted in Feigl & Sellars, 1949: 103–15.)

Russell, B. (1940). *An Inquiry into Meaning and Truth*. London: Allen & Unwin.

Russell, B. (1949). *A Critical Exposition of the Philosophy of Leibniz*. London: Allen & Unwin.

Ryle, G. (1949). *The Concept of Mind*. London: Hutchinson. (Reprinted Harmondsworth: Penguin Books, 1963.)

Ryle, G. (1957). 'The theory of meaning'. In C. A. Mace (ed.) *British Philosophy in the Mid-Century*. London: Allen & Unwin, 1957. (Reprinted in Zabeeh *et al.*, 1974: 219–44; Olshewsky, 1969: 131–50.)

Salmon, V. G. (1966). 'Language planning in seventeenth-century England'. In Bazell *et al.* (1966: 370–97).

Salomon, L. B. (1964). *Semantics and Commonsense*. New York: Holt, Rinehart & Winston.

Sampson, G. (1975). *The Form of Language*. London: Weidenfeld & Nicolson.

Sapir, E. (1921). *Language*. New York: Harcourt, Brace & World.

Sapir, E. (1944). 'On grading: a study in semantics'. *Philosophy of Science* 2. 93–116. (Reprinted in Sapir, 1949.)

Sapir, E. (1949). *Selected Writings in Language, Culture and Personality*, edited by D. G. Mandelbaum. Berkeley: University of California Press.

Saussure, F. de (1878). *Mémoire sur le Système Primitif des Voyelles dans les Langues Indo-Européennes*. Leipzig. (Reprinted in *Recueil des Publications Scientifiques de F. de Saussure*. Genève & Heidelberg, 1922.)

Saussure, F. de (1916). *Cours de Linguistique Générale*. Paris: Payot. English translation: *A Course in General Linguistics*. New York: Philosophical Library.

Saussure, F. de (1967–71). *Cours de Linguistique Générale: Édition Critique*, par Rudolf Engler. Wiesbaden: Harrassowitz.

Schaff, A. (1960). *Wstęp do Semantyki*. Warszawa. English translation: *Introduction to Semantics*. London: Pergamon, 1962.

Schaff, A. (1964). *Język i Poznanie*. Warszawa.

Schaff, A. (1969). 'A Marxist formulation of the problem of semantics'. (From the English translation of Schaff, 1960.) In Olshewsky (1969: 101–11).

Schank, R. C. (1975). *Conceptual Information Processing*. Amsterdam: North-Holland.

Schiffer, S. (1973). *Meaning*. Oxford: Oxford University Press.

Schillp, P. A. (ed.) (1963). *The Philosophy of Rudolph Carnap*. La Salle, Ill.: Open Court.

Schoenfield, J. R. (1967). *Mathematical Logic*. London: Addison-Wesley.

Schmitt, F. O. & Worden, F. G. (eds.) (1974). *The Neurosciences: Third Study Volume*. Cambridge, Mass.: M.I.T. Press.

Searle, J. R. (1958), 'Proper names'. *Mind* 67. 166–71.

Searle, J. R. (1969). *Speech Acts*. London & New York: Cambridge University Press.

Searle, J. R. (ed.) (1971). *The Philosophy of Language*. London: Oxford University Press.

Sebeok, T. A. (ed.) (1960). *Style in Language*. Cambridge, Mass.: M.I.T. Press.

Sebeok, T. A. (ed.) (1968). *Animal Communication*. Bloomington, Ind.: Indiana University Press.

Sebeok, T. A. (ed.) (1974). *Current Trends in Linguistics*, vol. 12. The Hague: Mouton.

Sebeok, T. A. & Ramsay, A. (eds.) (1969). *Approaches to Animal Communication*. The Hague: Mouton.

Seiffert, L. (1968). *Wortfeldtheorie und Strukturalismus*. Stuttgart: Kohlhammer.

Seuren, P. (ed.) (1974). *Semantic Syntax*. London: Oxford University Press.

Shannon, C. E. & Weaver, W. (1949). *The Mathematical Theory of Communication*. Urbana, Ill.: University of Illinois Press.

Sinclair, H. (= Sinclair-de-Zvart, H.) (1972). 'Sensorimotor action patterns as a condition for the acquisition of syntax'. In Huxley & Ingram (1972).

Sinclair, H. (1973). 'Language acquisition and cognitive development'. In Moore (1973: 9–25).

Skinner, B. F. (1957). *Verbal Behavior*. New York: Appleton Crofts.

Slobin, D. I. (ed.) (1971). *The Ontogenesis of Grammar*. New York & London: Academic.

Smith, A. G. (ed.) (1966). *Communication and Culture*. New York: Holt, Rinehart & Winston.

Smith, N. V. (1975). 'On generics.' *Transactions of the Philological Society 1975*.

Sommer, R. (1969). *Personal Space*. Englewood Cliffs, N.J.: Prentice-Hall.

Sørensen, H. S. (1963). *The Meaning of Proper Names*. Copenhagen: Gad.

Spang-Hanssen, H. (1954). *Recent Theories of the Nature of the Linguistic Sign*. *Travaux de Cercle Linguistique de Copenhague*, 9. Copenhagen.

Spang-Hanssen, H. (1961). 'Glossematics'. In Mohrmann *et al.* (1961: 128–62).

Sperber, H. (1930). *Einführung in die Bedeutungslehre.* Bonn & Leipzig. (3rd edition Bonn, 1965.)

Spradley, J. P. (ed.) (1972). *Culture and Cognition.* San Francisco, London & Toronto: Chandler.

Stampe, D. W. (1968). 'Towards a grammar of meaning'. *Philosophical Review* 77. (Reprinted in Harman, 1974.)

Steinberg, D. D. & Jakobovits, L. A. (eds.) (1971). *Semantics.* London & New York: Cambridge University Press.

Steiner, G. (1975). *After Babel: Aspects of Language and Translation.* London: Oxford University Press.

Stern, G. (1931). *Meaning and Change of Meaning.* Gothenburg. (Reprinted, Bloomington, Ind.: Indiana University Press, 1965.)

Stevenson, C. L. (1944). *Ethics and Language.* New Haven, Conn.: Yale University Press.

Strawson, P. F. (1950). 'On referring'. *Mind* 59. 320–44. (Reprinted in Caton, 1963: 162–93; Strawson, 1971; Olshewsky, 1969; Zabeeh *et al.*, 1974.)

Strawson, P. F. (1952). *Introduction to Logical Theory.* London: Methuen.

Strawson, P. F. (1959). *Individuals.* London: Methuen.

Strawson, P. F. (1964). 'Intention and convention in speech acts'. *Philosophical Review* 73. 439–60. (Reprinted in Searle, 1971 and Strawson, 1971.)

Strawson, P. F. (1971). *Logico-Linguistic Papers.* London: Methuen.

Strevens, P. D. (ed.) (1966). *Five Inaugural Lectures.* London: Oxford University Press.

Stroll, A. (ed.) (1967). *Epistemology.* New York & London: Harper & Row.

Sturtevant, E. H. (1917). *Linguistic Change.* Chicago: University of Chicago Press. (Reprinted, with a new introduction by Eric P. Hamp, Chicago: University of Chicago Press (Phoenix Books), 1961.)

Sturtevant, W. C. (1964). 'Studies in ethnoscience'. In Romney & d'Anrade (1964: 99–131).

Tarski, A. (1935). 'Der Wahrheitsbegriff in den formalisierten Sprachen'. *Studia Philosophica* 1. 261–405. English translation in Tarski (1956).

Tarski, A. (1944). 'The semantic conception of truth'. *Philosophy and Phenomenological Research* 4. 341–75. (Reprinted in Tarski, 1956; Olshewsky, 1969; Zabeeh *et al.*, 1974.)

Tarski, A. (1956). *Logic, Semantics and Metamathematics.* London: Oxford University Press.

Thorpe, W. H. (1972). 'The comparison of vocal communication in animals and man'. In Hinde (1972: 27–47).

Trier, J. (1931). *Der Deutsche Wortschatz im Sinnbezirk des Verstandes.* Heidelberg: Winter.

Trier, J. (1934). 'Das sprachliche Feld. Eine Auseinandersetzung'. *Neve Jahrbücher für Wissenschaft und Jugendbildung* 10. 428–49.

Trier, J. (1938), 'Über die Erforschung des menschenkundlichen Wortschatzes'. *Actes du IVème Congrès International des Linguistes,* pp. 92–7. Copenhague: Munskgaard. (Reprinted in Hamp *et al.*, 1966: 90–95.)

Trubetzkoy, N. S. (1939). *Grundzüge der Phonologie*. Prague: Cercle Linguistique de Prague. (French edition, *Principes de Phonologie*. Paris: Klincksieck, 1949.)

Turner, V. W. (1969). *The Ritual Process*. Chicago: Aldine.

Tyler, S. A. (ed.) (1969). *Cognitive Anthropology*. New York: Holt, Rinehart & Winston.

Uldall, H. J. (1944). 'Speech and writing'. *Acta Linguistica* 4. 11–16. (Reprinted in Hamp *et al.*, 1966: 147–51.)

Uldall, H. J. (1957). *Outline of Glossematics*. Travaux de Cercle Linguistique de *Copenhague*, 10. Copenhagen.

Ullmann, S. (1957). *The Principles of Semantics*, 2nd edition, Glasgow: Jackson & Oxford: Blackwell.

Ullmann, S. (1962). *Semantics*. Oxford: Blackwell & New York: Barnes & Noble.

Ullmann, S. (1972). 'Semantics'. In T. A. Sebeok (ed.), *Current Trends in Linguistics*, vol. 9: *Linguistics in Western Europe*. The Hague: Mouton.

Ullmann, S. (1973). *Meaning and Style*. Oxford: Blackwell.

Urban, W. (1939). *Language and Reality*. London: Allen & Unwin.

Urmson, J. O. (1956). *Philosophical Analysis*. Oxford: Clarendon Press.

Vachek, J. (1945/9). 'Some remarks on writing and phonetic transcription'. *Acta Linguistica* 5. 86–93. (Reprinted in Hamp *et al.*, 1966: 152–7.)

Vachek, J. (ed.) (1964). *A Prague School Reader in Linguistics*. Bloomington, Indiana: Indiana University Press.

Vachek, J. (1966). *The Linguistic School of Prague*. Bloomington: Indiana University Press.

Van Gennep, A. (1908). *Les Rites de Passage*. English translation: *The Rites of Passage*. Chicago: University of Chicago Press, 1960.

Vossler, K. (1932). *The Spirit of Language in Civilization*. London: Routledge & Kegan Paul.

Waismann, F. (1965). *The Principles of Linguistic Philosophy*. London: Macmillan.

Wallace, A. F. C. & Atkins, J. (1960). 'The meaning of kinship terms'. *American Anthropologist* 62. 58–60.

Warnock, G. J. (1958). *English Philosophy Since 1900*. London: Oxford University Press.

Watson, J. B. (1924). *Behaviourism*. New York.

Weaver, W. (1949). 'The mathematics of communication' (from *Scientific American* 181). In Smith (1966).

Weinreich, U. (1963). 'On the semantic structure of language'. In J. Greenberg (ed.) *Universals of Language*. Cambridge, Mass.: M.I.T. Press, 1963.

Weinreich, U. (1966). 'Explorations in semantic theory'. In T. A. Sebeok (ed.), *Current Trends in Linguistics*, vol. 3. The Hague: Mouton.

Weisgerber, L. (1939). *Die Volkhaften Kräfte der Muttersprache*. Frankfurt.

Weisgerber, L. (1950). *Vom Weltbild der Deutschen Sprache*. Düsseldorf: Schwann.

Weisgerber, L. (1954). 'Die Sprachfelder in der geistigen Erschliessung der Welt'. In *Festschrift... Trier.* Meisenheim: Hain.

Weiss, A. P. (1928). *A Theoretical Basis of Human Behavior.* Columbus, Ohio.

Westcott, R. W. (1971). 'Linguistic iconism'. *Language* 47. 416–28.

Whitaker, H. (1971). *On the Representation of Language in the Human Brain.* Edmonton, Alberta: Linguistic Research.

Whorf, B. L. (1956). *Language, Thought and Reality: Selected Writings of Benjamin Lee Whorf,* edited by J. B. Carroll. New York: Wiley.

Wiener, P. P. & Young, F. H. (eds.) (1952). *Studies in the Philosophy of Charles Sanders Peirce.* Cambridge, Mass.: Harvard University Press.

Wierzbicka, A. (1972). *Semantic Primitives.* Frankfurt: Athenäum.

Wiggins, D. (1967). *Identity and Spatio-Temporal Continuity.* Oxford: Blackwell.

Wilkins, J. (1668). *An Essay Towards a Real Character and a Philosophical Language.* London.

Winograd, T. (1975). 'Frame representations and the declarative-procedural controversy'. In Bobrow & Collins (1975: 185–210).

Wittgenstein, L. (1953). *Philosophical Investigations.* Oxford: Blackwell & New York: Macmillan.

Woods, W. A. (1975). 'What's in a link: foundations for semantic networks'. In Bobrow & Collins (1975: 35–82).

Wotjak, G. (1971). *Untersuchungen zur Struktur der Bedeutung.* Berlin: Akademie.

Wundt, W. (1912). *Völkerpsychologie,* Band 2. Leipzig.

Zabeeh, F., Klemke, E. D. & Jacobson, A. (1974). *Readings in Semantics.* Urbana, Chicago & London; University of Illinois Press.

Ziff, P. (1960). *Semantic Analysis.* Ithaca, N.Y.: Cornell University Press.

Zollinger, H. (1973). 'Zusammenhange zwischen Farbennennung und Biologie des Farbensehens beim Menschen'. *Vierteljahrschr. der Naturforsch. Gesellsch. in Zurich* 118. 227–55.

Zwicky, A. (1969). Review of Brown (1966). In *Language* 45. 444–57.

Index of Subjects

Asterisks indicate technical terms; bold type denotes the page number where a technical term is introduced.

dispositional theory of meaning*,
134, 135
distinctive features*, **232**, 245
distinguishers*, **326**, 328, 332
distribution*, **306**
distributional restriction, 307
distributive reference*, **187**
distributively*, 150, **178**
dominates*, **296**
duality*, **69**, 70, 71, 74, 75, 79, 87

echoic responses, 132
emotive meaning*, **175**
empiricism, 122, 225
empty class*, **157**
encapsulate*, **293**, 317
encapsulation*, **262**
encoded*, **37**, 38, 42, 45, 46
encoding stage, 98
Encyclopaedia of Unified Science 119,
126
England, 181
English, 29, 59, 60, 73, 77, 91, 101,
143, 149, 150, 151, 153, 156, 168,
176, 179, 185, 204, 208, 209, 211,
212, 215, 216, 219, 221, 222, 224,
225, 226, 227, 234, 237, 238, 241,
242, 243, 244, 246, 253, 254, 255,
258, 261, 262, 263, 266, 273, 275,
276, 277, 283, 284, 285, 292, 296,
297, 298, 299, 300, 302, 303, 304,
305, 308, 310, 312, 315, 318, 320,
324, 327, 328, 329, 334
Englishman, 112, 181, 222
English phonology, 76
entail*, **171**
entailed*, **202**
entailment*, **145**, 165
entitles, 77
entity, 298, 312
enumeration, 227
epistemology, 99, 140
equative sentence*, **185**, 201
equipollent opposites*, **279**
equivalence, 145
equivalence relations*, **154**
equivalent, 38
Eskimo, 242
Essay on Human Understanding, 99
essential proposition*, **195**, 196
etymological fallacy*, **244**
etymological meaning*, **222**

etymology*, **255**
European structuralists, 326, 327,
331
everyday language-behaviour, 216
evolutionary theory, 85
evolution of language, 89
Ewe, 60
exclamations, 55
exclusive disjunction*, **144**
existence*, **181**
existential proposition, 183, 184
existential quantifier, 150, 151, 189
expectancy, 42, 46
expressed*, **141**
expression*, 8, 18, **23**, 24, 25, 31,
138, 176, 177
expressive*, **50**, 51, 107, 174
expressive function, 53
expressive information, 50, 55
expressive meaning, 80
extension*, **158**, 176, 208, 291
extensional*, **146**, 160, 170, 171
extensional definition*, **158**
extensionality*, **146**, 200
extensionally identical*, **156**

face-to-face conversation, 63
factual information, 36, 50
false proposition, 161
feature*, **323**
feature-notation*, **322**, 323, 325,
326
feedback, 66
field (Feld), 251
field-theory*, **250**, 252, 256, 258,
259, 267, 268, 326, 327
finite class*, **155**
first-order predicate calculus*, **150**
floor-apportionment*, **66**
focal denotation, 246, 247
folk taxonomies*, **297** n
form*, **7**, 18, 23, 24, 25, 239
formal universality, 331
France, 182, 183, 185, 267
free variation*, **233**
French, 101, 168, 219, 222, 237, 238,
254, 262, 266, 300, 305, 322, 328
frequencies of occurrence, 43
frequency-counts, 20
function*, **146**, 149
functional*, **233**, 234
functional calculus, 147

Index of Personal Names

Abercrombie, 64, 65, 68, 106, 107
Alston, 207
Apresjan, 267, 332
Argyle, 51, 58, 65
Aristotle, 239
Augustine, St, 216
Austin, 56, 173, 186, 216, 218

Bacon, 300
Bally, 300
Bar-Hillel, 30, 47, 48, 49, 50, 106, 117, 118, 280
Barthes, 267
Berlin & Kay, 246, 283, 330, 332
Bidwhistell, 67
Bierwisch, 311, 313, 325, 327
Bloom, 92
Bloomfield, 17, 18, 21, 26, 114, 119, 125, 126, 127, 128, 129, 133, 209, 210, 265
Boas, 267
Bolinger, 327
Bréal, 104, 264
Brekle, 251
Brown, 51, 92, 134, 135, 302
Buck, 300
Bühler, 51, 52, 53, 54, 95, 107

Carnap, 47, 48, 49, 50, 114, 115, 116, 117, 118, 119, 126, 138, 200, 203, 204, 207, 291
Casares, 300
Cassirer, 231
Chase, 97
Cherry, 95
Chomsky, 21, 29, 76, 82, 90, 230, 302, 331
Chomsky & Halle, 76
Cicero, 199, 219, 220

Clark, 266, 276
Copleston, 112
Coseriu, 318, 326, 327, 331
Coseriu & Geckeler, 250, 318, 326
Croce, 51
Crystal, 64

Dalgarno, 74
Darwin, 85
Descartes, 300
Donnellan, 185, 186, 191, 192, 215
Dornsieff, 300
Durkheim, 239

Firth, 51, 70, 267
Frege, 111, 160, 176, 197, 198, 199, 207, 251

Gardiner, 34, 110
Gardner & Gardner, 91
Geach, 206, 214, 222, 223
Geckeler, 250, 251, 253, 259, 260, 300, 326
Gelb, 103
Gipper, 245
Goffman, 66
Goodenough, 318
Goodman, 211
Greimas, 267, 318, 322, 331
Grice, 34, 278

Halliday, 51
Hallig & Wartburg, 300
Harris, 26
Hayakawa, 97
Hayes & Hayes, 91
Herder, 231, 250
Hewes, 85, 88
Hinde, 80, 85